EDUCATION
and
DEAFNESS

EDUCATION
and
DEAFNESS

PETER V. PAUL
The Ohio State University

STEPHEN P. QUIGLEY
University of Illinois

Longman
New York & London

Education and Deafness

Longman 95 Church Street, White Plains, N.Y. 10601
A division of Addison-Wesley Publishing Co., Inc.

Associated companies:
Longman Group Ltd., London
Longman Cheshire Pty., Melbourne
Longman Paul Pty., Auckland
Copp Clark Pitman, Toronto

Senior editor: Naomi Silverman
Production editor: Marie-Josée A. Schorp
Cover design: Thomas W. Slomka, Thomas William Design
Text art: Vantage Art, Inc.
Senior production supervisor: Priscilla Taguer

Library of Congress Cataloging-in-Publication Data

Paul, Peter V.
     Education and deafness.
     Bibliography: p.
     Includes index.
     1. Deaf—Education—United States.   2. Deafness.
3. Deaf—Education—United States—English language.
4. Sign language.   I. Quigley, Stephen P. (Stephen
Patrick), 1927–   .   II. Title.
HV2545.P38   1989   371.91′2′0973   89-8312
ISBN 0-8013-0026-6

ABCDEFGHIJ-ML-99 98 97 96 95 94 93 92 91 90 89

Contents

Preface

This book is intended to be a comprehensive text on the education of hearing-impaired students. The main focus is on students with severe-to-profound hearing impairments; however, there is a chapter on students with less severe losses. Each chapter contains an in-depth discussion of the major issues, syntheses of research findings, and conclusions based on the available evidence.

The book is designed to be useful to anyone seeking an understanding of the intricate, challenging, and often fascinating, process of working with hearing-impaired individuals. Specifically, there is a substantial amount of basic information for prospective and practicing teachers, clinicians, counselors, and other professionals. The book should also appeal to linguists, psychologists, and other social scientists interested in studying a particular domain of deafness. These scholars can acquire sufficient background information to develop adequate evaluation tools or interpret the results of empirical investigations.

Chapter 1 presents historical perspectives on some of the major concerns in the education of hearing-impaired students. It provides an overview and some basic information on the various areas that are discussed in detail throughout the book. Topics include the interdependence of research and practice, language/communication, and academic achievement.

Chapter 2 discusses the anatomy and physiology of the ear and important principles of audiometry (the assessment of hearing). The etiology (cause), type, and degree of hearing impairment and their educational implications are also described. An attempt is made to differentiate individuals whose primary avenue for developing language and for communicating is vision from those individuals whose primary avenue is audition. The chapter emphasizes the importance of audition for the subsequent development of spoken language skills. Some aspects of hearing aids and classroom amplification systems are also discussed.

Although this book focuses mainly on severely to profoundly hearing-impaired students, Chapter 3 highlights some findings concerning the achievement of students with less severe hearing losses (i.e., hard-of-hearing students). The study of hard-of-hearing students, especially those integrated in regular-education programs, remains one of the most neglected areas of research and service. After presenting information on definitions, academic achievement, language and literacy, and the effects of placement on achievement and social development, the chapter concludes with a list of educational recommendations and needs.

Chapter 4 deals with certain psychoeducational and psychosocial issues and provides basic information and historical perspectives on cognitive and intellectual development. While it is debatable whether the cognitive development of severely to profoundly hearing-impaired students proceeds through stages similar to those of their hearing counterparts, there is little doubt that both cognition and language are interrelated and are important for the subsequent development of literacy. Other crucial topics covered are personal, social, and familial developments, occupational status, and the Deaf community and culture.

The language development of hearing-impaired students is presented in relation to oral English, American Sign Language, and English-based signed systems, the topics of Chapters 5, 6, and 7 respectively. The chapter on oral English describes the philosophy and the major components of oral education, namely, speech perception and production, speech reading, and auditory training/learning. It also synthesizes research data about the effects of oral-education approaches on the development of spoken and written English. The best overall academic results can be found in students who are educated in indisputably comprehensive oral programs or who are integrated into regular education programs.

Chapter 6 describes American Sign Language (ASL) and compares it to English and the English-based signed systems. It also summarizes the findings of research on linguistic, psycholinguistic, and neurolinguistic aspects of ASL, the effects of ASL on developing English, and the use of ASL in education programs. The research on bilingualism and second-language learning indicates that ASL should be used as an instructional approach for some hearing-impaired students. There is little agreement on how this should be accomplished, and there is even some debate on whether English should be taught at all. It is still not clear how hearing-impaired students can become literate in a spoken language after acquiring competence in a nonspeech-based sign language. The use of ASL in the classrooms is expected to receive increasing support from researchers and educators in the 1990s.

Chapter 7 focuses on the various English-based signed systems that have been developed for educational purposes. After describing the basic tenets, it shows the relationships of these systems to the structure of English. The chapter also synthesizes research findings on the use and effects of the signed systems on developing English. Although most systems have been used for at least 15 years, there is little evidence that many students have developed the ability to read and write English at a mature, adult level. Thus, it is concluded that using a particular signed system, albeit important, is not sufficient by itself to develop English literacy skills.

Most educators generally agree that developing adequate reading and writing skills is one of the most important goals in the education of students with hearing impairments. Reading and writing are discussed in the same chapter because they are interrelated and are crucial for success in other school subjects. The ability to write is contingent on the ability to read and both depend on the adequate development of a primary language. Chapter 8 shows the impact of deafness on the acquisition of English literacy skills. Current instructional and curricular practices are also examined. It is argued that there needs to be an interrelationship among theory, assessment, curriculum, and practice.

The educational placement, assessment, and achievement of severely to profoundly hearing-impaired students from preschool to postsecondary institutions are described in Chapter 9. Also discussed are the training of teachers, the use of curricular materials, the concept of the Individualized Educational Plan (IEP), and the use of educational interpreters. The findings on achievement reveal that the overall level of the average hearing-impaired student completing a secondary-education program is about six to seven grades lower than that of the average hearing counterpart. This is not surprising given the low levels of literacy. Even most prelinguistic severely to profoundly impaired postsecondary students have problems with reading and writing, which makes it difficult for them to obtain a four-year college or university degree. These low levels of achievement persist despite improvements in early intervention, amplification systems, and the construction of tests.

The focus of Chapter 10 is on hearing-impaired students with additional handicapping conditions. It provides some perspectives on definitions and incidence and discusses the relationships between additional handicaps and other variables such as degree of hearing loss, gender, and etiology. The chapter also presents some of the effects of current classification procedures on the training of preservice teachers, on curricula, and on instructional practices. A brief overview of residential alternatives and employment for handicapped adults is provided.

Chapter 11 summarizes our major conclusions and implications for further research and instruction. The discussion is organized around academic placement and achievement, literacy, and language/communication.

We are indebted to all the researchers and scholars who contributed the findings on which this book is based. We also express our gratitude to our colleagues who participated in a blind review of earlier versions of the manuscript. We thank Dr. Joseph O'Rourke, The Ohio State University, Columbus, and Dr. Jerry Crittenden, University of South Florida, Tampa, for providing valuable comments and support. Last, but certainly not least, we thank our wives, Mary Beth Pilewski Paul and Ruth Quigley, for putting up with us during the whole process.

EDUCATION
and
DEAFNESS

CHAPTER 1

Issues and
Historical Perspectives

MAJOR POINTS TO CONSIDER

Interdependence of research and practice

Characteristics of prelinguistically severely to profoundly
  hearing-impaired students

Educational philosophies of deafness

Language and communication issues

Language-teaching methods

Academic placement and achievement

The extent of the debate on the status of schools that occurred during the 1980s was unprecedented in the history of education in the United States (Gross & Gross, 1985). Numerous reports by commissions, committees, and task forces at local, state, and national levels were published. There were spirited discussions on how schools could be improved. Several statements common to these educational reform reports also appeared in earlier local, state, and national inquiries conducted in the late 1950s following the launching of Sputnik by the Soviet Union. According to Gross and Gross (1985):

> Then, as now, teacher education was criticized as intellectually flimsy. Higher salaries and more professional "career lines" for teachers were advocated—it was urged that "master teachers" should lead "teaching teams" in designing more effective instruction. The universities were admonished to get reinvolved with the schools. New technologies for teaching and learning were extolled—then it was television, now it's computers. The school curriculum was denounced as thin and outmoded. (p. 16)

1

The education of hearing-impaired children and adolescents has also been influenced by educational reform movements. Within the past 25 years, two national groups have evaluated the quality of education of hearing-impaired students in the United States. A committee established within the Department of Health, Education, and Welfare (HEW) reported its findings in 1965 (Babbidge Committee Report). More recently, Congress established the **Commission of Education of the Deaf** (CED) through the Education of the Deaf Act of 1986. Although there was some progress in the period between the reports of the two national groups, the first few lines of the latter report to Congress state (Commission on Education of the Deaf, 1988):

> The present status of education for persons who are deaf in the United States is unsatisfactory. Unacceptably so. This is the primary and inescapable conclusion of the Commission on Education of the Deaf. (p. viii)

Consequently, the CED offered 52 recommendations for improving the quality of education for hearing-impaired students. These recommendations were made in relation to seven broad topics: (1) prevention and **early identification,** (2) elementary and secondary education, (3) federal postsecondary education systems, (4) research, evaluation, and outreach, (5) professional standards and training, (6) the progress and potential of technology, and (7) **clearinghouses** and committees on **deaf-blindness.**

This chapter presents a brief introduction of and historical perspectives on some of the major issues and concerns in the education of hearing-impaired students, including those reported by the CED. The main purpose is to provide an overview of the basic information that is presented in detail in the rest of the book. The overview and related historical perspectives provide insights into the major prevailing issues and problems that have been documented in the two national reports on **deafness** and in the research and scholarly literature (e.g., Bender, 1970; Di Carlo, 1964; Lane, 1984; Schmitt, 1966; Scouten, 1984). A few enduring issues are singled out here to emphasize their importance.

INTERDEPENDENCE OF RESEARCH AND PRACTICE

A major reason for the slow and uneven progress in education in general is the use of inefficient and **unscientific** methods of collecting and applying knowledge (e.g., Behling, 1975; Borg & Gall, 1963, 1979; Kerlinger, 1973; Travers, 1978). Much of what is known about education and deafness has also been based on an uncritical acceptance of authority and an overdependence on personal experiences. Both approaches, although important as part of the decision-making process, have been shown to provide insufficient evidence for solving educational problems when used alone. For example, Borg and Gall (1963) stated that:

> Personal experience almost always constitutes insufficient evidence upon which to make decisions, even if the individual were able to remember and objectively evaluate his experience. We know from psychological research that the individual tends to remember

evidence that supports his opinion and to forget or distort evidence that does not. Personal experience often leads the individual to draw conclusions or assume relationships that are false. (p. 7)

Education, as other professions have done, needs to recognize the interdependence of research and practice. As Cole (1988) has stated:

Without a systematic way to accumulate and increase knowledge about education, the field will be characterized by fads that come and go, and practitioners will be forced to rediscover good practice largely for themselves. However, little change and improvement will actually occur. Only with good ongoing educational research can education have a recognized and growing base of knowledge. Such a knowledge base is the foundation of our profession, the source of our expertise as educators. As our knowledge grows we get better as a profession at educating each generation of students. (p. 4)

Knowledge in education should not only be systematically acquired but also be systematically applied. It should have an impact on educational areas such as preparation of teachers, development of curricular and instructional practices, and improvement of assessment. In relation to deafness, for example, more seems to be known about the processes of learning in areas such as language, reading, and writing than about how to *teach* and *develop* skills in these areas. Not much is known about the effectiveness of instructional practices and materials, and there is little ongoing research to rectify this situation (Clarke, Rogers, & Booth, 1982; King & Quigley, 1985). After reviewing the research on instruction and reading with deaf students, Clarke et al. (1982) reported that "the current state of instructional methodology is one of confused eclecticism" due to "the remarkable lack of empirical data in this critical area" (p. 65). Only a substantial, systematic, and sustained research effort is likely to correct this state of affairs.

Defining the Population

To generalize about the education of hearing-impaired students, there needs to be at least agreement that the research and scholarly findings are based on samples drawn from the same population. As stated by Quigley and Kretschmer (1982):

Much of the confusion in research and practice in the education of deaf children arises from incomplete descriptions of the populations under consideration and from generalization of findings to dissimilar populations. (p. 5)

A few descriptive variables have been found to influence significantly the educational achievement of hearing-impaired students: (1) **age at onset** and **degree of hearing impairment,** (2) the **hearing status,** level of involvement, and communicative ability of the parents/caregivers, (3) **intelligence,** and (4) **socioeconomic status.** Few investigations provide complete descriptions of the hearing-impaired **subjects** in these terms. Often, some vital information is not provided or not available to the researcher.

As discussed in detail in Chapter 2, this book is concerned primarily with the achievement of **prelinguistically,** severely to profoundly hearing-impaired students who are educated in **special schools,** special classes, or mainstreamed programs within public schools. These students have **sensorineural** hearing impairments of 71 **decibels** (dB) or greater in the better **unaided ear** that occurred before or at the age of about two years, that is, before basic development of **spoken,** verbal **language.** The primary mode for receiving communication input for a number of severely hearing-impaired students (71–90 dB) and many profoundly hearing-impaired students (91 dB+), even with the use of **amplification systems,** is vision. Audition, or **residual hearing,** serves as a secondary or supplemental channel for information input. This primary focus on vision is significant because it has been hypothesized that the eye perceives and structures information about spoken language differently from the ear, which could have profound effects on educational and psychological development, as discussed in Chapter 4.

Incidence.   About 8 percent of the general population has some degree of **hearing impairment,** including 1 percent who are severely to profoundly hearing-impaired. The annual survey by the **Center for Assessment and Demographic Studies** (CADS) at **Gallaudet University** reported that in 1982 there were approximately 68,000 hearing-impaired students between 6 and 17 years of age receiving special education **support services** (Ries, 1986). Most of these students had unaided severe (about 71 to 90 dB) and profound (91 dB+) hearing impairments. It was reported also that profoundly hearing-impaired students comprised about three-fifths of the hearing-impaired population in special schools or programs. Another one-fifth are severely hearing-impaired students (Allen & Osborn, 1984; Gallaudet Research Institute, 1985; Karchmer, Milone, & Wolk, 1979). In addition, it is estimated that more than 90 percent of all hearing-impaired students in special programs are prelinguistically hearing-impaired and the rest suffer hearing impairment **postlinguistically** (e.g., Allen & Osborn, 1984; Commission on Education of the Deaf, 1988).

Labels.   The use of classification labels in **special education,** which includes the education of severely to profoundly hearing-impaired students, is a matter of controversy. An excellent summary of arguments for and against their use can be found in Kirk and Gallagher (1986). Those who favor labels argue that they serve as a basis for further diagnosis and treatment, for research into **etiology** and prevention, and for communication among professionals. Opponents argue that some labels may foster misclassification (particularly in low-income families), do not lead to educationally relevant programs, and might be detrimental to the **self-concept** of the students.

Ross and Calvert (1984), for example, stated that if hearing-impaired students are labeled *deaf,* they are likely to be placed in educational programs that do not emphasize the development of speech and hearing skills. In addition, the researchers stated that teachers tend to hold low expectations for these students in developing **oral English** abilities. This situation is suspected to occur most often in **Total Communication** (TC) programs—that is, programs in which signing and speech are used simultaneously in some way (Connor, 1986; Geers, Moog, & Schick, 1984). Ross and Calvert argued for the use of the term *hearing impairment* as a generic label to refer to all hearing losses, reasoning that its use would be likely to ensure that most or all hearing-impaired students would be given an opportunity to develop their residual hearing and to acquire adequate speech skills. It may be that the use of the term *deaf* has actually resulted in greater use of signing with students who have only slight to moderate hearing impairments and who have no real need for signing.

Preparation of Teachers

The preparation of teachers for severely to profoundly hearing-impaired students is a complex and difficult process because it requires imparting to the future teachers knowledge and skills from many disciplinary and practical areas. To promote communication, language, **socioemotional,** educational, and vocational development, the future teacher needs to know much about each as it is related to **hearing** students as well as to hearing-impaired students. In general, however, this book deals with these areas only as they are related to hearing-impaired students. Communication, language, social-emotional growth, educational growth, and other domains of development are treated in detail as being important for future teachers and others seeking to understand the effects and problems of deafness. A few general topics are singled out here for emphasis because they are perceived to be either enduring issues of concern or emerging ones.

Educational Philosophies.   Every teacher of hearing-impaired students, most parents of hearing-impaired students, and the majority of those who work with hearing-impaired people in any extended capacity eventually develop an educational perspective or philosophy concerning the objectives that should be established and just how those objectives can be attained. Professionals working with severely to profoundly hearing-impaired students need to decide what forms of communication and language should be developed initially. This is the most important decision to be made in the home and school because it determines the future direction of the hearing-impaired child's life. It is a decision of awesome proportions even though it is often not perceived in that way. This matter is discussed in detail in Chapter 4.

Two bipolar perspectives or philosophies and several variations ranging between the two extremes should be considered (Baker & Cokely, 1980; Scouten, 1984; Silverman, Lane, & Calvert, 1978). At one extreme is the perspective that there is only one society, a hearing society, and that the main goal of education should be to enable hearing-impaired students to enter the **majority culture,** or mainstream of society. This viewpoint has been labeled the **clinical,** pathological, or medical model. The emphasis is on remedying the *deficiencies* in speech and language of hearing-impaired children and adolescents. Adherents of this view stress the importance of oral English communication skills (e.g., receptive and expressive speech skills) and the development of literacy (i.e., the ability to read and write). As much as possible, **academic placement,** curriculum, instruction, and assessment resemble those of hearing students in regular education programs. Finally, proponents of this viewpoint are likely either to reject the notion of the **Deaf community** or **culture,** or believe that it should play a minor role in the education of hearing-impaired students.

At the other extreme is the philosophical perspective that there are two societies, hearing and deaf, with only limited communication or interaction between them. (From this perspective, the word *deaf* can be interpreted audiologically as severe to profound hearing impairment, or culturally as individuals who support and advocate the use of sign communication systems). According to proponents of this position, most deaf individuals if given a choice, would spend most of their time in the comfort of the Deaf culture. Proponents claim that in the hearing society, deaf persons are treated as second-class citizens. Adherents to this perspective would suit the method of communication to the child; however, most of them argue for the use of signing, particularly **American Sign Language (ASL).** This viewpoint is also known as the **cultural model.** Deafness is not considered as a pathological condition that needs to be cured. One of the most important aspects of university-level teacher-training programs, according to this group, should be the establishment of fluent and intelligible communication between prospective teachers and students, primarily by the use of signing, preferably ASL. In addition, the teaching of reading and writing skills appears to be more important than the teaching of **oral-communication** skills. Finally, adherents to the cultural model are most supportive of **residential schools** and the development of **special instructional and curricular materials** that suit the individual needs of the deaf child.

The essence of this philosophy has been stated eloquently by Silverman, Lane, and Calvert (1978):

> The aim of the education of the deaf child should be to make him a well-integrated, happy deaf individual, and not a pale imitation of a hearing person. Let us aim to produce happy, well-adjusted deaf *individuals,* each different from the other, each with his own personality. If a child cannot learn to read lips well or cannot speak well, it is far better to encourage additional modes of expression and communication, writing and gesturing, than to make him feel ashamed and frustrated because he cannot acquire the very difficult art of speech and **lipreading.** Our aim must be a well-balanced, happy *deaf* person and not an imitation of a hearing one. (p. 440)

A summary of the most important tenets of the two extreme positions is illustrated in the list below (Baker & Cokely, 1980; Scouten, 1984; Silverman, Lane, & Calvert, 1978).

Philosophical Perspectives

Clinical (also known as medical or pathological) Model
   Emphasis is on remedying the deficiencies of deafness—for example, speech, language, and literacy.
   Favors mainstreaming, or regular-education programming: Educational goals and practices for hearing-impaired students should be like those for hearing students.
   Denies or minimizes the importance of a Deaf culture.
   Maintains that it's a hearing world and that deaf individuals must be able to interact with hearing individuals.

Cultural Model
   Emphasizes differences rather than deficiencies.
   Maintains that communication is important, primarily by using signing, preferably the American Sign Language.
   Maintains that the most appropriate education for most deaf students is in residential schools; favors the use of special instructional materials and practices.
   Argues that a well-adjusted, well-balanced deaf person is one who can communi-

cate and express needs; the ability to read and write are important but not highly valued; literacy is more important than well-developed oral communication skills.

Maintains that it is both a hearing and deaf world with only limited interaction between the two; deaf individuals may work in a hearing world, but they live in a deaf world.

Resolution of Perspectives.   As with most other either-or educational positions, it is probably best to incorporate elements from both extremes in the preparation of teachers at the university level. For example, a prospective teacher should be able to communicate fluently using both oral communication and signing skills and to teach severely to profoundly hearing-impaired students to develop their abilities in both skills. This means that teachers need to acquire and apply their knowledge of the development of oral skills such as speech, **speech reading,** residual hearing, and related areas. Likewise, they need to be well versed in signing, including the use of ASL as an instructional vehicle. Salient aspects of the Deaf culture, such as poetry, history, and storytelling, can be included in instruction and curriculum, and Deaf members of the culture can be invited to participate in classroom activities. As discussed in Chapter 6, the inclusion of the Deaf culture and members of the Deaf community in instructional and curricular activities is one of the most neglected areas in the education of severely to profoundly hearing-impaired students, particularly in TC educational programs. Developing **language and communication** skills, as well as exploring their effects on **cognitive, psychosocial,** and academic developments, is discussed briefly in the next section and in much greater detail in Chapters 4 through 7.

Knowledge of Academic Content Areas.   In addition to language and communication development, it is important for teachers to be knowledgeable in the various academic areas they are required to teach, such as reading, writing, mathematics, science, social studies, and career education. A competent instructor of reading requires a great deal of knowledge about the process and problems of reading encountered by hearing children as well as by hearing-impaired children. Teachers must have a strong background in **theory** and assessment as well as a familiarity with effective instructional strategies and practices. Teachers who become skilled in adapting curricular materials to meet the linguistic and cognitive needs of their students have an added advantage.

In general, research, curricular developments and materials, and the foci of university-level teacher-training programs have been on the development of communication skills, specifically speech, language, and signs (Corbett & Jensema, 1981; Lang, 1989; Moores, 1987; Quigley & Kretschmer, 1982). Consequently, teachers of hearing-impaired students are not always well trained in important subjects such as reading, mathematics, and science. A good review of the state-of-the-art instruction in mathematics, science, and social studies is in Lang (1989). Some insights into these subjects, including achievement, curriculum, and assessment, are provided in a later section of this chapter and in more detail in Chapter 9 of this book. Chapter 8 presents current thinking on the processes of reading and writing, charts the development of severely to profoundly hearing-impaired students in these areas, and gives general guidelines for improving instructional practices.

Other Major Issues

Early Intervention. One of the recent issues confronting researchers and educators of hearing-impaired children is the establishment of standards and procedures for **early intervention** programs. Because of the importance of the early childhood period for cognitive, communicative, social, and emotional development, there is an increasing interest in the establishment of preschool and other early intervention programs. The earlier emphasis was on programs for children between 3 to 5 years of age; now the focus is on infants from birth to 3 years old. Early intervention programs for hearing-impaired children, as well as for other **at-risk** children, are deemed to be critical for the development of hearing, speech, and language and also possibly important in fostering cognitive and psychosocial development. There is considerable controversy not on whether early intervention is important but on what types of services should be offered to most severely to profoundly hearing-impaired students. As expected, the controversy is affected by the philosophical perspectives on deafness discussed previously.

To establish adequate early intervention programs, improvements must be made in the screening, identification, and follow-up procedures of hearing-impaired infants. ''Identifying 'risk-factors' have been well delineated, but the fact is that the impairment is too frequently *not* identified until somewhere between the ages of 3 and 6'' (Commission on Education of the Deaf, 1988, p. 1). This may mean that the majority of hearing-impaired students are still not receiving formal education until they are 5 or 6 years old. This situation is similar to that of nearly 20 years ago (Hester, 1969). The importance of **early amplification** and intervention for hearing-impaired children is discussed briefly in Chapter 2 and in more detail in Chapter 9.

Educational Interpreters. Another emerging issue that has had a profound effect on **preservice** and **inservice** teachers and on the education of hearing-impaired students is the growing use of **educational interpreters** in regular education classrooms on the elementary, secondary, and postsecondary levels. **Interpreting** as a profession with training programs and standards has grown enormously since the establishment of the Registry of Interpreters for the Deaf (RID), a national certifying organization for interpreters, in 1965. Some of the major current problems of interpreters include salary, working conditions, and minimum standards for *educational* interpreters. The establishment of standards for oral interpreters is also a source of concern. Standards for sign interpreters, particularly educational sign interpreters, are affected by the prevailing thinking regarding the nature and use of ASL and the **English-based signed systems** (Chapters 6 and 7). Not much is known about the role and provisions for educational interpreters at the elementary and secondary educational levels. Another related concern is whether preservice and inservice teachers should pass exams in sign language competency that are similar or nearly similar to the ones required for interpreters. These issues and others are discussed in Chapter 9.

Multihandicapped Students. One of the most difficult problems facing researchers and educators is the understanding and planning of an appropriate education for the increasing number of multihandicapped hearing-impaired students. These students obviously complicate the tasks of classification, selection of instructional and curricular activities, and in some cases, the establishment of educational goals. It may be that current classification procedures lead to inappropriate educational practices, especially for some minority students. Despite the fact that nearly 30 percent of the hearing-impaired student population is reported to have additional handicaps (Wolff & Harkins, 1986), the nature and extent of the educational problems of members of this population have not been systematically explored. Chapter 10 provides more details on the educational problems (e.g., identification, assessment, teacher training, and programming) brought about by the increase of hearing-impaired students with additional handicaps.

LANGUAGE AND COMMUNICATION

The most enduring and controversial issue in the education of severely to profoundly hearing-impaired students is the language and/or communication system that should be used by and with the students in the home and school environments to develop receptive and expressive communication skills. More attention has been devoted to the development of language, particularly English, in these students than to any other instructional area (Corbett & Jensema, 1981; Lang, 1989; Moores, 1987). As discussed throughout this book, this issue has pervasive effects on all aspects of **academic achievement** and on cognitive and psychosocial developments. For example, the acquisition of English is important for the subsequent development of literacy, which is the cornerstone for success in school and throughout life (Anderson, Hiebert, Scott, & Wilkinson, 1985).

There are two major aspects of this issue: kind of language and form of communication (Quigley & Kretschmer, 1982; Quigley & Paul, 1984a). Specifically, there are two languages, American Sign Language and English, and two communication forms, oral and **manual.** The two languages and communication forms can be combined to produce a variety of approaches that can be categorized in three ways: (1) oral English, (2) **signed systems** or **manually coded English,** and (3) American Sign Language. These approaches (except for ASL) are part of one of two communication philosophies, oral education and Total Communication, as shown in the following lists:

Oral Education

Oral English Approaches
Primarily Auditory
    Also known as:
    Aural-oral
    Acoupedics
    Aural only
    Acoustic
    Unisensory
Multisensory
    Auditory-visual-oral
    Auditory-visual-tactile (including tactile-
      kinesthetic)
    Cued speech

American Sign Language

Total Communication

Manually Coded English Approaches
English-like signing
    Also known as:
    Pidgin sign English
    Sign English (or signed English)
    Simultaneous communication
Signed English
Manual English
Linguistic of visual English
Signing exact English
Seeing essential English
Rochester Method

In the development of the two major philosophies, many early programs implemented both oral and TC approaches. The differentiation between the two philosophies and their approaches emerged during the 18th century and was clearly established by the end of the 19th century.

Oralism

In the oral-communication philosophy, instructional methods involve the use of **auditory training/learning** and the development of speech and speech reading (lipreading) skills. The emphasis is on creating and proceeding in an instructional environment that is similar to that of typical hearing students in regular education programs. As discussed in Chapter 5, there is great variability with oral-education methods. For example, some programs emphasize the use of audition, or residual hearing, whereas others encourage the combination of vision and audition.

Historical Perspectives.   With some reservations that result from limited and sometimes contradictory historical reports, it is possible to chart the beginnings of the use of oralism in Europe with hearing-impaired children taught individually or in small groups. After using writing in conjunction with discrete objects to convey the concept of language, Ponce de Leon (1520–1584), an Augustinian monk and scholar, who is considered to be the first formal teacher of hearing-impaired students, is reported to have related the written form to speech (i.e., Spanish). Although accounts are sketchy, it is thought that he also taught the language to his students by using the **manual alphabet** (i.e., **finger spelling** or *dactylology*) in which the letters of the alphabet are represented by distinct handshapes.

During the 1700s and 1800s, formal organized education of hearing-impaired students commenced with the founding of several programs, some of which advocated the use of oral methods. For example, Johann Amman (1669–1724) of Holland is considered the father of pure oralism (Scouten, 1984). His work influenced that of Samuel Heinicke (1729–1790), who established a school in Germany (the first school supported by a government) and that of Thomas Braidwood (1715–1806), who established a school in Edinburgh, Scotland. Amman's methods are considered the precursors of those used today in working with not only hearing-impaired students but also individuals with speech problems such as **articulation** and **stuttering.** Braidwood is reported to have used signs and finger spelling in his instructional methods; however, his main emphasis was on the development of speech.

Heinicke is credited with initiating the formal controversy between oralism and manualism (Hester, 1969; Scouten, 1984). He tried to dissuade a colleague who was a professional educator from adopting the French method of manualism as developed by the Abbé de l'Epée (1712–1789), who established a school in Paris. Oral education in the United States during the 1800s was confined to a few programs such as the Clarke School for the Deaf, established in 1867 as the first residential school for deaf students, and the Horace Mann School for the Deaf, the first **day school** established in 1869.

After the International Congress on Deafness in Milan, Italy, in 1880, oralism became the predominant method in the education of hearing-impaired students. At this conference, the *superiority* of oral methods was asserted. As a result, a resolution was passed asserting that the use of manual communication (signing and finger spelling) by young children impedes their learning English and developing speech and speech reading skills. Subsequently, oral education methods became and remained dominant in the United States until the advent of the Total Communication philosophy during the late 1960s and early 1970s. A more detailed description of the oral methods and their use with hearing-impaired students is in Chapter 5.

Total Communication

Roy Holcomb, a deaf graduate of the Texas School for the Deaf and of Gallaudet College (now Gallaudet University), is considered the father of Total Communication (TC) (Gannon, 1981). Holcomb coined this term, which supposedly advocates the use of all forms of communication to teach language to hearing-impaired students. The TC philosophy spawned several signed systems that are based on the structural elements (e.g., vocabulary, **syntax**) of written **standard English** in the United States (see Chapter 7). Practitioners are supposed to sign and use speech simultaneously. By the late 1980s, educational programs were using signs with about 80 percent of profoundly hearing-impaired students, 75 percent of severely hearing-impaired students, and 30 percent of students with less severe hearing impairments (Gallaudet Research Institute, 1985). Most educators have not accepted the use of ASL as an instructional approach within the philosophy of Total Communication even though TC is reported to *endorse any or all forms of communication*. This complex issue is discussed in detail in Chapter 6.

Historical Perspectives.   The use of signed systems, or manual communication, simultaneously with speech is not new. The Italian mathematician and physician, Jerome Cardan (1501–1576), for example, attempted to teach children to read and write, and he remarked that "ideas could be expressed by the language of signs" (McClure, 1969, p. 3). After Ponce de Leon in Spain, Juan Bonet (1579–1620) advocated the use of teaching hearing-impaired children by using the one-handed manual alphabet, or finger spelling. This is the same manual alphabet that is used today in the United States. Bonet's approach of using finger spelling and speech simultaneously was the precursor of a similar approach called the **Rochester Method,** which was developed at the Rochester School for the Deaf in the United States in 1878, and was labeled **neo-oralism** by educators in the Soviet Union in the 1950s. Bonet also focused on teaching speech skills, particularly the articulation of sounds and syllables. These skills were taught before the introduction of literacy activities.

During the 17th century, manual approaches to teaching communication skills were also used in England, endorsed by major educational figures such as John Wallis (1616–1703) and George Dalgarno (1626–1687). The idea of adapting the signs of deaf persons to conform to the structure of a spoken language was developed and refined during the 18th century by the Abbé de l'Epée and his successor, the Abbé Sicard (1742–1822). As discussed in Chapter 7, de l'Epée modified the Sign Language of the French Deaf community into a signed system that reflected the vocabulary and syntax of French.

These efforts were the forerunners of the development of English-based signed systems in England and the United States during the 1960s and 1970s.

The signed methods of de l'Epée and Sicard were brought to America by Thomas Hopkins Gallaudet (1787–1851), who founded the first school, a residential school, for deaf students in Hartford, Connecticut, in 1817. Gallaudet persuaded Laurent Clerc (1785–1869), a deaf teacher and former student at the Paris school, to emigrate to the United States. "Thus began two traditions that have distinguished American education of deaf children from European systems—manual communication and deaf teachers" (Quigley & Paul, 1984a, p. 16). Although there were some attempts at oral instruction, particularly the teaching of speech, the early schools for deaf students in the United States predominantly used manual communication as their method of instruction for about 50 years. Similar to present day arguments, there were disagreements over what specific manual methods to use and how to use them. The combined system, the beginning of Total Communication in the 1970s, is reported to have been introduced, developed, and implemented in the first residential schools for deaf students in the United States during the 19th century.

Oral-Manual Controversy

As discussed previously, the **oral-manual controversy** developed formally with de l'Epée and Heinicke and continued with Edward Miner Gallaudet (1837–1917) and Alexander Graham Bell (1847–1922). At the International Congress in Milan, Italy, in 1880, the argument was on developing language and communication by using speech versus signs. Presently, the focus is on which method is most likely to develop adequately receptive and expressive skills in English.

From the perspective of Moores (1987):

> . . . it is technically inaccurate to speak of an oral-manual controversy. All educators of the deaf are aware of the benefits of the use of residual hearing, speech, and speech-reading. All educators of the deaf are by definition oralists and are concerned with developing a child's ability to speak and understand the spoken word to the highest degree possible. The difference is between oral-alone educators, who argue that all children must be educated by exclusively oral techniques, and oral-plus educators, who argue that at least some deaf children would progress more satisfactorily with **simultaneous** or combined oral-manual **communication.** (p. 10)

What is missing from the foregoing quotation and perhaps from most educators' perceptions of Total Communication is the possible use of ASL in the education of deaf students. Specifically, there is a growing belief that a number of severely hearing-impaired students and the overwhelming majority of profoundly hearing-impaired, or *deaf,* students may have a better opportunity to learn English, particularly reading and writing skills, if ASL is used in a **bilingual** or **second-language** program (Luetke-Stahlman, 1983; Paul, 1987; Quigley & Paul, 1984b; Reagan, 1985). Holders of this view believe that ASL should be taught to students as a first language, English as a second. As discussed in Chapters 6, 7, and 8, the use of *any manual communication approach by itself is not sufficient for the development of skills in a spoken language such as English.*

Nevertheless, ASL as an instructional approach has not been systematically used and assessed in the education of severely to profoundly hearing-impaired students in the 20th century (Lane, 1980, 1984; Quigley & Paul, 1984a, 1984b).

Natural Versus Structural Approaches

Related to the issue of methods is the debate on the use of **natural** or **structural** approaches to the teaching of language. The use of language-teaching approaches has affected, for example, the use of instructional and curricular activities for developing reading and writing skills (the focus of Chapter 8). Indeed, this issue may have pervasively influenced the use of educational activities and materials in the other academic subjects (see Chapter 9). The debate on natural versus structural approaches has a long history, and only a few highlights are presented here. The two approaches and their variations have been implemented in both oral and TC programs. A more detailed discussion can be found in McAnally, Rose, and Quigley (1987) and Quigley and Paul (1984a).

Practitioners of the natural approach try to develop language in hearing-impaired children in a holistic manner. In order for the students to discover rules and principles of English, for example, it is argued that they need to be exposed to a language-rich environment similar to that of their hearing peers. Proponents of the natural approach do not try to *teach* language but, rather, to provide numerous opportunities for deaf students to *acquire* it in natural, meaningful situations. The **grammar** of a language is not taught explicitly by definitions, examples, or abstract representations of parts of speech, or form classes, such as **nouns, verbs, adjectives, adverbs,** and so on. Exemplary proponents of the natural approach include Friedrich Hill in Germany in the 19th century, and Mildred Groht in the United States and van Uden in the Netherlands in the 20th century (Bender, 1970; Scouten, 1984).

Proponents of structural approaches maintain that language must be *taught,* at least partially, to hearing-impaired students. Students are expected to learn a language by analyzing and categorizing its various grammatical aspects, such as parts of speech. Specifically, they are required to understand the grammar within the constraints of a strictly sequenced curriculum. Students demonstrate their understanding by writing sentences, using patterns that have been taught. In most cases, grammatical aspects are categorized into specific slots of various **symbol systems** such as question words (e.g., *who, what,* and *where*). Exemplary representatives of this approach include de l'Epée and Sicard in France in the 18th century, Gallaudet and Clerc in the United States in the 19th century, and Edith Fitzgerald in the United States in the 20th century (e.g., Bender, 1970; Schmitt, 1966; Scouten, 1984).

Historical Perspectives.   The structural method and the language of signs was implemented in the first school for the deaf established in Hartford, Connecticut, now known as the American School for the Deaf. Based on Sicard's work, teachers at this school developed diagrams, or line drawings, to represent the grammatical aspects of English. Students were required to memorize rules and sentences and to read and write them. Influenced by the French method of teaching, almost all residential programs in the

United States in subsequent years used predominantly manual communication and structural methods of teaching language.

During the 19th century, a number of visual symbol systems, as well as curricula, texts, and readers, were developed to assist in teaching English by the structural approach (McAnally et al., 1987, and Quigley & Paul, 1984a). Among the creators of symbol systems were Frederick Barnard (straight-line and curved-line symbols), Richard Storrs (symbols written above words), George Wing (numbers, letters, and other symbols placed above words), and Katherine Barry (five slates or tablets of materials used for writing only, similar to the approach used by Sicard). Despite differences in the use of symbols, the common goal was to teach deaf children grammar and sentence patterns.

Even though structural approaches and special language materials dominated in the United States during most of the 19th century, the natural approach to teaching language began to attract the attention of educators and scholars. David Greenberger, principal of the Lexington School for the Deaf, an oral residential school in New York, espoused the principles developed earlier by Hill in Germany. Some principles of this approach were also implemented in other schools, particularly residential schools such as the Rochester School for the Deaf in Rochester, New York, where the natural approach was used with preschoolers age 4 to 7 years by communicating with speech and finger spelling simultaneously.

The development of special materials for teaching language and the use of both structural and natural techniques continued into the 20th century. Most of the materials and methods reflected the prevailing linguistic thinking of the period. Linguistic thinking has shifted from an emphasis on **phonology** (study of sounds) to syntax (word order) to **semantics** (meaning), and finally, to the current emphasis on **pragmatics** (function or use of language) (Quigley & Paul, 1984a).

Perhaps the most widely known structural approach for teaching language, and one that is still used in a number of programs today, is the Fitzgerald Key developed by Edith Fitzgerald, a deaf teacher at the Wisconsin School for the Deaf. This program is described in her book *Straight Language for the Deaf* (1929). Although the Fitzgerald Key is based on some of the principles developed by Katherine Barry for her Five Slate System, it expanded on earlier principles (McAnally et al., 1987). The Key has six columns, each headed with words and symbols as follows: (1) subject *(who, what)*, (2) verb and predicate words, (3) **indirect** and **direct objects** *(what, whom)*, (4) phrases and words denoting place *(where)*, (5) other phrases and word modifiers of the main verb *(for, from, how, how often, how much)*, and (6) words and phrases dealing with time *(when)*. Fitzgerald asserted that the purpose of the Key is to enable deaf students to learn some of the rules of English and to construct and evaluate their written productions (1929).

The natural approach gained momentum with the publication of *Natural Language for Deaf Children* by Mildred Groht (1958). Influenced by her predecessor, David Greenberger, Groht, who was principal of the Lexington School for the Deaf, espoused the notion of *developing* language rather than teaching it through analytical drills and exercises. The focus was on helping children to *induce,* or *discover,* how language works. Some principles advocated by Groht (1933) were as follows:

1. The child's needs should dictate the content of language rather than lists of words and language rules.
2. Natural language is learned by a number of meaningful situations rather than by drills and exercises.
3. The functions of language can be taught best through conversations, discussions, writing, and the academic subjects.
4. Language principles that need to be taught should be introduced incidentally in natural situations, explained by the teacher in real meaningful situations, and practiced by children in numerous activities such as games, questions, stories, and conversations.

Since the early 1950s, several special language materials have been developed and some educators have advocated *a structured approach to teaching language in a natural manner* (Blackwell, Engen, Fischgrund, & Zarcadoolas, 1978; Heidinger, 1984; Streng, 1972). The latest thrust seems to indicate that a combination of some of the best principles from the two general approaches—natural and structural—is more acceptable than an either-or situation. Some of the publications along these lines include books such as *A World of Language for Deaf Children* (van Uden, 1977) and *Analyzing Syntax and Semantics* (Heidinger, 1984), and special language materials such as *Sentences and Other Systems* (Blackwell et al., 1978), the *Apple Tree* curriculum (Anderson, Boren, Caniglia, Howard, & Krohn, 1980), and the *TSA Syntax Program* (Quigley & Power, 1979). Detailed discussion of the present use of natural and structural approaches and special materials, specifically special reading series, is in Chapter 8 of this book.

The debate on language and communication continues to focus on the best methods for teaching or developing the English language skills of hearing-impaired children. A number of questions still need to be answered; for example:

How important is residual hearing for the development of speech? for language? for reading?

How do hearing-impaired children's language abilities relate to the development of their thinking abilities, particularly **higher-level skills** such as reasoning, problem-solving, and **inferencing?**

How are children's social and emotional developments affected by their language skills?

Can most severely to profoundly hearing-impaired children learn to speak intelligibly?

Is speech ability related to reading ability?

Can children adequately learn an English-based signed system?

Is it possible to speak and sign simultaneously in a systematic, consistent manner?

Are signed systems truly representative of the structure (i.e., syntax and grammar) of English?

Can American Sign Language be used to teach English as a second language?

How do hearing-impaired children's signing abilities relate to reading and writing abilities?

Throughout the book, we try to synthesize the available research and scholarly literature to provide an examination and discussion of these questions as well as to suggest some tentative answers.

ACADEMIC PLACEMENT AND ACHIEVEMENT

When the Commission on Education of the Deaf (1988) observed that the present status of the education of deaf students was unsatisfactory, one of the problems discussed was the low levels of academic achievement. The Commission stated that these low levels were caused mainly by low levels of reading achievement, which affected all other academic areas. This assertion has been made by many other scholars (Babbini & Quigley, 1970; DiFrancesca, 1972; Quigley & Paul, 1986; Trybus & Karchmer, 1977). Indeed, reading is an essential tool that students need in order to master other academic areas. A lack of reading skill is a major reason for the low levels of educational achievement that have been documented in hearing-impaired students since the beginning of formal assessment (Quigley & Paul, 1986).

Assessment and Achievement

Achievement is usually determined by performance on **secondary-language** measures, that is, on tests that require students to read and to write their responses. Such tests demand at least competency in the language in which the students are supposed to read and write, as well as knowledge of subjects such as mathematics, social studies, and science. Some students may know the answers to questions that are presented to them through speech and/or signs, but their knowledge is evident only if they are permitted to answer the questions in the same expressive mode or modes. Students may not, however, be able to evince their knowledge through reading and/or writing as required by **standardized tests** and other similar assessments. Thus, it seems that achievement tests often measure the level of English language competency of hearing-impaired students rather than their level of achievement in the various academic subjects. This issue is related to the present debate on whether hearing-impaired students should be required to take the same minimum competency examinations as do typical hearing students, or to take special tests designed for them (Bloomquist, 1986). As with other educational debates, the viewpoints of educators and scholars are influenced by their personal philosophies of education and deafness. In brief, are they focusing on deafness as a clinical or a cultural entity or as some combination of the two? In any event, it can be argued that achievement tests measure the ability of students to understand information presented at a certain literate level in the **majority language** of mainstream society.

Curriculum, Instruction, and Achievement

Several other nonstudent factors influence achievement—theoretical perspectives, test tasks, curricula, and instruction. For example, tests of reading are influenced by theories regarding the nature of the reading process. If test-makers define reading as a series of subskills, then their tests might be designed to measure such skills as main idea, word parts, and so on.

It is often overlooked that there are, or should be, close interrelations among tests, curricula, and instruction. To provide an accurate picture of achievement, the objectives and content of standardized tests, for example, should be reflective of the objectives and content of academic courses common to a national sample of schools. The tests should assess information that is contained in the curriculum and that is an integral part of instruction (Anastasi, 1982; Pearson & Valencia, 1986; Salvia & Ysseldyke, 1985). If these conditions are met, one can compare the scores of individuals from various schools at similar grade or age levels. More detailed discussions of the standardization process and other aspects of the development of tests are presented in Chapter 9.

Placement and Achievement

Because of **Public Law 94–142,** increasing attention is being given to academic placement and its effects on academic achievement of hearing-impaired students. Placement has a history as long and as contentious as do language and communication methods and language-teaching approaches. According to Quigley and Frisina (1961):

> Organized education for deaf children in the United States began with the opening of the American School for the Deaf in West Hartford, Connecticut, in 1817. This was a residential school which provided boarding facilities for its students as well as educational facilities and programs. During the next 50 years, state residential schools for the deaf spread throughout the country. Then, in 1869, a change occurred. In that year, the first day school for the deaf was opened in the United States in Roxbury, Massachusetts. Since then, day schools have been established in many cities. The day school provided only educational facilities, and the children live at home. At about the turn of the century, day classes for deaf children were opened in Chicago, Illinois. Day classes differ from day schools in that they have fewer students and are part of regular public schools rather than being located in a separate facility. Both day classes and day schools have the presumed advantage of permitting the deaf child to live at home with his family. (p. 1)

Recent Perspectives.   Since about 1945, there has been a consistent trend for hearing-impaired students to be enrolled in **day programs** (day schools or public school classes). By the mid-1960s, the majority of students were in day programs. This shift in enrollment from residential to day programs was accelerated by the passage of Public Law 94–142 in 1975, and the concept of the **least restrictive environment** came into effect. It was argued, as it had been for a century or more, that residential and other segregated schools and programs were not the best educational placement for the majority of hearing-impaired students. This argument also applied to students in other special-education populations (Heward & Orlansky, 1988; Kirk & Gallagher, 1986).

Although the current trend is on placing students in regular education programs as much as possible, fewer than 50 percent of hearing-impaired students are academically integrated (mainstreamed) at least part time in regular education classrooms (Karchmer, 1984; cf., Libbey & Pronovost, 1980; Wolk, Karchmer, & Schildroth, 1982). Most of these students have hearing losses that range from slight to moderate. Very few students with severe to profound, prelinguistic hearing impairments are mainstreamed in regular classes (Allen & Osborn, 1984; Moores & Kluwin, 1986; Wolk et al., 1982). In addition, most severely to profoundly hearing-impaired students in public schools spend most of their time in **self-contained** classrooms, or they are mainstreamed in nonacademic classes such as physical education and art education.

Even though enrollment has declined over the years, a large number of severely to profoundly hearing-impaired students (about one-third) still attend residential schools. Many residential students are adolescents, and about 40 percent commute to the school rather than live in dorms (Moores, 1987). There is also some speculation that residential schools have been receiving the bulk of the increasing population of deaf students with additional handicaps.

In recent years, additional programs have emerged that are a product of services offered in public education programs in an attempt to meet the special needs of hearing-impaired students. For example, there are **resource rooms** in which students receive special individualized services from resource teachers in English, reading, and writing, and in academic subjects such as math, science, and history. In addition, there are now **itinerant programs** in which students who typically attend regular education classes receive special support help from teachers who travel to several schools to provide **individualized instruction.** Finally, there are variations of the education programs discussed here; some programs combine elements from several other programs. A brief description of the various program models follows (Moores, 1987; Ross, Brackett, & Maxon, 1982):

Special Schools

Residential Schools
>   Education for hearing-impaired students only.
>   Housing facilities available.
>   In areas accessible to large populations.
>   About 40 percent of students commute to school.

Day Schools
>   Education for hearing-impaired students only.
>   Located in large metropolitan areas.
>   No housing facilities available.
>   Students commute to school.

Regular Education Programs

Day Classes
>   Located in public schools.
>   Hearing-impaired students commute to school.
>   Hearing-impaired students may attend regular education or self-contained classes.

Resource Rooms
>   Located in public schools.
>   Hearing-impaired students commute to school.
>   Typically for students who spend all or most of the day in regular education classrooms.
>   Regular and remedial instruction, speech, tutoring, and other support services.

Itinerant Services
    Located in public schools.
    Typically for students who spend all day in regular education classrooms.
    Students receive support services from teachers and other personnel who travel to
        several schools.

Chapter 9 provides further details of the relationships between academic achievement and other areas of long-standing problems such as language and communication methods, academic placement, and student and test characteristics and provides information on which to base tentative conclusions regarding the academic achievement of severely to profoundly hearing-impaired students leaving secondary-education programs. Students in postsecondary institutions, which have experienced an increase in enrollment, are also discussed. There is an extensive system for the education of hearing-impaired students from preschool to college in the United States but not for children from birth to about 3 or 4 years of age (Commission on Education of the Deaf, 1988).

SUMMARY

The primary focus of this chapter was to provide an introduction to and some historical perspectives on the major enduring issues in the education of severely to profoundly hearing-impaired students that are discussed in detail throughout the book. One of the main points was that there is a need for the acquisition and application of knowledge. Very little is known about the most effective methods and techniques for teaching the students. Research and scholarly literature indicates that there is very little ongoing instructional investigation. In addition, much of what exists concerns the development of language, specifically English. There is also a need to investigate instruction in other academic disciplines such as mathematics, science, and social studies.

To advance and apply knowledge, it is important for researchers to provide an adequate description of the population under study. This chapter listed several important variables—for example, degree and age at onset of hearing impairment. One of the most important benefits of adequately describing the population is to help prevent the generalization of findings to dissimilar populations.

With the foregoing issues in mind, this book is concerned primarily with the achievement of groups of typical prelinguistically, severely to profoundly hearing-impaired students in special education programs and/or classes. These students have sensorineural hearing losses of 71 decibels (dB) or greater in the better unaided ear that occurred before the age of about 2 years. The problems of language, communication, and academic achievement of these students are markedly different from those of other students with less severe hearing impairments.

One of the most important areas of research and practice is the preparation of teachers at the university level. It was argued in this chapter that teacher-training programs, including the selection of communication methods, language-teaching approaches, and curricular viewpoints, are influenced pervasively by two educational philosophies, or perspectives, on deafness. The basic tenets of the two bipolar perspectives—that is, clinical and cultural models—and some implications for instruction and curriculum were discussed.

Another area that needs attention is teachers' receiving more training in academic content other than that of language skills. Because of the enduring emphasis on the development of language, specifically English, many teachers are not adequately qualified to teach several academic courses that they may be required to teach. They take a number of university-level classes that emphasize language-teaching methods, but they may take only one or two classes that focus on mathematics, reading, science, and social studies.

Some brief remarks were provided on other emerging issues that have had an impact on the preparation of teachers. These include educational interpreting, the establishment of adequate early intervention programs, and the increase in the population of hearing-impaired students with additional handicaps. Many of these issues have become evident, in part, because of the passage of Public Law 94–142 and its amendments. Despite their impact on educational programs and programming, most of the emerging areas are still in need of consistent and systematic investigation.

Perhaps the most enduring and controversial issue in the education of severely to profoundly hearing-impaired students deals with language and communication. Since the beginning of the formal education period, more attention has been given to language teaching and development than to any other academic area. The two aspects of this issue are kind of language (American Sign Language and English) and form of communication (oral and manual). The two can be combined to create a number of communication approaches. Instructional use of the approaches is influenced by two bipolar communication philosophies, oralism and TC.

This chapter showed that neither the philosophies nor their methods and controversies are new. One puzzling question, however, is why ASL has not been used systematically as an instructional approach in the 20th century. Despite the philosophy of TC, which advocates the use of any or all communication approaches catered to the individual needs of the child, ASL is not widely used in TC educational programs.

The salient principles of two general language-teaching models—the natural and structural approaches—were discussed. The debate on natural versus structural methods has a long contentious history. At present, the most effective methods for developing language and communication skills in prelinguistically, severely to profoundly hearing-impaired students are still not known.

The academic placement and achievement of hearing-impaired students is a complex issue affected by several variables. Much of what is known about the educational achievement of these students is based on their performances on secondary-language tests. That is, achievement is measured by standardized and other similar tests that require students to read and write at some level. The decision to use tests developed for hearing students or those specifically designed for hearing-impaired students is affected also by educators' perspectives on deafness (e.g., clinical versus cultural models).

Presently, we can say that the education of hearing-impaired students has become primarily the responsibility of public education agencies in the area where students and their families live. To meet the individual needs of many students in public education programs, several new educational program models have emerged—for example, the use of itinerant and resource teachers. Despite these trends, a considerable portion of prelinguistically severely to profoundly hearing-impaired adolescents still attend residential schools. In addition, residential schools have been admitting a significant number of students with additional handicaps.

In sum, there is a well-established, extensive system for educating hearing-impaired students from preschool to postsecondary institutions. The only exception is the lack of educational programs for children between birth and 3 years of age.

COMPREHENSION

1. TRUE or FALSE? The Commission on Education of the Deaf (1988) stated that the present status of education of deaf students in the United States is satisfactory.
2. Education, as other professions have done, needs to recognize the interdependence of research and practice. What does this statement mean?
3. To generalize and understand research findings, Quigley and Kretschmer argued that researchers must provide complete descriptions of their hearing-impaired subjects. List three important descriptive variables.
4. Which of the following statements is/are TRUE about prelinguistically severely to profoundly hearing-impaired students?
   a. They have sensorineural hearing losses of 71 dB or greater in the better unaided ear.
   b. Their hearing losses occurred after the age of 2 years.
   c. Their primary mode for receiving communicative input is audition.
   d. Most students enrolled in special schools or classes have prelinguistic severe to profound hearing impairments.
   e. All of the above.
5. Label the following statements as *clinical* or *cultural:*
   a. A belief in only one society, a hearing society.
   b. The emphasis is on remedying the deficiencies (e.g., speech) of hearing-impaired students.
   c. There are two societies, hearing and Deaf, with only limited communication or interaction between them.
   d. Deafness is not a disease or something to be cured.
   e. The method of communication should be suited to the child; however, signing, particularly ASL, is very important.
   f. There is no Deaf community.
   g. The aim of education should be to make the deaf child a well-integrated, happy individual and not a pale imitation of a hearing person.
6. What may be the best way to deal with the two bipolar educational perspectives in teacher-training programs?
7. TRUE or FALSE? University teacher-training programs have focused mainly on the development of language and communication skills rather than on the development of skills in academic subjects.
8. What are the two languages and two forms associated with language/communication? What are the three major categories that account for the various combinations of the languages and forms?
9. TRUE or FALSE? The differences between oralism and Total Communication did not become clear until the 1970s.
10. How did Heinicke in Germany initiate the controversy between oralism and manualism?
11. TRUE or FALSE? Until 1880, most programs in the United States used manualism.

12. Which of the following statements is/are TRUE about Total Communication?
   a. The term was coined by a deaf man.
   b. The concept advocates the use of all forms of communication to teach language.
   c. The use of signed systems began with TC in the 1960s.
   d. American Sign Language has been systematically used in TC programs.
   e. All of the above.

13. Label the following statements as *natural* or *structural:*
   a. Language should be developed in a holistic manner.
   b. Language must be taught.
   c. Students must be provided opportunities to *acquire* language.
   d. Students learn a language by analyzing and categorizing its parts.
   e. In the beginning, almost all residential schools for deaf students used analyses and categories in teaching language.

14. What factors cause the shift in enrollment from residential to day programs for hearing-impaired students?

15. TRUE or FALSE? Most severely to profoundly hearing-impaired students are mainstreamed, that is, they spend all or most of the school day in regular education classes.

16. Describe the various placement options for severely to profoundly hearing-impaired students.

SUGGESTED ACTIVITIES

1. Obtain a copy of Public Law 94–142 from your library. What is the purpose of this law? According to the document, what is considered the least restrictive environment (LRE)?

2. Plan a visit to the following:
   a. A residential school
   b. A special day school
   c. Special classes in public schools for hearing-impaired students
   Make a list of similarities and differences among the various placements. Be sure to note the nature of the communication method (e.g., oralism or Total Communication) and the language-teaching methods (e.g., natural, structural, or combined). Solicit the opinions of the various educational personnel (i.e., principals, teachers, interpreters) on Public Law 94–142.

3. Find out whether your state has established a competency testing program for teachers of hearing-impaired students. If so, what content areas are assessed? Does your state also have a sign communication competency exam for teachers? If not, why not?

4. Make a list of the major journals in the field of deafness.

FURTHER READINGS

Beveridge, W. (1980). *Seeds of discovery: The logic, illogic, serendipity, and sheer chance of scientific discovery.* New York: Norton.

Beyer, L. (1988). *Knowing and acting: Inquiry, ideology, and educational studies.* New York: Falmer Press.

Boatner, M. (1959). *Voice of the Deaf: A biography of Edward Miner Gallaudet.* Washington, DC: Public Affairs Press.

Bruce, R. (1973). *Bell: Alexander Graham Bell and the conquest of solitude*. Boston, MA: Little, Brown.

Garnett, C. (1968). *The exchange of letters between Samuel Heinicke and the Abbé Charles Michel de l'Epée*. New York: Vantage Press.

Lash, J. (1980). *Helen and teacher*. New York: Delacorte Press/Seymour Lawrence.

National Center for Law and the Deaf. (1986). *Legal rights of hearing-impaired people* (3rd ed.). Washington, DC: Gallaudet University Press.

National Commission on Excellence in Education (1983). *A nation at risk: The imperative for educational reform*. Washington, DC: U.S. Government Printing Office.

Watson, D. (Ed.). (1973). *Readings on deafness*. New York: New York University, Deafness Research and Training Center.

Winefield, R. (1987). *Never the twain shall meet: Bell, Gallaudet and the communications debate*. Washington, DC: Gallaudet University Press.

Wright, D. (1969). *Deafness*. New York: Stein & Day.

CHAPTER 2

Hearing Science

MAJOR POINTS TO CONSIDER

Anatomy and physiology of the ear

Nature and perception of sounds

Measurement of hearing

Nature and causes of hearing impairment

Individual and group amplification systems

Hearing impairment affects the communication process, particularly the use of speech and hearing in typical spoken conversations. The root of the problem, however, lies in the impact of the impairment on the acquisition of oral, or spoken, symbols—that is, **experiential** and meaningful stimuli necessary for the development of spoken language. It is not always obvious that even a relatively slight hearing loss can negatively affect spoken language, literacy, and academic achievement of children (Paul & Quigley, 1987a; Ross, Brackett, & Maxon, 1982). Audition, the meaningful use of hearing, plays an important role in the internalization, storage, and retrieval of spoken-language structures for cognitive and linguistic functions.

Typically, speech comprehension and production occur after the development of inner, or internalized, spoken-language structures. Inner, or **internalized, language** results from the process of relating incoming, meaningful auditory symbols to appropriate visual, tactual, and **kinesthetic** images (Ling, 1986; Ling & Ling, 1978; Ross, 1986a). The internalization of symbols is made possible by the use of auditory perceptual abilities—namely, the ability to attend to, discriminate, recognize, and retain sensory input.

The development of adequate auditory perceptual abilities depends on reasonably intact peripheral mechanisms of hearing, involving the outer, middle, and inner parts of the ear. The proper functioning of the central nervous system mechanisms and the auditory cortical structures of the brain are also necessary for the transmission, integration, assimilation, and interpretation of incoming auditory stimuli.

The development of spoken-language structures requires at least the exploitation of reliable, consistent **auditory/articulatory** experiences at as early an age as possible. Early detection and intervention of hearing impairment is also important for preventing the occurrence of **auditory sensory deprivation.** It has been claimed that (Ross et al., 1982):

> . . . if the auditory system does not experience some critical quantity of meaningful, patterned sound at some early period after birth, the system will demonstrate certain morphological and physiological abnormalities that will forever limit its performance below what it might have been. (p. 6)

For hearing-impaired students, the educational intervention tools that typically have been used to develop auditory perceptual abilities are auditory learning/training (Cole & Gregory, 1986), speech (Ling, 1976), speech reading (O'Neill & Oyer, 1981), visual aids, tactile aids, hearing aids, and other amplification systems (Ling, 1986; Ross, 1986a).

We can say the educational development of audition requires the teacher to have a basic knowledge of (1) the nature of hearing and of hearing impairment; (2) the functions and limitations of amplification systems; and (3) strategies for developing children's residual hearing in classroom situations. This chapter discusses information pertinent to the first two. Techniques for developing receptive and expressive spoken communication skills are discussed in Chapter 5. First, a brief overview of the anatomy and physiology of the ear and important principles of **audiometry,** or the assessment of hearing, are provided. Next, the etiology (cause), type, and degree of hearing impairment along with educational implications are described. Finally, some of the important features of hearing aids and classroom amplification systems are covered.

ANATOMY AND PHYSIOLOGY OF THE EAR

The overall function of the ear is to gather sounds from the environment and change them into a form that can be interpreted by the brain (Davis, 1978; Harris, 1986; Meyerhoff, 1986). As sound energy passes through the structures of the ear, it is converted into mechanical, electrical, and finally, neural impulses. The changing of energy from one form to another is called **transduction.** Like events in other perceptual and learning processes, the events in the transduction process occur almost simultaneously. Nevertheless, we can discuss the anatomy and physiology of the ear in relation to the journey of sound waves through the hearing mechanism. Sound energy proceeds from the outer ear into the middle ear, then into the inner ear, and finally, into the brain. The three parts of the ear and some structures in each are illustrated in Figure 2.1.

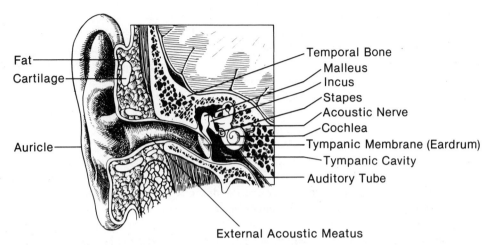

Fat
Cartilage

Auricle

Temporal Bone
Malleus
Incus
Stapes
Acoustic Nerve
Cochlea
Tympanic Membrane (Eardrum)
Tympanic Cavity
Auditory Tube

External Acoustic Meatus

Figure 2.1. Some structures of the outer, middle, and inner ear.
The Human Ear, ANAMOD™ (Anatomical Cross-Sectional Models) Series No. 13005. Oxford, CT: Redco Science, 1979. Reprinted by permission.

Anatomy: Outer Ear

The structures of the outer or external ear include the pinna (auricle) and the ear canal (external auditory meatus). The pinna is the visible flaplike part of the ear. It is a cartilage framework covered with soft tissue. The ear canal is an irregularly shaped tubelike passage that stretches horizontally for about one inch toward the center of the head. It ends at the eardrum, more properly called the drumhead or drum membrane because it is only one surface of a three-dimensional structure. The drum membrane (tympanic membrane) is considered the boundary between the outer and the middle ear.

In some animals, the pinna (auricle) is highly developed and plays important roles in gathering and locating sounds and keeping foreign materials out of the ears (Bess & McConnell, 1981; Davis, 1978). For example, rabbits, squirrels, and cats make judgments about the source of sounds without turning their heads. Other animals such as seals and moles manipulate their external ear parts so that water and other debris cannot enter their ear canals. In humans, however, the pinna has a minor role, mainly to collect sound waves into the ear canal. In relation to hearing, the external ear contributes only about five to seven decibels (dB), especially in the perception of high **frequencies** (decibels and frequencies are discussed later).

Like the pinna, the ear canal (external auditory meatus) varies from individual to individual in size and shape (Harris, 1986; Schneiderman, 1984). It is lined with skin that is continuous with the surface of the pinna. The portion of the canal closest to the external ear contains stiff hairs and glands. The glands secrete earwax (cerumen), which keeps the skin of the canal and the ear drum (tympanic membrane) from drying out. The earwax and the hairs also prevent foreign particles from entering the canal.

Anatomy: Middle Ear

The components of the middle ear include the drum membrane, an air-filled cavity, and other such items as three tiny bones (ossicles) and two small muscles (stapedius and tensor tympani). Another important structure, the Eustachian tube (a duct that opens into the air cavity), connects the middle-ear cavity to outside air. The drum membrane separates the cavity from the ear canal (external auditory meatus). According to Davis (1978) this ". . . entire structure is known as the eardrum from its resemblance to the familiar musical instrument" (p. 47).

The main function of the Eustachian tube, which is normally closed, is to ventilate the middle-ear cavity. This keeps the cavity from becoming filled with fluid. Ventilation also equalizes air pressure on both sides of the drum membrane. Typically, the Eustachian tube opens when an individual yawns or swallows.

Attached to the inner layer of the drum membrane is one of the three tiny bones, or ossicles, called the malleus (hammer). The bulky upper end of the malleus extends into the air cavity and fits into the socket of the second of the ossicles, the incus (anvil). The incus is attached to the head of the third ossicle, the stapes (stirrup). The ossicles are held in place by the two small muscles, stapedius and tensor tympani, and several ligaments (tough bands of tissue). The base of the stapes, known as the footplate, nestles into an opening of the middle-ear cavity near the inner ear. This opening is called the oval window. It is a path through which sound energy enters the inner ear. Just below the oval window in the medial wall of the middle-ear cavity is another membrane-covered opening, the round window. The round window relieves the pressure of the fluid of the inner ear that is set in motion by the vibrations of the oval window. Other important anatomical structures of the middle ear are discussed elsewhere (see Bess & McConnell, 1981; Davis, 1978; Harris, 1986; and Meyerhoff, 1986, for details).

Anatomy: Inner Ear

The most complicated and essential organ of hearing is the inner ear, which consists of a labyrinth of channels and cavities enclosed within the temporal bone, the hardest bone in the body. The labyrinth contains the receptor organs for the senses of hearing and balance. The oval and round windows of the middle ear open into the elements of the inner ear.

The hearing part of the inner ear is the cochlea. The word *cochlea* means *snail;* indeed, the cochlea does resemble the body of a snail. The cochlea is the space within connected tubes or passages that resemble the coil of a snail. The basal end of the cochlea is next to the middle ear, specifically the oval window. The apical end (the apex, or peak, of the coil) is the farthest away from the oval window. The cochlea is divided into two fluid-filled cavities. The fluid-filled structure (i.e., space) that forms the dividing line is called the cochlear duct, or partition (the scala media).

Two other important structures within the scala media are the basilar membrane and the organ of Corti. The basilar membrane forms the base, or floor, of the scala media and is more elastic at the apical end of the cochlea. On top of the basilar membrane lies the spiral organ of Corti, which contains hair cells crucial to the sensation of hearing. Additional details on other important structures of the inner ear can be found elsewhere (Davis, 1978; Harris, 1986; Schneiderman, 1984).

The basic anatomical structures discussed here are part of the **peripheral hearing system.** An in-depth discussion and illustration of the higher-order hearing mechanisms in the auditory center of the brain are beyond the scope of this book. The reader is referred to other sources for basic information (Schneiderman, 1984; Zemlin, 1968).

Physiology

How we hear and eventually understand sounds is an interesting and complex process (Berlin, 1984; Harris, 1986). Advances in knowledge of the physiology of hearing have been made in the 1980s, but there is still much to learn, especially about the brain's role in the interpretation of auditory stimuli. Some basic information on the physiological process of hearing is presented in the following paragraphs.

Sound waves (i.e., acoustical energy) enter the ear canal and are amplified as they move toward the drum membrane. The drum membrane moves in and out in response to changes in sound pressure. These movements transduce (change into another form) acoustical energy into mechanical energy. The vibratory motion of the membrane transfers the energy to the ossicles (malleus, incus, and stapes) in the middle ear.

The ossicular chain in the middle ear amplifies sound pressure. For most sounds of normal intensities, the malleus and the incus move as a single unit, exhibiting a rocking motion. Then, the stapes with its footplate vibrates like a piston, that is, it moves in and out of the oval window. The transduction process of the footplate of the stapes is best described as a hydraulic action. This vibration causes the fluid in the inner ear to move. At this point, sound energy has been transmitted from the middle ear to the inner ear. The arrangement of the ossicles and the footplate work together to deliver sound energy from the middle ear to the inner ear with very little loss of energy. This process is known as immitance matching (Davis, 1978; Harris, 1986), and its purpose is to increase the vibrations of the stapes relative to the drum membrane.

For sounds of high intensities, the two small muscles in the middle ear, stapedius and tensor tympani, collaborate to reduce the amount of sound energy to protect the ear. These muscles contract reflexively when loud sounds enter the ear. As a result, they stiffen the drum membrane and the ossicles. Thus, vibrations are reduced and so is sound energy at low frequency levels. Instead of moving in and out, the stapes pivot on a horizontal axis located in the middle of the footplate. This results in a less efficient transfer of energy to the inner ear, particularly since less fluid in the inner ear is displaced.

Sound can also reach the inner ear by two other routes that are less efficient. For example, sound energy can proceed directly across the middle ear to the round window membrane by air waves instead of through the ossicular chain. Sound can also be transmitted to the inner ear through vibrations on the bony structures of the skull. This latter process is known as **bone conduction,** which is described later (Harris, 1986; Schneiderman, 1984). Because these routes result in an enormous loss of energy, they do not contribute much to audition under typical conditions.

The complex stages of the hearing process begin with the movements of structures in the inner ear (Davis, 1978; Harris, 1986). The motion of the stapes (in the middle ear) generates pressure in the cochlea, causing the round window to bulge into the middle ear cavity. As the stapes rapidly moves back and forth, fluid pressure displaces the cochlear partition (scala media), permitting a more direct path for the sound energy to use in going from the stapes to the round window. The bulge, called a traveling wave, then moves more slowly along the basilar membrane.

Each section of the basilar membrane is responsive to a particular range of frequencies that are amplified as the wave proceeds over the membrane. Higher frequencies are amplified nearer the basal end and lower frequencies nearer the apical end. Activity of the basilar membrane results in a shearing force that is applied to the hairs on the sensory (or nerve) cells in the organ of Corti. The shearing action on the hairs produces neural impulses that are eventually understood by the brain.

Nerve information leaves the cochlea through the nerve endings at the base of the hair cells and travels along the eighth nerve (i.e., auditory pathway) to the brain stem through a hole in the temporal bone. The length of the eighth nerve is about one-fourth inch. Nuclei between the eighth nerve and the **auditory cortex** in the brain process the auditory signals and transmit them to higher levels.

In general, the auditory cortex responds in an organized way to tones of various levels of frequency. That is, tones of successively higher frequency are directed to specific locations. The cortex, however, is not particularly responsive to auditory sensitivity, or discrimination, of **pitch** (the psychological correlate of frequency) and loudness (the psychological correlate of **intensity**), but it seems to be critical for the processing of sounds with high information content. The auditory cortex performs several functions simultaneously: (1) it receives information about sounds, (2) it processes this input, (3) it sends the processed information to other cortical areas, and finally, (4) it sends signals back to lower centers to modulate their activity (Bess & McConnell, 1981; Davis, 1978; McClelland, 1978).

MEASUREMENT OF HEARING

The measurement of hearing is one of the domains of **audiology,** a recently developed discipline. Audiology, which means basically the study of hearing, is often said to include the entire field of hearing science (Martin, 1986a). To obtain a basic understanding of how the professional audiologist measures hearing acuity, we must discuss the nature and perception of sounds.

The Nature of Sound

Everyone has some intuitive knowledge about the nature and perception of sound. For example, we know that sounds are produced by vibrating objects such as a drum, a rubber band, or our voices. We can feel and hear these vibrations and, typically, interpret them as high or low, loud or soft. In addition, we know that sound travels from one point in time to another. Sound is loudest at its original place of vibration, and it diminishes as it travels.

We can describe sounds objectively by using physical terms such as waveform, frequency, intensity or pressure, and phase relations (Bess & McConnell, 1981; Boothroyd, 1986; Davis, 1978). The simplest vibratory waveform is called the sine wave, or sinusoid. Many free vibratory movements (e.g., oscillation or up and down movements) such as the swing of pendulums and watch springs are sinusoid in nature. A simple sinusoid oscillation is labeled a pure tone. Most sounds that include speech, music, and environmental noises are complex tones; that is, they vibrate in more complicated recurring patterns. We can analyze complex tones into a set of component pure tones, each with a definite frequency and intensity.

Frequency refers to the number of similar, recurring up-down movements, or cycles, per unit of time, typically one second. The more vibrations that occur within a second, the higher the frequency. For example, if a vibratory movement makes 100 complete up-down oscillations per second, it is said to oscillate at a frequency of 100 cycles per second. A frequency of one cycle per second is known as a hertz (Hz) in honor of the German physicist Heinrich Hertz (Davis, 1978). A tone of 100 cycles per second is a 100 Hz tone.

Intensity refers to sound pressure. The vibration that produces sound, or acoustical pressure, results from an applied force (energy) over a given area. Pressure is often viewed by laypersons as a steady force; however, sound is an alternating pressure that continually exerts force in opposite directions. The intensity of a sound refers to the magnitude of vibration that exists in a sound wave (Boothroyd, 1986).

The intensity of a sound is measured in decibels (dB), named in honor of Alexander Graham Bell (Davis, 1978). The decibel scale is based on ratios and thus has no fixed absolute values. It describes the ratio of one unit to another—that is, whether a unit is greater or less than another unit. The scale is also logarithmic. Logarithms are exponents (a number superimposed above another number) that are referred to a specified base number, typically base 10. In logarithms, the base number is multiplied by itself the number of times indicated by the exponent. Thus, in base 10, each logarithmic unit represents a *10-fold* increase. For example, for sounds of similar frequency levels, a sound level of 10 dB has 10 times more intensity than a sound that is barely audible. Each 10 dB increment represents a 10-fold increase in intensity. A 20 dB sound is 100 times as intense as a barely audible sound, and a 30 dB sound is 1,000 times as intense (Bess & McConnell, 1981; Boothroyd, 1986).

It should be clear that a decibel is the logarithm of a ratio. To express a ratio, however, there must be a reference point. Typically, the most commonly used reference level is a 1,000 Hz tone at the faintest audible sound-pressure level (SPL), which is represented by 0 dB on the **audiogram** (a chart for recording **hearing threshold** levels). A given pressure can be described as being twice, three times, ten times, or a hundred times the reference pressure. The sound-pressure levels of some common environmental sounds are given in Table 2.1.

The Perception of Sound

The psychological counterpart of frequency is pitch. The human ear perceives the frequency of a sound as pitch. The pitch of a sound can range on a scale from low (bass) to high (treble). The higher the frequency of a sound, the higher the pitch. The human ear is capable of perceiving sounds from about 20 Hz (or cycles per seconds) to about 20,000 Hz. The ear, however, cannot hear all sound frequencies equally well. It is most

TABLE 2.1. Hearing Threshold Levels and Some Common Environmental Sounds

Hearing Threshold Levels	Decibels	Environmental Sounds
Pain	140	Shotgun blast
Discomfort	130	Jet takeoff
	120	Loud rock music
	110	
	100	Powered lawnmower
	90	
	80	Party with 100 guests
	70	
Conversational speech	60	
	50	
	40	
	30	Inside a library
Whisper (5 feet)	20	
	10	
Threshold of hearing (1,000 Hertz)	0	

SOURCE: Based on Bess & McConnell (1981).

sensitive to 1,000 Hz tones; that is, a sound presented at this frequency can be heard at less intensity than other lower or higher frequencies. Most of the important speech information occurs within the frequency band of 500 to 2,000 Hz.

The psychological counterpart of intensity is loudness. The ear perceives intensity as loudness. The more intense the sound, the louder it is perceived. The most intense sound that can be heard without discomfort is about 120 dB greater than the faintest audible sound. In relation to sound intensity, this loud tolerable sound is about 1 trillion times as intense as the faintest audible sound (Bess & McConnell, 1981; Boothroyd, 1986). The level at which sounds become intolerably loud or painful regardless of frequency is about 135 to 140 dB SPL.

The hearing of sounds involves perception of phase or time relations. For example, frequencies and their corresponding intensities vary from moment to moment. Our perception of pitches depends on rhythm (ordered alternation of weak and strong stress patterns) and tempo (rate, or speed, of movements).

Pure-Tone Audiometry

One of the most important tasks of the audiologist is to measure hearing acuity. A basic audiological examination includes **pure-tone** air and **bone conduction,** speech tests, and immittance (formerly impedance) tests (Martin, 1986b; Roeser, 1986). Immittance testing does not measure hearing per se; rather, it assesses the mechanical transfer function of sound in the outer and middle ear, and provides information about the function of the auditory nerve in the brain stem. **Pure-tone audiometry** is the principal basis of a hearing evaluation. The major objectives of pure-tone tests are screening (e.g., the identification of a hearing problem), diagnosis (e.g., the location of the problem), and intervention (e.g., prescribing **hearing aids** or placement in special education programs).

Audiometer. To assess hearing acuity, audiologists use an electronic machine called an audiometer. Although audiometers vary in type, size, and sophistication, some characteristics are basic to all of them. There is a frequency selector dial that the examiner uses to present pure-tone frequencies. The examiner may use an interruptor switch to turn the tone switch on and off. Typically, the interruptor switch is off, and a tone is presented by depressing the tone bar to the *on* position. A hearing level dial controls the intensity of the signal. Most audiometers can present a tone from 0 to 120 dB in 5 dB increments. An output selector determines whether the pure tone will be presented through earphones (air conduction) or, occasionally, through a bone vibrator (bone conduction). The more elaborate audiometers provide means of measuring **speech reception** and **speech discrimination** abilities.

In pure-tone testing, tones of varying frequencies are presented at varying intensities, typically through earphones (air conduction) or a bone vibrator (bone conduction). In an air-conduction test, the auditory signal enters the external ear canal, proceeds across the middle ear cavity into the inner ear, and finally ends in the brain. In a bone-conduction test, tones are transmitted through a bone vibrator that is placed on the skull, typically behind the ear. The tone causes the skull to vibrate, thus bypassing the outer and middle-ear structures and directly affecting the cochlea. From there, the signal proceeds to the brain.

In either air- or bone-conduction testing, the lowest frequency commonly used is 125 Hz. Other frequencies are at octave (doubling in frequency) intervals: 250, 500, 1,000, 2,000, 4,000, and 8,000 Hz. Hearing can also be measured without earphones or bone vibrators through the use of loudspeakers, which is known as field testing. This technique is similar to normal listening conditions because it involves both ears simultaneously.

Pure-Tone Audiogram. On the audiogram, frequency is represented by vertical lines and intensity by horizontal lines (see Figure 2.2). As discussed previously, the ear is sensitive to certain frequencies in that it does not hear all of them equally well. Thus, the audiometer is calibrated to account for differences in threshold sensitivity at various frequency levels.

Hearing threshold levels for the selected frequencies are recorded on an audiogram. A threshold level is defined as the lowest (softest) SPL needed for an individual to detect a tone approximately 50 percent of the time. The recorded values for each ear are compared to normal threshold values (labeled 0 dB on the audiogram) to determine hearing sensitivity.

Typically, **pure-tone averages** (PTA) across the **speech frequencies** (500, 1,000, and 2,000 Hz) are reported. Consider the audiogram illustrated in Figure 2.3. It can be seen that the hearing thresholds for this child across the speech frequencies are 75, 80, and 85 dB for the right ear, and 90, 95, and 100 dB for the left ear. To compute PTAs, divide the total decibels for the speech frequencies by three for each ear. Thus, the PTA for the right ear is 80 dB and the PTA for the left ear is 95 dB. Results obtained from

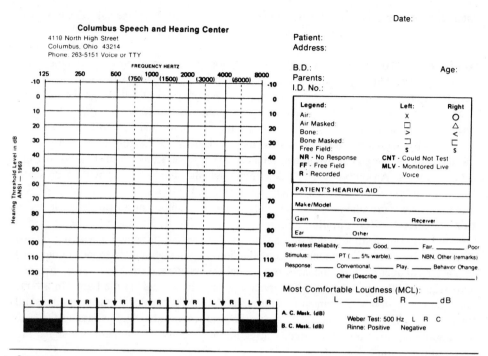

Figure 2.2. Example of a pure-tone audiogram.
Courtesy of the Columbus Speech and Hearing Center. Reprinted by permission.

the audiogram can be used to describe and classify the extent of the hearing impairment, which is discussed later. Notice that the reference on the audiometer is SPL whereas the reference on the audiogram is hearing level (HL) (i.e., hearing threshold level).

Pediatric Audiology

With most children from about age 3 and older, it is possible to use **conventional behavior audiometry**—that is, instructing children to raise a finger when they hear a sound and to lower it when they do not (Davis, 1978; Roeser & Yellin, 1987; Wilson & Thompson, 1984). However, for younger and immature children, including members of special populations such as those with hearing impairments, considerable modifica-

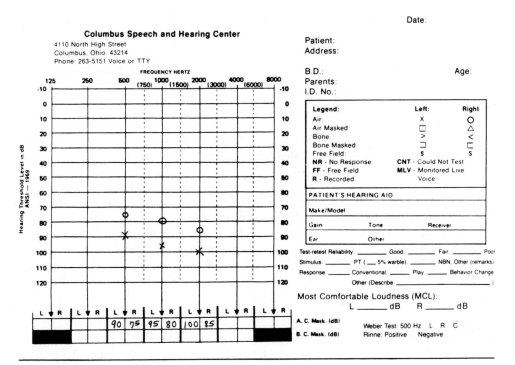

Figure 2.3. Example of pure-tone average on an audiogram.
Courtesy of the Columbus Speech and Hearing Center. Reprinted by permission.

tions of behavior audiometry techniques are required. For screening and follow-up (i.e., threshold) testing, **play audiometry** and test-training testing are often conducted in a sound field setting. Visual reinforcement may be used in some instances (e.g., movements and noises of toys). These techniques depend on some voluntary response from the child. For children under 3 months of age, it is necessary to elicit involuntary responses to sounds, such as startle reactions, eye blinks, or changes in respiration or heart rate. In other cases, physiological audiometry may be used in which the examiner measures responses from the auditory nerve (or brain) or from the sweat glands in the skin.

Most audiological testing procedures used with young children can be categorized as follows: **behavior observation audiometry** (BOA), **classical conditioning audi-**

ometry such as conditioned orientation reflex (COR), visual reinforcement audiometry (VRA), and **operant conditioning audiometry** such as tangible reinforcement operant conditioning audiometry (TROCA), and conditioned play audiometry. The salient principles of each category are briefly discussed. More detailed information, including advantages and disadvantages of the various tests and procedures, can be found elsewhere (Roeser & Yellin, 1987; Wilson & Thompson, 1984).

Behavior Observation Audiometry.   Behavior observation audiometry is considered passive because children are not conditioned to respond. Rather, their reactions to sounds are observed. Testing can be conducted with earphones or in a sound field. Typically, two examiners participate in the assessment. One examiner observes the child within the test room, and the other observes the child from outside the room. The outside observer presents the test stimuli. A warble tone or narrow-band noise stimulus is presented at an increasing level of intensity until a response is observed. Responses may include head turning, looking at examiner, eye-widening or blinking, cessation of play activity, verbalization, increased or decreased sucking, or searching activity (Roeser & Yellin, 1987). Results are often interpreted as minimum response levels rather than true thresholds of hearing (Thompson & Weber, 1974).

Classical Conditioning Audiometry.   In classical conditioning audiometry, a stimulus is presented to elicit a response or a change in behavior (Roeser & Yellin, 1987). The two response modes are unconditioned and conditioned responses. An *unconditioned response* (e.g., a startle reaction) is a reaction to a stimulus without prior learning. A *conditioned response* occurs when the unconditioned reflex is transferred to a neutral event such as a light. Eventually, the neutral event (in this case, the light) elicits the desired response. Examples of classical conditioning testing include the COR and VRA.

In COR testing, an auditory stimulus is paired with a light stimulus (neutral event). In the beginning, after a light stimulus is presented, the child looks toward the source of the light. Later, the child can be trained to look at the light source only when the sound stimuli alone are perceived. Thus, if the child looks at the light when sound stimuli are presented, then the light comes on (as a reward). Auditory stimuli are presented until a response is observed. The intensity of the stimuli is decreased until a threshold is established.

A commonly used form of COR testing is The Puppet in the Window Illuminated *(PIWI)* (Haug, Baccaro, & Guilford, 1967). When an appropriate response is observed, a box containing a puppet is illuminated. This test can be used with children who cannot perform fine motor tasks. The PIWI accepts a wide range of responses such as eye orientation reflex, startle reactions, and searching behaviors.

The COR is not appropriate for hearing-impaired individuals because they have difficulty following the procedures. The criteria and response mode of the COR, however, have been modified to accommodate the needs of this population. The altered form is called visual response audiometry (VRA) (Liden & Kankkunen, 1969). The VRA has a wider range of response modes (e.g., reflexive behavior, widening of the eyes, or changing of the facial expression). There is more flexibility in the type of responses that are acceptable.

Operant Conditioning Audiometry.   From about age 3 and older, the child has suffi-ciently matured to permit more structured procedures to be used in audiometric testing. Techniques frequently used are those of conventional audiometry and those known as operant conditioning audiometry such as tangible reinforcement operant conditioning audiometry (TROCA) or conditioned play audiometry (also known as play conditioning audiometry, or PCA).

TROCA is a highly structured test procedure originally developed for assessing **mentally retarded** children (Lloyd, Spradlin, & Reid, 1968). Typically, tangible ob-jects (i.e., reinforcers) such as candy or little toys are dispensed if a child depresses a button on a box after hearing a sound. If the child depresses the button in the absence of a sound stimulus, no reinforcement is provided. Sometimes a visual reinforcer is used instead of a tangible one.

Play conditioning audiometry is the most acceptable and most reliable technique for establishing hearing thresholds of young children (Roeser & Yellin, 1987). PCA makes audiological testing a game by involving a child in some form of play activity such as putting blocks in a box or placing pegs in a hole. The child is conditioned to perform this play activity after hearing a sound stimulus. Thus, the play activity, as well as the accompanying social praise of parents or caregivers, serves as a reinforce-ment for appropriate responses. The child is prevented from engaging in the play activ-ity if an inappropriate response is made.

Speech Audiometry

To obtain a complete picture of hearing sensitivity, it is important to assess an individ-ual's understanding of spoken language. **Speech audiometry** is a useful tool for mea-suring the detection, discrimination, and comprehension of speech stimuli (Davis, 1978; Jerger, 1984; Martin, 1986b, 1987). The procedure is similar to pure-tone audiometry, except that speech sounds are presented through the earphones or in a sound field en-vironment (field testing). Speech sounds are more complex (and meaningful) than pure tones. Presentations may be live (i.e., the examiner speaks into a microphone with controlled speech) or prerecorded. It is recommended that prerecorded materials be used to ensure that speech test stimuli are presented at a consistent level of intensity.

Speech audiometry is not as objective or precise as pure-tone audiometry. Unlike pure-tone test stimuli, speech stimuli change within the time it takes to utter a single word or parts of words. Changes may occur in intensity, frequency, rate, rhythm, and duration. In addition, speech test materials and methodologies are difficult to standard-ize. The sources of variability in speech audiometry are greater than those in pure-tone audiometry. Thus, there is more room for error, particularly with the examiner, the materials, methods, and the client/individual. The two basic measures of speech audi-ometry discussed in the following paragraphs are *speech reception threshold* and *speech discrimination.*

Speech Reception Threshold.   Speech reception threshold (SRT) refers to the hearing level in decibels at which an individual is able to understand speech approximately 50 percent of the time. The SRT, now often referred to as the ST (Martin, 1986b), plays three important roles in the measurement of hearing sensitivity. *One,* it can be used to check the validity of the pure-tone average thresholds. Typically, the PTA and the ST scores should be similar or nearly similar. *Two,* ST scores can be used as guidelines for selecting and administering speech discrimination tests. And *third,* speech reception measures are useful for assessing young children. Speech threshold scores are easier to obtain than pure-tone threshold scores, mainly because speech is a more meaningful stimulus than is a pure tone.

Typical ST materials are lists of spondaic words (i.e., two-syllable words such as *hot dog, sidewalk,* and *baseball* and others) on auditory tests such as those developed at the Central Institute for the Deaf in St. Louis, Missouri (Davis, 1978; Martin, 1987). The words on the lists should be perceived at about the same intensity level above threshold and should also be within the intelligence and language abilities of the individual taking the test. To determine the ST of children, many audiologists still adhere to guidelines reported by Keaster (as cited in Martin, 1987):

1. The test must have sufficient appeal to maintain the child's attention long enough for threshold to be determined.
2. Most young children have a brief attention span, requiring a rapid procedure.
3. Since verbal comprehension is more highly developed than verbal production in small children, nonverbal responses are preferred.
4. Children's short attention spans must not be exceeded nor their abilities to understand the task.
5. Test words must be within the child's vocabulary. (p. 274)

An example of a speech reception threshold is shown in Figure 2.4 (middle section).

Speech Discrimination.   Speech discrimination tests have been developed to assess an individual's ability to discriminate among different speech sounds at a comfortable hearing level. A variety of test stimuli (sounds, syllables, words, sentences) and formats (multiple-choice, written responses, oral responses) have been used (Jerger, 1984; Martin, 1987). Test materials are composed of nonredundant, real words such as monosyllabic words. (See Figure 2.4 for recording speech discrimination thresholds.)

The most commonly used tests are those that employ lists of phonetically balanced monosyllabic words, that is, lists of single-syllable, commonly used words that adequately represent speech sounds in typical English conversations. Examples of test items include words such as *bean, boat, burn, chalk,* and *choice.*

Common speech discrimination tests that are appropriate for older children and adults are the *PAL–50* lists developed at Harvard Psychoacoustic Laboratories (Egan, 1948), the *CID–W22* lists developed at Central Institute for the Deaf (Hirsh, Davis, Silverman, Reynolds, Eldert, & Benson, 1952), and the *NU–6* lists developed at Northwestern University. Despite the differences in the tests, research has shown that the scores on one assessment correlate with those on the other tests. In other words, an individual scoring high or low on one test also scores high or low on the others (Bess, Freeman, & Sinclair, 1981).

Discrimination tests have also been developed for use with children under 10 years of age. One test is the *PBK–50* (Haskins, 1949), which contains phonetically balanced words from the International Kindergarten Union Vocabulary list. Another assessment containing monosyllabic words that appear in the recognition vocabulary of children

Date:

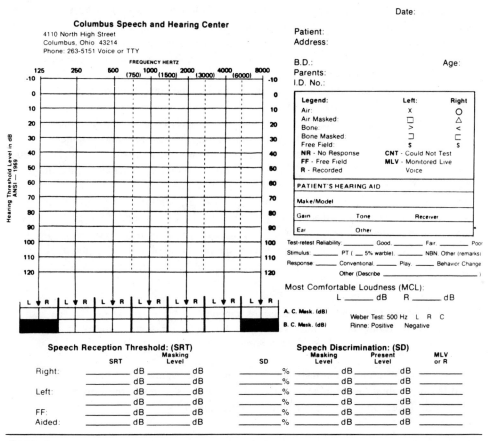

Figure 2.4. Speech reception and speech discrimination on an audiogram.
Courtesy of the Columbus Speech and Hearing Center. Reprinted by permission.

over $2\frac{1}{2}$ years old is the Northwestern University Children's Perception of Speech (Nuchips) test (Elliott & Katz, 1980). Another frequently used test is the Word Intelligibility by Picture Identification (WIPI) test (Ross & Lerman, 1970). The WIPI is comprised of four lists of 25 plates (flat sheets of material) with six pictures on each plate. Relatively new in the battery of speech discrimination tests for children is the Pediatric Speech

Intelligibility (PSI) test (Jerger & Jerger, 1982; Jerger, Lewis, Hawkins, & Jerger, 1980), which contains both sentences and monosyllabic words and can be used with children who have high and low receptive language abilities. Other tests use nonverbal signals (e.g., sound effects) or simplified verbal materials (e.g., numbers) (Jerger, 1984). Although test materials vary, test procedures are fairly similar. Most use a closed set paradigm in which children are instructed to point to the correct alternative picture from a set of four or five pictures.

It is extremely difficult to use speech tests, especially speech discrimination tests, with children who have severe to profound hearing losses. In some instances, results may be achieved if the participants are permitted to use their eyes to receive visual cues during the assessment. Typically, tests such as the Nonsense Syllable Discrimination Test (NSDT); or Ling's Five-Sound Test (Ling & Ling, 1978) may be used. In the NSDT, the examiner presents 50 syllable pairs (e.g., ma-la) to the child who selects from the two alternatives of same or different. In the Five-Sound Test, children try to identify five sounds, three vowels (/a/, /u/, /i/) and two consonants (/s/, /sh or ʃ/). Ling and Ling state that this test is useful as a quick check of a child's potential speech discrimination.

According to Martin (1987):

> Speech discrimination measurements are important in the diagnosis of the type and degree of hearing disorder in children as well as in the decisions necessary for appropriate remediation, ear choice for a hearing aid, and so forth. (p. 285)

Thus, speech discrimination tests are important in the evaluation of hearing ability. If it is difficult to obtain reliable scores, then the audiologist can use the information on the ST (Speech Reception Threshold) and the pure-tone tests.

HEARING IMPAIRMENT

Hearing impairment is a generic term referring to all types, causes, and degrees of hearing loss. To understand the educational implications of hearing impairment, four major factors should be considered: degree of loss, age at onset, location of the lesion, and cause (etiology) of impairment. A fifth factor, parental acceptance, is discussed primarily in Chapters 4 and 6.

Degree of Hearing Impairment

An individual's hearing threshold level is indicated on the audiogram as a pure-tone average (PTA) across the range of speech frequencies. The pure-tone audiogram is designed to chart hearing sensitivity from 0 dB to about 110 dB (Acoustical Society of America, 1982). Typically, hearing is considered normal up to a hearing threshold level of about 26 dB. Some researchers prefer a more lenient classification of a 15 to 16 dB threshold level (Ross, 1986a). The degree of hearing impairment can be categorized from slight to profound (or extreme), as illustrated in Table 2.2.

Individuals in the slight, mild, and moderate categories have been labeled **hard-**

TABLE 2.2. Categories of Hearing Impairment

Degree of Impairment	Description	Label
Up to 26 decibels	Normal	Normal hearing
27 to 40 decibels	Slight	Hard-of-hearing
41 to 55 decibels	Mild	Hard-of-hearing
56 to 70 decibels	Moderate	Hard-of-hearing
71 to 90 decibels	Severe	Hard-of-hearing, or Deaf
91+ decibels	Profound (Extreme)	Deaf

NOTE: Decibel loss refers to results from the better unaided ear averaged across the speech frequencies, according to the International Standards Organization (ISO).

of-hearing whereas those in the profound, or extreme, category are considered *deaf*. The fourth category has been referred to as "the zone of uncertainty" because it is observed that "some individuals are socially deaf (i.e., *their social behaviors resemble those of deaf persons*) but more of them are merely hard-of-hearing" (Davis, 1978, p. 88; emphasis added). It has been argued, however, that most hearing-impaired children, including some children with profound hearing losses, can perform like hard-of-hearing individuals if they receive effective early intervention training that develops at least their residual hearing (Ross, 1986a, 1986b; Ross & Calvert, 1984).

Even with early intervention and early amplification, there may be a point on the audiological continuum at which the extent of hearing impairment is sufficiently severe to preclude the adequate development of auditory receptive skills. Evidence suggests that this occurs at approximately 91 dB, or what is considered the profound range (Conrad, 1979; Davis, 1978; Erber, 1974, 1975; Quigley & Kretschmer, 1982). At best, most individuals with this degree of impairment receive a fragmented acoustic message or no acoustic information at all. These persons are linked to the world of vision; their primary mode for receiving linguistic input is through the eye rather than the ear, even when they use adequate amplification systems such as hearing aids or **group aids** (Quigley & Paul, 1984a). With advances in technology, the point of deafness may be pushed to a higher degree of impairment such as 95 to 100 dB; however, we may be reaching the limits of amplification systems.

Age at Onset

Age at onset refers to the age at which an individual sustains a hearing loss. This factor is often considered in relation to the optimal period for acquisition of verbal (i.e., spoken) language, usually from birth to about 2 years. The more severe the impairment, the more crucial age at onset becomes for the development of auditory-articulatory experiences that provide the foundations for the development of spoken language.

Two terms associated with age at onset are *prelinguistic hearing impairment* and *postlinguistic hearing impairment*. Prelinguistically hearing-impaired students sustain their hearing losses before the establishment of spoken language. Students with postlinguistic hearing impairments sustain hearing losses after the age of about 2 years. When degree of impairment is considered in conjunction with age at onset, one sees significant effects on the development of **primary language** and secondary language skills (King & Quigley, 1985; Quigley & Paul, 1984a; see also Chapters 7 and 8 of this book). A child who becomes deaf after age 2 has language, communication, and educational needs that are very different from those of a child who becomes deaf before the age of 2. For the most part, prelinguistically hearing-impaired children will not have established an auditorially based language developed through aural/oral (i.e., listening/speaking) interactions similar to those to which typical hearing children are exposed.

This book is concerned mainly with children who have suffered prelinguistic, severe to profound hearing impairments. Children with less severe hearing losses (i.e., hard-of-hearing children) are discussed in some detail in Chapter 3. Hard-of-hearing children are receiving increasing attention from researchers and educators. There is still a need, however, to identify and study more members of this group, especially those who are integrated into regular education programs (Ross et al., 1982).

Location of the Lesion

Hearing impairment may occur alone or in conjunction with certain diseases. In the latter condition, an individual may have other symptoms such as tinnitus (head noise), balance problems, pain, and discharge from the ear (Bess & McConnell, 1981; Davis, 1978; Meyerhoff, 1986). There are four types of hearing losses—**conductive, sensorineural, mixed,** and **central.**

Typically, *conductive losses* pertain to abnormalities or malfunctions of the outer and middle ear. For example, the external ear (auricle) may be absent or gathering sounds in an inefficient manner. The ear canal may be obstructed or filled with wax and other debris. A loss can also occur if the drum membrane or ossicles are immobile, resulting in an incomplete or inefficient transfer of energy to the cochlea. A conductive impairment may also include the inner ear. For example, it is possible for the basilar and tectorial membranes in the cochlea to undergo physical changes, resulting in a reduced transfer of energy to the hair cells. Most conductive losses are medically reversible.

Sensorineural hearing impairments refer to damage to a "sensory unit . . . ; that is, an auditory nerve fiber plus the hair cell or cells that excite it" (Davis, 1978, p. 95). This damage (i.e., absence or malfunctioning of sensory units) may occur in the cochlea, the auditory nerve, or even in the central auditory system (i.e., central sensorineural hearing impairment; Meyerhoff, 1986). Sensorineural hearing losses can occur concurrently with conductive problems in the middle or inner ear or both. This combination of sensorineural and conductive disorders is referred to as a *mixed hearing impairment*.

At present, most sensorineural hearing impairments are medically irreversible. Even one of the most recent medical phenomena, cochlear implants, has been only somewhat successful with only a few profoundly hearing-impaired persons (Miller & Pfingst, 1984). Individuals with sensorineural hearing impairments may receive limited benefits from the use of amplification devices such as hearing aids.

Central hearing impairments involve damage to the auditory nerve (eighth nerve) pathways from the brain stem to the auditory cortex. Disorders can also occur concurrently with sensorineural impairments. In-depth treatments of hearing disorders can be found in Davis (1978) and Meyerhoff (1986).

Etiology

Hearing impairment can be classified as exogenous (having a cause outside of the body) or endogenous (having a cause within the body), and sustained during prenatal (before birth), perinatal (during birth), or postnatal (after birth) periods (Brown, 1986; Morgan, 1987; Vernon, 1987a). Exogenous causes include disease (e.g., meningitis), toxicity (e.g., drugs, antibiotics), and accident or injury. Typically, part of the auditory system becomes damaged, thus reducing its capacity to receive and transmit sounds. Endogenous hearing impairments result from the transmission of genetic characteristics from parents to the child—that is, inherited or hereditary traits. Although this classification scheme is useful, it is still difficult to ascertain the causes of hearing impairment because of incomplete or inaccurate records or a lack of complete understanding of genetic factors. In addition, a large percentage (estimates range from 25 to about 40 percent) of hearing impairment in children is a result of unknown causes (Brown, 1986). The following paragraphs provide a brief description of some common causes of hearing impairment within the three periods of onset.

Prenatal Period.   Two common causes of deafness sustained during the prenatal period are heredity and maternal rubella (German measles). Rubella, one of the prenatal infectious diseases, is seasonal (spring and early summer) and typically accounts for about 10 percent of sensorineural hearing impairment. It has been reported that the rubella epidemic of 1963 to 1965, however, was the source of the hearing impairment of more than 50 percent of all hearing-impaired children in special education programs (Brown, 1986; Vernon, 1987a). Many children deafened by rubella have other handicapping conditions such as mental retardation, vision problems, heart disorders, and **emotional and behavioral problems.** Because of effective immunization programs, it is not likely that this disease will strike a large number of pregnant women in the future.

One of the most interesting and least understood causes of deafness is heredity. Shaver and Vernon (1978) stated that 40 to 60 percent of all deafness can be attributed to heredity. It is generally accepted that deafness is inherited at least 50 percent or more of the time (Konigsmark & Gorlin, 1976). In fact, according to Vernon (1987a), "Genetic factors have been the leading cause of deafness throughout this century except during certain epidemic periods of rubella" (p. 32).

There are more than 200 types of hereditary hearing impairments. Most types are typically accompanied by other disabling conditions such as vision and heart problems. Several types occur with no additional handicaps (Konigsmark & Gorlin, 1976). It may be that most children with genetic deafness have one of these types because these children have often been reported to perform better academically and socially than children with nongenetic deafness (Moores, 1987; Quigley & Kretschmer, 1982).

Hereditary hearing impairment is governed by Mendelian laws of inheritance; the inherited traits can be dominant, recessive, or sex-linked. Dominant trait transmission accounts for about 15 percent of all childhood deafness, recessive about 33 percent, and sex-linked transmission about 2 percent (Taylor, 1980). Genes are located on chromosomes, which occur in pairs (except for the sex chromosomes of males). Humans have 22 pairs of nonsex-determining chromosomes (autosomes) and one pair of sex-determining chromosomes. The child inherits one member of each gene pair (and a corresponding member) from each parent. Thus, half of the child's genes are from the mother and half from the father.

Of interest here is the inheritance of autosomal dominant or autosomal recessive genes. In autosomal dominant inheritance, the trait is present in the genes (nonsex chromosomes) of only one parent and can be passed on to 50 percent of the offspring. The dominant trait is carried vertically from one generation to another.

The parents of a child deafened from an autosomal recessive trait are carriers of a single abnormal recessive gene. That is, each parent carries two different genes, one normal and one abnormal in relation to a particular gene pair. Their offspring can inherit two normal or two abnormal genes, or one of each. The offspring becomes merely a carrier for the trait if only one abnormal gene is transmitted. If two abnormal genes are passed on, the offspring is affected and also carries the trait. There is a 50 percent chance of inheriting the abnormal gene from the father or from the mother. Thus, the probability of an offspring being both affected and a carrier is about 25 percent, and the probability of an offspring being a carrier only is 50 percent. This type of deafness is common in consanguinity (marriage between close relations, usually first cousins). Morgan (1987) surmised that the disability of from one-third to one-half of children with profound sensorineural hearing impairment and a large proportion of children whose hearing impairment is unknown could be the result of autosomal recessive inheritance. The majority of children inherit their hearing impairment during the prenatal period.

Perinatal Period.   Some causes of hearing impairment during the perinatal period are prematurity, pregnancy complications, trauma, sexually transmitted diseases, and blood type (Rh) incompatibility. These perinatal factors have been known to cause sensorineural hearing impairment. Determining the cause of perinatal hearing impairment is extremely difficult because of a number of complex factors. Perinatal factors are often considered after prenatal and postnatal factors have been ruled out. Hypoxia (oxygen deprivation) and prematurity (birth before the ninth month) are probably the most suspected causes of perinatal sensorineural hearing impairment (Morgan, 1987). Morgan (1987) stated that "These circumstances are most often beyond the control of those in attendance" (p. 45).

Postnatal Period.   Hearing impairment acquired during the postnatal period can be a result of a variety of causes such as bacterial and viral infections, injury, and even heredity (e.g., otosclerosis in which the stapes become immobilized). Otitis media, a bacterial infection in the middle ear, is the most common cause of conductive hearing impairment (Morgan, 1987). The most common bacterial infection causing sensorineural hearing impairment is probably meningitis, which is an inflammation of the meninges covering the brain and spinal cord. This infection can destroy the auditory nerve and the organ of Corti (in the cochlea), resulting in severe and profound bilateral hearing impairment. Despite the many advances made in medicine, meningitis remains the most frequent postnatal cause of hearing impairment in school-age children (Brown, 1986).

Incidence of Hearing Impairment

It is difficult to determine the exact number and the characteristics of hearing-impaired students in the general population, in general education, or in special education programs. As mentioned in Chapter 1, about 8 percent of the general population has some degree of hearing impairment, including 1 percent who are severely to profoundly hearing-impaired. Based on an annual survey conducted by the Center for Demographic and Assessment Studies (CADS) at Gallaudet University, it is estimated that in 1982 there were about 68,000 hearing-impaired students between the ages of 6 and 17 years receiving some type of special education services. According to Ries (1986), "It appears that males and blacks were proportionately overrepresented among these hearing impaired students" (p. 29). About 23,000 of these students were categorized as deaf—that is, with profound hearing impairment. The remaining students had lesser degrees of hearing impairment. The overwhelming majority of students in the survey, however, had severe to profound hearing losses.

The findings of the CADS surveys may not be representative of hearing-impaired students in the general population, in general education programs, or of all students receiving special education services. For example, most hearing-impaired children in general education programs have mild to moderate losses, but many of these children have not been identified (Ross et al., 1982). Keeping in mind that it is difficult to determine type of special educational service, it is possible that the students in the survey overrepresent those students with profound hearing impairments who are receiving full-time special educational services.

AMPLIFICATION AND HEARING IMPAIRMENT

Probably the most important consideration in the rehabilitation/habilitation of hearing impairment is amplification (Ling, 1986; Pollack, 1980; Sanders, 1982). To facilitate the acquisition of receptive and expressive spoken communication skills, it is necessary to develop the residual hearing of hearing-impaired children as early and as effectively as possible. As aptly stated by Ross and Tomassetti (1980): ". . . for most hearing impaired children the early and appropriate selection and use of amplification is the single most effective tool available to us" (p. 214). Audiologists are primarily responsible for the selection and assessment of the most appropriate hearing aids. Teachers should be responsible for helping hearing-impaired students to make maximum use of their residual hearing, either through the use of the students' personal hearing aids or classroom educational aids.

It is convenient to categorize amplification systems as being of three kinds (Bess & McConnell, 1981; Byrne, 1983; Pascoe, 1986): (1) individual hearing aids, (2) group hearing aids in classroom settings, and (3) other assistive devices (e.g., visual aids, tactile aids, and electrode implants). This section presents basic information relevant to the first two kinds of aids only because they are widely used. Despite differences between individual and group hearing aids, the end goal is the same: to amplify and deliver sounds in a manner that enables the user to comprehend them.

The Nature of Amplification

The purpose of amplification is to increase the intensity of the acoustic signal so that it is above the hearing threshold of the user. The signal is converted into electrical energy, amplified, and then converted back into acoustic energy so that the ear can perceive it. Three basic units are common to all amplification systems—the microphone, the amplifier, and the receiver. The microphone converts acoustic sound waves into a weaker but similar electrical energy. The amplifier, driven by a power supply (usually a battery), increases the amplitude (voltage) of the electrical signal. The receiver converts the electrical signal back into acoustic energy. The ear perceives the amplified signal by means of a coupler system (e.g., an earmold or bone-conduction coupler).

The assessment of a hearing aid's performance is related to characteristics such as gain, output, and frequency response (Bess & McConnell, 1981; Byrne, 1983; Hodgson & Skinner, 1981; Pascoe, 1986; Sanders, 1982). The information on performance is obtained from measurements made within isolation boxes that recreate the acoustic environment of a real ear. Measurements are recorded automatically, usually in graphs or numerical data.

The acoustic gain of a hearing aid is defined as the increase in sound pressure level (SPL) of pure-tone stimuli from the microphone to the receiver. The increase indicates how much the input signal has been amplified. For example, if the incoming signal is 30 dB and the amplified output signal is 80 dB, then the acoustic gain is 50 dB—the difference between the values of the two signals. All hearing aids have a maximum power output (MPO) level that represents the output limitations across the frequency range of the hearing aid. The purpose of this standard level is to protect the hearing aid user from loud, damaging acoustic signals (Pascoe, 1986).

The frequency response describes the modification of the acoustic signal by the hearing aid. For example, a hearing aid may amplify some frequencies and reduce the gain of others, depending on the needs of the user. Frequency response is the relationship between gain and frequency. The frequency response provides information regarding the amount of acoustic gain and the frequencies at which the hearing aid is most sensitive (Bess & McConnell, 1981; Byrne, 1983).

Detailed descriptions of the specifications of other performance characteristics of hearing aids can be found elsewhere (Pascoe, 1986; Sanders, 1982). In addition to basic performance standards, the Food and Drug Administration regulates the selection, usage, and sales of amplification systems to protect the hearing aid consumer. For example, a medical examination by a specialist is recommended for the adult consumer and *required* for children less than 18 years old.

Individual Hearing Aids

Personal hearing aids are of two broad categories: air conduction and bone conduction. In each category are two types of aids: body aids and on-the-head aids (Pascoe, 1986; Sanders, 1982). Among the various on-the-head styles are behind-the-ear (BTE) style, in-the-ear style (ITE), the eyeglass style, and in-the-canal style (ITC) (see Figure 2.5).

Body Aids.   The largest air-conduction systems are the body aids. Typically, body aids are used by young children with severe to profound hearing impairments. The aid may be placed in a user's pocket or in a specially designed case worn on the body. The case contains the microphone, amplifier, and battery. A cord connects the aid to a receiver that is fastened to an earmold. There may be one or two cords providing signals to one or two receivers. The separation of the microphone and of the receiver by the cord

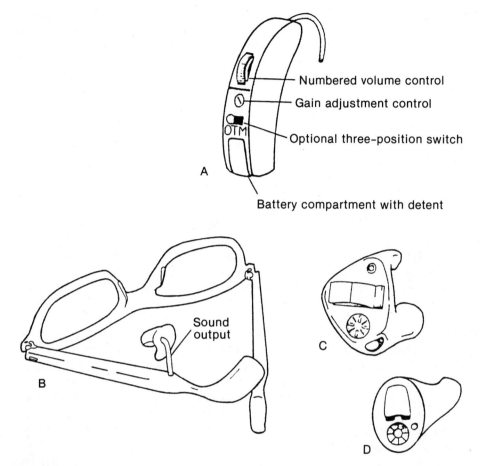

Numbered volume control

Gain adjustment control

Optional three–position switch

Battery compartment with detent

Sound output

Figure 2.5. Examples of on-the-head hearing aids: A: behind-the-ear; B: eyeglass; C: in-the-ear; D: in-the-canal.
D. P. Pascoe, *Hearing Aids*. Austin, TX: PRO–ED, 1986. Reprinted by permission.

reduces the probability of feedback (an audible, acoustic squeal that escapes from the aid). In general, body aids are used only when on-the-head aids are not feasible.

On-the-Head Aids. The on-the-head, or ear-level, instruments include those that can be fitted behind the ear, in the ear or ear canal, or in the frame of eyeglasses, with the sound entering the microphone near the ear. The most widely worn type of hearing aid is the BTE aid (Sanders, 1982). The BTE and eyeglass aids are placed on the back of the outer ear. Sound reaches the ear through plastic tubing inserted into an earmold. The components of the ITE hearing aid are contained within the plastic earmold, and no tubes are inserted into the ear. The ITC aids are similar to the ITE, only they are much smaller and fit into the ear canal.

A CROS (contralateral routing of signals) aid is another on-the-head aid (Pascoe,

1986; Sanders, 1982). A microphone is placed over one ear, and sounds are delivered to a receiver on the other ear by a cord or the use of radio frequencies in a wireless model. This instrument is useful for individuals with good hearing in one ear. A CROS aid can be a BTE, eyeglass, or ITE aid. It may be single (one microphone) or bi-CROS (two microphones), especially if the *good* ear needs some amplification.

One advantage of on-the-head aids is that they improve the localization of the sources of sounds, especially if two aids are worn. There is evidence that binaural hearing aids improve sound localization and speech discrimination in noise (Sanders, 1982). On-the-head aids are less conspicuous and always preferable to body aids for children as they approach upper elementary school age. Ear-level aids have been improved so much that many severely to profoundly hearing-impaired children can benefit from them.

Bone-Conduction Aids.   Body, BTE, and eyeglass aids are also available as bone-conduction aids. As in bone-conduction audiological testing, the amplified sound reaches the ear through a vibrator, instead of a receiver, that is placed on the mastoid bone behind the ear. No earmold is needed. Individuals who have abnormalities of the external ear (auricle) or who suffer from chronic middle-ear infections may require bone-conduction aids.

Hearing Aid Controls.   Hearing aids may have a variety of manipulable external or internal controls. Some common external controls are volume, or gain, which is usually a rotating wheel, or dial, with numbers, and an on-off switch (Niemoeller, 1978; Pascoe, 1986; Sanders, 1982). On-off switches can have other functions as well. For example, they may allow the user to receive magnetic emissions, which are converted and amplified, from a telephone. When the aid switch is in the *T* position, the user can hear only the sound from the telephone. Another position, *B,* is available that permits the user to hear telephone and face-to-face conversations simultaneously. Some of the more recent models permit individuals to use their personal aids with an FM attachment (see discussion of FM in ''Group Amplification Systems'' later in this chapter.

The internal controls include adjustments that can be made in acoustic gain, frequency response, and maximum power levels. These adjustments require special tools and should be made by the professional, not the user of the aid.

Earmolds.   A component of a hearing aid that is as important as the electrical components is the earmold. This custom-made structure affects the acoustic characteristics of the signal as it flows through the ear canal. Earmolds are made from wax impressions of the individual's ears. Typically, they are constructed to fit the area just outside the ear canal and to extend into the canal.

Care must be exercised in the production of earmolds. It is important to make a mold that does not cause discomfort or pain to the user. In addition, earmolds should deliver sounds to the ear canal at the specified gain and frequency levels of the aid without the problem of feedback (the acoustic squeal that occurs when amplified sound escapes). A more detailed discussion of earmolds and other important aspects of individual hearing aids can be found elsewhere (Niemoeller, 1978; Pascoe, 1986; Sanders, 1982).

Group Amplification Systems

Group amplification systems, or group hearing aids, are sometimes used in special education classrooms for hearing-impaired students. Typically, a teacher wears and speaks into a microphone that delivers amplified speech to each student. The students use their individual aid (if they are so equipped) or earphones that are part of a system. There are several transmission modes for group aids: hard-wired systems, wireless or induction-loop systems, radio-frequency transmission systems, and infrared light systems (Pascoe, 1986; Sanders, 1982).

Hard-Wired Systems.   Wired systems were developed and implemented in many special schools for deaf students. As the name implies, electrical wiring is used to make connections among the various units. The teacher's microphone and students' individual units are connected to a nonportable amplifier. Additional microphones may be available to the students so that they can monitor their voices. Students receive speech through earphones or receivers fastened to their earmolds. Today, hard-wired systems are not used widely because they impose restrictions on teacher and student mobility (Pascoe, 1986; Sanders, 1982).

Induction-Loop Systems.   Induction-loop systems, or wireless systems, operate on the principle of induction. Amplified speech signals from the input microphone are transmitted by an induction coil that produces electromagnetic fields. The coil is looped around a classroom at established places. Because no connecting wires are needed, this system solves the mobility problem and permits students to monitor their own voices through their personal hearing aids set on the T coils (i.e., the same as is used for telephones). Induction-loop systems are not widely used, however, because of difficulties with installation and the provision of strong, reliable signals (Pascoe, 1986; Sanders, 1982).

Radio-Frequency Systems.   Radio-frequency systems are becoming acceptable to educators, especially for hearing-impaired students in either mainstreamed or regular education settings (Ross, 1986a; Sanders, 1982). The teacher speaks into a microphone with a built-in transmitter, and speech is transmitted through frequency-modulated (FM) signals to the students' FM receivers, which can be attached to their personal aids. The systems "represent miniature FM radio stations or Radio Frequency units, broadcasting to a classroom audience who listen to the teacher's 'station' on their private wearable FM hearing aid" (Sanders, 1982, p. 232).

Infrared-Light Systems.   One of the most recently developed group amplification aids is the infrared-light system (Pascoe, 1986). This transmission system is often found in theaters and can be used as an aid in listening to television. Typically, the teacher's microphone and an amplifier are connected by a wire. Speech signals reach an amplifier that activates an infrared-light generator placed near the ceiling of the classroom. An invisible oscillating light fills the room and is detected by special receptors worn by the students. The receptors convert the light signal into sound.

Use of Group Systems.   A number of educators do not accept group amplification systems (Pascoe, 1986). They maintain that individual hearing aids should be used because they represent conditions that are typical outside of classrooms. One of the important benefits of the various group systems, however, is that they can provide a constant level of input that does not decrease as teachers and students move around the room. No matter where the teacher stands in the classroom, students can receive speech signals at the same level of intensity as specified by their group units or individual aids. More detailed descriptions of advantages and disadvantages of the various group systems can be found elsewhere (Sanders, 1982). In sum, if a particular group amplification system is implemented, it should: (1) permit students to monitor their own voices, (2) be flexible enough to adapt to a variety of classroom settings, (3) allow for student–student and teacher–student communication exchanges, (4) be relatively easy to install, maintain, and repair, and (5) suit the acoustical needs of each individual student (Byrne, 1983; Ross, 1986a; Sanders, 1982).

Candidacy and Expectation for Hearing Aids

That it is important for hearing-impaired children to receive early amplification is generally accepted. Research has shown that even the use of fragmentary hearing can be of enormous benefit (Erber, 1982). There is intense ongoing debate, however, on who should wear a hearing aid, when a person should be fitted for an aid, and what type of aid is beneficial (Ling & Ling, 1978; Pollack, 1980; Ross, 1986a, 1986b).

Candidacy for a hearing aid can be determined by the amount of hearing loss across the speech frequencies in the better unaided ear of an individual (Bess & McConnell, 1981). It should be emphasized, however, that even a slight hearing impairment has been shown to affect academic achievement negatively (Paul & Quigley, 1987a; Quigley & Thomure, 1968; Chapter 3 of this book). Auditory sensitivity alone is not sufficient to determine whether a person should wear an aid. Decisions about a hearing aid should not be restricted to a specific type or degree of hearing loss. Hearing aids may be necessary for any child (at the earliest age possible) whose hearing impairment affects adversely the development of spoken language abilities.

SUMMARY

The major purpose of this chapter was to introduce the reader to some basic aspects of hearing science. The nature of hearing and hearing impairment, the assessment of hearing, and the functions and limitations of hearing aids and group amplification systems were discussed. It was emphasized that audition plays an important role in the acquisition of primary (i.e., speech) and secondary (i.e., reading, writing) forms of spoken language. It was also stressed that early amplification is critical for the optimal development of auditory perceptual skills. In short, early amplification should be an integral part of early intervention programs for hearing-impaired students.

The chapter described some important structures and functions of the ear in relation to three broad anatomical areas: outer ear, middle ear, and inner ear. The outer ear plays only a minor role in the hearing process. The structures of the middle ear change acoustical energy into mechanical energy and then into hydraulic energy as sound proceeds into the inner ear. The most complicated and essential mechanisms of peripheral hearing are located in the inner ear, specifically the cochlea. In essence, the shearing actions of the hair cells in the cochlea generate neural impulses that travel along the auditory nerve to the auditory cortex into the brain where they are interpreted.

After presenting some salient aspects of the nature and perception of sound, such as waveform, frequency, and intensity, a basic introduction to audiometry, or the assessment of hearing, was provided. Pure-tone audiometry, using either air-conduction or bone-conduction tests or both, is the principal basis of a hearing evaluation. Special modifications are necessary when testing the hearing sensitivity of young children, particularly hearing-impaired children. A number of techniques that have been developed are based on principles of behaviorism, notably classical and operant conditioning.

Speech audiometry, or the use of speech stimuli, was reported to be a useful, meaningful tool for complementing the results of pure-tone testing. Although not as objective as pure tones in pure-tone audiometry, speech stimuli are meaningful and are important in assessing children. The chapter described some speech tests commonly used with adults and children for obtaining speech reception thresholds and speech discrimination scores.

The nature of hearing impairment was discussed in relation to four factors: degree of loss, age at onset, location of the lesion, and cause (etiology). The term *deaf* was defined as the point on the audiological continuum at which individuals become linked to vision for language and communication, despite the use of early intervention and amplification. The impact of severe to profound hearing impairment on the development of spoken language is most noticeable when it is sustained before the age of about 2.

Most severely to profoundly hearing-impaired children have sensorineural losses and sustained their hearing impairments during the prenatal period. The common causes of deafness during the prenatal period are maternal rubella and heredity. Heredity remains one of the most interesting and difficult aspects to detect and understand. About 50 percent of deafness is attributed to heredity. During the postnatal period, the most common cause of conductive hearing losses is otitis media. Meningitis is the most common cause of sensorineural hearing impairments.

It was emphasized that early amplification is of prime consideration in the rehabilitation/habilitation process of hearing-impaired children. After discussing the nature of amplification, the chapter described some of the important components and functions of amplification systems in relation to two broad areas: individual hearing aids and group hearing aids. The most commonly used individual hearing aids are the on-the-head models, particularly the behind-the-ear aids. Of the group aids, the radio-frequency models are widely accepted. These models are best equipped to handle the panorama of amplification needs in classroom settings. Although there is ongoing debate regarding the use of group aids, it was argued that group amplification systems do offer some advantages over individual aids. In addition, they are beneficial for hearing-impaired students who attend regular education or mainstreamed programs.

Finally, it was noted that it is difficult sometimes to determine who should wear a hearing aid, when it should be fitted, and what type of aid is necessary. Using only the degree of hearing impairment to determine candidacy is not sufficient, although it is a useful guideline. Given the negative effects of even a slight hearing loss on academic achievement, it is important to provide adequate amplification aid to hearing-impaired children as early as possible.

COMPREHENSION

1. Decide where the following structures are located: *outer, middle,* or *inner* ear:
   a. Ossicles
   b. Fluid-filled cavities
   c. Pinna (auricle)
   d. Cochlea
   e. Air-filled cavity
   f. Ear canal (external auditory meatus)
2. Discuss briefly how we hear and eventually understand sounds. Be sure to describe the physiology of structures such as the *ossicles, oval window, round window, basilar membrane, organ of Corti, eighth nerve,* and *auditory cortex.* The discussion has been started for you:

    Sound waves enter the ear canal and are amplified as they move toward the drum membrane. The drum membrane moves in and out and transfers the energy to the *ossicles* in the middle ear. The movements of the drum membrane change acoustical energy into mechanical energy. The ossicles . . .
3. TRUE or FALSE? The two small muscles in the middle ear collaborate to increase the amount of sound energy in the ear.
4. Determine whether the following statements refer to *intensity* or *frequency:*
   a. The more vibrations per second, the higher is the number of similar, recurring up-down movements or cycles per unit of time.
   b. Sound pressure is the magnitude of vibration that exists in a sound wave.
   c. Sound pressure is measured in cycles or hertzs.
   d. It is measured in decibels.
   e. It is perceived as loudness.
   f. It is perceived as pitch.
5. TRUE or FALSE? A 20 dB sound contains two times as much intensity (i.e., it is twice as loud) as a 10 dB sound.
6. TRUE or FALSE? The ear can hear all sound frequencies equally well.
7. What are the three major objectives of a pure-tone hearing assessment?
8. How is air-conduction testing different from bone-conduction testing?
9. Compute the pure-tone averages in the following examples.

	250	500	1,000	2,000	3,000	4,000	5,000	6,000	8,000
Left Ear	50	65	60	70	95	—	—	—	—
Right Ear	20	20	35	40	35	40	35	40	40
Left Ear PTA									
Right Ear PTA									
Left Ear	40	60	55	60	70	70	85	80	85
Right Ear	25	25	30	30	30	35	—	—	—
Left Ear PTA									
Right Ear PTA									
Left Ear	60	85	90	100	—	—	—	—	—
Right Ear	60	95	100	110	—	—	—	—	—
Left Ear PTA									
Right Ear PTA									

10. Label the following as *behavioral observation audiometry, classical conditioning audiometry, operant conditioning audiometry,* or *play audiometry.*
    a. Passive testing; children not conditioned to respond
    b. Conditioned orientation reflex (COR)
    c. TROCA
    d. Visual reinforcement audiometry (VRA)
    e. Audiological testing as a game
11. TRUE or FALSE? Speech audiometry is not as objective or precise as pure-tone audiometry.
12. Define speech reception and speech discrimination.
13. List three important roles that speech reception tests play in the measurement of hearing sensitivity.
14. Define *prelinguistic* and *postlinguistic* hearing impairment.
15. Label the following statements as *conductive, sensorineural, mixed,* or *central* hearing loss:
    a. Combination of conductive and sensorineural disorders
    b. Generally medically irreversible loss
    c. Damage to the sensory unit in the cochlea or auditory nerve
    d. Damage to the auditory nerve (eighth nerve) pathways from the brain stem to the auditory cortex
    e. Typically related to abnormalities or malfunctions of the outer or middle ear
    f. Mostly medically reversible losses
16. What are two common causes of deafness during the prenatal period?
17. The most frequent postnatal cause of sensorineural hearing impairment in school-age children is one of the following:
    a. Rh incompatibility
    b. Trauma
    c. Meningitis
    d. Otosclerosis
18. What are the three broad categories of amplification systems?
19. The most widely worn type of individual hearing aid is one of the following:
    a. Body aid
    b. In-the-ear aid
    c. In-the-canal aid
    d. Behind-the-ear aid
20. What is one of the most important advantages of group amplification systems as compared to individual hearing aids?

SUGGESTED ACTIVITIES

1. Place cotton and ear plugs into your ears to simulate hearing impairment. Engage in the following activities and record your observations.
   a. Watch TV, particularly the news and one of your favorite programs.
   b. Converse with your friends and relatives on a range of topics.
   c. Go to the grocery store and ask for the location of a few items.
   d. Go to the post office and ask for information regarding the use of Express Mail.
   Note: Do not drive any motorized vehicle. Ask a friend or relative to take you to the various suggested places.
2. Visit your local speech and hearing center or hearing-aid center. Ask personnel to show you the following:
   a. Various kinds of individual hearing aids

b. How they make a wax impression of the ear

c. Examples of other assistive devices such as telecommunication devices (TDDs) and volume amplifiers for telephones

FURTHER READINGS

Berger, K. (1984). *The hearing aid: Its operation and development* (3rd ed.). Livonia, MI: National Hearing Aid Society.

Boothroyd, A. (1976). *The role of hearing in education of the deaf.* Northampton, MA: Clarke School for the Deaf.

Bradford, L., & Hardy, W. (Eds.). (1979). *Hearing and hearing impairment.* New York: Grune & Stratton.

Davis, H., & Silverman, S. R. (1978). *Hearing and deafness* (4th ed.). New York: Holt, Rinehart and Winston.

Martin, F. (1986). *Introduction to audiology* (3rd ed.). Englewood Cliffs, NJ: Prentice-Hall.

Northern, J., & Downs, M. (1984). *Hearing in children* (3rd ed.). Baltimore, MD: Williams & Wilkins.

Stark, R. (Ed.). (1974). *Sensory capabilities of hearing-impaired children.* Baltimore, MD: University Park Press.

CHAPTER 3

Hard-of-Hearing Students

MAJOR POINTS TO CONSIDER

Definition of hard-of-hearing students

Difference between hard-of-hearing and deaf students

Academic achievement of hard-of-hearing students

Effects of placement on achievement and social development

Early intervention

Support services

Although this book focuses mainly on severely to profoundly hearing-impaired students, it is important to highlight some findings concerning the achievement of students with less severe hearing losses—that is, hard-of-hearing students. The study of hard-of-hearing students, especially those integrated into regular education programs, is one of the most neglected areas of research and service (Berg & Fletcher, 1970; Davis, 1986; Ross, Brackett, & Maxon, 1982). The education of these students is markedly different from that of many, and perhaps most, severely and profoundly hearing-impaired (or deaf) students. As stated by Ross et al. (1982):

> The hard of hearing child is developing, or has developed, his basic communication skills through the auditory channel. His residual hearing is sufficient, with or without amplification, to serve as the basis for his evolving speech and language skills. Although these skills are more often deficient than not, he is, nonetheless, basically an auditory rather than a visual communicator. Thus he has much more in common with a normally hearing child than he does with a deaf child. (p. 2)

Because of the complexity of instructing these students, an in-depth treatment of educational issues is beyond the scope of this chapter. Instead, we discuss briefly definitions, academic achievement, language and literacy, and the effects of placement on achievement and social development. The chapter concludes with a presentation of educational recommendations and needs.

DEFINITION OF HARD-OF-HEARING STUDENTS

In defining hard-of-hearing students, it is important to consider several factors discussed previously—degree of impairment, age at onset, etiology, and intelligence. Other critical factors are the amount of speech, language, and auditory training, the age at onset of the training, and the auditory and language environment of the home and school (Ross, 1986a; 1986b; Silverman, Lane, & Calvert, 1978).

In Chapter 2, hearing impairment was defined as the average hearing threshold level of pure audiometric tones in the better unaided ear across the speech frequencies of 500, 1,000, and 2,000 Hz. Hearing impairment was divided into five categories. Certain educational implications associated with the categories are listed in Table 3.1. Students with hearing losses up to 70 dB in the better unaided ear are considered the typical hard-of-hearing group. Depending on their use of residual hearing, students in the fourth category (i.e., from 71 to about 90 dB) may also be considered hard-of-hearing.

Early amplification and early intervention are important for helping hard-of-hearing students to function effectively in a primarily auditory mode. Most hard-of-hearing students can learn to listen, speak, read, and write a spoken language on a level commensurate with their hearing peers. As mentioned in Chapter 2, it has been argued that most students with severe losses (up to 90 dB) and many students with profound or extreme hearing impairments should also be able to learn through the use of audition (Ross, 1986a, 1986b; Ross & Calvert, 1984).

The incidence of hard-of-hearing students has been estimated at about 16 for every 1,000 students in preschool, elementary, and secondary education levels (Ross et al., 1982). About half of these students have unilateral hearing impairments and do not wear personal hearing aids (Davis, Shepard, Stelmachowicz, & Gorga, 1981; Shepard, Davis, Gorga, & Stelmachowicz, 1981). In addition, it has been found that about 71 percent of integrated students with bilateral mild to severe losses wear personal hearing aids compared to only 29 percent of their hearing-impaired counterparts in self-contained classes.

Much of the available research findings concerns hard-of-hearing students who are receiving special education services. These data might not be representative of students with similar characteristics in regular education programs who are unidentified and are not receiving special education services. These students (Ross et al., 1982):

> . . . are, rather, scattered in 'mainstream' settings throughout the country, with no single public school administration, at any hierarchical level, able or interested in developing and collecting the information regarding their performance. (p. 16)

TABLE 3.1. Categories of Hearing Impairment and Educational Implications

Degree of Impairment	Label	Educational Implications
Up to 26 dB	Normal	Regular education placement
27 to 40 dB	Slight	Regular education placement; favorable seating; may need training in speech and speech reading; may need other support services; academic progress should be monitored.
41 to 55 dB	Mild	Regular education placement; favorable seating; should use hearing aid; may need instruction in speech, speech reading, and auditory training; may need help in language and reading; may need other support services; academic progress should be monitored.
56 to 70 dB	Moderate	Regular education placement; favorable seating; training and use of hearing aid; instruction in speech and speech reading; special help in language and reading; use of other support services such as tutoring and note taking; progress should be monitored.
71 to 90 dB	Severe	Regular education placement if possible; favorable seating; full-time special education program may be necessary; part-time integration whenever possible; training in use of hearing aid; instruction in speech, speech reading, and auditory training; comprehensive support services must be available; academic progress should be monitored.
91+ dB	Profound	Special education program likely; training in both oral and signing communication skills; comprehensive support services must be available; part-time integration only for carefully selected children.

SOURCE: Based on discussions in Ross (1986a, 1986b) and Silverman, Lane, & Calvert (1978).

EDUCATIONAL ACHIEVEMENT

Two general conclusions can be reached about the effects of hearing impairment on the education of hard-of-hearing students. *One,* it is well accepted that even a slight hearing loss can negatively affect academic achievement as well as the development of spoken and **written language** abilities (Paul & Quigley, 1987a; Ross et al., 1982). Thus, the academic development of hard-of-hearing students proceeds at a slower rate than that of their hearing peers. *Two,* despite this slower rate of progress, hard-of-hearing students are reported to proceed through learning stages of speech and language that are similar to those of their hearing counterparts. These conclusions emphasize the need for a comprehensive early intervention program, particularly in the development of oral communication skills such as speech, speech reading, and the use of residual hearing. Improvements in the identification process should also be considered because many of the unidentified fully integrated students may need important educational support services such as speech therapy, auditory training, **note taking,** and tutoring.

In a review of studies from the time of Pintner and Lev (1939) to the more recent ones (Blair, Peterson, & Viehweg, 1985), it has been found that the academic achievement of average hard-of-hearing students, in either mainstreamed or special education programs, lags behind that of their hearing peers (see the following list for a brief description of the major findings of several studies).

Studies on Achievement and Hearing Impairment	**Major Points**
Kodman (1963)	Achievement level of group (20 to 65 dB) about 2 years behind that of hearing students; only one-third of students wore hearing aids.
Quigley & Thomure (1968)	Inverse relationship between hearing impairment and academic achievement; slightly impaired students about 1 year behind; moderately hearing-impaired students about 3 years behind.
Jensema (1975)	Inverse relationship between hearing impairment and achievement in a national sample of students in special education programs.
Davis & Blasdell (1975)	Syntactic development of hearing-impaired students quantitatively reduced but qualitatively similar to that of younger hearing students.
Reich, Hambleton, & Houldin (1977)	Fully integrated students performed as well as hearing peers on language and reading tasks.
Davis, Shepard, Stelmachowicz, & Gorga (1981)	Students with mild to moderate impairments performed as well as did their hearing peers on reading, mathematics, and spelling. The gap between hearing and hearing-impaired students becomes significant for students with losses greater than 50 dB.
Blair, Peterson, & Viehweg (1985)	Academic lag of hearing-impaired students not as great as that reported by Quigley and Thomure (1968). Impressive results can be obtained with early, adequate auditory management.

In some cases, the achievement gap of hard-of-hearing students increased with age. That is, as students become older, their achievement becomes even slower and lags further behind that of their hearing counterparts. The educational achievement of the students is related to their degree of impairment and the quality of support services.

TABLE 3.2. Hearing Impairment and Mean Achievement Scores

Degree of Impairment	Vocabulary	Reading	Mathematics	
			Concepts	Computation
Up to 26 dB	1.28	0.78	0.50	0.19
27 to 40 dB	0.85	0.65	0.58	0.28
41 to 55 dB	0.59	0.51	0.39	0.24
56 to 70 dB	0.22	0.18	0.16	0.08
71 to 90 dB	−0.03	0.02	−0.04	−0.02
90+ dB	−0.16	−0.12	−0.09	−0.04

Age deviation scores; 1.00 represents the 84th percentile; −1.00, the 16th percentile. SOURCE: Adapted from Jensema (1975).

Achievement, Hearing Loss, and Support Services

Kodman (1963) analyzed the performances of 100 mainstreamed hard-of-hearing students whose hearing impairments ranged from 20 to 65 dB in the better unaided ear. The average academic achievement level of these sixth-grade students was 3.8 grades, slightly more than 2 years below that of their hearing grade peers. It was reported also that only one-third of the students wore hearing aids and about one-fourth received support services in speech and language.

Similar results were documented in a later study by Quigley and Thomure (1968), who examined the educational achievement of all hearing-impaired students (173) in a city in Illinois. An inverse relationship was observed between hearing impairment and academic achievement. For example, Quigley and Thomure reported that a slight hearing loss (see Table 3.1) can result in a lag of about 1 year when compared to the performance of hearing peers. The performances of students with moderate hearing impairments showed a 3-year retardation. One of the researchers' main points was that even a very slight hearing impairment can have a negative effect on educational achievement.

That academic achievement is negatively related to the severity of hearing loss and the quality of support services has been documented by several more recent studies. For example, Balow, Fulton, and Peploe (1971) found that the **mean** reading scores of the few mildly impaired students in their study were about one grade higher than those for the severely to profoundly impaired students in residential and/or special day school programs. A similar pattern can also be seen in a comprehensive review by Jensema (1975), whose findings are based on the results of national surveys conducted by the Center for Assessment and Demographic Studies (CADS) at Gallaudet University in Washington, D.C., on about 7,000 students in special programs. The educational achievement of hearing-impaired students was compared to other hearing-impaired students, not to normal-hearing students. Table 3.2 shows that the vocabulary, reading, and mathematics scores decreased as hearing impairment increased.

It has been shown that with early amplification, early intervention, and adequate classroom management, the academic achievement gap between many hard-of-hearing students and their hearing peers can be reduced. For example, McClure (1977) reported

TABLE 3.3. Comparison of Hearing-Impaired and Hearing Students in Grades 1 to 4 on
Reading Achievement

	Mean Grade Scores			
Grade	1	2	3	4
Hearing-impaired	2.0	3.3	3.5	4.5
Hearing	2.3	3.7	4.7	6.3

Hearing-impaired students are on grade level but still lower than their hearing peers who took the same test (Iowa Test of Basic Concepts). SOURCE: Adapted from Blair et al. (1985).

that 14 mainstreamed moderately to severely hearing-impaired students achieved age-level or average scores on the reading subtest of the Wide Range Achievement Test. Reich, Hambleton, and Houldin (1977) also reported less severe academic lags for their Canadian hard-of-hearing students. The fully integrated students in this study performed as well as their hearing peers on language and reading tasks. The success of the hearing-impaired students was attributed to factors such as early diagnosis, use of hearing aids, involved and educated parents, and highly developed oral-communication skills. In a more recent study, Davis et al. (1981) found that the achievement of mildly to moderately impaired students was similar to that of their hearing counterparts in reading, mathematics, and spelling on standardized achievement tests. Significant gaps in the performances between hearing and hearing-impaired students were observed only when the degree of unaided impairment exceeded 50 dB.

In relation to adequate **auditory management,** Blair et al. (1985) stated that the academic performance of the hearing-impaired students in their study was related positively to the length of time the students had worn personal hearing aids. The researchers compared the achievement levels of students with unaided hearing losses ranging from 25 to 45 dB with those of their hearing grade peers (i.e., in grades 1 to 4). The results revealed that the hearing students still had significantly higher scores on the reading, vocabulary, and mathematics subtests of the Iowa Test of Basic Concepts. The academic lag of the hard-of-hearing students was not as great, however, as that reported by Quigley and Thomure (1968). The mean grade scores of the hard-of-hearing students at the end of the fourth grade were not much different from the **norms** (see Table 3.3).

Quantitative and Qualitative Issues

In language development, **quantitative** lags have also been reported, but the process of development has been found to be similar in sequence for both normally hearing and hard-of-hearing students (Davis & Blasdell, 1975; Davis et al., 1981). Hard-of-hearing students make language errors similar to those of profoundly hearing-impaired, or deaf, students; however, they make fewer of them. Although these students do not acquire language at the same rate as their normally hearing counterparts, hard-of-hearing students do acquire language structures in the same manner. That is, they proceed through developmental stages and produce errors that are similar to those of younger normally hearing students.

For example, Pressnell (1973) and Wilcox and Tobin (1974) studied the performance of students with moderate or greater hearing impairments on aspects of the verb system of English. On the basis of analyses of **spontaneous language samples** and the results of the Northwestern Syntax Screening Test, Pressnell found evidence for quantitative delays and **qualitative** similarities. Using a sentence repetition task, Wilcox and Tobin reported similar findings.

Davis and Blasdell (1975) examined the syntactic abilities of both hard-of-hearing and hearing students between the ages of 6 to 9 years. The hard-of-hearing students had hearing impairments ranging from 35 to 75 dB in the better unaided ear. The researchers were interested in the students' abilities to comprehend medially embedded **relative clauses** (as in *The man who chased the sheep cut the grass*). As expected, hard-of-hearing students produced more errors than did their hearing counterparts at all age levels compared, and the gap between the two groups increased with age. The errors of the hearing-impaired students, however, were similar to those made by their hearing peers.

ACADEMIC PLACEMENT

As discussed in Chapter 1, increasing attention is being paid to academic placement and its effects on educational achievement and social development. Several placement options are available for hearing-impaired students—residential schools, day schools, self-contained public school classes, full integration in public schools, and the use of resource rooms and itinerant programs (see Chapter 1 for brief descriptions). There are variations of these categories, and some have overlapping features. For example, Ross (1968a) argues that:

> In actual practice, the self-contained class and the resource room overlap in organization and function; one school district may include both types of programs, permitting lateral transfer of the children when this is deemed appropriate. (p. 25)

As discussed previously, most students with hearing impairments up to moderate levels are fully integrated (and often unidentified) in regular education programs. Typically, these students are exposed to methods and materials used by regular education teachers. Some students who have been identified are receiving support services such as speech and hearing training, note taking, and tutoring. Some moderately hearing-impaired students and many severely hearing-impaired students are enrolled in special education programs. Students in self-contained or other special programs may be exposed to a variety of **unisensory** or **multisensory** approaches through signing or, more likely, speech, depending on whether the program endorses an oral or a Total Communication (TC) philosophy.

To compare hard-of-hearing students in educational settings, there should be agreement that the comparisons concern groups of students with similar characteristics. For example, the academic achievement of prelinguistic moderately hearing-impaired students in self-contained classes in public schools can be compared with that of other prelinguistic moderately impaired students fully integrated in regular education programs. Many important variables, such as intelligence and socioeconomic status, must be controlled for the comparisons to be valid. Comparisons of students in special schools

TABLE 3.4. Program Type and Mean Achievement Scores

Type of Program	Vocabulary	Reading	Mathematics	
			Concepts	Computation
Residential	−0.09	−0.06	−0.10	−0.09
Day	−0.13	−0.14	−0.11	−0.11
Full-time special class	0.04	−0.01	0.02	0.02
Resource	0.19	0.22	0.17	0.13
Part-time special class	0.24	0.37	0.31	0.28
Itinerant	0.69	0.71	0.56	0.42

Age deviation scores; 1.00 represents the 84th percentile; −1.00, the 16th percentile. SOURCE: Adapted from Jensema (1975).

with those in public schools are important. The results, however, are sometimes difficult to interpret because of numerous factors beyond experimental control.

Very few studies have adequately compared hard-of-hearing students in various educational settings (Davis, 1986). Some data can be found on the effects of academic placement on achievement and social development. Most of the findings reported here concern students with hearing impairments *up to* the severe level. The few studies involving severely hearing-impaired students and those with profound impairments are discussed in Chapter 9.

Placement and Achievement

That integrated hard-of-hearing students have higher achievement levels than those of their nonintegrated counterparts is shown by the results of the annual surveys conducted by the Center for Assessment and Demographic Studies (CADS) at Gallaudet University. The data provided by Jensema (1975) indicated that the academic achievement of students improved as the program shifted from special to regular education (see Table 3.4). Reich et al. (1977), discussed previously, examined the performance of 195 hearing-impaired students with varying degrees of impairment in four educational programs in Canada. When important factors such as degree of impairment, age at onset, and **ethnic status** were taken into account, the researchers reported that integrated students were achieving at or above grade level whereas students attending special classes lagged by 1 to 2 years. The results of these studies have been confirmed by more recent analyses of the national survey data collected by CADS (Allen & Osborn, 1984).

As for placement and achievement, it should be emphasized that integration is not an all-important factor. Several researchers have shown that integration accounts for only a small amount of achievement variation (Allen & Osborn, 1984; Wolk, Karchmer, & Schildroth, 1982). Other important variables must be considered, among them the quality of instruction and curricula and the expectations and training of teachers (Kluwin & Moores, 1985). Despite some exceptions (Antia, 1982; Doehring, Bonnycastle, & Ling, 1978), it has been argued that these favorable instructional variables and others (such as demanding use of oral-communication skills) are more likely to be found in integrated classrooms (Ross, 1986a, 1986b; Ross et al., 1982).

Social Development

The social development, particularly social interaction skills, of hearing-impaired students in both integrated and special classrooms in regular schools has been documented in several studies. For example, Kennedy, Northcott, McCauley, and Williams (1976) compared the socialization skills of fully integrated hearing-impaired students (the mean degree of impairment was 82 dB) with those of their hearing classmates in grades 1 through 4. The researchers found that hearing-impaired students preferred to interact with their teachers rather than with hearing peers. They also found that hearing students interacted more successfully with one another. Kennedy et al. concluded that hearing-impaired students received more socially rewarding interactions from teachers than from their peers.

In a more recent study, Antia (1982) reported similar findings. Antia compared the social interactions of partially integrated hearing-impaired students (the range of impairment was from 25 dB to 108 dB) with both their hearing and hearing-impaired peers in integrated classrooms and resource rooms from five schools. Four of the five schools used oral communication, and the fifth used simultaneous communication. Four groups of behaviors were categorized: physical proximity, interaction, mode of communication, and unusual behavior. The results indicated that integrated hearing-impaired students did not experience physical isolation. They did, however, interact more frequently with their teachers and with other hearing-impaired students than with their hearing peers. Antia also observed that hearing-impaired students used more oral communication in resource rooms than in integrated classrooms, and hypothesized that the increased use in resource rooms may have resulted from the demands and expectations of the teacher. In addition, Antia concluded that physical integration was not sufficient for promoting the development of adequate oral communication and social interaction skills.

A few researchers have attempted to develop or adapt intervention techniques to improve the social interactions of hearing-impaired students with their hearing peers. Vandell, Anderson, Erhardt, and Wilson (1982) provided hearing children with information about hearing impairment and opportunities to interact with their hearing-impaired preschool classmates. No significant increase in the social interactions between the two groups was found. More positive results have been documented in other recent studies on young children with slight to severe unaided hearing impairments (Antia & Kreimeyer, 1987; Antia & Kreimeyer, 1988). The results were attributed to the use of teacher instruction and modeling in teaching positive social interaction skills. This intervention program also involved structuring the classroom environment and activities that facilitate and provide numerous opportunities for peer interactions. In addition, it was suggested that the intervention procedures should be withdrawn gradually rather than abruptly to ensure the maintenance of the increased level of interactions between hearing and hearing-impaired children. More research is needed on the maintenance of peer interaction skills for an extended period.

SUMMARY

Regardless of degree of loss, it is clear that hearing impairment has a negative effect on students' language and academic achievement levels. The impact on achievement is related to the severity of the impairment. Research has also shown that the language development of hard-of-hearing students is slower than, albeit similar to, that of normally hearing students. These patterns are evident for hearing-impaired students in all kinds of educational placements.

There is some evidence that integrated hearing-impaired students do better academically than nonintegrated students. Integration itself may not be the critical factor. Other important factors are the qualifications and attitudes of teachers and the use of effective instructional and curricular practices. In addition, it is important to establish and maintain an early, intensive auditory management program that encourages the development of residual hearing. More emphasis should be placed also on the socioemotional growth of integrated hearing-impaired students. As indicated by recent investigations, integrated students need additional opportunities for interacting with hearing peers, and they *need to be taught effective socialization strategies*. Hearing students also need to learn how to interact with their hearing-impaired peers.

It is thought that the academic lag between many hearing-impaired students and their hearing peers can be reduced with early, intensive amplification and intervention, which also includes the involvement of parents/caregivers. Most students with slight to moderate losses and many with severe impairments can benefit from placement in regular education programs with adequate auditory management, parental involvement, and comprehensive support services. Hard-of-hearing students are receiving increasing attention from educators and researchers; yet there is still a need to identify and study more members of this group, especially those in integrated classrooms. The following recommendations are suggested (Davis, 1977; Ross, 1986a; and Ross et al. 1982):

1. Improvements in early identification and identification of hard-of-hearing students in regular education programs.
2. Encouragement of parents/caregivers to become involved in the education of their children and in efforts to improve communication skills.
3. Establishment and maintenance of an early, intensive auditory management program, involving training in the use of residual hearing and promoting the use of early amplification.
4. Comprehensive support services available for *all* students regardless of degree of hearing impairment and educational placement.
5. Systematic records kept on the academic and socialization progress of students, especially those in regular education programs.
6. As much as possible, the placement of hearing-impaired students with slight to severe losses in regular education programs, with orientation to hearing impairment for regular education teachers and administrators.
7. Additional research studies on the spoken and written language development of hard-of-hearing students.
8. The establishment of successful intervention procedures to increase and maintain high levels of socialization skills.

COMPREHENSION

1. TRUE or FALSE? The study of hard-of-hearing students, especially those integrated into regular education programs, is one of the most neglected areas of research and service.
2. Select some of the variables that are important in defining hard-of-hearing students from among the following:
    a. Degree of impairment
    b. Age at onset
    c. Amount and quality of speech and auditory training
    d. All of the above
    e. Items *a* and *b* only
3. Traditional hard-of-hearing students are those individuals with hearing losses in the better unaided ear from slight to
    a. Mild.
    b. Moderate.
    c. Severe.
    d. Profound.
    e. Slight only.
4. TRUE or FALSE? The authors believe that most students with severe impairments (up to 90 dB) and many students with profound impairments are able to learn through the use of audition.
5. TRUE or FALSE? Research has shown that hard-of-hearing students (i.e., those with mild to severe losses) in integrated classes are more likely to wear personal hearing aids than are their peers in self-contained classes.
6. What are the two general findings that have been made about the effects of hearing impairment on the education of hard-of-hearing students?
7. Research on the academic achievement of hard-of-hearing students has revealed that (select all that apply)
    a. Most students perform on a par with their hearing peers.
    b. The achievement of students with a slight loss is about 3 years behind that of their hearing peers.
    c. An inverse relationship exists between hearing impairment and achievement; the greater the impairment, the lower the achievement.
    d. Most students are reading on grade level.
    e. With early amplification and adequate classroom management, the gap between hard-of-hearing and hearing students can be reduced.
8. In relation to language development, the performance of hard-of-hearing students is
    a. Quantitatively and qualitatively similar to that of their hearing peers.
    b. Quantitatively different but qualitatively similar.
    c. Qualitatively different but quantitatively similar.
    d. Both quantitatively and qualitatively different.
    e. None of the above.
9. TRUE or FALSE? Quantitatively similar means that the language acquisition processes of both hearing-impaired and hearing students are developmentally similar.
10. What are the academic placement options available for hard-of-hearing students?
11. TRUE or FALSE? Most students with hearing losses up to moderate levels are fully integrated into regular education programs.
12. The research on placement indicates that (select all that apply)
    a. Integrated students have higher achievement levels than do their nonintegrated hearing-impaired peers.

b. The act of integration alone has a major effect on achievement.

c. Integration results in greater development of oral communication and social interaction skills.

d. Integrated hearing-impaired students interact more often with teachers than with their hearing peers.

e. Integrated hearing-impaired students need to be taught effective socialization strategies.

13. List five recommendations for improving the education of hard-of-hearing students.

SUGGESTED ACTIVITIES

1. Interview several hard-of-hearing students in the various educational placements. Find out (with the teacher's help, if necessary) the following:

a. Their hobbies and interests

b. How they feel about their hearing aids

c. How they feel about school

d. The amount of time they spend in integrated classrooms

e. Whether they have hearing-impaired and/or hearing friends

f. If they like to read

g. If they know how to sign

2. Ask several hard-of-hearing students to read a story to you. Tape the readings.

a. Which of the readings are most intelligible? Least intelligible?

b. Is there a relationship between intelligibility and hearing impairment? (If possible, obtain the latest audiological exam of the students.)

FURTHER READINGS

Berg, F., & Fletcher, S. (1967). The hard of hearing child and educational audiology. *Proceedings of International Conference on Oral Education of the Deaf* (pp. 874–875). Washington, DC: Alexander Graham Bell Association for the Deaf.

Boothroyd, A. (1982). *Hearing impairments in young children.* Englewood Cliffs, NJ: Prentice-Hall.

Jaffe, B. (Ed.). (1977). *Hearing loss in children: A comprehensive text.* Baltimore, MD: University Park Press.

Martin, F. (Ed.). (1987). *Hearing disorders in children: Pediatric audiology.* Austin, TX: Pro-Ed.

O'Neill, J. (1964). *The hard of hearing.* Englewood Cliffs, NJ: Prentice-Hall.

Quigley, S. (1978). Effects of hearing impairment on normal language development. In F. Martin (Ed.), *Pediatric audiology* (pp. 35–63). Englewood Cliffs, NJ: Prentice-Hall.

Ross, M., & Giolas, T. (Eds.). (1978). *Auditory management of hearing-impaired children: Principles and prerequisites for intervention.* Baltimore, MD: University Park Press.

CHAPTER 4

Psychology and Deafness

MAJOR POINTS TO CONSIDER

Notions of cognition and intelligence

Cognitive/intellectual functioning of severely to profoundly hearing-impaired students

Relations between cognition and language

Piagetian and information processing models

Psychology of deafness

Psychosocial aspects of deafness

Characteristics of the deaf community and Deaf culture

Many lay persons, educators, and researchers have asked, and sometimes sought answers to, a variety of psychological questions concerning hearing-impaired individuals. Examples of inquiries that have an impact on the education of severely to profoundly hearing-impaired students include the following:

What do hearing-impaired students think in?

Are their cognitive/intellectual processes similar to or different from those of hearing students?

Can hearing-impaired students engage in abstract thinking, reasoning, and problem solving?

Is speech important for cognitive development?

What is the mental health status of hearing-impaired individuals?

Is there a Deaf culture?

Is there a **psychology of deafness;** that is, are there certain behavioral traits uniquely attributed to deafness that are different from those associated with the typical, nondisabled population?

Adequate answers to these and other questions could help to provide a better perspective on the academic, language, literacy, personality, and socioemotional development of severely to profoundly hearing-impaired students.

Many issues related to psychology and deafness are influenced by an understanding of the nature of the language/communication system between hearing-impaired children and significant others such as parents/caregivers and teachers. The development of children's educational potential is pervasively affected by language and communication. It has been said that "The education of deaf children has to be judged . . . by its success in providing a child with a language for thought. . . . a language upon which the development of cognitive process can advance." (Conrad, 1979, p. 6). It should also be a language that can advance socioemotional and other developmental processes.

This chapter describes briefly the **cognitive**/intellectual, social, and **personality development** of students with severe to profound hearing losses. Because of the focus on education, we are interested in the impact of this development on the academic and social progress of the students. This interest is representative of much of the recent research on cognition and deafness. This trend, however, does not diminish the importance of more work in the area of deafness and psychosocial issues. To answer some of the questions posed earlier, the interrelationships among cognition, intelligence, language, and reading are discussed. Within this conceptual framework, the chapter synthesizes the research findings on selected cognitive/intellectual processes and on mental health and familial development. Finally, some salient characteristics of the adult deaf community, including the existence of the Deaf culture, are presented. As is discussed later, it is difficult to provide generalizations on the various psychological issues related to deafness because (1) much of the research on cognition is not driven by theory, (2) some researchers provide incomplete descriptions of their samples of hearing-impaired subjects, and (3) research findings are sometimes generalized to dissimilar populations.

COGNITION, INTELLIGENCE, AND DEAFNESS

To obtain a basic understanding of the research on the cognitive/intellectual functioning of severely to profoundly hearing-impaired students, it is necessary to discuss cognition and intelligence. **Cognition** can be defined as the acquisition, organization, and application of knowledge (Sternberg, 1986). **Cognitive structure** refers to what is being acquired or represented. **Cognitive process** is the activity responsible for the acquisition or representation of knowledge (or structure). This process consists of two levels: representational and executive (Anderson, 1975; Gagné 1977). Thus, it is important to discuss individuals' ability to represent environmental information in the brain and their ability to execute, or use, this knowledge. Cognitive process also refers to the awareness that individuals have of their thinking and reasoning abilities. Some theorists, particularly those concerned with reading ability, prefer to label this awareness *metacognition* (Baker & Brown, 1984; Chapter 8 of this book).

At first, it may seem that cognitive functioning and intellectual functioning should be synonymous. Until quite recently, however, intelligence has not been considered as cognitive competence. As pointed out by Moores (1987):

> A great deal of confusion has arisen out of the tendency to subsume within one area two quite different sets of activities: (1) the investigation of cognitive development and functioning and (2) the **IQ** (intelligence quotient) **test** movement. Each has different goals, procedures, and even terminology. (p. 146)

There is general agreement that current IQ tests such as the Leiter International Performance Scale *(LIPS;* Leiter, 1979) and the Wechsler Intelligence Scale for Children–Revised *(WISC–R;* Wechsler, 1974) provide a very narrow concept of intelligence (Sternberg, 1986). Scores are determined by performances on two scales: verbal and nonverbal. These tests measure verbal intelligence by performance on tasks of verbal comprehension and achievement (e.g., vocabulary and general knowledge subtests). Nonverbal ability is assessed by spatial reasoning tasks such as block design and matrices.

There is a need to construct intelligence tests that are based on theory and research in cognitive processing to make possible more effective decisions on the academic or vocational performance of students. For example, it has been reported that the Hiskey–Nebraska Test of Learning Aptitude (H–NTLA) (Hiskey, 1966) does not correlate highly with academic achievement. The H–NTLA might be more reliably predictive, however, if used in conjunction with other tests in planning the academic program of hearing-impaired students (Watson, Goldgar, Kroese, & Lotz, 1986). Nevertheless, individual cognitive variability can be better understood from a perspective of cognitive processing. This, in turn, would improve the diagnostic functions of the tests and provide a conceptual base on which intervention programs could be established.

In sum, there is a need for a strong theoretical framework rather than revisions of old intelligence tests that continue to focus on content rather than process (Naglieri & Das, in press; Sternberg, 1984, 1986). It is important to move away from the conception of intelligence as a unitary trait that can be measured by IQ or PIQ (Performance IQ) tests. Intelligence tests should reflect cognitive processes and be based on theoretical models of cognitive processing. For example, the tests might focus on areas such as speed of processing and problem-solving strategies. It has also been proposed that cognitive processes be used as a modern term for intelligence and IQ (Naglieri, 1987).

Historical Perspectives

With the foregoing caveats in mind, a historical perspective on intelligence and deafness follows. A number of researchers have compared the cognitive abilities of severely to profoundly hearing-impaired individuals to those of their normally hearing peers. Specifically, they have sought to answer the question: Are the abilities of the two groups qualitatively (i.e., manner of acquisition) and quantitatively (i.e., rate of acquisition) similar? Up until the beginning of formal testing in the early 1900s, deaf individuals were often labeled *deaf and dumb*—that is, as being both mute (without speech) and of inferior intelligence (Moores, 1987). From the early 1900s to the present, there were three successive stages of thought concerning intelligence and deafness: (1) The Deaf are inferior individuals, (2) the Deaf learn through their experiences with concrete objects and actual events, and (3) the Deaf are normal. It should be remembered that some subjects in these studies had moderate and severe hearing losses, thus, the word *deaf* referred to individuals with moderate to profound hearing impairments (Quigley & Kretschmer, 1982).

Pintner and his associates (Pintner, Eisenson, & Stanton, 1941; Pintner & Paterson, 1917; Pintner & Reamer, 1920) advanced the inferiority hypothesis. On the basis of results of paper-and-pencil intelligence tests, these researchers reported that deaf subjects evidenced an average retardation of 10 IQ points when compared to their normally hearing counterparts. It was concluded that the cognitive functioning of deaf individuals was quantitatively reduced. It is not clear whether Pintner and his associates believed that the intellectual functioning of their deaf subjects was qualitatively similar or dissimilar to that of their hearing peers.

The work of Myklebust and his collaborators (Myklebust, 1964) represents the second stage of thinking about the deaf: that deaf individuals grow intellectually through their perception of actual events and things. On the basis of global test scores from nonverbal IQ tests, the researchers argued that there were no differences between deaf and hearing subjects. A close inspection of the scores on the various subtests, however, revealed a pattern of qualitative differences between the two groups. The cognitive functioning of deaf individuals was reported to be quantitatively equal but qualitatively inferior to that of their hearing counterparts. In addition, Myklebust argued that the performances on tests assessing abilities to comprehend abstractions indicated that deaf individuals have difficulty dealing with abstract thoughts and ideas. Myklebust and Brutton (1953) remarked that deafness "restricts the child functionally to a world of concrete objects and things" (p. 93). They hypothesized that this condition results from the hearing impairment that forces the individual to perceive the world differently because of a reliance on the other intact senses—vision, touch, taste, and smell. Not only do deaf individuals perceive the world differently; they also exhibit personal and social behaviors different from those of normally hearing individuals. It is apparent that Myklebust believed in a *psychology of deafness*—namely, that certain behavioral traits that are different from those associated with the typical, nondisabled population can be uniquely attributed to deafness.

The third stage is characterized by the idea that deaf individuals are intellectually normal (Furth, 1966; Rosenstein, 1961; Vernon, 1968, 1969a). It is argued that cognitive differences between the two groups can be accounted for by (1) difficulties with conveying test instructions, (2) language and cultural biases implicit within the assessment, and (3) experiential deficits caused by inadequate development of a language or communication system. Evidence can be found to support these arguments. There are still some problems, however, in resolving numbers 2 and 3. For example, many nonverbal intelligence tests can be as culturally loaded as language tests (Anastasi, 1982; Naglieri & Das, in press). As discussed previously, one way to produce a nonbiased test is to focus on process rather than content.

In relation to number 3, it has been shown that most *deaf* (i.e., profoundly hearing-impaired) students do not learn a language adequately by the time they finish school. If deaf students know or acquire a language, it is most likely to be American Sign Language (ASL) (for further details, see Chapters 6 and 7). Much of the research on cognitive processes involves many deaf students who do not have a *language for thought* (Conrad, 1979). Related also to issue number 3 is the notion that many deaf individuals may have adequate cognitive functioning ability but lack the skills to apply it on linguistic and cognitive tasks (Karchmer & Belmont, 1976; Liben, 1984). If communication between teacher and student is sufficient, then deaf students may be able to learn effective strategies.

From another perspective, it may be that the intellectual ability of deaf individuals cannot be explained adequately by previously assumed factors such as language/communication and parental/caregiver interactions (Conrad & Weiskrantz, 1981; Kusché, Greenberg, & Garfield, 1983). For example, the superior performances of deaf children of deaf parents as compared to deaf children of hearing parents have been attributed to the faster speed with which the former group processes information (Braden, 1987). In a cognitive-processing theoretical framework, speed of processing is considered important, along with strategies and decision-making (i.e., metacognitive) skills. The extent to which these skills are influenced by educational intervention has not been studied. As discussed previously, current IQ or PIQ tests are unitary tests that focus on a narrow view of intelligence. Thus, differences between the groups, as well as a better understanding of intelligence, may emerge only when a cognitive-processing paradigm is used.

COGNITION AND LANGUAGE

In this section, some current thinking on the relationship between cognition and language is briefly discussed. Also presented are some insights that are gleaned from the research on deaf individuals. The nature of this relationship has not only theoretical but also practical significance. For example, if cognition is dependent on language, then deficits in language development affect cognitive development. If language is dependent on cognition, then cognitive deficits affect language development and, subsequently, reading and writing abilities. If cognition and language are not related to each other, then development in one domain does not affect development in the other domain.

As stated eloquently by Snyder (1984):

> The study of the relationship between language and cognitive development is like the carnival huckster's shell game. The player—try as he might to keep his eye on the pea—often finds that it is not under the shell he has selected. Unfortunately for the individual interested in the child's acquisition of language, the problem often becomes confounded by the addition of many more shells than the player can follow. When one looks for instances where the acquisition of linguistic and cognitive structures may be related, it is often difficult to discern with which cognitive shell the linguistic pea is located. Cognition represents such a broad domain that it adds many more shells to the game. (p. 107)

On one level, there seems to be some relationship between cognition and language, as is evident in the idea that language is a symbol system used for communication and thought (Bloom & Lahey, 1978). The symbols (i.e., sounds, words, phrases, sentences) represent ideas and knowledge about the world that people have in their minds. Language symbols represent the knowledge associated with objects, events, people, and the relationships among these entities as perceived by speakers and listeners. For example, the word *chair* stands for a concept and related concepts as well as for the object that might be present in front of the language users.

Many theorists (MacNamara, 1972, 1977) argue that the ideal of language as a symbol system is the only one that exists. Language and cognition, however, have been viewed from several perspectives that are based on prevailing theories of language development. At one extreme is a **language-dominant** position characterized by Chomsky's (1957, 1965, 1968, 1975) nativist hypothesis and its variations. On the other end of the continuum is the **cognitive-dominant** position, also known as the constructivist hypothesis, which has several forms (MacNamara, 1972; Miller, Chapman, & Bedrosian, 1977). Between these two extreme positions are many other perspectives (McNew & Bates, 1984; Muma, 1986; Snyder, 1984).

The crux of the nativist hypotheses is that individuals have innate language mechanisms that predispose them to learn the rules of a language. Language mechanisms are considered innate because of children's ability to learn detailed and complex structures in a short period, despite being exposed to limited, albeit representative, bits of information. In essence, only language, not cognitive, mechanisms, can account for the acquisition of specific, structural rules. For example, to understand complex syntactic structures such as relative clauses (The boy *who kissed the girl* ran away) and the **passive voice** (The boy *was hit* by the girl), individuals need specific knowledge of the linguistic structures that cannot be provided by the concepts behind them. That is, in the sentence containing the relative clause, they need to understand that the boy kissed the girl and he also ran away.

Perhaps the strongest version of the language-dominant position is the theory of linguistic determinism (Sapir, 1921; Whorf, 1956). Linguistic determinism asserts that the languages of individuals *determine* or *define* their thoughts, that there is a one-to-one relationship between language and cognition. Thus, language can be used to determine the breadth and depth of cognitive skills. In addition, it is argued that as languages differ across cultures, so do concepts or views of the world. For example, the view of the world of a Chinese is thought to be different from that of a Briton. It could be inferred that a person who is bilingual, that is, who knows two languages, has two world views! At present, the linguistic determinism hypothesis is not widely accepted.

Several nativist hypotheses have been conceptualized; among them are little linguist (i.e., child as linguist), lexicon, and learnability (McNew & Bates, 1984; Snyder, 1984). The differences among them are centered on (1) the processes regarding the acquisition of syntactic structures and (2) the role of cognition in the process of language acquisition, particularly the acquisition of specific structures beyond the word level. The weakest version of these hypotheses suggests that cognition does play a role, albeit a minor one (Schlesinger, 1977).

The basic tenet of constructivist hypotheses is that children acquire knowledge about the world, including language, through their interactions with objects, events, and mature users of language. Children's cognitive development influences the hypotheses that they formulate about how their language works. This is an interactive process between the child and the environment; children use their schemata (i.e., knowledge structures) to build their own model of what the world means. They may apply their existing schemata to the environment or modify their model of understanding after considering input from the environment. "The give and take of this continuous interaction is the mechanism of the child's cognitive development" (Snyder, 1984, p. 111).

Until recently, there were two groups of constructivist hypotheses: strong and weak. The strong constructivist hypothesis asserts that specific cognitive structures provide the foundation for language development. It says that there is a one-to-one correspondence between cognitive development and language development and that cognition can adequately account for children's ability to learn a language (Karmiloff-Smith, 1979; Miller et al., 1977). The weak cognitive hypothesis contends that cognition is necessary for language but that it is not sufficient to explain the complete development of language (Cromer, 1976). Children need both linguistic skills and cognitive skills in order to acquire a language. From another perspective, the weak cognitive hypothesis implies that the influence of language structures may be equal to or less than, but never greater than, that of cognitive structures (Miller et al., 1977).

The most recent perspective on the relationship between cognition and language is the correlational hypothesis (Miller et al., 1977). This hypothesis suggests that cognition and language are strongly related because they share similar underpinnings. Developmental changes that occur in the underpinnings can be observed as individuals engage in linguistic or cognitive tasks. Examples include children's performances on the various Piagetian tasks, some of which are discussed later. A more detailed discussion of this hypothesis can be found elsewhere (Bates, Benigni, Bretherton, Camaioni, & Volterra, 1979; Snyder, 1984).

A review of the literature reveals some support for the correlational cognitive hypothesis for the prelinguistic period (i.e., before the first words) and the emergence of syntax (i.e., the two-word stage). Much of the evidence on the relationship of cognition and language is equivocal for the **one-word stage** and most other linguistic structures. Thus far, there is little evidence to support the strong nativist position or the strong or weak version of the cognitive constructivist position. In sum, the available data suggest that cognition, language form, and language function all play a role in language development. Nevertheless, we are still a long way from a complete, or even an adequate, understanding of the nature of that role.

Cognition, Language, and Deafness

The prevailing thinking in any particular era about the relationship between cognition and language has influenced that era's interpretations of the intellectual development of hearing-impaired individuals (Moores, 1987; Quigley & Kretschmer, 1982). Until the 1970s, many educators and researchers ascribed to a language-dominant hypothesis, especially linguistic determinism. For example, both Pintner and Myklebust attributed the intellectual lag of deaf subjects to language deficiencies. Myklebust concluded that deaf individuals perceive the world differently from normally hearing persons. In addition, he argued that they have difficulty understanding abstract concepts because they need to rely on their other intact senses. According to Myklebust (1964), deaf individuals have to communicate and learn by means of signs that are not part of a bona fide language. Before the late 1970s, the language of signs was not considered a rule-governed system capable of expressing abstract concepts and ideas.

Many researchers who believed that deaf individuals are intellectually normal disagreed on the role of language in the development of cognition (Levine, 1976; cf., Furth, 1966, 1973). One prominent line of research suggested that studying deaf subjects should provide additional insights into the relationship of cognition and language because deaf subjects do not have a language. As Furth (1971) argued:

> The simple fact is that Piaget is the one great psychologist who holds a theory of thinking that makes sense of the fact that deaf children can grow up into thinking human beings even though they do not know much language. (p. 9)

Although Furth's research methods and interpretations have been questioned (Moores, 1987; Quigley & Kretschmer, 1982), there is some merit in the foregoing quotation. As discussed previously and elsewhere in this book (see Chapters 6 and 7), most severely to profoundly hearing-impaired students do not acquire a spoken language by the time they finish high school, although they may know ASL. A better understanding of the relationship between cognition and language in hearing-impaired students requires at least the identification of subgroups according to levels of development in a language, either spoken and/or signed. It is also argued that the development of *any* language in the students requires instruction in both language (e.g., vocabulary, syntax) and cognition (e.g., inferencing and reasoning skills).

PERFORMANCE ON COGNITIVE TASKS

Several sources are available that provide reviews of severely to profoundly hearing-impaired individuals' performances on various cognitive tasks (Conrad, 1979; Greenberg & Kusché, 1989; Martin, 1985; Ottem, 1980; Rodda & Grove, 1987; Quigley & Kretschmer, 1982). A common theme running through all these sources is that it is difficult to provide a clear understanding of the cognitive processes of these individuals. We stated our perspectives on this issue at the beginning of the chapter. Similar views can be found in Wolk (1985) who evaluated the research on deafness and cognition presented at an international symposium at Gallaudet University in Washington, DC. Wolk concluded that there was an:

> (a) . . . absence of a guiding and consistent theoretical or conceptual orientation underlying the research question or questions across research studies and (b) . . . inconsistent and often confusing use of divergent research methodologies and related operational definitions. (p. 202)

It is convenient to discuss hearing-impaired students' performance on some tasks that are related to two theories of cognition: the Piagetian theory and the **information processing** theory. It is not proposed that all studies can be placed in one or the other category, or that these are the only two theories for categorizing cognitive studies (Quigley & Kretschmer, 1982; Sigel & Brinker, 1985). A synthesis of the work in these areas, however, provides a representative picture of the cognitive abilities of the students.

Piagetian Tasks

Jean Piaget, the Swiss psychologist, conceived of cognitive development as a sequence of stages through which all children pass in order to reach a mature, adult level of functioning (Piaget, 1955; Piaget & Inhelder, 1969). As children proceed through each stage, they acquire more complex motor and cognitive abilities. Each stage is characterized by a different set of behaviors, and the transition between them is gradual. The four stages are labeled **sensorimotor, preoperation, concrete operation,** and **formal operation.** Much of the discussion that follows is based on the writings of Flavell (1977) and Yussen and Santrock (1978).

Sensorimotor Stage.   The sensorimotor stage covers the period from birth to about age 2. Children's understanding of the world involves only objects, events, and people that they experience. They may discover actions by accident, repeat them, and then apply them to new situations. For example, if a child wants a toy that is above the crib, the child may repeat the actions of visually searching for and grasping it until these actions are coordinated in a plan. Near the end of the sensorimotor stage, children acquire *object permanence,* or the ability to develop mental images. They come to understand that objects exist by themselves. For example, they know that their mother still exists even after she has left the room.

Preoperational Stage.   The preoperational stage extends from about age 2 through 7 years. During this period, children develop most of their language abilities. On the basis of their own perceptions and experiences (i.e., egocentricity), children use more complex mental images and symbols to represent world knowledge. Because they have limited experiences, they make up explanations for events and relations they do not understand. Children in this stage are not yet able to think in a logical manner. For example, consider the following. An examiner pours water from a tall, narrow glass into a short, wide glass. When questioned, a child may answer that the tall narrow glass contains more water because the water level is higher. During the preoperational stage, a child's thought is said to differ dramatically from that of an adult.

Concrete Operational Stage.   From ages 7 through 11, children proceed through the concrete operational stage. They are now able to perform mental operations (i.e., action performed in the mind) similar to the volume activity (water level) described earlier (i.e., the principle of conservation). In the previous stage, children can count from 1 to 10 in a rote fashion. During the concrete operational stage, they understand that *one* stands for something. Thus, they are able to add, subtract, multiply, and divide in their minds. The primary characteristic of operational thought is its *reversibility*. That is, children know that something can be added or subtracted; they can mentally reverse the direction of their thoughts. In addition, children can mentally arrange objects along some quantitative dimension such as size or weight (i.e., seriation). Operations are labeled *concrete* because they apply only to objects that are physically present.

Formal Operational Stage.   Formal operation, the last stage, begins at about age 11. During this stage, children are able to perform operations on objects or events that are not present. That is, they can think about abstract and hypothetical ideas such as the future, space, and time. Children engage in rational and systematic thought. For example, they can conceive of various ways to view and solve a problem. They can also perform metacognitive activities; that is, they can think about their own thinking processes. According to Piaget, the formal operational stage marks the end of the development of mental structures. From here on, cognitive development consists of an increase of breadth and depth of knowledge.

Research.   In general, Piagetian tasks pertain to the executive level of cognitive processing (i.e., application of knowledge) as mentioned previously. Most of the studies involving hearing-impaired individuals focused on (1) comparing their performances to those of hearing subjects and (2) examining the effects of modifying the tasks or procedures (e.g., to see if these effects explain differences between groups) (Best & Roberts, 1976; Dolman, 1983; Murphy-Berman, Witters, & Harding, 1985; Rittenhouse, 1977; Witters-Churchill, Kelly, & Witters, 1983).

When compared to hearing infants, deaf infants have been observed to demonstrate similar developmental progress through the sensorimotor stage. The only difference between the two groups was in the area of vocal imitation (Best & Roberts, 1976).

During the preoperational and concrete operational stages, similarities and differences can be observed between hearing and hearing-impaired children. For example, the performance of the hearing-impaired children was inferior to comparable hearing children on tasks involving seriation (ranking items in order), reversibility (changing directions), and classification of objects. The differences between the groups decreased when the experimenter (1) provided more information on the tasks (i.e., more than what is typically given to hearing children), and (2) demonstrated how to perform the tasks. The fact that hearing-impaired children improved their performance was interpreted as evidence of experiential deficits that resulted in a delay of their development.

In relation to conservation, a number of researchers have documented significant developmental delays (Furth, 1964, 1966, 1973; Rittenhouse, 1977; Rittenhouse, Morreau, & Iran-Nejad, 1981). Conservation involves the ability to recognize that objects may change in shape but not in weight or volume. On some conservation tasks such as liquid quantity, length, and area, severely to profoundly hearing-impaired children have been reported to be as much as 6 years behind their hearing counterparts. The delay in the understanding of conservation tasks persists despite improvements and modifications in task instructions.

Not much research has been conducted on formal operations and deafness, and the available data do not provide a clear picture because there is much variability in the performance of subjects. For example, some severely to profoundly hearing-impaired adolescents can be trained to perform some formal operational tasks. Other adolescents, however, continue to have difficulty in learning the tasks.

In working on Piagetian tasks, hearing-impaired children begin to demonstrate some developmental delays after the sensorimotor stage. No differences between groups or improvements by the hearing-impaired individuals are seen on tasks that depend primarily on visual attention and perception (e.g., seriation). When more than one attribute of a task must be considered (as in conservation tasks), a heavy reliance on only visual perception results in a lack of conceptualization. Severely to profoundly hearing-impaired individuals' problems with most concrete operational tasks and subsequently with formal operational tasks (e.g., reasoning and problem solving) have been attributed to their difficulty with simultaneous processing of data (Greenberg & Kusché, 1989; Quigley & Kretschmer, 1982).

We suggested previously, as have others (Conrad, 1979; Greenberg & Kusché, 1989) that language is important for the development of cognition. It may be that hearing-impaired students' inadequate development of language (i.e., *any* language) contributes to their poor performance in the concrete and formal operational stages. It seems that basic concept development during the sensorimotor and preoperational stages does not require a sophisticated development in language. Most of the tasks during these stages seem to depend on adequate visual perception and processing. Language may play a more important role, however, in the development of concrete and formal operational thinking skills, including higher-order cognitive skills such as inferencing. Language may also have a strong effect on memory processes, as discussed in the next section.

Information Processing

Information processing refers to the processes of the human mind—that is, the mind's ability to perform tasks such as remembering, comprehending, and inferencing. About solving problems, Carroll (1986) has said, ". . . we nearly have multiple ways of doing things, and . . . we generally choose the easiest, fastest, or most efficient strategy that will work'' (p. 45). A general model of information processing shows how information is encoded, stored, and retrieved. The model assumes that the same process is used for all information—remembering a telephone number or someone's birthday, and solving an algebraic equation. The classical model consists of three mental structures, **sensory registers,** or stores, **short-term memory,** and **long-term memory.** It is also said to consist of control processes (e.g., strategies) that facilitate the flow of information through the structures (Craik & Lockhart, 1972; Rumelhart, 1977). Examples of the control processes include rehearsing (repeating), elaborating (relating new to old information), and organizing, or chunking (grouping or classifying).

Sensory Registers.   The sensory registers, or stores, are the first of several stages in the sequence of processing information. They take in new unanalyzed information for a very short time. The amount of time, however, is sufficient for more extensive processing to be undertaken by the other mental structures if necessary. Most of the information fades away because it is not relevant to an individual's needs. It is speculated that there is a sensory register, or store, for each of our senses. Much of what is known in this area pertains to visual and auditory stores (Carroll, 1986).

Short-term Memory.   The second stage is short-term (STM), or **working, memory.** Working memory provides an important temporary storage for information that is currently occupying a person's attention. From another perspective, STM can be considered the immediate state of awareness. To solve simple and complex problems, individuals must hold a certain amount of information in their working memory. The amount of information that can be held in STM is about seven (the range is from five to nine) items (e.g., seven numbers such as 8926456). Short-term memory is important, perhaps critical, for facilitating the flow of information into permanent, or long-term memory. As is discussed later (and in Chapter 8), many reading problems of severely to profoundly hearing-impaired students, and perhaps problems with English in general, may be due to the nature and content of their STM system.

Long-term Memory.   Long-term, or permanent, memory, is the third stage in processing information. Long-term memory (LTM) contains a person's knowledge of the world—that is, linguistic and cognitive knowledge related to objects, events, people, and relationships. Long-term memory stores past or prior information that individuals are not currently using. This stored knowledge is used to interpret new experiences (such as reading a story) that are in turn added to a storehouse of experiences. New information is understood by relating, or interpreting, it in terms of what is already known.

There are two types of LTM: episodic and semantic (Rumelhart, 1977). Episodic memory holds information that is related to a specific time or event. It is a very personal kind of memory. Examples of information in episodic memory might include what individuals were doing when President Kennedy was assassinated, what they ate for breakfast yesterday, and their favorite musical group while growing up. Thus, episodic memory varies from person to person. Semantic memory contains general organized classes of knowledge such as ". . . motor skills (typing, swimming, bicycling), general knowledge (grammar, arithmetic), spatial knowledge (the spatial layout of your room or house), and social skills (how to begin and end conversations, rules for self-disclosure)'' (Carroll, 1986, p. 47). Both types of memory interact during the processing of information.

The model of information processing presented here is also called a *stage-of-processing viewpoint*. This model has been criticized and others have been proposed (Craik & Lockhart, 1972). Nearly all the research on deafness and information processing, however, has been conducted within the stage-of-processing model (Greenberg & Kusché, 1989; Martin, 1985; Quigley & Kretschmer, 1982). Much of this research attempted to answer our earlier question: What do hearing-impaired individuals think in? Or, to answer what Conrad (1979) has asked: What do deaf individuals *memorize* in? In addition, investigators compared the short-term memory abilities of hearing-impaired and hearing subjects.

Research on Short-term Memory.   Blair (1957) conducted the first major study of the visual short-term memory processes of hearing-impaired children. Blair compared the ability of hearing-impaired and hearing children to remember items presented sequentially (i.e., in a sequence or order) and simultaneously, or spatially (i.e., two or more items presented at a time). The scores on the memory tasks were also related to the reading achievement levels of the children. The results indicated that the scores of hearing-impaired children were inferior to those of hearing children on sequential memory tasks in which the subjects had to recall sequences of digits, pictures, dominoes, and reversed digits. No differences in the scores of the two groups were reported on the simultaneous memory tasks. Blair concluded that (1) the auditory memory ability of hearing-impaired children was inferior to that of hearing children, and (2) auditory memory ability was related to reading ability.

Since the seminal work of Blair, numerous studies have documented similar findings (Conrad, 1979; Greenberg & Kusché 1989; Rodda & Grove, 1987). Using a variety of stimuli, including the use of signs, severely to profoundly hearing-impaired children and adults do not perform as well as their hearing counterparts on memory tasks requiring the processing of sequentially or temporally presented stimuli. This situation persists even when meaningful information is presented. For example, hearing subjects were superior in remembering semantically, grammatically correct English phrases and additive sets of numbers. In addition, Kusché (1985) wrote that her:

> Cross-sectional pilot data . . . indicated that the short-term memory development appears to show little improvement after the age of 9½ (strikingly reminiscent of the asymptote generally reported for reading comprehension scores. (p. 115)

Several researchers, however, reported no differences in the scores of the two groups in the serial recall of nonverbal, nonmeaningful stimuli, particularly shapes (Kool, Pathak, & Singh, 1983; O'Connor, 1979). To complicate matters, some research data do not support hearing individuals' preference for temporal/sequential processing or hearing-impaired individuals' inclination toward spatial processing (Beck, Beck, & Gironella, 1977). These findings are discussed again later in the section on the relationship between short-term memory and the development of English. To better understand this relationship, it is important to discuss the results of studies that attempt to answer the question: What do deaf individuals think or memorize in?

A number of interesting research designs have been developed to determine the nature of the information held in the short-term memory of deaf individuals. Researchers have tried to describe the strategies that individuals use to recode (or rehearse, associate) verbal stimuli (letters, words) for a short period. Their descriptions are based on the kinds of errors subjects made or the manner in which the information was remembered.

The following simple example should clarify our point. Suppose that hearing-impaired students are required to read and remember two short lists of words. One list of printed words is also presented with signs; that is, the students can read the words and see the sign associated with each word:

Printed Only	Printed and Signed
Soccer	Sandwich
Computer	Popcorn
Table	Pretty
Sidewalk	Hamburger
Happy	Lawyer
Picture	Football
Shoe	Clock
Doorknob	Ice cream
Hot dog	Homework
Confused	Angry

Next, the students are requested to write all the words they remember. In our hypothetical experiment, suppose that the students remember more printed words accompanied by signs than printed words without signs. We can hypothesize that our subjects used a sign-recoding strategy to recall printed words. Thus, they remember best those items that are consistent with their **internal mediating system.** The memorized items are similar in nature to the strategies that individuals use to memorize them. The same is true for analyses of errors. The errors that subjects make on memory tasks have features that are similar in nature to their short-term recoding strategies.

On the basis of error and memory analyses, it appears that many severely impaired and most profoundly hearing-impaired students use a **nonspeech-based** recoding strategy—for example, sign, visual or graphemic (print), and finger spelling (a certain handshape corresponding to each letter of the alphabet (Greenberg & Kusché, 1989; Martin, 1985; Quigley & Kretschmer, 1982). There is much variability in the recoding strategies used by individuals. It has also been documented that severely to profoundly hearing-impaired individuals may rely on more than one recoding strategy, especially during reading (Lichtenstein, 1985). (See Chapter 7 for more details.)

Differences between the short-term memory abilities of the two groups may be related to the nature of the short-term memory recoding strategies used by most severely to profoundly hearing-impaired persons. It is hypothesized that hearing children develop an internal representation of the spoken language (i.e., auditory/articulatory experiences) to which they are typically exposed (see Chapter 2). This predominantly **speech-based code** for short-term memory is considered important for the development of spoken and written language skills. Specifically, a speech-based recoding strategy may be most efficient for (1) handling linguistic information presented in a temporal-sequential fashion such as verbal stimuli (letters, words, phrases), and (2) understanding complex sentences during reading (see Chapter 8 for more details). Thus, most profoundly hearing-impaired, or deaf, individuals may have inferior short-term memory ability because they do not use a predominantly speech-based code. There is some evidence that deaf individuals who use a predominantly speech-based code have higher achievement levels in intelligible speech, speech reading, and reading than those individuals who use a predominantly nonspeech-based code (Conrad, 1979; Hanson, 1985; Lichtenstein, 1985). The speech-based recoders are also superior in remembering sequential stimuli. Deaf speech recoders, however, still do not do as well as hearing speech recoders (see Chapter 8).

In summary, speech-recoding strategies seem to be prevalent in hearing-impaired individuals with slight to moderate hearing losses, greater intelligence, and higher educational achievement levels. Native signers with these characteristics are most likely to engage in sign-recoding strategies. These findings are similar to one of the recurring themes in this book: The cognitive, linguistic, and communicative skills of severely to profoundly hearing-impaired students are related to the nature of the language/communication systems to which they are exposed in infancy and early childhood.

From another perspective, it can be argued that there is a point on the hearing continuum (see Chapter 2) at which the short-term memory strategies of hearing-impaired students are *different* from those of hearing students. Individuals who use these different strategies depend on vision for cognitive, linguistic, and communicative purposes. This may mean that their short-term memory is better suited for encoding simultaneous-based or spatial-based information. It may also mean that the majority of these individuals find it easier to learn a sign language rather than a spoken language and its written equivalence (see discussion in Chapter 6). This is true if it is accepted that sign languages contain predominantly simultaneous- and spatial-based information whereas spoken languages are mainly temporal/sequential in nature.

Finally, as discussed previously, there is some evidence that deaf individuals have difficulty processing verbal sequential but not nonverbal sequential information (Kool et al., 1983), which seems to support the hypothesis that their short-term memory strategies are different rather than deficient. Specifically, it suggests that differences between deaf and hearing individuals in the processing of sequential tasks appear only when spoken language stimuli are used (see also the discussion in Cumming & Rodda, 1985). More research is needed in this area because of important educational implications for, among other things, the teaching of effective visual strategies that may facilitate the acquisition of reading and writing skills.

Research on Long-term Memory.   Much of the research on long-term memory has been concerned with the transfer of information from short-term memory and its retrieval in performing cognitive tasks such as making inferences and answering questions. In addition to the nature of the encoded stimuli, it is of interest to know the location in the brain where knowledge is encoded and retrieved. The end goal of research is to present a comprehensive model, or theory, of knowledge. The intention is to describe what we know, how we know what we know, and where this knowledge, or what we know, is stored in the brain.

A stage-of-processing theoretical framework suggests that information is encoded in semantic (i.e., meaning) form in long-term, or permanent, memory. One of the first major studies dealing with this issue using hearing individuals was the work of Sachs (1967). His subjects were shown a list of sentences and were required to repeat them after a delay. The hearing individuals usually forgot the surface structure (i.e., the exact words) and provided only the gist of the sentences.

The findings of Sachs have been documented in a number of subsequent investigations (Carroll, 1986; Lindsay & Norman, 1972; Rodda & Grove, 1987). Similar results have been reported for deaf individuals. For example, Hanson and Bellugi (1982) presented sentences in ASL and required their subjects to recognize the sentences under two conditions: immediately and delayed for 45 seconds. The deaf subjects had to judge whether subsequent sentences were similar to the test sentences. After 45 seconds, it was found that deaf individuals, like hearing individuals in other studies, remembered only the meaning of the sentences rather than the surface form (in this case, the exact signs that were used).

Even if the long-term memories of both hearing and hearing-impaired persons are semantically, or meaning, based, it does not follow necessarily that the encoding processes and storage of knowledge in the brain are also similar in nature. The impetus for this line of thinking is based on the assumption that deaf individuals are inclined predominantly to process and store information visually and spatially in both short-term and long-term memory, a strategy that is purported to be different from hearing individuals' processing and storing of information auditorially and temporally. For hearing individuals with spoken language skills, the left hemisphere of the brain is considered to be mainly responsible for processing and storing verbal, sequential, and temporal information. The right hemisphere is the area for nonverbal, visual-spatial, and simultaneous-based stimuli (Greenberg & Kusché, 1989; Wilbur, 1987). If hemispheric specialization is influenced by environmental factors, it is argued, differences in the language and communication environments (i.e., sign versus spoken language) of deaf and hearing individuals may result in differences in hemispheric development and processing.

As discussed later in Chapters 6 and 7, severely to profoundly hearing-impaired individuals are exposed to a variety of language and communication methods. Thus, this population is not a homogeneous group in relation to hemispheric processing and storage. This is the case even for individuals who are native ASL users. No definitive conclusions can be stated regarding the hemispheric development and processing of native ASL signers (e.g., see discussions in Wilbur, 1987, and in Chapter 6). Although understanding ASL involves temporal-sequential processing strategies, it entails the use of more visual-spatial and simultaneous processing strategies than English or the English-based signed systems (signed systems are discussed in Chapter 7).

Psychology of Deafness

At this point, we present our thinking on one of the questions posed earlier: Is there a psychology of deafness? Our remarks pertain to research based on the stage-of-processing theoretical framework. The data on long-term memory and deafness are inconclusive. More research is needed on the long-term memory strategies of native signers and bilingual individuals, both hearing and deaf, who know a sign language or system and a spoken language.

No definite conclusions can be gleaned from the results of short-term memory research and deafness. An interesting trend is developing, however. Recent research indicates that severely to profoundly hearing-impaired individuals' short-term memory capacity (i.e., for both sequential and simultaneous processing) may not be deficient but, rather, *different* from that of their hearing peers. Any differences that exist are due to the use of verbal or spoken language stimuli in the tasks. In other words, deafness may have a noticeable effect on only those cognitive tasks that are associated with audition (or articulatory/auditory experiences; see Chapter 2).

If the foregoing discussion is supported by further research, then many of these students may have considerable difficulty in acquiring competency in spoken language and its written equivalent. Most students have problems encoding verbal sequential stimuli in short-term memory. This in turn affects their ability to read and write at a literate level. As long as both educational achievement and assessment are based on literacy, the low achievement levels of students with *normal* cognitive functioning will continue to plague educators and researchers. It is critical for professionals to obtain a better understanding of the relationship between memory processes and the development of verbal (or spoken) language skills.

 PSYCHOSOCIAL ASPECTS OF DEAFNESS

The subject of this section is the impact of deafness on psychosocial variables such as familial interactions, social and personality development, and the establishment of a subculture, namely, the Deaf culture. We have discussed the influence of cognition on both language and literacy. Here, the focus is on the interactions between cognition and psychosocial development. It is well established that, in both normally hearing and hearing-impaired students, psychosocial development is related to academic achievement, one of the major themes of this book, and to other factors such as IQ and parental socioeconomic status (Hagborg, 1987). The question is: How does deafness affect psychosocial development?

From one perspective, it can be stated that hearing impairment itself alters psychosocial development. Development is affected because many individuals cannot adequately encode auditory/articulatory stimuli in short-term memory and are inclined to organize information spatially and visually. This emphasis on, in the words of Rodda and Grove (1987), the primary consequences of deafness is similar to the arguments proposed by the early investigators of intellectual development (see discussion on the three stages of cognitive development). We argue, as have others (e.g., Greenberg & Kusché, 1989), that the primary consequences of deafness may affect the ability to communicate with members of a hearing society. Thus, the cognitive functioning of most severely to profoundly hearing-impaired students may be conducive to the development of a language of signs rather than a language of sounds.

The emerging viewpoint is that psychosocial and other aspects of development are influenced by the by-products, or secondary consequences (Rodda & Grove, 1987), of the language and communication situation of deafness. The difficulties that families and significant others have in developing effective communication skills have led to an inadequate development of cognitive, linguistic, social, and personal experiences in hearing-impaired children. As with intellectual development, it is thought that deafness alone does not pervasively affect psychosocial development.

Familial Interactions

> The probability of normal affective maturation in deaf children may well be threatened by a breakdown of communication between mother and child. Parents have social and psychological needs of their own that must be met through communication. The lack of reaction or the bizarre response they receive from their child may change their behavior toward him/her, resulting in the withdrawal of verbal stimulation and affection. (Watts, 1979, p. 495)

Typically, the foregoing quotation refers to the initial stage in the family environment of severely and profoundly hearing-impaired children with hearing parents, especially those parents who place too much emphasis on their children developing oral communication skills. Although oral communication skills are important, many children are not likely to meet the expectations of parents/caregivers and professionals. It is normal for parents/caregivers to experience reactions such as anger, guilt, denial, confusion, helplessness, and grief (Mindel & Feldman, 1987). The parents'/caregivers' ability to cope with these emotional reactions, however, has a significant impact on the home environment and subsequently, on the educational achievement of their children.

Perhaps the major factor in familial interactions is the extent of parental/caregiver acceptance of deafness. A number of studies have shown that hearing mothers treat their deaf children differently from (1) their other children who are hearing, (2) deaf mothers with deaf children, and (3) other hearing mothers with hearing children. This factor is often discussed in relation to one all-encompassing factor—the type of communication (i.e., sign versus speech) between parents/caregivers and their children. Many researchers have argued, however, that fluent and intelligible communicative interaction is more important than the kind of communication (Greenberg & Kusché, 1989; Moores, 1987; Quigley & Kretschmer, 1982; Rodda & Grove, 1987). There may also be other influential factors. For example, some hearing mothers harbor unrealistic or lowered expectations for their children (Stinson, 1974, 1978).

Much of what is known about familial interactions comes from the few studies of mother-child dyads. The interactions of hearing mothers using oral communication with their children have been compared to those of hearing mothers with hearing children (Cheskin, 1982; Henggeler & Cooper, 1983; Schlesinger & Meadow, 1972, 1976; Wedell-Monnig & Lumley, 1980). In general, mothers with severely to profoundly hearing-impaired children were found to be less flexible and creative and to provide fewer instances of approval of their children's behaviors. They were also more controlling, directing, didactic, and intrusive, and less responsive to their children's needs. The children were also observed to engage in fewer spontaneous attempts at communication and independent play. In some cases, they were less compliant as compared to hearing children.

Some deviations from the foregoing profile appear when quality of communicative interactions is considered. For example, the ratings (e.g., interactions, creativity, positive effects from mothers) on children who had more advanced communication skills were similar to those of hearing children and better than other hearing-impaired children with poor communication skills. Finally, in most cases, mothers of hearing-impaired children seem to be as satisfied with their children and their marriages as mothers with hearing-impaired children. The level of satisfaction, however, is related to low parental stress and high life satisfaction.

A few researchers compared mothers using oral communication with their children to mothers using total or manual communication (Greenberg, 1980a, 1980b; Greenberg & Marvin, 1979). There were generally no differences in the communicative competency of the two kinds of dyads. Mothers who signed with their children, however, engaged in more and longer, complex, reciprocal interactions. They were also more responsive to their children's needs and seemed to be less anxious and controlling of their children's behaviors. Higher levels of maternal satisfaction, trust, and acceptance were found in mothers who signed to their deaf children. Despite differences between signing mothers and speaking mothers, deaf children and their speaking mothers did not experience profound communicative and interactional problems. In fact, the oral (i.e., speaking) deaf children were successful academically.

Neither of the foregoing groups performed as well as the deaf children of deaf mothers in a study by Meadow, Greenberg, Erting, and Carmichael (1981). The researchers compared four groups: (1) deaf children of deaf parents, (2) hearing children of hearing parents, (3) oral deaf children of hearing parents, and (4) signing deaf children of signing hearing parents. On most measures, there were no significant differences between the deaf child–deaf mother and the hearing child–hearing mother dyads. The interactions of the deaf child–deaf mother dyads, however, were more frequent, complex, and reciprocal than deaf children in both speaking and signing mother–child dyads.

We can conclude that parental acceptance and adequate communicative competence are important in familial interactions as well as for educational and vocational success (see Chapter 9 of this book and Quigley & Paul, 1986). These conditions are most likely to be found in hearing-impaired children with deaf parents; however, communication competence, not kind, is the critical factor (Brasel & Quigley, 1977; Corson, 1973). In short, the findings of Meadow et al. seem to support the notion that the primary consequences of deafness (Rodda & Grove, 1987), or deafness per se, do not lead to inferior parent-child interactions. More research is needed on mother-child dyads using severely to profoundly hearing-impaired children beyond the preschool or early elementary school years.

About 90 percent of hearing-impaired children have hearing parents. On discovering that their children are not *normal,* the initial response of the parents may be anxiety and depression. Many hearing parents may need counseling in coping with their deaf children, particularly in relation to expectations and communication. Typically, they are not experienced in rearing a deaf child, and many do not know other parents of deaf children (Luterman, 1984; Mindel & Feldman, 1987). With proper care and guidance, there is no reason why the interactions of deaf children of hearing parents cannot be as rich or rewarding as deaf children of deaf parents.

Social and Personality Development

We have argued, as have others (Greenberg & Kusché, 1989; Levine, 1981; Liben, 1978; Rodda & Grove, 1987), that the social and personal development of many severely to profoundly hearing-impaired individuals is influenced also by the quality of communication experiences during infancy and early childhood. These include, but are not limited to, parental attitudes, acceptance, child-rearing practices, and individuals' self-perceptions. The discussion in this section is divided into three parts: (1) personality, (2) social maturity, and (3) **psychological/behavioral problems.** The intent is to provide a summary of the few studies on deafness in each area. We agree, however, with other researchers, particularly Moores (1987), that:

> With only a few notable exceptions—for example, the Minnesota Multi-Phasic Inventory (MMPI)— . . . reliable and valid measures of personality do not exist. The process is much more subjective, and interpretation of results is susceptible to a greater degree to the bias of interpreters. Because most of the more commonly used measures either require a relatively high level of reading . . . or should involve substantial communication between tester and testee . . . , their applicability to deaf individuals may be limited. (p. 168)

In addition to the foregoing, much of what we claim to know about the psychosocial aspects of deafness is based on tests that have been normed on nonhearing-impaired populations, particularly normally hearing individuals.

Personality.   Personality has been defined in numerous ways by theorists. In general, one can consider personality as "an integration of traits which can be investigated and described in order to render quality of the individual" (Chaplin, 1975, p. 381). Personality traits that have been studied are self-concept (i.e., the individual's self-evaluation) and impulsivity (i.e., engaging in activities without reflection). The findings of studies presented here should be considered with the caveats expressed by Moores (1987) in mind.

A number of studies have reported lower self-concept ratings in severely to profoundly hearing-impaired individuals when they are compared to their hearing counterparts (Garrison & Tesch, 1978; Meadow, 1968). The results may have been a result of general language/communication deficits, negative environmental (e.g., familial) interactions, and the person's perception of social experiences. In addition, self-concept was found to be positively related to academic achievement.

A few studies exist on the relationship of academic placement to self-concept and sociometric (e.g., social acceptance and interactions) ratings (Gresham & Elliott, 1987). For example, Farrugia and Austin (1980) found that deaf students in residential school settings had higher self-concept ratings than those in day schools or public schools. Preliminary results of a more recent study, however, found no differences between severely to profoundly hearing-impaired students in both residential and public school settings in self-concept and social skills (Cartledge, Paul, Jackson, & Drumm, 1988). Thus, it is still not clear whether deaf students in public schools experience the degree of social isolation and rejection that has previously been assumed. In another study, sociometric ratings were reported to be related to both IQ and academic achievement but not to kind of school (Hagborg, 1987). Students with high ratings of social acceptance were also judged to be well adjusted behaviorally. A more detailed discussion of academic placement and related issues is presented in Chapter 9.

Additional studies have documented other personality characteristics presumed to be common across severely to profoundly hearing-impaired individuals: egocentricity (self-centeredness), rigidity (inflexibility), immaturity, submission, dependency, lack of empathy, passivism (characterized by submissiveness in sexual relations), and impulsivity (Altshuler, Deming, Vollenweider, Rainer, & Tendler, 1976; Bachara, Raphael, & Phelan, 1980). Several researchers have argued, however, that earlier studies underestimated the abilities of hearing-impaired students, especially in egocentricity and empathy (Greenberg & Kusché, 1989).

Quigley and Kretschmer (1982) have argued that many of the behaviors given in the foregoing paragraph are indicative of a psychological phenomenon labeled **external locus of control,** or **learned helplessness.** Individuals may react passively to the world, may not take responsibility for their actions, and in general, may feel that they have no control over their lives. Eventually, this attitude can lead to underachievement (McCrone, 1979). A lack of motivation to participate or achieve seems to be related to impulsivity, which is considered one of the most significant psychosocial problems in the deaf population.

These assertions are supported by the findings of a more recent study showing that, in general, deaf children are more impulsive than hearing children (O'Brien, 1987). In addition, the differences between the two groups did not diminish with age (from 6 to 15 years). Finally, no differences were observed between deaf students in total communication programs (i.e., speech and signing) and those in oral programs (i.e., speech only). O'Brien stated: "This appears to support the view that the type of language, manual or verbal, is not important for the regulation of impulsive behavior" (p. 216).

Social Maturity.   Social maturity has been defined as "an individual's development of the skills and customs characteristic of the group" (Chaplin, 1975, p. 499). From another perspective, social maturity refers to the degree to which individuals take care of themselves and of others. Social maturity has been typically measured by the Vineland Social Maturity Scale (Doll, 1965) and, more recently, as part of the Meadow/Kendall Social-Emotional Assessment Inventory (SEAI) (Meadow, Karchmer, Peterson, & Rudner, 1980). These tests use a structured interview (i.e., prepared questions and statements) to assess skills such as self-help, self-direction, communication, emotional maturity, social adjustment, and social relations.

On the basis of the results of the Vineland Social Maturity Scale, a number of investigations have concluded that the social maturity of severely to profoundly hearing-impaired children and adolescents is lower than that of their hearing peers (Greenberg & Kusché, 1989; Meadow, 1980). Myklebust (1964) also indicated that the discrepancy between the two groups *increased* with age. He attributed this phenomenon to individuals' lack of competency in standard English. This assertion seems valid. In fact, Greenberg (1980a) has argued that the Vineland Scale is an inappropriate instrument for some hearing-impaired persons because it requires oral English language skills to complete some of the tasks. In addition, Meadow (1980) observed that many of these studies did not use control groups and failed to provide complete descriptions of the subjects.

More recent studies indicate few or no differences between severely to profoundly hearing-impaired subjects and hearing subjects. For example, Greenberg (1980b, 1983), using the Alpern-Boll Developmental Profile (Alpern & Boll, 1972), found no difference between the social age of hearing-impaired preschoolers and that associated with hearing norms. Greenberg also reported that students in total communication programs received higher ratings than those in oral programs. This seems to support a recurring theme in all areas of psychosocial research: The quality of communication between parent/caregiver and the child is significantly related to the child's social maturity. Nearly similar findings on children and adolescents were documented by Meadow (1980, 1983) and Farrugia and Austin (1980) by using the SEAI, one of the first instruments standardized on the deaf population. Contrary to Greenberg and to Farrugia and Austin, Cartledge et al. (1988), using the SEAI, did not find any significant differences between Total Communication and oral hearing-impaired students or between residential and public school students.

In sum, we reiterate that social maturity is a very complex psychological construct that is influenced by the interaction of several factors that we have discussed previously, among them, parental/caregiver attitudes, acceptance, and communicative abilities. As in the research on cognition and deafness, there is a growing trend to relate social adjustment of the students to causes other than hearing impairment, and *not only* to communication/language competency. As a final example, consider the work of Quarrington and Solomon (1975), who studied students in a residential school setting in which students stay in dorms as is the case in boarding schools. One of their findings was that social maturity was related positively to an increased number of visits that students made to their homes.

Psychological/Behavioral Problems.   A recent study conducted a survey of counseling services in programs for the deaf in California (Briccetti, 1987). Respondents indicated that the predominant causes of student problems were the family and the home environment. In addition:

> Many respondents ranked learning problems (and consequent emotional and behavior problems) as a significant referral reason for hearing-impaired students. Other problem areas included peer relations, emotional instability and/or mental deficiency, and reactions to the hearing loss (such as denial, embarrassment and using the loss to gain sympathy). (p. 281)

In addition, it is surmised that a number of deaf children and adolescents have been sexually victimized or abused (Sullivan, Scanlan, & La Barre, 1986; Sullivan, Vernon, & Scanlan, 1987). It is feasible, therefore, to hypothesize that a higher incidence of psychological/behavioral problems may be present in hearing-impaired children and adolescents. As is discussed later, however, an unequivocal pattern does not emerge from the research literature.

The prevalence rates for behavioral problems in hearing-impaired students have been reported to be as low as 6 percent to as high as 33 percent (Jensema & Trybus, 1975; Meadow, 1980; Wolff & Harkins, 1986). The reasons for this discrepancy in incidence figures are not clear. It may be that there is lack of agreement about what constitutes a severe behavioral problem. For example, many classroom problems are thought to indicate behavioral adjustment or communication problems, not severe psychological/behavioral problems. Another possible explanation is that a number of hearing-impaired students have additional handicaps, yet those handicaps are not identified because deafness is considered the overriding factor. Some educators do believe, however, that multihandicapped students are increasing in number and that many of them are not receiving adequate services (Briccetti, 1987) (see also Chapter 10). It is thought that the major reason for the discrepancy in incidence figures is the lack of standardized tests or **diagnostic assessments,** or the use of tests that are narrow in scope (Cohen, 1980).

dents have more behavior problems than do their hearing peers. There is continuing debate, however, on how these results should be interpreted, although there is some agreement that most problems do not reflect severe psychiatric illnesses. The incidence rates for psychiatric illnesses are considered to be similar to those for the typical hearing population.

There is a need for increased counseling and mental health services for individuals and their families (Briccetti, 1987; Moores, 1987; Quigley & Kretschmer, 1982). Some exemplar, pioneer programs that offer various forms of supportive and direct mental health services include the St. Elizabeth Hospital program in Washington, DC; the Languley Porter Hospital in San Francisco; the New York State Psychiatric Institute; and the Michael Reese Medical Center Psychiatric and Psychosomatic Institute in Chicago. These programs have developed models for providing inpatient and outpatient services, parental counseling, and training professional personnel. Referring students for counseling services outside the school continues to be a difficult task, however, because of a limited number of adequate resources and qualified personnel that are available. This problem is critical in cities away from large metropolitan areas and for low-income families.

With few exceptions (e.g., residential schools), many of the problems regarding mental health and counseling services, including lack of parental involvement, also apply to most educational programs for hearing-impaired students. On the positive side, one of the most important recent developments in educational services is called *home-infant instruction* (Briccetti, 1987). This intervention program is for preschool children and their families. Briccetti said:

> This intervention, which provides early enrichment to deaf preschool children as well as some training and support for their parents, can be described as a preventive intervention. (p. 281)

Many schools, however, may lack the necessary funding to support this type of service.

We can conclude that our knowledge of the social and personality development of severely to profoundly hearing-impaired children and adolescents is less clear than that of cognitive development. Like the current views on intellectual development, there is some agreement that the secondary consequences of deafness, not deafness per se, have the most influential impact on psychosocial development. Some of the important consequences are the quality of familial and significant others' interactions. Thus, many of the behavioral problems may be the result of unhealthy parent-child relationships and inadequate opportunities for socialization and independence. Many of these conditions occur for deaf children with hearing parents/caregivers who may need counseling and mental health services. There is also growing support for the argument that many of the discrepancies in the studies may be that most researchers have viewed deafness from a pathological, or clinical, perspective, rather than from a cultural perspective. This is a complicated, controversial issue, and it is discussed in the next section on the Deaf culture.

In sum, there is no question that there is a need for more counseling and mental health services and the development of well-trained personnel for hearing-impaired individuals in the schools and in the communities. In addition, preservice and inservice teachers should be required to take courses in cognitive, social, and personality development. Finally, more effort and research should be placed on developing effective psychosocial intervention programs such as Providing Alternative Thinking Strategies (PATHS) (Greenberg, Kusché, Calderon, Gustafson, & Coady, 1983). It is important to develop programs that focus on teaching appropriate cognitive and psychosocial skills, as well as to develop more appropriate measurements for these skills.

THE DEAF CULTURE

This section provides some perspectives on the major characteristics of members of the adult deaf community, particularly those individuals who are members of the *Deaf culture*. (Hearing individuals can become members also; however, the focus is on the hearing-impaired members). After describing attempts to define community and culture, the role that the Deaf culture or the deaf community should play in the education of hearing-impaired students is discussed. A more detailed account of these complex issues may be found elsewhere (Gannon, 1981; Higgins, 1980; Hoffmeister, 1985; Padden, 1980; Stokoe, 1980).

In recent years, a conceptual framework for understanding the deaf community or Deaf culture has been proposed (Baker & Cokely, 1980; Maxwell, 1985a; Padden, 1980). There is also some discussion that *community* and *culture* are not synonymous. For example, members of the Deaf culture are members of the deaf community; however, not all members of the deaf community are members of the Deaf culture. It is argued that perspectives on deafness can be grouped into two extreme categories: pathological (i.e., clinical, medical) and cultural.

Views of Deafness

The pathological perspective focuses on preventing, curing, or overcoming deafness. It views deafness as a pathological condition that can lead to communication problems and isolation. The communication abilities, academic achievement, and psychosocial and vocational patterns of deaf persons are compared with their normally hearing counterparts, or members of the *hearing world* (i.e., the mainstream of society). The main goal of all educational and psychological efforts should be to overcome the pathological conditions of deafness so that the individual can become integrated into the mainstream. Baker and Cokely (1980) have remarked that "In a sense, this is the 'outsider's view'— a view which focuses on how deaf people are different from hearing people and which generally perceives these differences negatively" (p. 54). Moores (1987) describes this view as a "deviance model" in which "the emphasis is on identifying ways in which deaf persons are different from a norm or standard established for a hearing population" (p. 166). It is hypothesized that this viewpoint has dominated the thinking of educators and psychologists and is still widely accepted.

The cultural perspective may be more difficult to describe because opinions differ on what constitutes a culture (Demerath & Maxwell, 1976) or a community (Hillery, 1974); or, whether a culture is different from a community (Baker & Cokely, 1980; Padden, 1980; Maxwell, 1985a). We can state that the cultural perspective focuses on the "language, experience, and values of a particular group of people who happen to be deaf" (Baker & Cokely, 1980, p. 54). From this perspective, deafness is not a pathological condition. The communication and isolation problems are secondary consequences of deafness that are due, in part, to (1) the isolation of hearing persons who cannot communicate effectively with deaf persons by signing, and (2) attempts to prevent deaf persons from learning the language of signs (Lane, 1984). The major goal should not be the creation of a *normal* person integrated into the mainstream but, rather, the development of a healthy, integrated deaf person.

There is a growing trend that views deafness from a cultural perspective. Thus, the language, customs, and values of the Deaf culture should have important roles in the education of students. For example, students need to be exposed to salient aspects of the Deaf culture and to ASL. In addition, adult deaf members of the deaf community or culture should be participants in classroom activities (or should be encouraged to become certified teachers of hearing-impaired students). The extent and nature of the involvement of the Deaf culture is controversial, probably as a result of the lack of agreement and understanding about the existence of this culture. As discussed previously, one's view of deafness (i.e., whether it is pathological or cultural) may contribute to the confusion. For example, proponents of a clinical or pathological perspective seem to deny the existence or importance of the Deaf culture in the education of hearing-impaired children.

Community or Culture?

Traditionally, many educators and researchers have used the term *deaf community* in describing the communication abilities, educational achievement, psychosocial development, marriage patterns, and employment characteristics of deaf individuals, mostly those with *prelinguistic* severe to profound hearing impairments (Schein, 1978; Schein & Delk, 1974; Terzian & Saari, 1982). For example, it is argued that many deaf people are underemployed; most deaf employees are likely to be found in manufacturing industries such as automobile and steel, working as craftsmen or technicians. Very few deaf persons are employed in sales, service occupations, or management, and even fewer are in professional positions that require a four-year college degree (Vernon, 1987b; Welsh, Walter, & Riley, 1988; for an interesting contrast, see Ogden's (1979) account of members of the oral deaf community). In general, the income levels of most deaf employees and professionals are not commensurate with those of their hearing counterparts.

Members of the deaf community form a heterogeneous group. Levine (1981) says:

> For example: there are deaf persons who can speak and read the lips with exceptional proficiency; others who can speak but are only indifferent lipreaders; still others who can read the lips fairly well but whose speech is barely comprehensible; and some deaf persons can do neither. There are deaf individuals who are masters of all forms of communication and can move as easily in deaf as in hearing society; and at the other extreme, there are some who have never acquired any conventional mode of communication and must convey messages through pantomime and home-made signs and gestures. . . . Some deaf persons have no contact whatsoever with other deaf individuals because of family prohibition, lack of opportunity, or personal preference; and others live a full rich life with both deaf and hearing friends. There are deaf persons who cannot communicate freely with members of their hearing families for lack of a mutually understood method, and others who cannot communicate with certain of their own deaf peers for the same reason. (p. 155)

As mentioned previously, not all members of the deaf community are members of the Deaf culture (strictly speaking, it should be the Deaf *subculture*). Some educators and researchers have used the two terms interchangeably. With the advent of the language status of ASL, the culture of Deaf individuals may have become more closed than is the deaf community (Maxwell, 1985a; Padden, 1980; Rodda & Grove, 1987).

Basically, individuals who share and work toward common goals in a particular geographic location comprise a community (Edwards & Jones, 1976; Hillery, 1974; Poplin, 1972). A community of people also has the power to make decisions about its own functions and goals. Communities may be small and closed, or they may contain a large number of mixed groups. Depending on the size and number of groups, members may unite on some issues but disagree on others. Thus, as Padden (1980) says:

> A deaf community is a group of people who live in a particular location, share the common goals of its members, and in various ways, work toward achieving these goals. A deaf community may include persons who are not themselves Deaf *culturally* [emphasis added], but who actively support the goals of the community and work with Deaf people to achieve them. (p. 92)

In relation to a cultural perspective, the Deaf culture has its own organizations, values, customs, social structures, attitudes, and *language*. Using the convention adopted by a number of sociological researchers, the capitalized *Deaf* refers to cultural aspects whereas the lower case *deaf* refers to noncultural aspects such as degree of hearing impairment (see the definition of *deaf* in Chapter 2). The differences between the deaf community and the Deaf culture may be seen in the following discussion of cultural values such as language, attitude, social relations, and literature.

Language. Deaf members of the deaf community may exhibit a broad range of communicative abilities. The single, unique, most important value of the Deaf culture, however, is the use of American Sign Language. Some members are native signers; that is, they learned ASL from their Deaf parents. Most Deaf individuals acquired ASL from native users either during their school years or their adulthood. If severely to profoundly hearing-impaired students acquire or learn a language competently, it is most likely to be a sign language such as ASL (see discussion in Chapter 6). Thus, ASL is promoted in the Deaf culture and is used (and preferred) in a majority of communicative exchanges and functions. Although some Deaf individuals may also use oral communication in certain situations, most of them tend to consider speech and related mouth movements as inappropriate or unacceptable behaviors (Padden, 1980).

Attitude. Members of the Deaf culture have what Baker and Cokely (1980) label **"attitudinal deafness"** (p. 55). Members identify with and are involved in supporting social and political activities, events, values, and customs of the culture. They are also accepted by other long-standing members. As some researchers have discovered, "there is Deaf culture and Deaf language, and . . . that 'Deaf is beautiful' " (Maxwell, 1985a, p. 97).

Social Relations. Like other minority groups, members of the Deaf culture consider social and familial relationships to be very important. These relationships result in sharing experiences and in maintaining contact with other Deaf members. Continuous involvement in social events such as class reunions at residential schools, the special Olympics, and gatherings with **captioned films** has created a very close, trusting group. As noted by Padden (1980):

> It has frequently been observed that Deaf people often remain in groups talking late, long after the party has ended, or after the restaurant has emptied of people. One reason is certainly that Deaf people enjoy the company of other like-minded Deaf people. They

feel they gain support and trusting companionship from other Deaf people who share the same cultural beliefs and attitudes. (p. 97)

These close ties are also evident in the family and marriage patterns of the culture's members. For example, after finishing or leaving school, many Deaf individuals tend to seek employment in the limited number of places that have hired other Deaf persons. In addition, at least 90 percent of adults marry others who are members of the Deaf culture (Schein, 1978; Schein & Delk, 1974).

Literature.   From one perspective, it is possible to argue that the literature (primarily, art and poetry) of deaf individuals may reflect their desire to conform and belong to a majority, or hearing, culture. What is now considered examples of Deaf literature cannot be found in books or magazines (except for historical purposes). Much of the cultural experiences of the Deaf are expressed by ASL in art forms such as plays, poetry, mime, and storytelling (Baker & Cokely, 1980; Gannon, 1981; Klima & Bellugi, 1979; Lane, 1984; Padden, 1980; Rodda & Grove, 1987). Keep in mind that many members of the Deaf culture cannot read or write adequately. Thus, cultural aspects of their lives are often experienced in acceptable, valued, nonliterate forms such as signing and art.

Examples of Deaf literature include plays such as *Sign Me Alice* (Eastman, 1974) and poetry such as *Gestures: Poetry in Sign Language* (Miles, 1976). Perhaps the most popular art form is storytelling, particularly "success stories" such as the model provided by Padden, 1980 (remember the difference between *deaf* and *Deaf* as discussed previously).

. . . a *deaf* person grows up in an oral environment, never having met or talked with *Deaf* people. Later in life, this *deaf* person meets a *Deaf* person who brings him to parties, teaches him Sign Language and instructs him in the way of *Deaf* people's lives. This person becomes more and more involved, and leaves behind his past as he joins other *Deaf* people. (pp. 97–98)

Involvement in Education

In addition to sharing experiences, members of the deaf community and/or Deaf culture often participate in advocacy activities through organizations such as the National Association of the Deaf and the Oral Deaf Adults (of the Alexander Graham Bell Association for the Deaf; see the Appendix for some examples of regional, national, and international organizations). Moores (1987) speculated, "The establishment of the Deaf Community as a self-conscious entity may be traced to a growing awareness among deaf people of the erosion of their position within society in general and within education of the deaf in particular" (p. 192). For example, there were no deaf superintendents of residential schools from 1900 to the 1970s, and presently there are only a few superintendents who have severe to profound hearing impairments (see also the discussions in Gannon, 1981 and Lane, 1984). Gallaudet University (formerly Gallaudet College), the only liberal arts university for hearing-impaired individuals in the world, received its first deaf (postlingually deafened) president in March 1988, nearly 125 years after it was established in Washington, DC.

Whether hearing-impaired students are in total communication or oral communication classrooms, appropriate adult Deaf role models can and should be invited to participate in classroom activities. In addition, hearing-impaired individuals should be encouraged to seek careers in education. Discussion of the complexity of this issue is beyond the scope of this book. It should be emphasized, however, that if bilingual programs (i.e., those involving ASL and English) are established for hearing-impaired students, then members of the Deaf culture should be involved. They can serve as excellent role models and can establish a **bicultural** environment for the students (Paul & Quigley, 1987b). This and other aspects of a bilingual education program for severely to profoundly hearing-impaired students are discussed in depth in Chapter 6.

SUMMARY

This chapter presented an overview of the cognitive and psychosocial developments of individuals with severe to profound hearing impairments. It also discussed the interrelationships among cognition, language, and psychosocial development. Finally, characteristics of members of the deaf community and Deaf culture were described. Remember that generalizations on these issues should be accepted with caution because there is still much disagreement on the nature and interpretation of the available data.

Cognition and Deafness

Until quite recently, research on cognitive skills and research on intelligence were two separate movements. This has influenced prevailing perspectives on the cognitive functioning of severely to profoundly hearing-impaired individuals. That functioning can be categorized into three stages: inferior, concrete, and normal. There is increasing belief that current intelligence tests reflect a very narrow view of intelligence. It is argued that cognitive functioning and variability can best be understood from a cognitive processing perspective. Tests should focus on skills such as speed of processing and metacognition (e.g., problem solving), which may provide additional insights into the relationship between cognition and language. There is still debate, however, on the nature of the cognitive processing model that should be adopted, whether stage-of-processing or some other paradigm.

The current view of intelligence and deafness is that the distribution of individuals along the IQ scale is similar or nearly similar to that of normally hearing individuals. It is hypothesized that deviations can be explained by reference to test bias or experiential deficits caused by inadequate development of a language or communication system. A better understanding of the relationship between cognitive/intellectual development and language comprehension requires at least the identification of subgroups of students according to levels of development in a language, whether spoken or signed. In view of the results of traditional intelligence testing, it must be concluded that most severely to profoundly hearing-impaired students are not reaching their educational achievement potential. It remains an open question whether similar results will be found for intelligence tests based on recent models of cognitive processing.

Significant differences between hearing-impaired and hearing individuals have been reported in studies related to two theories of cognition: Piagetian and information processing. In relation to Piagetian tasks, severely to profoundly hearing-impaired students have difficulty with several activities requiring concrete and formal operational thinking skills. Language may play an important role in the development of higher-level cognitive skills in these Piagetian stages. On the basis of a cognitive processing model, there is some evidence that speed of processing is affected by exposure to language, particularly a sign language, for severely to profoundly hearing-impaired students.

Research on the stage-of-processing model reveals that language, particularly the kind of language, influences memory ability. Although no definite conclusions can be inferred, there is growing support that some hearing-impaired individuals' short-term memory capacity may be different—not deficient—from that of their normally hearing counterparts. Deviations from this pattern are thought to result from the artifacts of the tasks. In short, some researchers interpret the results of the stage-of-processing research model to reflect a psychology of deafness—that is, that certain *cognitive* behavioral traits uniquely attributed to deafness are different from those of the typical, nondisabled population. As discussed in this chapter and in Chapter 8, these results have pervasive implications for teaching literacy skills. It may be that different strategies and methods for teaching reading and writing need to be developed, or that teaching these skills is impractical for use with the majority of students with severe to profound hearing losses.

Psychosocial Development

The psychosocial development of severely to profoundly hearing-impaired individuals was discussed in relation to familial relationships, personality, social maturity, and the prevalence of psychological/behavioral problems. It was concluded that we know less about psychosocial development than we do about cognitive functioning. Many researchers agree that the secondary consequences of deafness, rather than deafness per se, affect psychosocial development. For example, hearing mothers have been observed to be more directive and controlling of their deaf children's behaviors than deaf mothers are with their deaf children. The behaviors of hearing mothers may be caused in part by factors such as poor communication interactions and parental acceptance of deafness.

Differences between hearing-impaired individuals and hearing counterparts may also reflect test biases or artifacts (such as lack of standardization) or the interpretations of professionals who view deafness as pathological. Some behaviors such as impulsivity do seem to persist and may have a negative effect on academic achievement. There is some consensus, however, that many psychosocial problems would be resolved with increased counseling and mental health services for hearing-impaired individuals and their families, and with improvement in the training of professionals who work with them.

Deaf Culture

This section stated that most philosophical perspectives on deafness can be grouped into two categories: pathological and cultural. These views have influenced theories, research, and practices in disciplines such as education, psychology, and linguistics. They also have some effect on debate about the existence of a Deaf culture (or subculture).

Many educators and researchers have used the terms *deaf* (or *Deaf*) *community* and *Deaf culture* interchangeably, but a few have suggested that the terms may not be synonymous. The culture of Deaf individuals may be more closed than that of the deaf community because the former group places more value and emphasis on the use of ASL. ASL is considered the language of *Deaf* individuals and is the primary form of communication for familial, social, and political interactions. It also plays an important role in expressing cultural values and customs through theater, poetry, and storytelling activities.

There is no question that members of the deaf community and/or Deaf culture should be involved in education. They would be excellent role models for appropriate groups of hearing-impaired children. If bilingual education programs involving ASL and English are being established, then it is necessary to involve members of the Deaf culture. Creative models for including Deaf adults in mainstreamed programs also need to be explored.

Finally, it is important for preservice and inservice teachers to receive additional training in the psychology of deafness. For example, several intervention programs focus on the development of adequate thinking skills and behaviors in severely to profoundly hearing-impaired children. Within the conceptual framework of recent cognitive processing models, it is argued that critical higher-level cognitive skills such as problem solving, decision making, and other metacognitive strategies can be learned. If so, the learning could have an impact on cognitive and psychosocial developments, and, as discussed in Chapter 8, the development of literacy skills.

COMPREHENSION

1. Define the following terms:
   a. Cognition
   b. Cognitive structure
   c. Cognitive process
   d. Metacognition
2. TRUE or FALSE? Most current intelligence tests are based on theoretical models of cognitive processing.
3. Select a stage of thought, that is, *inferior, concrete,* or *normal,* that corresponds with the following statements concerning hearing-impaired individuals:
   a. Cognitive functioning is quantitatively reduced. Qualitativeness of intellectual functioning is not explicitly stated.
   b. Intellectual development is similar to that of the general population.
   c. Cognitive differences between deaf and hearing individuals can be explained in part by language and cultural bias associated with the assessments.
   d. Cognitive functioning is quantitatively equal but qualitatively inferior to that of their hearing counterparts.
   e. There is definitely a psychology of deafness.
4. The following statements pertain to the relationship between cognition and language: TRUE or FALSE?
   a. The nativist hypothesis and its variations reflect a cognitive-dominant position.
   b. The constructivist hypothesis reflects a cognitive-dominant position.
   c. The strongest version of the language-dominant position is linguistic determinism.

    d. The available data suggest that both cognition and language play a role in language development.

    e. Until the 1970s, many educators and researchers in deafness subscribed to a cognitive-dominant hypothesis.

5. The four Piagetian stages are *sensorimotor, preoperation, concrete operation,* and *formal operation.* Select a stage that corresponds with the following statements:

    a. Children can think about abstract and hypothetical ideas such as the future, space, and time.

    b. During this stage, children develop *most* of their language abilities.

    c. During this stage, children are able to perform mental operations that apply only to objects that are physically present.

    d. Near the end of this stage, children acquire the concept of *object permanence* (i.e., that objects exist by themselves).

    e. Children can perform metacognitive activities (i.e., they can think about their own thinking processes).

6. TRUE or FALSE?

    a. In general, there are no significant differences between deaf and hearing individuals on preoperational and concrete operational tasks.

    b. Not much research has been conducted on formal operations and deafness.

    c. Deaf children begin to demonstrate some developmental delays after the sensorimotor stage.

    d. Deaf individuals' problems with some formal operations have been attributed to their difficulty with visual attention and perception.

7. List and briefly describe the three major stages of information processing.

8. The research on short-term memory indicates that (select all that apply)

    a. The scores of severely to profoundly hearing-impaired students are inferior to those of their hearing peers on simultaneous memory tasks.

    b. Little improvement in short-term memory processes of deaf individuals occurs after the age of $9\frac{1}{2}$ years.

    c. Some data do not support hearing-impaired individuals' inclination toward spatial processing.

    d. Many deaf individuals use a speech-based recoding strategy.

    e. A speech-based recoding strategy is most efficient for understanding complex sentences during reading.

9. TRUE or FALSE? Much of the research on long-term memory has been concerned with organization of information.

10. Discuss the two perspectives on the manner in which deafness affects psychosocial development.

11. In the few studies on mother-child dyads (select all that apply)

    a. Mothers who used oral communication were found to be more flexible, creative, and more responsive to their deaf children's needs than were mothers of hearing children.

    b. Mothers of hearing-impaired children seem to be satisfied with their children and their own marriages.

    c. No differences in communicative competence were observed between mothers who used oral communication and mothers who used total or manual communication.

    d. Mothers who used oral communication were less anxious about and controlling of their children's behaviors than were mothers who used total or manual communication.

    e. Neither the speaking-hearing mothers nor the signing-hearing mothers performed as well as deaf mothers.

12. TRUE or FALSE? Parental acceptance and adequate communicative competence are most likely to be found in hearing parents who use total or manual communication with their hearing-impaired children.

13. Research on psychosocial aspects showed that (select all that apply)
    a. Less is known about social and personal development than about cognitive development of severely to profoundly hearing-impaired children.
    b. Hearing-impaired students in residential schools clearly have higher self-concept ratings than do their counterparts in special day schools or public school classes.
    c. Much of what is known is based on tests that have been normed on hearing-impaired populations.
    d. More recent studies indicate little or no difference between severely to profoundly hearing-impaired children and hearing children in social maturity.
    e. There is little need for counseling and mental health services for deaf individuals and their families.

14. Discuss the similarities and differences between the deaf community and Deaf culture.

SUGGESTED ACTIVITIES

1. Visit a local Deaf club. Find out the following:
   a. The purpose of the club
   b. How the club was established
   c. Activities in which members become involved
   d. The method of communication among the members
   e. Who can become members

2. Visit a community center for the deaf (i.e., a center that provides specialized services such as interpreting, counseling, etc.). Find out the following:
   a. How and why the center was established
   b. If the director is hearing-impaired
   c. The range of services provided by the center
   d. If and how the center maintains contact with members of the Deaf culture

3. Write your own definition of deafness (you may wish to reread Chapters 2 and 4). What are the educational implications of your definition? Does your definition have clinical or cultural aspects, or both?

FURTHER READINGS

Baker, C., & Battison, R. (1980). *Sign Language and the Deaf community: Essays in honor of William C. Stokoe*. Silver Spring, MD: National Association of the Deaf.

Benderly, B. (1980). *Dancing without music*. Garden City, NY: Doubleday.

Clark, H., & Clark, E. (1977). *Psychology and language: An introduction to psycholinguistics*. New York: Harcourt Brace Jovanovich.

Garnett, C. (1967). *The world of silence: A new venture in philosophy*. New York: Greenwich Book Publishers.

Greenberg, J. (1970). *In this sign*. New York: Holt, Rinehart and Winston.

Jacobs, L. (1980). *A deaf adult speaks out* (rev. ed.). Washington, DC: Gallaudet University Press.

Lane, H. (1976). *The wild boy of Aveyron*. Cambridge, MA: Harvard University Press.

Ogden, P., & Lipsett, S. (1982). *The silent garden: Understanding the hearing-impaired child*. New York: St. Martin's Press.

Padden, C., & Humphries, T. (1988). *Deaf in America: Voices from a culture*. Cambridge, MA: Harvard University Press.

CHAPTER 5

Oral English Development

MAJOR POINTS TO CONSIDER

Anatomy and physiology of the speech mechanisms

Classification of speech sounds

Speech production errors of hearing-impaired students

Oral education approaches

Components of aural rehabilitation

In many education programs for hearing-impaired students, the development of speech, or spoken language, is an important component. The emphasis placed on and the instruction used in teaching speech may vary from program to program. Programs that place a great deal of value on the acquisition of speech support the concept that good oral communication skills increase educational and vocational opportunities and, subsequently, the socioeconomic status of hearing-impaired individuals in society (Quigley & Kretschmer, 1982; Ross, Brackett, & Maxon, 1982).

Oral English development and communication skills are the major goals of oral education programs (Ling, 1984a; Mulholland, 1981) using speech, speech reading, and residual hearing. Adequate oral skills are considered necessary for the later development of reading and writing. According to Ling (1984a):

> The philosophy of oral education is that hearing-impaired children should be given the opportunity to learn to speak and to understand speech, learn through spoken language in school, and later function as independent adults in a world in which people's primary mode of communication is speech. (p. 9)

101

It is argued that *only* through oral education methods can hearing-impaired students gain access to the auditory/articulatory code on which spoken and written language is based.

There is a variety of oral methods and approaches for helping hearing-impaired students develop receptive and expressive spoken-language communication skills. The approaches vary according to the emphasis placed on the kind of sensory input. Oral education procedures include speech training, auditory training/learning (i.e., the use of residual hearing), speech reading, and the use of assistive devices such as hearing aids, auditory trainers, tactile aids, and visual aids. Some oral training procedures such as the use of speech reading and auditory training/learning, may supplement or be supplemented by others (Ling, 1986; Ross, 1986a).

This chapter focuses on the oral English development of prelinguistically, severely to profoundly hearing-impaired students in oral programs. First, basic information is provided on the philosophy and the major components of oral education, namely, **speech perception** and production, speech reading, and auditory training/learning. Next, some research data are presented on the effects of several common oral communication systems on the development of spoken and written English. The best overall results are associated with those hearing-impaired students who are educated in indisputably **comprehensive oral programs** or who are integrated most of the school day into regular education programs. Many of these students constitute a select group; they have above-average IQs and highly involved parents of above-average socioeconomic status (see Geers & Moog, 1989).

SPEECH SCIENCE

In the evolution of humans, the emergence of speech as the basic, most efficient primary communication mode is probably a result of the physiological properties of the central nervous system (Boothroyd, 1986; Ling, 1976, 1984a). Speech is not language but, rather, a representation of language by sound patterns and movements. As discussed in Chapter 6, language can also be represented by **visual-gestural-spatial** movements as in a sign language. Language is seated in the brain, primarily in the left hemisphere. What is produced on the hands or by the lips are manifestations of the activity that occurs in that part of the brain that controls language.

In normally hearing individuals, analyses of speech production may provide reasonably good estimates of their competence in a particular language. This relationship between speech production and **language competence** is far from perfect. In fact, it has been argued that such analyses cannot yield a complete description of an individual's language competence (Chomsky, 1968; Slobin, 1979). It is also difficult to analyze the spoken utterances of children, especially in the early stages of development. There is continuing debate on when children produce their first words (Pettito, 1986). To resolve these and other problems, researchers should continue to define and construct adequate measures of speech intelligibility. Before discussing hearing-impaired students' perception and production of spoken language, some basic information on the process and production of speech is presented.

Speech Mechanisms and Production

Speech communication can be viewed as a series of stages (Boothroyd, 1986; Levitt, 1989; Ling, 1976). First, speakers construct their ideas and thoughts in their heads. Then, the ideas and thoughts are coded in language patterns, that is, words and sentences. Next, speech patterns are generated by neural signals in the brain that control the movements of the **speech mechanisms** (e.g., lungs, **larynx,** tongue). These movements produce speech sounds that travel through a medium such as air. Listeners perceive the speech sounds through their auditory systems. Finally, the message or thought of the speaker is interpreted in the brain of the listener.

The speech mechanisms include body structures that also participate in breathing and eating activities—the lungs, larynx, tongue, and lips (Boothroyd, 1986; Ling, 1976; Zemlin, 1968). The **oral** (mouth), **pharyngeal** (throat), and **nasal** (nose) cavities (i.e., chambers) are important, especially for **resonance** (i.e., the quality imparted to **voiced** sounds). Some important speech structures are illustrated schematically in Figure 5.1.

In the production of speech, the lungs exhale a flow of air that passes through the **vocal tract.** The air flow produces sound when it is obstructed or constricted by the speech mechanisms. For example, the larynx contains the **vocal folds,** or vocal cords (two muscular flaps), which interrupt the flow of air by coming together and separating. Before sound proceeds through the lips, it is modified by the resonant qualities of the oral and nasal cavities.

There are three categories of sound source in the production of speech: voicing, frication, and stop-plosion (Boothroyd, 1986; Levitt, 1989; Zemlin, 1968). The sound sources are responsible for the production of two groups of sounds: vowels and consonants.

Voicing.   The most important source of speech sounds is voicing, which occurs in the larynx, especially in the vibrations of the vocal folds. The space between the vocal folds is called the *glottis.* When the folds are pulled together, the glottis closes and thus obstructs the flow of air from the lungs. Pressure builds up on the bottom of the glottis and eventually forces it to open and the vocal folds to come apart. This permits a pulse of air to escape into the vocal tract. The opening and closing of the glottis and, in particular, the escaping air pulses cause the vocal folds to vibrate, generating voiced sounds. "The air is thus released in brief, repetitive bursts, generating a complex tone, called voicing" (Boothroyd, 1986, p. 18).

The frequency of vibration of the vocal folds is called the *fundamental frequency* of voicing and is perceived as pitch. The average frequency values vary across the speech of men, women, and children because of differences in the size and weight of the vocal folds. Thus, the voices of men are at a lower frequency range than those of women, and women's voices are lower than children's. The variations of frequency during speech production are perceived as the **intonation** of speech.

Frication.   Frication refers to the random turbulence produced when air is forced through a narrow opening. This constriction of air can be caused by any of the speech mechanisms at various places along the vocal tract. The place where the narrow opening occurs is called the *place of articulation.* Some places of articulation are between the

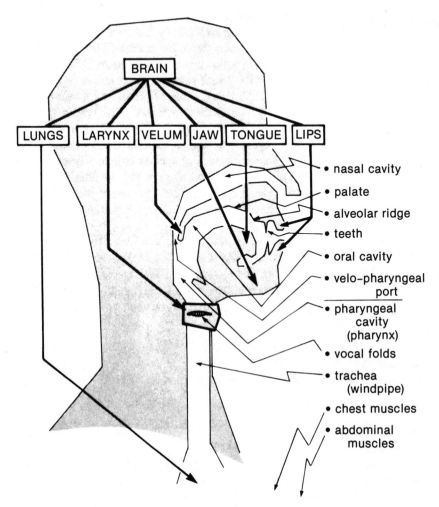

Figure 5.1. A schematic view of some important speech structures.
A. Boothroyd, *Speech Acoustics and Perception.* Austin, TX: PRO–ED, 1986. Reprinted by permission.

lips (bilabial), between the lower lip and upper teeth (labiodental), and between the partially closed vocal folds (glottal). An example of a labiodental placement is the /f/ sound (as in *f*oot).

Sounds such as /f/ and /s/ (as in *s*ound) that are generated by the random turbulence of air alone are called **voiceless** sounds. If the random turbulence is combined with the source of voicing, the result is voiced sounds. For example, the voiced counterpart of /f/ is /v/ (as in *v*oice), and that of /s/ is /z/ (as in *z*ebra).

Stop-plosive.   A third sound source results when the air flow is stopped completely and then released quickly by the build-up of air pressure. This source is the plosive, stop-plosive, or stop-consonant. It is referred to here as stop-plosive (Boothroyd, 1986).

TABLE 5.1. Consonants

		Position of Articulation					
Manner	**Bilabial**	**Labio-dental**	**Inter-dental**	**Apico-alveolar**	**Fronto-palatal**	**Dorso-velar**	**Glottal**
Stop	p (pin)			t (tin)		k (kit)	
	b (bid)			d (dog)		g (get)	
Affricate				t ʃ (chop)			
				dʒ (jet)			
Fricative	wh (why)	f (fin)	θ (thin)	s (sit)	ʃ (ship)		
	v (vie)		∂ (that)	z (zip)	ʒ (azure)		h (hit)
Nasal	m (me)			n (noon)		ŋ (sing)	
Lateral				l (loom)			
Semivowel	w (wad)			r (bar)	j (yet)		

NOTES: Stop = plosive; voiceless = p, t, k; voice = b, d, g.
  Affricate = voiceless = t; voice = d.
  Fricative = voiceless = wh, f, θ, s, ʃ; voice = v, ∂, z, ʒ, h.
  Lateral = glide.
  Semivowel = glide.
  Nasal, lateral, and semivowel are voiced.
SOURCE: Based on Creaghead & Newman (1985) and Shelton & Wood (1978).

Stop-plosive sounds are produced at various places along the vocal tract in which air can be completely stopped. Examples of stop-plosive sounds are /p/ (put), /b/ (but), /t/ (tall), and /g/ (got). Notice that one cannot produce these sounds in isolation; they can be produced only in conjunction with another sound, typically a vowel. For example, the production of /t/ or /p/ sounds like *ta* or *pa* respectively (short *a* sound).

As mentioned previously, the oral and nasal cavities modify speech sounds primarily by changing the dimensions (shape and size) of the vocal tract. These resonant cavities emphasize or de-emphasize certain frequencies of sound. Three configurations of the cavities are possible. One, the **velum** can be raised, resulting in the use of an oral cavity alone. Most speech sounds are produced in this manner. Two, the velum can be lowered, resulting in a blocked oral cavity. In this case, the air flows through the nasal cavity for sounds such as /m/ and /n/. Finally, in the use of both oral and nasal cavities, the velum is lowered, but the oral cavity is still open. Further discussion on the functions of the oral and nasal cavities can be found in Boothroyd (1986) and Zemlin (1968).

Classification of Speech Sounds

It is convenient to discuss speech sounds in relation to two groups: consonants and vowels. Because of differences among speakers of the same language, it is difficult to provide the exact number of consonants and vowels in a particular language (Creaghead & Newman, 1985; Shelton & Wood, 1978). A chart of the most commonly observed consonants and vowels in English is shown in Table 5.1 and Table 5.2, respectively.

TABLE 5.2. Vowels

	Front	Center	Back
		Tongue Positions	
High	i (*eat*)		u (*food*)
	I (*it*)		U (*cook*)
Mid	e (*hate*)	ɝ (*bird*)	o (*boat*)
	ɛ (*ever*)	ʌ (*cup*)	ɔ (*paw*)
		ɚ (*butter*)	
		ə (*about*)	
Low	æ (*at*)		ɒ (*pot*)
	a (*lass*)		ɑ (*father*)

SOURCE: Based on Creaghead & Newman (1985) and Shelton & Wood (1978).

Consonants.   Consonants involve the use of air turbulence produced by the constriction or obstruction of speech mechanisms along the vocal tract. Consonants can be classified according to three features of articulation: place, manner, and position. Another feature is the absence or presence of voicing (i.e., whether or not the vocal folds vibrate).

The places of articulation are similar to those discussed previously in frication, which is one of the sound sources for consonants. The articulation places correspond to the speech mechanisms that are involved in producing the sound. The various places with their descriptions and consonants associated with them are shown in Table 5.1.

Typically, consonants are categorized according to the manner of their articulation: stop-plosive, affricate, fricative, nasal, and vowel-like consonants (also called *glides*). These groups and the consonants associated with them are also shown in Table 5.1.

In producing stop-plosive consonants, the articulators (i.e., speech mechanisms) stop the air flow, and air pressure is built up behind the occlusion. Then, the articulators release the air. This results in a burst of air that escapes and produces a stop or plosive sound as in /p/ or /b/. English has six common stop-plosive sounds. Half of the sounds involve the use of voice, and half are voiceless. Voiced sounds have two sound sources: voicing and stop-plosion. The source for voiceless sounds is voicing only. The oral cavity only is responsible for resonance.

There are only two **affricates** in English, one voiced and one voiceless (Boothroyd, 1986; Creaghead & Newman, 1985; Shelton & Wood, 1978). These sounds are similar to the stop-plosives except that the air pulses are sustained for a slightly longer time. Two sound sources are needed to produce the voiceless affricate whereas all three sound sources are necessary for the voiced affricate. The voiced affricate is the only sound in English that requires the use of all three types of sound sources. Resonance is provided by the oral cavity only.

In English, there are six voiceless and four voiced **fricatives** (Boothroyd, 1986; Shelton & Wood, 1978). In the production of fricatives, the air flow is channeled through a narrow opening (i.e., place of articulation), resulting in a turbulent stream of noise. Voicing and frication are the sound sources for voiced fricatives, and frication only is the source for voiceless fricatives. For both types of consonants, the oral cavity is the only resonator.

In the production of nasal sounds, the velum is lowered and the vibrated air flows through the nose rather than the mouth. Thus, the nasal cavity is the sole resonator for the three nasals in English. The only sound source for nasals is voicing.

The last group of consonants are the vowel-like consonants (Boothroyd, 1986; Creaghead & Newman, 1985; Shelton & Wood, 1978). As their name implies, these consonants are similar to vowels. Specifically, the oral cavity provides resonance, and voicing is the sole sound source. Vowel-like consonants are also referred to as glides, either lateral glides or semivowel glides. There is considerable disagreement on the manner in which vowel-like consonants should be classified. It is usually agreed, though, that there are four common vowel-like consonants in English.

Vowels.   All vowels are voiced with voicing as the typical sound source and the oral cavity as the sole resonator. Differences among vowels are determined primarily by the placement of the tongue. The configurations of the lips and the pharyngeal cavity also play important roles in the production of the vowels.

In relation to tongue positions, vowels can be classified as front, center, and back, or high, middle, and low. For example, the /i/ vowel, as in the word m*ea*t, is produced by placing the arch of the tongue high up and forward in the oral cavity. Thus, the /i/ vowel is classified as a high, front vowel. As shown in Table 5.2, other possible combinations are midfront, low front, high back, midback, low back, and midcentral vowels. The vowel chart in Table 5.2 illustrates "ideal positions, reflecting isolated sound production, and these ideal positions are rarely reached during running speech" (Shelton & Wood, 1978, p. 68). This table and its accompanying descriptions of vowels are important, however, for teaching vowel production.

Vowels can also be classified according to whether they are *tense* or *lax*. Tense vowels require more muscular tension and adjustments of the tongue than do lax vowels. Tense vowels also are longer in duration than their lax counterparts. As for the duration, it is useful to consider tense vowels as having long vowel sounds and lax vowels as having short sounds. Examples of words with long vowels are *sew, see, meat,* and *cope.* Some words with short vowel sounds are *sit, hit, set,* and *book.*

The last group of vowels to be discussed are diphthongs. In one view, these vowels are considered to be "double vowels" (Boothroyd, 1986, p. 41). The dimensions of the vocal tract and the positions of the tongue change during the production of diphthongs. For example, the tongue may start to produce a low or midlong vowel and end with a high short one. The vocal tract configurations and the tongue positions modify the resonance and quality of the vowel. "Two resonances may occur, one blending into another, creating a diphthong" (Creaghead & Newman, 1985, p. 18). Some common diphthongs are /eI/ as in vac*a*tion, /aI/ as in h*i*de, /aU/ as in h*ow*, and /oU/ as in bl*ow*.

Running Speech Production

Thus far, this chapter has discussed isolated speech sounds that are rarely produced in isolation except for specific training purposes. To understand what happens when an individual speaks, it is necessary to focus on the interactions and modifications of speech sounds. Some important common aspects of running speech are intonation, **rhythm,** and coarticulation (Boothroyd, 1986; Levitt, 1989).

Intonation represents the various patterns of fundamental frequency produced over a period. Intonation is the rise and fall of pitch during speech production. Typically, this speech quality is the result of voiced speech sounds such as vowels and vowel-like consonants.

The timing patterns of speech are called *rhythm,* which refers to the duration of specific sounds and **syllables** as well as the periods of time between stressed sounds and syllables. The position and duration of pauses also contribute to speech rhythm.

In coarticulation, the production of a sound is influenced by the characteristics of the speech mechanisms used to produce the preceding or following sound. Consider the example discussed by Boothroyd (1986). In the word *team,* the velum is raised so that the /t/ sound and the /i/ (for *ea*) sound are produced through the oral cavity. In the production of the /i/ sound, however, the velum may be lowered (oral cavity still open) in anticipation of the last sound, /m/, which is nasal. In this sense, we coarticulate, or combine, the sounds of the /i/ and the /m/. Some coarticulatory effects may involve the combinations of three or four sounds as in the production of diphthongs, stop-plosives, and vowel-like consonants such as glides. At present, a widely accepted theory of coarticulation does not exist (Fowler, 1985; Levitt, 1989).

SPEECH PERCEPTION AND DEVELOPMENT

To comprehend speech, individuals must receive and interpret (or process) incoming, reasonably unambiguous speech stimuli. Speech comprehension, however, involves more than just the discrimination and interpretation of isolated sounds. Individuals are concerned with the underlying meaning of the speaker's message. As stated by Ross et al. (1982):

> Normally hearing persons . . . can often grasp the meaning of an utterance using only a fraction of all the potentially available information. They can bypass much of the acoustic, phonetic, lexical, and grammatical information contained in a speech signal because they share with the speaker much of the same intuitive grasp of the language. (p. 19)

Theories regarding phonological development can be grouped according to the prevailing linguistic thinking of a particular era—for example, **behaviorism, structural linguistics, psycholinguistics** (i.e., transformational generative grammar), and **socioculture** (particularly pragmatics). A good treatment of this issue, as well as theories of speech perception, can be found elsewhere (Boothroyd, 1986; Creaghead, 1985).

Most normally hearing children acquire speech and other important aspects of the phonological system of their language with little or no difficulty. During the prelinguistic stage, certain aspects of **phonation,** such as duration, stress, and intonation, develop initially, followed by the production of vowels and consonants. The first words emerge by the time children are about a year old, marking the beginning of linguistic development. The beginning of grammar, particularly syntax, occurs when children reach the two-word stage, typically by the end of their second year. Some children can produce most of the **phonemes** (i.e., speech sounds) by age 3, and most children can be understood by strangers by age 4. Phonological development is essentially complete by age 7 or 8 (Creaghead, 1985).

From the three-word stage and beyond, much of the linguistic development focuses on complex word forms (i.e., **morphology** and vocabulary) and **metalinguistic** knowledge (i.e., thinking with and about language). Most children reach linguistic maturity by 12 years of age. That is, they have mastered nearly all the rules concerning the form (phonology, syntax), content (semantics), and function (pragmatics) of language.

SPEECH AND DEAFNESS

Most students with hearing impairments no worse than severe can develop spoken communication by audition with or without assistive hearing devices such as hearing aids and group amplification systems. The same is true for some profoundly hearing-impaired students. In general, most prelinguistically, severely to profoundly hearing-impaired students require alternative methods for speech perception and production—for example, the use of vision and taction (touch). To comprehend and produce intelligible speech, it is not essential to hear all speech sounds; however, it is important to receive a substantial portion of them (Bess, Freeman, & Sinclair, 1981; Ling, 1984a; Ross, 1986a).

As discussed in Chapter 2, several factors are related to the speech perception and production abilities of hearing-impaired students. The speech errors of many students seem to be linked to the nature of their impaired perception (Gold, 1980; Smith, 1975). That is, the errors reflect aspects of ambiguous speech signals that students receive through audition and/or speech reading. A more detailed discussion of these and other factors, and their interactions, can be found elsewhere (Ling, 1976; Ross et al., 1982; Wolk & Schildroth, 1986).

Perception, Production, and Hearing Level

It has been documented that speech perception and production are affected pervasively by degree of impairment (Boothroyd, 1984; Levitt, 1989; Ling, 1976; Wolk & Schildroth, 1986). The greater the hearing impairment, the less intelligible the speech, and the more difficult it is for speech to be developed. In speech perception, students with mild hearing impairments may have difficulty hearing **sibilants** such as /f/, and /s/, and stop-plosives such as /p/ without amplification. Students with severe hearing impairments may not perceive voiceless consonants and most of the voiced consonants. They may also have difficulty with some vowels. Profoundly hearing impaired, or deaf, students may perceive only some low-frequency vowels and nasals, even with the use of adequate amplification systems.

Despite individual differences, the speech production errors of severely to profoundly hearing-impaired students can be described (Calvert & Silverman, 1983; Erber, 1982; Levitt, 1989; Ling, 1976). In many cases, patterns can be observed within **segmental** and **suprasegmental** categories. Thus, these patterns can be viewed as part of a phonological system rather than as unrelated errors (Dodd, 1976). There are exceptions; however, as noted by Levitt (1989):

Exceptions occur at either end of the intelligibility scale; that is, children with very good speech intelligibility (close to 100%) make insufficient errors for a pattern to be discernible and children with very poor speech (intelligibility close to zero) often have gross idiosyncratic errors, many of which are not easily defined in conventional phonetic terms. (p. 30)

Suprasegmental Errors.   A number of studies have reported errors in respiration, rate, rhythm, stress pattern, and duration (Erber, 1982; Levitt, 1989; and Ling, 1976). Typical problems include excessive prolongation of vowels and other continuant sounds, and prolonged and improperly inserted pauses in running speech. Difficulties with the production of syllables have been attributed to the use of inappropriate utterance rates, inadequate differentiation of stressed and unstressed syllables, and improper grouping of syllables.

Other suprasegmental problems that affect voice pitch and quality are **breathiness,** too much or too little **nasality,** and inappropriate variations and pauses in pitch. The voice quality of many severely to profoundly hearing-impaired students has been labeled as *breathy* or *tense*. This quality may be caused by the students' inability to position their vocal cords properly during speech production (Calvert & Silverman, 1983; Erber, 1982; Ling, 1976).

Many of these problems have an adverse effect on the speech intelligibility of hearing-impaired students. Intonation is negatively affected by excessive prolongation of speech sounds and improper control of voice pitch. It has been argued that some of these errors are caused by inadequate control of breath and the speech mechanisms (Levitt, 1989; Ling, 1976; Nickerson, 1975). Specifically, there appears to be little coordination between the articulators (tongue, lips, velum, and jaw) and the breath-voice system. It may also be that students have not been taught to breathe and articulate at proper rates during speech production. Whatever the cause, problems with certain aspects of breath and voice have persisted in many students despite the use of systematic instructional procedures. These procedures have been successful only for those students who can take advantage of their residual hearing, especially with assistive hearing devices.

Segmental Errors.   Many hearing-impaired students experience much difficulty in producing appropriate vowel quality. Their vowel productions show insufficient intensity (i.e., amplitude) and are often accompanied by excessive aspiration and nasality. The common vowel errors have been classified as substitutions, neutralization, dipthongization, and nasalization (Calvert & Silverman, 1983; Erber, 1982; Levitt, 1989; Ling, 1976). Common errors include the substitution of lax vowels for tense vowels such as /I/ for /i/ (e.g., h*i*t for h*ea*t). The substitution of tense vowels for lax ones also occurs frequently. Substitutions by central vowels (e.g., b*e*t to b*u*t) are common. Dipthongization of vowels occurs less frequently; the student may produce a sound that is heard as a neighboring vowel or as a diphthong.

The difficulties that many hearing-impaired students have in clearly differentiating vowels may be a result of their inadequate range of tongue movement. This limited range of articulation may also affect the intelligibility of adjacent consonants. There seems to be a relationship between the total number of vowel errors and the total number of consonant errors. Thus, it is important for teachers to recognize that adequate vowel production is necessary for improving the intelligibility of students' speech.

Unlike errors in vowel production, the most common consonantal errors are omissions (Erber, 1982; Levitt, 1989; Ling, 1976). Hearing-impaired students are likely to omit consonants produced near the center or back of the mouth (/t/, /l/, /k/, /g/) rather than those made near the front of the mouth (/p/, /b/, /f/, /v/, /m/). Similarly, consonants occurring in the middle or final position of a word are more likely to be omitted than are those in the beginning position. Omission errors involving unstressed syllables or verb endings (e.g., -s, -ing) also appear in the spoken and written language of students. Although some of these errors may result from an inadequate command of language principles (Quigley & Paul, 1989), others might be caused by "perceptual deficiencies" (Erber, 1982, p. 161). That is, some hearing-impaired students produce errors involving unstressed **affixes, plurals,** and **prepositions** because these sounds are difficult to see (speech read) or hear.

Another common set of errors is that of substitution. Typically, consonants are substituted for consonants and vowels for vowels. These substitutions involve the same place of articulation, especially for consonants produced at the front of the mouth. For example, students may have difficulty differentiating voiced (/b/) from voiceless consonants (/p/). In addition, they make errors involving manner of production, particularly high-frequency consonants (/s/, /ʃ/) and **consonantal blends** /bl/ and **clusters** (/str/).

The poor velar (soft palate) control of many hearing-impaired students contributes to difficulties in distinguishing between nasals (/m/, /n/, /ŋ/) and their counterparts, voiced stops (/b/, /d/, /g/), that involve the same place of articulation. Substituting voiced stops for nasals also occurs but not as frequently. It is also difficult for students to produce intelligible consonant clusters involving nasals (/nd/, /mp/).

Substitution errors have been observed with the use of fricatives and affricates. Stop consonants with a similar place of articulation (e.g., /t/ for /s/) often substitute for fricatives. Occurring less frequently is the substitution of fricatives for stops. Substitutions of affricates for other consonants are rare; however, affricates are usually substituted for affricates (Levitt, 1989).

A number of researchers have attributed the segmental speech errors of hearing-impaired students to poor control of the speech mechanisms and problems with rhythm or timing (Erber, 1982; Levitt, 1989; Ling, 1976). These sources of error also apply to the suprasegmental problems discussed previously. From another perspective, Levitt (1989) argued that:

> By far the most common source of error, however, is that of lack of effort. The most obvious manifestation of this problem is the omission of consonants, particularly at the end of a word or phrase. Other related errors involve partial omissions in the production of diphthongs, affricates and blends. The neutralization of vowels is also a manifestation of lack of effort and should not be regarded simply as improper placement of the articulators. (p. 30)

Speech Development and Signing

Perhaps the most interesting and controversial correlate of speech production is the *method* of communication (Moores, 1987; Quigley & Paul, 1984a). It is the heart of the oral-versus-manual debate, and more recently, of mainstreaming versus residential or special classrooms. In relation to the development of adequate oral communication and literacy skills, there is debate whether hearing-impaired students should be educated with oral or manual (sign) communication methods or in mainstreamed (regular education) or special education settings.

It is not clear whether the use of a signed system or a sign language has any direct causative effects, either negative or positive, on the development of spoken English and on English literacy skills (see Chapters 6 and 7 for further details). One of the most prevalent inferences made from a synthesis of studies is that signed communication is not detrimental to the development of speech skills (Moores, 1987; Quigley & Kretschmer, 1982; Wilbur, 1987). There is some evidence, however, that training in speech and residual hearing (i.e., auditory training/learning) and amount of oral language input may not be adequate in many Total Communication and/or nonintegrated educational programs (Connor, 1986; Huntington & Watton, 1986; Ross & Calvert, 1984). Thus, the speech production and oral English language development of students in these programs could be affected.

As discussed previously and documented elsewhere (Levitt, 1989; Ling, 1976), speech intelligibility is strongly related to degree of hearing impairment. In fact, degree of impairment is probably "the strongest and most consistent correlate of speech intelligibility" (Wolk & Schildroth, 1986, p. 152). Degree of hearing loss by itself, however, does not account for all the variation in the intelligibility ratings. Ethnicity and integration may also influence speech intelligibility. In relation to communication mode, Wolk and Schildroth (1986) examined two data bases on a national sample of students and reported:

> Student communication method relates very strongly to speech intelligibility. Again, the relationship is a direct one, independent of other relationships, particularly that involving degree of hearing loss. Intelligible speech was consistently reported for students who relied primarily on speaking as a communication mode. A nearly perfect opposite relationship exists for those students who relied upon signing to communicate: Nearly all were reported to have speech that was not intelligible. Students who used both speaking and signing to communicate were nearly as likely to be reported as having intelligible speech as they were to have speech that was not intelligible. (p. 152)

Speech Instruction and Deafness

It is clear that the major thrust of oral education for hearing-impaired students has been on the development of speech and, subsequently, of English literacy skills. Chapter 1 indicated that the teaching of speech to hearing-impaired students has a long, contentious history, and some scholars have argued that no superior theory or model has emerged (Calvert, 1986; Di Carlo, 1964). Calvert (1986) stated that, for students with severe to profound hearing impairments:

> . . . there has been neither a clear record of steady improvement in teaching methods nor significant breakthroughs that have either markedly reduced the level of effort or significantly increased quality of the result for 400 years. (p. 167)

Calvert also said that much of the research on speech development and deafness is still in the descriptive stage. Moores (1987), however, presented several critical points. *One,* not much is known on how severely to profoundly hearing-impaired students acquire speech or use it in natural, communicative situations. *Two,* there are no data available on the relative merits of the various methods of speech instruction. And *three,* speech instructional methods do not have a theoretical base.

Several speech programs are available (Calvert & Silverman, 1983; Ling, 1976). Most programs place a strong emphasis on the systematic training and assessment of auditory skills (i.e., the use of residual hearing). A well-organized speech-training program can improve speech skills in some severely to profoundly hearing-impaired students. It is an open question, however, whether these improvements have an effect on the overall speech intelligibility of most of the students. Recently, computer-assisted techniques have been developed that seem to be powerful motivators for students (Calvert, 1986; McGarr, Head, Friedman, Behrman, & Youdelman, 1986). They are also useful to teachers and other professionals because of the automation of tedious tasks such as keeping records and monitoring performance.

One can classify techniques of teaching speech according to natural or structural methods of teaching language, particularly the teaching of writing (see Chapter 8). It is more convenient, however, to classify the techniques by their emphasis on the various sensory modes: (1) **primarily auditory,** (2) multisensory (i.e., auditory and visual), and (3) tactile-kinesthetic (i.e., touch) (Calvert, 1986; Connor, 1986; Erber, 1982; Ling, 1986). There are numerous variations (labeled *methods* by Calvert, 1986) within and across these approaches. After discussing some of the basic tenets of each approach, we describe briefly two general rehabilitative procedures, auditory training/learning and speech reading, which are part of one or more approaches. These approaches and their variations can be used to teach not only speech development (i.e., perception and expression) but also language and literacy in oral education programs.

Primarily Auditory Approach.   The major focus of this approach is on the development of residual audition. As discussed in Chapter 2, the use of residual hearing is extremely important for the development of speech reception and production. Most variations of this technique concentrate on using audition alone in activities, encouraging parents to be actively involved in the education of their children, and using amplification and auditory training/learning techniques with the child as early as possible. Auditory training/learning refers to activities that facilitate the development and use of sound perception in hearing-impaired children. The use of speech reading (i.e., using visual cues such as reading the lips) is minimized as much as possible. Within this framework, the primarily auditory approach can be labeled as aural-oral, aural, acoupedic (Pollack, 1984, 1985), acoustic (Erber, 1982), auditory, auditory global (Calvert & Silverman, 1975, 1983), or unisensory (Beebe, Pearson, & Koch, 1984). A more detailed description of this approach and its variations can be found in Ling (1984a).

Multisensory Approach.   The multisensory approach focuses mainly on the development of the auditory and visual senses of hearing-impaired children. It is the traditional oral approach and has an intensive speech-training component (Ling, 1984a; Ling, 1976; Ling & Ling, 1978). As in the primarily auditory approach, the early and consistent use of amplification and auditory training/learning, as well as encouraging the involvement of parents, is emphasized. Attention is also given to the development of adequate speech reading skills. There is some evidence that developing both audition and vision (i.e., speech reading) skills has a greater impact on speech reception and production than the development of audition alone for some severely to profoundly hearing-impaired students (Novelli-Olmstead & Ling, 1984). Although the primary emphasis is on the auditory and visual senses, this approach may also have a tactile-kinesthetic component and can thus be named auditory-visual-tactile or auditory-visual-oral (Messerly & Aram, 1980).

Cued speech can also be called a multisensory *oral* approach (Cornett, 1967, 1984). The major goal of cued speech is to enable the hearing-impaired child to perceive the spoken signal in a clear, unambiguous manner. The focus is on the development of speech perception and production skills. Both vision and audition are considered important. To facilitate the development of speech and speech reading skills, the child is expected to perceive manual cues (handshapes) that accompany speech (thus, the name *cued speech*).

In cued speech, consonants are represented by eight handshapes, and vowels correspond to four positions near the facial area (see Figure 5.2). The combination of handshapes and positions is used to produce all the phonemes of speech in a given language that cannot be differentiated solely by speech reading (e.g., *ma, pa*). The manual cues are meaningless unless used in conjunction with speech.

According to Cornett (1984), cued speech ". . . has enjoyed a steady but slow growth since its inception, culminating in a rapid acceleration beginning in 1979" (p. 5). It is estimated that cued speech is used in approximately 350 programs in the United States. More than 300 of these programs, however, contain five children or fewer.

Tactile-kinesthetic Approach.   Calvert (1986) said that the tactile-kinesthetic approach "is that which emphasizes a strong tactile-kinesthetic feedback pattern associated with speech production" (p. 178). Typically, it is used with hearing-impaired children who have difficulty with techniques that focus primarily on audition and/or vision in the development of speech. Based on a motor theory of speech perception and known also as the *association method,* tactile-kinesthetic feedback incorporates speech reading, auditory training, reading, and writing with specific step-by-step training in the production of speech sounds (Calvert, 1986).

Aural Rehabilitation

The two most important components of aural rehabilitation (i.e., speech perception and production) are auditory training/learning and speech reading (Giolas, 1986; Ross, 1986a). Ross argues that these components are interwoven in practice and thus should not be treated as separate entities. Nevertheless, each component receives varying degrees of emphasis in the various approaches discussed previously. This section describes auditory training/learning and speech reading in relation to the development of speech and language in hearing-impaired children.

Auditory Training/Learning.   It is difficult to find a widely used definition of auditory training/learning. Until recently, the term *auditory training* was used to describe a set of procedures that facilitates the development of audition in hearing-impaired children (Ling, 1986). In a handbook published by the Clarke School for the Deaf (1971) in Northampton, Massachusetts, auditory training is defined as ". . . the structuring of an individual's environment to facilitate the development and use of sound perception" (p. vii). Examples of structuring or creating special communication conditions include "wearing a hearing aid; participating in auditory exercises; having attention drawn to meaningful sounds; using sound for warning and arousal; modifying your own behavior so that the student must understand all or part of what you say through hearing alone; advising parents of the use of hearing and hearing aids, etc." (p. vii). Many of these examples and others have been reiterated in more recent, widely used teaching manuals on auditory training (Erber, 1982; Sanders, 1982).

Traditional auditory training programs began with discrimination among nonverbal sounds, such as bells and drums. Then, children were required to discriminate among speech sounds, words, and sentences. With the advent of powerful amplification systems, the focus is now on teaching the child to *learn to listen* and *learn by listening,* rather than to learn to hear (Ling, 1986). This new focus, *auditory learning,* can be related to each child's spoken language development using real-life experiences (Cole & Gregory, 1986). Auditory learning emphasizes and extends the fourth and highest level of auditory skills, that is, the comprehension of meaningful sounds. It is argued that the other three levels—detecting, discriminating, and identifying sounds—are important but are not sufficient for developing listening skills. Auditory learning is a predominantly pragmatic (i.e., emphasis is on the function and meaning of sounds) approach to the development of listening abilities in hearing-impaired children. Although the term is new, the emphasis of the approach is not; natural methods of teaching speech and developing audition, as well as teaching language, have been in use for many years (Moores, 1987; McAnally, Rose, & Quigley, 1987).

Speech Reading.   Speech reading refers to the process of understanding a spoken message through observation of the speaker's face (Berger, 1972; Jeffers & Barley, 1971; O'Neill & Oyer, 1981). It is debated whether speech reading should be considered as involving vision only (i.e., without voice or auditory cues) or as complementing audition through the use of visual cues (i.e., lip movements, facial expressions, and so on) (Farwell, 1976; Ross, 1986a). Because of the effects of varying degrees of hearing impairment on speech development, it has been argued that it is important to study speech reading with and without the use of auditory cues (Conrad, 1979; Paul, 1988a; Perry & Silverman, 1978).

Traditionally, the process has been labeled lipreading. More recently, terms such as *visual communication* and *speech reading* have been used because the process of understanding speech involves more than simply reading the lips. Although *speech reading* is commonly used, some researchers still prefer the traditional term *lipreading* (Conrad, 1979; Ross, 1986a).

Speech reading ability can be categorized as follows: (1) speaker-sender, (2) environment, (3) lipreader-receiver, and (4) code-stimulus (O'Neill & Oyer, 1981). *Speaker-sender* refers to speaker-based factors such as rate of speech, visibility and characteristics of the speaker's face, and dialect of the speaker. The *environment* includes lighting, distractions, and distance between the speaker and the speech reader. Some lipreader-receiver factors are personality characteristics, prior or world knowledge, linguistic

CONSONANT CODE AND CUESCRIPT CHART

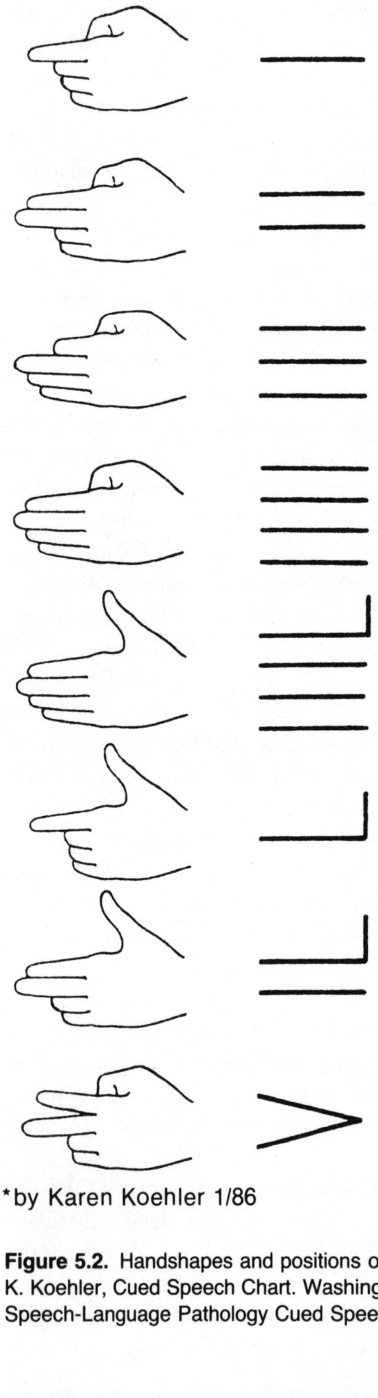

HANDSHAPE	CUESCRIPT	HANDSHAPE CODE NUMBER	/PHONEMES/ *("PHUNNY" PHRASES)
	—	1	/d, zh, p/ ("déjà pu")
	=	2	/tH, k, v, z/ ("the caves")
	≡	3	/h, r, s/ ("horse")
	≣	4	/b, hw, n/ ("By when?")
		5	/m, f, t/ ("miffed")
		6	/w, l, sh/ ("Welsh")
		7	/j, g, th/ ("joggeth")
	>	8	/ch, y, ng/ ("Chai Yung")

*by Karen Koehler 1/86

Figure 5.2. Handshapes and positions of cued speech.
K. Koehler, Cued Speech Chart. Washington, DC, Gallaudet University, Department of Audiology and Speech-Language Pathology Cued Speech Team, 1986. Reprinted by permission.

VOWEL CODE AND CUESCRIPT CHART

(note: vowels alone are cued with *OPEN* handshape ☰)

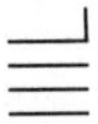

POSITION	CUESCRIPT	/PHONEMES/ *("PHUNNY" PHRASES)
Mouth		/ur, ee/ ("fir tree")
Chin	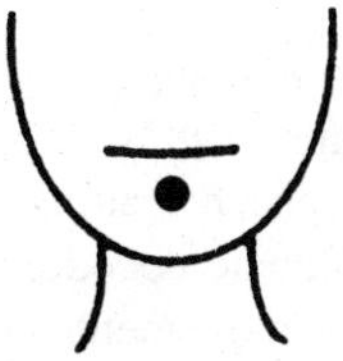	/ue, aw, e/ ("too tall Ted")
Throat	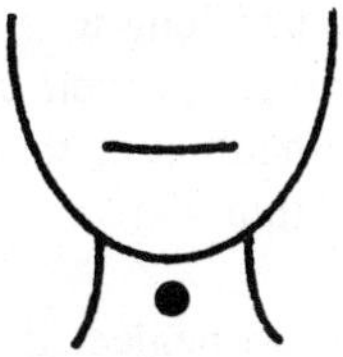	/oo, a, i/ ("Look at it.")
Side	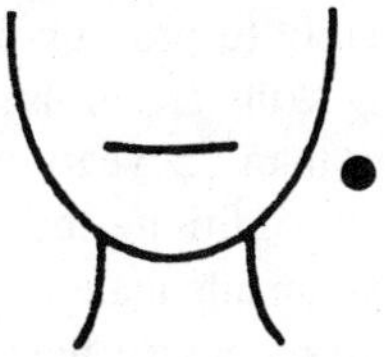	↑/oe, ah/, /u/↓ ("Joe got one.")
Chin–Throat Glide	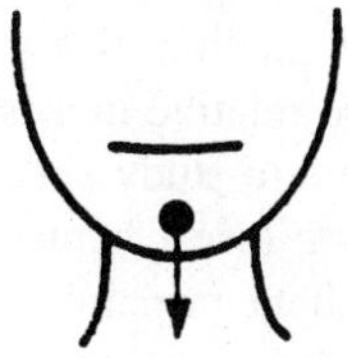	/ae, oi/ ("Hey, Roy!")
Side–Throat Glide	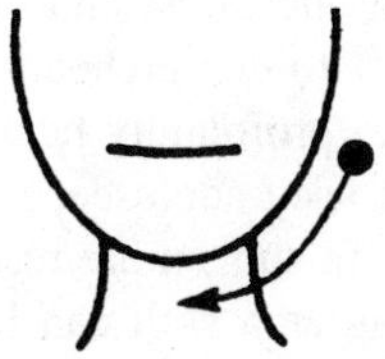	/ie, ou/ ("eyebrow")

*by **B🌂** 1/86

Figure 5.2. *(Continued)*

competence, and certain cognitive areas such as memory and visual perceptual abilities. *Code-stimulus* refers to the spoken message itself, including visibility of sounds, rate of transmission, vocabulary levels, and length and types of sentences.

It is beyond the scope of this chapter to provide a comprehensive treatment of the effects of these on speech reading ability. Good reviews of research studies can be found elsewhere (Erber, 1982; Farwell, 1976; Jeffers & Barley, 1971; O'Neill & Oyer, 1981; *Volta Review,* 1988). Conrad (1979) has argued, however, that the results of most investigations of speech reading and the effect of the degree of hearing impairment are confounded by linguistic competence. "Whether the procedure uses silent speech or vocal speech, whether the subjects wear hearing aids or not, it is unclear whether language knowledge or the ability to 'read' lips is being measured" (p. 179). It is difficult to develop tests that distinguish between knowledge of language and visual recognition of language aspects.

It is useful to compare speech reading ability with the ability to read printed text (Perry & Silverman, 1978; Williams, 1982), especially in view of current interactive theories of reading. For example, speech reading and textual reading require **decoding** and comprehension skills. With adequate decoding skills, good speech readers can proceed from perceiving articulatory movement/sound correspondence to constructing meaning. They also use information in long-term memory and certain cognitive skills such as inferencing and predicting to check their understanding of the spoken message. Speech reading may be a more difficult task than textual reading, however, because there is a great deal of variability within and across the four groups of factors discussed previously.

Speech reading is one of the most neglected areas of research in the development of English language skills in severely to profoundly hearing-impaired students. Several methods of teaching speech reading skills are in use, but these methods have not changed much from those developed more than 75 years ago (Berger, 1972; Jeffers & Barley, 1971; O'Neill & Oyer, 1981). In addition, they have been developed primarily for hearing-impaired persons who have an adequate knowledge of a spoken language. Using speech reading to teach students to recognize what they already know is different from and much easier than using speech reading as a language-teaching tool. Very little experimental data are available on the relative merits of the various approaches.

It may be useful for researchers to study speech reading from an interactive model that is used for the study of reading (see Chapter 8). Even the construction of speech reading tests can adhere to the salient principles of good reading tests—using longer intact passages, asking inferential questions, and taking into account the effects of prior or world knowledge on the ability to comprehend speech reading. There is also a need to use prelinguistically severely to profoundly hearing-impaired students as subjects because most previous studies have used adolescents or adults with postlinguistically less-than-severe hearing impairments. In sum, more research is necessary because "We have very little evidence that lipreading as a skill can be improved after training; we do not know whether the differences that sometimes occur before and after training reflect innate factors or specific aspects of the teaching process, or whether the improvements that may occur are stable and result in improved communication outside of the therapy setting" (Ross, 1986a, p. 40).

ORAL HEARING-IMPAIRED STUDENTS

The oral education methods described earlier are most likely to be used with severely and profoundly hearing-impaired students in special schools and classrooms. Results of the research on several of the methods are available. Most of the results on speech and language development, however, are from case studies or studies involving only a few students. Some data from large groups on reading and academic achievement are available.

Two general comments can be made about the achievement of oral students. *One,* when oral education methods are used in a systematic, consistent way, favorable results can be seen in the development of speech and language. *Two,* these results have been observed with a select group of oral students who comprised only a very small portion of severely to profoundly hearing-impaired students who had been educated in *incontestably, comprehensive oral education programs* such as the Clarke School for the Deaf, the Central Institute for the Deaf, and the St. Joseph School for the Deaf or in regular education programs (Connor, 1986; Quigley & Paul, 1984a). Many, if not most, of these students were able to exploit their residual hearing effectively by the use of assistive amplification devices. Because of the limited data available, Lane (1976a) has argued that there is a need for "well documented research, demonstrating the value and need for oral methods" (p. 137). This assertion has been repeated in a more recent investigation (McCartney, 1986).

Cued Speech

The effects of cued speech on the development of English have not been extensively documented. Much of what is known about cued speech is available in newsletters that are sent to members of professional organizations (Cornett, 1984). Few experimental or descriptive data are available, and most of the findings concern hearing-impaired students in countries other than the United States. The studies discussed here focus mainly on speech reception abilities, with only one study reporting on the language production of severely and profoundly hearing-impaired students (see also the study by Luetke-Stahlman, 1988a in Chapter 7 of this book).

Ling and Clarke (1975) and Clarke and Ling (1976) assessed the receptive abilities of Canadian hearing-impaired students who had been exposed to cued speech for about two years. The researchers presented cued (i.e., cues and speech) and noncued (i.e., speech only) words, phrases, and sentences to their subjects. They analyzed the students' written responses. The results showed that the scores on cued materials were better than those on uncued materials. In addition, cued words were easier to read than cued phrases, which were easier than cued sentences. Most students, however, performed very poorly beyond the level of the cued word. One of the most important findings was that students' errors could be categorized. Thus, the researchers stated that it is possible to establish a remedial program for improving the receptive skills of the students that was based on the patterns, or categories, of errors.

In a more recent study, it was shown that cued speech did not negatively affect the speech reading skills or the use of residual hearing in Australian hearing-impaired students (Nicholls & Ling, 1982). In fact, the inclusion of speech reading with cued speech (with or without accompanying voice) increased the speech reception scores of the students. The researchers concluded:

> . . . that more widespread use of cued speech would be merited, particularly as an oral option for those children who have very limited residual hearing, are totally deaf, or who are failing to make adequate progress in more conventional programs. (p. 268)

Only one study was found that assessed the language development of students exposed to cued speech (Mohay, 1983). There were only three subjects—two profoundly hearing-impaired and one severely hearing-impaired—who had received their previous training in a conventional oral program. After being exposed to cued speech, the children's use of word combinations (i.e., two- or three-words utterances) began to increase. Because of the lack of scientific control, it is not known if the increase in the children's spoken utterances was caused by factors other than cued speech—for example, growth in linguistic and cognitive abilities.

More recent studies involving hearing adults (Abraham & Stoker, 1984; Chilson, 1985) and hearing-impaired adults (Gregory, 1987) have supported the earlier findings about the positive effects of cued speech on speech reading skills. In these investigations, adults obtained significantly higher speech reading scores on speech stimuli presented with cues than on stimuli without cues. This seems to indicate that cued speech should be used primarily as a receptive oral-communication tool. Cued speech may be effective in improving severely to profoundly hearing-impaired students' ability to receive spoken information.

Traditional Oral Education Programs

If the text by Ling (1984a) is representative of intensive, comprehensive, early oral intervention programs, then it seems that the most effective oral options focus on the development of residual hearing, particularly by using the primarily auditory method. In some programs, multisensory approaches, especially the use of visual and tactile senses, may be used in the beginning stages. In other programs, speech reading instruction may be added at a later stage, particularly for students who are having difficulty with primarily auditory approaches. All programs stress the importance of developing auditory skills in early infancy for speech and language development.

This section discusses the findings of a few studies that assess the effects of oral English methods on the speech, language, and reading abilities of severely to profoundly hearing-impaired students. We have included investigations on students exposed *only* to unisensory and/or multisensory oral techniques, particularly in indisputably intensive programs. In these programs, parents and teachers tried to provide a language environment similar to that provided for hearing children of comparable ages.

The benefits of unisensory methods, especially the acoupedics approach, have been documented in several case studies (Pollack, 1984). For example, Long, Fitzgerald, Sutton, and Rollins (1983) reported on the achievement of a $4\frac{1}{2}$-year-old deaf girl exposed to the method for about 1 year. Analyses of spoken language utterances revealed that the girl produced "complete, adult-like sentences 76% of the time" (p. 35) during the last 6 months of the study. In fact, the deaf girl was acquiring language at a rate similar to that of her hearing peers.

Similar or nearly similar levels of achievement in speech perception and production were documented in other case studies (Beebe et al., 1984). Several investigations on groups of students reported improvements in speech reception abilities when speech reading was used in conjunction with residual hearing (Erber, 1982; Hack & Erber, 1982). Improvements in hearing-impaired students' speech production and generalization of speech skills have also been noted, especially in programs that focus on speech training (Novelli-Olmstead & Ling, 1984; Perigoe & Ling, 1986). For some students, it appears that speech and auditory training/learning methods are more effective in developing speech and language skills than the use of auditory training/learning alone. These students still need periods in which auditory training/learning techniques are used alone, however.

Some of the most impressive results of the early use of oral education methods can be seen in the few investigations on students enrolled in the indisputably comprehensive oral programs and/or integrated in regular education programs. For example, Doehring, Bonnycastle, and Ling (1978) studied the language comprehension abilities of unaided severely and profoundly hearing-impaired students from 6 to 13 years old. Some of these students were also enrolled in regular education programs. In general, the hearing-impaired students performed as well as or better than their hearing counterparts on reading-related tasks. On the language tasks, however, the students performed below grade level. It was argued that the inferior scores on these tasks were a result of artifacts (e.g., conditions) of the test and were not indicative of the true abilities of the students. The researchers stated: "The auditory-oral training of these children seems to have enabled them to acquire many of the oral reading skills needed in classes for normally hearing children" (p. 407).

Additional support for the success of students in comprehensive oral programs or integrated for all or most of the day in regular education programs can be found in more recent studies (Geers & Moog, 1989; Geers, Moog, & Schick, 1984; Messerly & Aram, 1980; Moog & Geers, 1985).

For example, Geers and Moog (1989) analyzed the primary language, secondary language, and cognitive performance of profoundly hearing-impaired students enrolled in oral education and regular education programs in the United States and Canada. Eighty percent of the students were mainstreamed for all or most of the school day. Results indicated that many students have well-developed primary language and secondary language skills. The researchers concluded that

(a) It is possible for profoundly hearing-impaired children, by the time they are 16 years of age, to achieve reading skills commensurate with those of normal-hearing students (between 24% and 34% of students in this sample achieved at this level on the various reading measures administered).

(b) Children with profound hearing impairment who have a combination of favorable factors—including at least average nonverbal intellectual ability, early oral education management and auditory stimulation, and middle-class family environment with strong family support—have a potential for developing much higher reading, writing, and spoken language skills than is reported for hearing-impaired people in general (e.g., 7th- to 8th-grade reading skills rather than 3rd-grade reading levels).

(c) The primary factors associated with the development of literacy in this orally educated sample are good use of residual hearing, early amplification and educational management, and—above all—oral English language ability, including vocabulary, syntax, and discourse skills. (p. 84)

Other interesting insights regarding the success of the few exceptional orally trained students can be gleaned from two survey investigations (McCartney, 1986; Ogden, 1979). One study focused on former oral students in three comprehensive oral programs; the other study included former oral students, parents, and teachers of students in oral programs. The former oral students in both studies were successful educationally and vocationally. In fact, it was remarked that "this group is atypical in comparison to both the national population and the national hearing-impaired population," that is, they "have better than average education, careers, and annual salaries" (McCartney, 1986, p. 135).

The results provided support for the factors listed previously—early education, parental involvement, and oral communication skills. In addition, the more recent study (McCartney, 1986) emphasized the importance of oral personality and values. That is, students, parents, and teachers need to be committed to and value the development of adequate oral communication skills and literacy. It is also important to desire to be integrated in regular education classrooms and into the mainstream of society. As aptly stated by McCartney (1986), oral students "must have innate qualities to be oral" (p. 140).

SUMMARY

This chapter discussed the development of oral English skills in students enrolled in indisputably comprehensive oral education programs or in public school programs for most or all of the school day. It described the philosophy of oral education and its major components: speech, speech reading, and auditory training/learning. Data were presented on the effects of several common oral methods and techniques used to develop spoken and written English in students with severe to profound hearing losses. Finally, some conditions for success in oral education programs were presented.

Basic information on the anatomy and physiology of speech mechanisms was provided, particularly for the structures in the throat and mouth such as the larynx, vocal folds, tongue, velum, and lips. In general, in the production of speech, air is exhaled by the lungs and is obstructed or constricted by the various speech mechanisms. Before leaving the lips, air is modified by the resonant qualities of the oral and/or nasal cavities.

The three sources of speech sounds were described: voicing, frication, and stop-plosive. These sound sources are responsible for all speech sounds, which can be categorized into two broad areas: consonants and vowels. Consonants were classified and discussed according to three features of articulation: place, manner, and position. Vowel classification was discussed in relation to the positions of the tongue within the oral cavity. Examples of consonants and vowels were provided, and it was emphasized that their descriptions reflect ideal positions and sound production. In order to discuss running speech production, the chapter covered intonation, rhythm, and coarticulation. To complete the basic introduction to speech science, the phonological development of normally hearing children was briefly described.

In relation to speech and deafness, it was argued that some of the major correlates of speech intelligibility were degree of hearing impairment, use of residual hearing, and the modes of communication to which students are exposed in infancy and early childhood. It was emphasized that severely to profoundly hearing-impaired students' problems with speech production are not organic; there is nothing wrong with their speech mechanisms. Their hearing impairment makes it difficult for the students to proceed with the physiological aspects of speaking. They need to exert more effort in learning how to breathe properly, where to put the tongue, and how to manipulate their speech mechanisms appropriately during speech production. Despite the best efforts of teachers and other professionals, there has been little steady progress in developing speech in prelinguistically severely to profoundly hearing-impaired students.

Some students do learn to speak intelligibly. Speech instruction, as well as the teaching of language and literacy, was classified and described according to three broad oral methods: primarily auditory, multisensory, and tactile-kinesthetic. The chapter also described two major aural rehabilitation aspects of these methods: auditory training/ learning and speech reading. These aspects receive varying degrees of emphasis in the commonly used oral approaches. Although new models such as the use of computers have been suggested for studying and using auditory training/learning and speech reading techniques, much research work still needs to be done in these areas.

Research on the oral English development of severely to profoundly hearing-impaired students were presented in relation to two areas: cued speech and traditional oral education methods. The focus was on students educated in incontestably comprehensive oral programs and/or regular education classes because these environments exemplify the philosophy of oralism. Limited data available indicate that it is possible to develop adequate speech, language, and reading skills in the students. It was emphasized, however, that many of these students represent a select group and comprised only a very small portion of all severely to profoundly hearing-impaired students in special education programs, possibly in *all* education programs. It seems that the language and reading development of most of these students proceed at a slower rate but in a similar manner when compared with hearing counterparts.

Very few investigations have been conducted on the merits of cued speech. Cued speech may aid in the development of speech reception skills, especially if it is used in conjunction with audition and speech reading. As a multisensory approach, cued speech may be useful to oral students who cannot receive much benefit from traditional oral education programs.

Research data were provided on severely to profoundly hearing-impaired students educated in comprehensive, traditional oral programs and/or in regular education programs. Despite differences in the approaches, we can list some common conditions that seem to promote success in these programs. Perhaps the most important factor is the development of residual hearing. In fact, it was argued that this factor helps students gain access to the auditory/articulatory code on which spoken and written language is based. The development of residual hearing requires, at least, early identification, early amplification, and adequate early intervention procedures. For many hearing-impaired students, it is necessary to add speech reading training in order to enhance language and reading comprehension abilities. A large number of students performed at or above grade level when compared to their hearing peers. The academic success of oral severely to profoundly hearing-impaired students was attributed to their well-developed oral skills—speech, speech reading, and the use of residual hearing.

The remarkable success of orally trained students was also revealed in two survey investigations. It was reported that the educational and vocational attributes of oral hearing-impaired adults were higher than those for the typical general population and for hearing-impaired students educated in other education programs. Both surveys indicated that students, parents, and teachers were committed strongly to the philosophy of oralism and its major goal of successful integration into the mainstream of society. The participants valued oralism so much that it was implied that they had developed an oral personality, that is, the desire to communicate through speech.

COMPREHENSION

1. Describe the series of stages of speech communication. The description has been started for you.
   First, speakers construct their ideas and thoughts in their heads. Then . . .
2. What are the three categories of sound sources in speech production?
3. TRUE or FALSE? The variations of frequency during speech production are perceived as intonation.
4. Provide one example (using a word) for the following categories of consonants:
   Example: nasal - - /m/ as in *mother*.
   a. Stop-plosive
   b. Affricate
   c. Fricative
   d. Nasal
   e. Vowel-like (glide)
5. Provide one example (using a word) for the following categories of vowels:
   Example: high front - - /i/ as in *eat*.
   a. High front
   b. Low front
   c. High back
   d. Low back
   e. Midfront
6. TRUE or FALSE? The greater the hearing impairment, the less intelligible the speech, and the more difficult it is for speech to be developed.
7. Classify the following errors as *suprasegmental* or *segmental:*
   a. Substitution of vowels
   b. Rhythm
   c. Respiration
   d. Omission of consonants
   e. Dipthongization of vowels
   f. Prolonged and improperly inserted pauses
8. TRUE or FALSE? The most common consonantal errors are omissions.

9. Label the following as examples of *primarily auditory, multisensory,* or *tactile-kinesthetic* approaches:
   a. Focuses mainly on developing auditory and visual senses.
   b. Focuses mainly on developing residual audition.
   c. Includes acoustic and acoupedics.
   d. Used with children who have difficulties with approaches that focus on audition and vision.
   e. Includes cued speech.
   f. Based on a motor theory of speech perception.
10. TRUE or FALSE? It has been clearly shown that the use of signed communication is detrimental to the development of speech skills.
11. How does the traditional auditory training program differ from the current auditory learning program?
12. What are the four categories of factors related to speech reading ability? Provide one example for each category.
13. TRUE or FALSE? Speech reading methods have not changed much since those developed more than 75 years ago.
14. Which of the following is/are TRUE about the research on cued speech?
    a. Effects on English language development have not been extensively studied.
    b. Most findings concern hearing-impaired students in the United States.
    c. Major thrust of research has been on developing literacy.
    d. Students score better on cued materials than on uncued materials.
    e. Students' errors can be categorized.
15. TRUE or FALSE? The most impressive results of the use of oral education methods can be seen for students in comprehensive special oral programs and for those integrated in regular education programs.
16. List three important factors that are said to account for the success of oral deaf students.
17. What does it mean to have an oral personality?

SUGGESTED ACTIVITIES

I. Ask a few of your friends to take the following speech reading test. Stand about 6 feet in front of them and say the sentences without voice. Try not to exaggerate your lip movements. Give one point for each correct sentence. It is all right to miss a word or two as long as the gist of the sentence is correct. Record what your friends say about their attempts to understand you.*

   1. All right.
   2. Where have you been?
   3. I have forgotten.
   4. I have nothing.
   5. That is right.
   6. Look out.
   7. How have you been?
   8. I don't know if I can.
   9. How tall are you?

---

*Source: Utley Sentence Test, Form A in Jeffers & Barley (1971).

10. It is awfully cold.
11. My folks are home.
12. How much was it?
13. Good night.
14. Where are you going?
15. Excuse me.
16. Did you have a good time?
17. What did you want?
18. How much do you weigh?
19. I cannot stand him.
20. She was home last week.
21. Keep your eye on the ball.
22. I cannot remember.
23. Of course.
24. I flew to Washington.
25. You look well.
26. The train runs every hour.
27. You had better go slow.
28. It says that in the book.
29. We got home at six o'clock.
30. We drove to the country.
31. How much rain fell?

II. Visit classrooms for hearing-impaired students that use oral instructional methods.
1. Ask teachers to describe their oral education methods. How do they teach speech, speech reading, and auditory training/learning skills?
2. Can you place their descriptions into one of the categories discussed in this chapter?
3. What tests do they use to assess the speech and hearing abilities of their students?
4. Ask teachers to provide some differences between oral classrooms and Total Communication classrooms.
5. Ask teachers if any of their students know how to sign.

FURTHER READINGS

Connor, L. (Ed.). (1971). *Speech for the deaf child: Knowledge and use*. Washington, DC: Alexander Graham Bell Association for the Deaf.

DeLand, F. (1968). *The story of lip-reading*. Washington, DC: Volta Bureau.

Jakobson, R. (1971). *Studies on child language and aphasia*. The Hague: Mouton.

Kaplan, H., Bally, S., & Garretson, C. (1987). *Speechreading: A way to improve understanding* (2nd ed.). Washington, DC: Gallaudet University Press.

Newman, P., Creaghead, N., & Secord, W. (1985). *Assessment and remediation of articulatory and phonological disorders*. Columbus, OH: Merrill.

Van Riper, C. (1978). *Speech correction: Principles and methods* (6th ed.). Englewood Cliffs, NJ: Prentice-Hall.

Vorce, E. (1974). *Teaching speech to deaf children*. Washington, DC: Alexander Graham Bell Association for the Deaf.

Weiner, F. (1979). *Phonological process analysis*. Baltimore, MD: University Park Press.

Winitz, H. (1975). *From syllable to conversation*. Baltimore, MD: University Park Press.

CHAPTER 6

American Sign Language

MAJOR POINTS TO CONSIDER

The first or primary language of severely to profoundly hearing-impaired students

Similarities and differences between sign languages and spoken languages

Manual and nonmanual aspects of American Sign Language

How ASL differs from English and the English-based signed systems

Effects of ASL on English language development

Why and how ASL should be used to teach English literacy skills

Historically, much of what is known about language acquisition and development has come from the study of spoken languages such as French, German, and English (Blumenthal, 1970; Naremore, 1984). Many language scientists, or linguists, have assumed that all languages are primarily spoken and that other forms, such as writing and signing, are based on the spoken form. Sign languages as used by native deaf signers have been labeled alinguistic, or nonlanguages; that is, they do not have a grammar or a finite set of rule-governed principles. Another view has been that the languages are substandard versions of the signing that teachers used with deaf children in educational environments. Recently, however, linguists and psychologists who study language development have revised their thinking on the nature and function of nonverbal, or sign, languages. The study of the acquisition of sign language has increased our understanding of language development in general. The importance and extent of research in sign language was evident at the Third International Symposium held in Rome, Italy, in 1983, where presentations covered a number of sign languages—Italian Sign, Brazilian Sign, Chinese Sign, Danish Sign, and American Sign (Stokoe & Volterra, 1985).

This chapter focuses on American Sign Language (ASL) and its effects on communication, language, and achievement in the education of hearing-impaired students. After describing briefly some linguistic, psycholinguistic, and **neurolinguistic** aspects of ASL, the chapter shows how ASL differs from English and from the English-based signed systems that are discussed in detail in Chapter 7. Finally, we present tentative answers to two of the most important questions facing educators: (1) What is the first, or primary, language of severely to profoundly hearing-impaired students? and (2) Is it possible for these students to learn a spoken language through the use of a sign language?

SIGN LANGUAGES AND SPOKEN LANGUAGES

American Sign Language is a rule-governed and visual-gestural language (Lane & Grosjean, 1980; Wilbur, 1987). To facilitate understanding, it is important to highlight these two major characteristics of ASL and demonstrate similarities and differences between sign languages and spoken languages.

Like English and other spoken languages, ASL is governed by rules. It is possible to describe a grammar of ASL that consists of a set of statements about how this language works. American Sign Language has its own grammar with rules that pertain to the major components of a language such as (1) pragmatics (functions of a language), (2) semantics (meaning), (3) syntax (structure and organization of sentences), and (4) phonology (sound or phonetic system). For example, ASL syntax basically adheres to a **subject-verb-object** order as in the sentence, *I like football* (Friedman, 1977; Liddell, 1980). It also has rules for producing **morphemes,** the smallest part of a word having meaning. This can be seen in the production of inflectional morphemes (e.g., plurality, as in tree*s*) and derivational morphemes (e.g., affixes, as in slow*ly*).

As a visual-gestural language, ASL (and other sign languages) is particularly structured to accommodate the eye and motor capabilities of the body. The grammatical structure of ASL is spatially based. Space and movement play important linguistic roles such as marking **verb aspects** (e.g., present, past, or future tenses), noun plurals, and differentiating morphologically verb-like signs from related noun-like signs (e.g., the sign pairs, SIT, CHAIR; IMPROVE, IMPROVEMENT; FLY, AIRPLANE).

Most of the information in ASL is presented and conveyed in front of the signer's body. Instead of using speech, native signers communicate by executing systematic manual and nonmanual body movements simultaneously. Manual movements refer to the shapes, positions, and movements of the hands; nonmanual movements consist of gestures involving the shoulders, cheeks, lips, tongue, eyes, and eyebrows.

Unlike most spoken languages, ASL and other sign languages do not have a standardized secondary form. Thus, it is not possible (at present) to read or write in a sign language. This is a major reason why many educators have disregarded the value of using ASL with severely to profoundly hearing-impaired students. They cannot see how ASL can be used to teach English, particularly literacy skills.

The fact that ASL is a visual-gestural, spatially based language needs to be emphasized to provide the foundation for understanding how ASL is different linguistically from English and from the English-based signed systems. In addition, these characteristics of ASL address the question of whether English as a spoken, auditory language can be developed through the use of a signed or manual mode that does not incorporate space and movement as part of its grammar. Thus, the use of ASL to teach English offers insights regarding the development of language, either spoken or signed, in most deaf students (Paul, 1987, 1988b; Quigley & Paul, 1984a).

LINGUISTIC DESCRIPTION

Linguistic analyses of ASL began with the seminal work of William Stokoe (1960), who proposed that signs were comprised of a finite number of linguistic traits that can be combined to produce a number of concepts in a lexicon (i.e., the vocabulary items of a language). Within a structural linguistic philosophical framework, Stokoe studied the formation of signs, which he labeled *cherology* (from the Greek root *cheir* for hand). Cherology is similar to phonology (i.e., the study of speech sounds). For example, just as words can be divided into smaller phonemic elements (/t/, /f/), so also can signs be broken down into smaller cheremic (hand-signal) elements. These are (1) handshape (designator, or *dez*), (2) location (tabulation, or *tab*), and (3) movement (signation, or *sig*). Stokoe and his associates developed a notational system for writing and studying signs (Stokoe, Casterline, & Croneberg, 1976). A sample of this system is shown in Figure 6.1.

To illustrate how this system works, consider the sign, KNOW, as an example. Using Stokoe's notations, we can describe the phonological/cheremic parameters of the sign. Typically, KNOW is executed on the forehead or in proximity to the forehead. The *tab* symbol that represents the forehead or upper brow is used here. The handshape for KNOW resembles a flat-hand salute with the palm facing the floor. This combination requires representation by a *dez* symbol and another *tab* symbol. Finally, the *sig* symbol for this sign is one that indicates movement toward the signer or tapping of the fingertips on the forehead. Thus, the notation for the sign, KNOW, shown in Figure 6.2, can be written as: *Tab∩, Dez* B_{TX} (the *sig* symbol is written as a subscript after the *dez* symbol).

Since the work of Stokoe, there have been some major alterations in the understanding of sign formation (Lane & Grosjean, 1980; Wilbur, 1987). For example, a proposed fourth cheremic feature, orientation, was added to the original three. Orientation refers to the direction that the palm of the hand is facing, that is, up, down, or to the right or left. This is important, for instance, in differentiating the sign for SHORT (meaning "brief") from the sign for TRAIN (meaning "vehicle for travel").

More recent research on ASL has focused on other crucial linguistic elements such as rate and movement of the signs **(modulation),** the direction and size of the path of signing **(directionality),** and nonmanual aspects such as eye gazing and head tilting or shaking (Newport & Meiser, 1986). An important area of sign formation not discussed by Stokoe in his original work was the nonmanual aspects of ASL. As mentioned previously, these refer to nonsign movements such as facial expressions that are used as grammatical devices for questions, **negation,** and various types of clauses. For example,

Figure 6.1. Notational system for signs.
W. C. Stokoe, Jr., D. C. Casterline, and C. G. Croneberg, *A Dictionary of American Sign Language on Linguistic Principles.* Linstok Press, 1976. Reprinted by permission of the author.

Tab symbols

Ø zero, the neutral place where the hands move, in contrast with all places below
∩ face or whole head
∧ forehead or brow, upper face
ʊ mid-face, the eye and nose region
ᴗ chin, lower face
} cheek, temple, ear, side-face
π neck
[] trunk, body from shoulders to hips
\ upper arm
√ elbow, forearm
ɑ wrist, arm in supinated position (on its back)
ᴅ wrist, arm in pronated position (face down)

Dez symbols, some also used as tab

A compact hand, fist; may be like 'a', 's', or 't' of manual alphabet
B flat hand
5 spread hand; fingers and thumb spread like '5' of manual numeration
C curved hand; may be like 'c' or more open
E contracted hand; like 'e' or more clawlike
F "three-ring" hand; from spread hand, thumb and index finger touch or cross
G index hand; like 'g' or sometimes like 'd'; index finger points from fist
H index and second finger, side by side, extended
I "pinkie" hand; little finger extended from compact hand
K like G except that thumb touches middle phalanx of second finger; like 'k' and 'p' of manual alphabet
L angle hand; thumb, index finger in right angle, other fingers usually bent into palm
3 "cock" hand; thumb and first two fingers spread, like '3' of manual numeration
O tapered hand; fingers curved and squeezed together over thumb; may be like 'o' of manual alphabet
R "warding off" hand; second finger crossed over index finger, like 'r' of manual alphabet
V "victory" hand; index and second fingers extended and spread apart
W three-finger hand; thumb and little finger touch, others extended spread
X hook hand; index finger bent in hook from fist, thumb tip may touch fingertip
Y "horns" hand; thumb and little finger spread out extended from fist; or index finger and little finger extended, parallel
8 (allocheric variant of Y); second finger bent in from spread hand, thumb may touch fingertip

Figure 6.1. (continued)

Sig symbols

∧	upward movement	
∨	downward movement	vertical action
ᴎ	up-and-down movement	
>	rightward movement	
<	leftward movement	sideways action
ᴢ	side to side movement	
⊤	movement toward signer	
⊥	movement away from signer	horizontal action
ɪ	to-and-fro movement	
ɑ	supinating rotation (palm up)	
ᴅ	pronating rotation (palm down)	rotary action
ω	twisting movement	
ŋ	nodding or bending action	
◻	opening action (final dez configuration shown in brackets)	
♯	closing action (final dez configuration shown in brackets)	
ᴊ	wiggling action of fingers	
⊚	circular action	
⟩⟨	convergent action, approach	
×	contactual action, touch	
⊐	linking action, grasp	
✦	crossing action	interaction
⊙	entering action	
÷	divergent action, separate	
⟨⟩	interchanging action	

raising the eyebrows while signing identifies **yes/no questions** as in the sentence, *Do you want a cup of coffee?*

This can be signed as:

$$\underline{\qquad\qquad \text{q}}$$

YOU WANT COFFEE?

The *q* refers to the nonmanual signal for the yes/no question, which is raising the eyebrows (Baker & Cokely, 1980). Pulling the eyebrows together and/or shaking the head expresses negation as in the sentence, *I am not hungry.* One way to sign this is:

$$\underline{\qquad\qquad \text{neg}}$$

HUNGRY ME.

The *neg* refers to a nonmanual signal as in nodding the head.

KNOW
Fingers of palm–in hand hit
forehead lightly; may repeat

Figure 6.2. The sign for KNOW.
G. Gustason, D. Pfetzing, and E. Zawolkow, *Signing Exact English*. Los Alamitos, CA: Modern Signs Press, 1980. Reprinted by permission.

It is important to remember that a complete description of ASL signs entails both manual and nonmanual movements. Focusing on one or the other but not on both results in a misinterpretation of the signed message. Although linguistic differences between ASL and the English-based sign systems can be discussed in relation to both kinds of movement, typically most of the emphasis has been placed on the manual differences. In fact, lack of knowledge about the nonmanual aspects of ASL has contributed to the difficulty many educators encounter in understanding and describing the signed utterances of deaf students (Maxwell, 1985a, 1985b; Woodward, 1986). Many educators are not even aware of the various manual aspects of signs. They do not know that ''. . . the number of ASL signs greatly exceeds what is usually found in the manuals used in sign classes'' (Wilbur, 1987, p. 113). Clearly, the list of signs in these manuals do not include, for example, the nonmanual aspects, **classifiers** (pronoun forms plus verb system), noun-verb pairs, reduplicated forms (TREE into TREES or FOREST), compound signs (HOME + WORK = HOMEWORK), or derived, idiomatic forms (WRONG with an elbow rotation meaning SUDDENLY, UNEXPECTEDLY).

PSYCHOLINGUISTIC DEVELOPMENT

We have learned a great deal about language development from investigators in a subfield of cognitive psychology called *psycholinguistics*. Psycholinguists are interested in the mental processes involved in language comprehension and production. Research on psycholinguistic development and ASL has centered mainly on linguistic processes such as perception, comprehension, production, and memory of signs (Lane & Grosjean, 1980; Newport & Meier, 1986; Wilbur, 1987). Interesting findings have been reported on, for example, the comprehension and production of the first signs, the development of finger spelling by ASL-using deaf children, and how signs are stored in memory. The ways in which deaf individuals process and use ASL are influenced by the age at which they acquire ASL and the age at onset of deafness. Although the results are based on data from only a few studies, we can conclude that in general developmental stages and processes are similar to those found in individuals who are learning and using spoken languages.

Parallels in processes between ASL and English have been observed in hearing and deaf adults. Studies of memory with hearing adults indicate that their recall errors are related to the phonological properties of words. That is, in the absence of semantic (meaning) information, adults confuse acoustically similar letters or words such as *d* and *t* or *hat* and *cat*. There is evidence that the same is true for memory for signs. It has been reported that deaf adults have difficulty remembering lists of signs of similar form such as handshape or movement (Bellugi, Klima, & Siple, 1974). For example, the sign for SHORT is often confused with the sign for TRAIN.

Other acquisition parallels between ASL and English have been observed in children. As in the case of first-language learners of English, the learning process of deaf children is replete with **hypothesis-testing** strategies and trial-and-error patterns. In the development of negative structures (e.g., the use of *no, not, never*), both hearing and ASL-using deaf children proceed through similar developmental milestones (Hoffmeister & Wilbur, 1980). Typically, they begin by placing *no* or *not* before the main sentence as in *No want milk* or *No money*. Then the negative element is included within the sentence as *You can't write* or *He no have money*. Eventually, the children move on to mastering negation properties.

Additional evidence for similarity between the developmental stages of ASL and English can be found in other syntactic areas (e.g., the use of **pronouns** and verbs), semantics, and even in pragmatics (functions of language), the most recently developed linguistic component. The research on pragmatics reports that deaf mothers engage in communication behaviors similar to those of hearing and speaking mothers. For example, they modify the structure of their language to facilitate communication with their children (Kantor, 1980; Maestas & Moores, 1980). Specifically, when deaf mothers sign to their children, they use simple and more direct signed utterances. Hearing mothers continue to talk to their babies even when the infants' eyes are closed or when they are falling asleep. Likewise, deaf mothers continue to sign to their infants.

One of the most important areas of psycholinguistic research has been on the role of iconicity in the memory and acquisition of ASL signs. *Iconicity* is the *pictorial* relationship between a sign and its meaning. The formation of a sign can be traced to a real-world attribute. For example, the sign for CAT involves the stroking of the upper side or sides of the lip, indicating the whiskers of a cat. The concept of iconicity is probably the most misunderstood aspect of sign languages because it leads to the assumption that signs are pictorial or ideographic in nature and thus are not part of a real language (Markowicz, 1980; Wilbur, 1987).

Research on adults and children indicates that iconicity does not determine the relationship between a sign and its meaning. When signs were presented to nonsigners, it was found that the subjects could not guess the meaning of the signs on the basis of the obviousness or "guessability" of the signs. There is also evidence that iconicity does not play a major role in the acquisition of initial signs or in the memory of signs (Klima & Bellugi, 1979; Orlansky & Bonvillian, 1984). Thus, similar to the relation between a spoken word and its referent, the relation between a sign and its referent is also arbitrary and must be learned.

Comparisons have also been made between the ages at which children produce their first words and at which they produce their first signs. Hearing children have been reported to speak their initial words between the ages of 10 and 13 months (de Villiers & de Villiers, 1978). A broader age range has been documented for the production of the first signs by deaf children, from about 7 months (Hoffmeister & Wilbur, 1980; Orlansky & Bonvillian, 1985) to about 13 months (Schlesinger & Meadow, 1972).

These results should be interpreted with caution. It is difficult to determine the first words because of problems with the speech intelligibility of very young children. Another source of confusion is whether the pointing behaviors of young deaf children should be considered as different from those of young hearing children (Pettito, 1986). This is important because deaf children are given credit for gestures and pointing in the production of their first signs. Hearing children, however, are given credit only for speaking the actual words; their pointing behaviors are viewed as prelinguistic behaviors. Although more data are needed, it has been hypothesized that sign languages are not acquired earlier than spoken languages.

NEUROLINGUISTIC RESEARCH

Neurolinguistics is a growing, scientific discipline in the United States. One of the main tenets of this specialty is that a proper and adequate understanding of language depends on synthesizing information from a variety of fields concerned with the structure and function of both language and brain. Two of these important fields are neurology and linguistics. Critical insights can be gathered about the functions of the brain in the acquisition of language.

Research studies on language and brain functions have suggested a division of labor of the cerebral hemispheres for linguistic and nonlinguistic processes (Naremore, 1984). The left hemisphere seems to be specialized for language and other types of thinking and reasoning tasks whereas the right hemisphere is responsible for tasks that are generally visual-spatial in nature. There has been some research on cerebral dominance and the processing of sign language, as discussed earlier in Chapter 4. (See also the reviews in Obler, Zatorre, Galloway, & Vaid, 1982, and Poizner & Lane, 1979.) The focus has been on whether ASL is specialized in the left hemisphere because it is a language or in the right hemisphere because of its visual-spatial nature.

In a number of studies, a combination of printed words, drawings of signs and finger spelling, and/or geometric shapes were presented simultaneously to hearing and deaf individuals. It was reported that hearing adults showed a significant left hemisphere advantage for tasks involving the processing of English letters or words. Deaf adults also showed a trend in that direction. Both groups, however, evidenced right hemisphere advantages for finger spelling, ASL signs, and nonlinguistic input. In some cases, no hemispheric dominance was observed for geometric shapes, for signs and words combined, or for signs only (for deaf adults).

On the basis of these findings, it appears that ASL is processed predominantly by the right hemisphere of the brain. It has been argued, however, that most of these studies contained methodological problems (Neville & Bellugi, 1978; Poizner & Lane, 1979). For example, it is not certain that the deaf adults were native or near-native users of ASL. More important, there is debate whether tachistoscopical presentation of static (i.e., still pictures) signs reflects real-world processing of ASL.

In one study (Poizner, Battison, & Lane, 1979), deaf signers viewed English words, static signs, and signs portrayed with movements. Hearing participants viewed only printed words. Results indicated a left hemisphere advantage for words for both hearing and deaf persons. In addition, deaf persons showed a right hemisphere advantage for the static signs; however, no hemisphere advantage was observed for the moving signs. One interpretation of these findings was that signs may be bilaterally processed—that is, it is likely that signs are processed in both hemispheres of the brain (Neville & Bellugi, 1978; Obler et al., 1982).

Additional insights might be gained from a research review on bilingualism. It has been concluded that bilinguals show much greater right hemispheric processing than do monolinguals. The reasons for this phenomenon are not clear. It might be caused by, for example, culture-specific language and reading habits or by language-teaching methods. If deaf ASL signers are bilingual (e.g., if they know ASL and English), they may show greater right hemispheric specialization than those deaf persons who know only ASL. Several issues need to be considered, and more research is necessary to determine the hemispheric specialization of ASL. In sum, it is still not known whether sign languages are processed in the same area of the brain as spoken languages.

Up to now, the major purpose of linguistic, psycholinguistic, and neurolinguistic research on ASL has been to demonstrate that ASL is a bona fide language with developmental milestones that parallel those of spoken languages. At present, there is a need for researchers to explore how ASL can be used as an instructional tool in a bilingual program and/or a program to teach English as a second language (ESL). One of the major goals in these programs should be the development of English literacy skills. Before discussing what is known about the effects of ASL on English language development, it is important to describe how ASL differs from English and the English-based signed systems.

AMERICAN SIGN LANGUAGE AND ENGLISH

Given that ASL is one language and English is another language, it is or should be obvious that the grammars of ASL and English are not identical. American Sign Language has its own grammar, which is not derived from that of English (Lane & Grosjean, 1980; Klima & Bellugi, 1979; Wilbur, 1987). Thus, the rules pertaining to the various linguistic components are different for the two languages. For example, although ASL syntax primarily follows a subject-verb-object pattern, it is still less rigid than that of English, which is affected mainly by the sequential order of words. The grammar of ASL, like that of any other **minority language** coexisting in a majority-language culture, is influenced by the grammar of English. This can be observed in the use of finger-spelled loan signs as the sign, NG, which can be translated as *no good*.

Another example is the production of adjective signs before noun signs as in *SMART DOG*. As with any other two languages, it is generally possible to translate ASL utterances into English phrases or sentences, and vice versa. It is much less likely, however, to be able to translate individual ASL signs into individual English words or to go from words into signs.

As indicated previously, the most important difference between ASL and English is *form*. This is obvious in that English is a spoken language, making use of auditory and articulatory features (see Chapter 2), whereas ASL is a sign language and depends on the use of visual and gestural aspects. A closer inspection of this crucial difference, however, reveals that speech is predominantly processed in a sequential manner, and this influences the formation of the grammar of English. On the other hand, ASL grammar is organized and processed predominantly nonsequentially owing to its spatial-based nature (Supalla, 1986; Wilbur, 1987).

Consider inflectional morphology as an example. In English (and other spoken languages), inflectional morphemes such as plural (e.g., *-s*) and progressive (*-ing*) markers typically occur sequentially and affixally (i.e., at the beginning or end of the root word). In ASL, inflectional morphology is neither sequential nor affixal. Instead, morphemes are combined simultaneously in a spatial fashion. For example, the pluralization of *tree* in English requires a plural form such as *-s* that appears at the end of this word in a sequential manner. In ASL, the sign for *trees* entails the simultaneous occurrence of TREE and a sign morpheme marker (in this case, **reduplication** of the sign for TREE) in space.

The visual-spatial dimensions of ASL also provide other types of syntactic information such as subject-object relation and pronominal (e.g., pronouns) reference. This can be observed in the use of classifier forms, which contain more syntactic information than do single words of English (Kantor, 1980; Wilbur, 1987). By combining several morphemes in one sign, some forms involve the use of subject, direct and indirect objects, and verbs. Several signs are needed to convey the same message in the English-based signed systems. Figure 6.3 illustrates examples of classifiers. It can be seen that one of the most important differences between ASL and the English-based signed systems is the use of space to convey a complex array of linguistic and paralinguistic (e.g., intonation, intensity) information that is within the visual capabilities of the eye.

ASL and English-Based Signed Systems

If it is clear how ASL differs from English, it should also be evident that ASL is different from the English-based signed systems (discussed in detail in Chapter 7). Signed systems are forms of English-based signing; that is, they were constructed to represent manually to various degrees the syntactic structure of written, standard English (Quigley & Paul, 1984a; Quigley & Paul, 1987). In using these systems, there is an attempt to create artificially a one-to-one correspondence between a word in English and a sign in ASL for the purpose of teaching English grammar to deaf students.

Although the lexicon (i.e., vocabulary items) of ASL forms the basis of many signs in the English-based signed systems, it should be emphasized that there are several important modifications based on the structure of English. First, the signs are frozen. That is, they are executed only in their citation glosses (as presented, for example, in

CL:Å

For any stationary object such as a house, a vase, a statue, a lamp, a company, a business.

CL: ⊬

For winged aircraft.

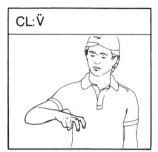

CL:V̈

For any small or crouched animal or human such as a frog, a mouse, a child sitting down, or a horse lying down.

Figure 6.3. Examples of classifiers.
T. Humphries, C. Padden, and T. J. O'Rourke, *A Basic Course in American Sign Language.* Silver Spring, MD: T. J. Publishers, 1980. Reprinted by permission.

dictionaries of signs), and thus do not retain their original syntactic and semantic properties as evident in the context of ASL. Second, contrived sign markers are used to reflect inflectional and derivational morphology, and these are presented sequentially rather than simultaneously. Finally, certain kinds of linguistic and paralinguistic information conveyed by spatial and nonmanual dimensions in ASL is seldom used in signed systems.

A simplified comparison of signed utterances in these two modalities illustrates some of the differences. Consider the following sentence: *Two boys are running to the chair.* In many signed systems (Gustason, Pfetzing, & Zawolkow, 1980), this sentence can be described as: (1) a sign for *two* (typically, two fingers that represent the number two), (2) a sign for *boy* (similar to the ASL sign) plus a contrived morphological marker for the plural *-s* (s-shaped, finger-spelled handshape), (3) a contrived sign for *are* (using an *r*-shaped, finger-spelled handshape coming off the lips), (4) a sign for *run* (starting at the signer and moving straight forward) plus a contrived morphological marker for *-ing* (*i*-shaped, finger-spelled handshape moving from one side to the other), (5) a sign for *to,* (6) a sign for *the,* and (7) a sign for *chair* (two fingers sit on thumb of *c*-shaped finger-spelled handshape). Thus, this utterance can be signed as:

TWO BOY + S ARE RUN + ING TO THE CHAIR.

There are several ways to sign this English sentence in ASL, depending on the context. The following is representative: (1) a sign for *boy* plus a sign for the number *two;* establish the boys in space to the signer's right; (2) a sign for *chair* (in ASL, this is a reduplication of the sign for *SIT,* that is, the sign is recorded as a double movement) (Humphries, Padden, & O'Rourke, 1980); establish the chair in space to the signer's left; (3) a sign for *run;* move the sign from the right to the left in a continuous, circular fashion (this reflects the progressive aspect of the verb and also indicates directionality). Thus, this utterance in ASL can be signed as:

> BOY, TWO (Classifier 1–1,
> hold classifier to the right); SIT–SIT (chair),
> POINT–LEFT; move the sign RUN Classifier 1–1 from
> right to left.

A more detailed description of the differences between ASL and some of the English-based signed systems can be found elsewhere (Supalla, 1986; Wilbur, 1987).

ASL and English Language Development

The effects of having learned ASL in infancy and early childhood, particularly in terms of educational achievement and the development of English literacy skills, have not been systematically investigated (Paul & Quigley, 1987a, 1987b; Quigley & Paul, 1989). These limited findings need to be interpreted with caution. First, most of the studies were conducted before an extensive description of a grammar of ASL was available. More important, it is not clear whether bilingualism (i.e., knowledge of ASL and English) was adequately evaluated (Paul, 1987; Stewart, 1985). Thus, the signing behaviors of deaf children and/or their parents may not have been accurately described.

To evaluate the effects on the acquisition of English of knowing ASL as a first language, most of the early investigations employed the paradigm of comparing deaf children of deaf parents (DCDP) with deaf children of hearing parents (DCHP). In a study of the academic behaviors of students (mostly in residential and day schools), it was reported that DCDP significantly outperformed DCHP in overall educational achievement, intelligence, psychosocial development, reading, written language, speech reading, finger spelling, and signing abilities (Meadow, 1968; Quigley & Frisina, 1961; Stuckless & Birch, 1966). Even having only one deaf parent was found to correlate with significant positive effects on achievement (Balow & Brill, 1975). The superior performances of deaf children of deaf parents were reported to be the result of exposure to early manual communication (presumably ASL) and a higher degree of parental acceptance.

The two factors, parental acceptance and manual communication, have been further investigated. Although parental acceptance influences academic success, it is not limited to parents who *sign* to their children. It can be found in home environments where both deaf or hearing parents use *speech* with their children (Corson, 1973; Messerly & Aram, 1980). Focusing mainly on the parental acceptance factor, one researcher reported that children of speech-using deaf parents performed better than those of sign-using deaf parents (Corson, 1973).

The work of Brasel and Quigley (1977) has demonstrated that the kind and use of manual communication are also important. They studied four groups of deaf students. One group had deaf parents who used English-based signing, a second group had deaf parents who used ASL, a third group had hearing parents who obtained and used intensive oral methods, and a fourth group of parents left the oral training of their children to the general school system. The group exposed to English-based signing was found to be significantly superior to the other groups on almost all the language and educational variables tested. The ASL group and the group exposed to intensive oral education performed about equally, whereas the group with average oral education was significantly inferior to all other groups. Brasel and Quigley concluded that early manual communication produced greater educational benefits than early oral communication and that English-based signing provided benefits over ASL for these deaf students.

What type of English-based signing—that is, which specific signed system to use—is still an open question (Luetke-Stahlman, 1988a, 1988b; Strong & Charlson, 1987; Chapter 7 of this book). In addition, it is still debatable whether manual communication is better than oral English communication or ASL in developing English skills. It may be that an effective communication mode is one that is fluent and intelligible to the child, is used consistently, and closely corresponds to written English (Quigley & Kretschmer, 1982). This can be seen in one study in which the academic achievement of students of hearing parents who used speech was reported to be significantly higher than that of matched counterparts, that is, students of deaf parents who used signing (Messerly & Aram, 1980).

In the earlier studies on manual communication, it is possible also that some, or even most, of the students who performed well on educational assessments might have had a range of competency in ASL as well as in English. Some support for this assertion can be found in more recent investigations (Hatfield, Caccamise, & Siple, 1978; Stewart, 1985). For example, Stewart (1985) examined the signing behaviors of students in Vancouver, British Columbia, Canada. Teachers and judges selected by the researchers described and rated the signing of high-school students in relation to ASL and **signed English** (i.e., English-based signing), which was supposedly used in the school. The students were required to view videotaped stories presented in the two communication systems and to retell the stories. All students were judged to be bilingual; however, most of them were labeled ASL-dominant. That is, the students' preferred mode of communication was reported to be ASL according to the results of the ratings, as was subsequently evident in their retelling of the stories.

Additional support for the bilingual hypothesis can be gleaned from studies that analyzed the signing of severely to profoundly hearing-impaired students supposedly exposed only to some form of English-based signing in the home and classroom environments (Kluwin, 1981a, 1981b; Livingston, 1983; Maxwell, 1985a; Supalla, 1986). It appears that most of these students who did not know ASL as a first language learned it or acquired it as they interacted with others who were native users or who incorporated many features of ASL in their signing. It was also argued that despite being exposed to a form of English-based signing for a number of years, these students had not achieved a high level of sign competency in English (see also the discussion in Chapter 7 of this book). The ease of acquisition of ASL is assumed to be mainly a result of its being better structured than the English-based signed systems for meeting the capabilities of the eyes for communication.

More research on the effects of ASL on the development of English is needed. As is discussed elsewhere in this book, however, studying the acquisition of English from this perspective only is not sufficient. In addition to communication system, educational achievement has been shown to be influenced by factors such as involvement of staff and school administration, content of curricula, competency of teachers, and the presence of oral communication skills such as speech and speech reading.

BILINGUALISM AND SECOND-LANGUAGE LEARNING

In recent years, a number of researchers have suggested that the language development of severely to profoundly hearing-impaired students should be investigated in relation to bilingualism and learning English as a second language (ESL) (Quigley & Paul, 1984b; Reagan, 1985). These issues, however, are shrouded in controversy and confusion. Part of the problem is a lack of understanding of what constitutes bilingualism, or second-language learning. There is also disagreement on what language or languages students know when they begin school. Many students are not assessed for language and/or system dominance (Luetke-Stahlman, 1982; Luetke-Stahlman & Weiner, 1982). In addition, debate continues on the most useful type of program and instructional methods to implement. As stated by Paul & Quigley (1987b):

> . . . should American Sign Language and English be developed concurrently in infancy and early childhood as in a bilingual environment? Or, should ASL be taught as a first language to all deaf students, and then English as a second language? Finally, should English be taught as a second language only to students who know ASL as a first language or to all deaf students? (p. 139)

The answers to these questions are influenced by an understanding of how English can be acquired through the use of ASL. After discussing briefly bilingualism, second-language learning, and language competence of severely to profoundly hearing-impaired students, we argue why and how ASL should be used to teach English literacy skills.

Language and Culture

A widely used, acceptable definition of bilingualism, or second-language learning, does not exist in the literature (Cummins, 1984). There is agreement that a complete description should include at least the degree of competence in comprehension and production of both the spoken and written modes of *two* languages. In addition, it is important to consider the home environment or culture of the students. In general, the distinction between bilingualism and second-language learning depends on when the languages are learned. This distinction is important for the implementation of instructional programs, methods, and goals. It is also critical for the comparison of the processes of second-language learning with those of first language learning, and comparison should include limited users of a language. A more detailed treatment of these issues can be found in Quigley and Paul (1984a).

Describing the language and culture of hearing-impaired students is not a simple matter and must be considered in relation to the type of communication taking place at home during infancy and early childhood. It is also necessary to consider the results of linguistic and educational assessments. A case can be made for the instructional use of ASL and the teaching of English as a second language for some, perhaps most, severely to profoundly hearing-impaired students (Paul, 1987; Paul, 1988b; Paul & Gramly, 1986; Quigley & Paul, 1984b).

In the home environments of hearing-impaired children in the United States, at least three languages have been identified and investigated: English, Spanish, and ASL (King, 1981; Schildroth & Karchmer, 1986). In addition, it is possible to use one or more communication modes, that is, speech, signs, or both simultaneously (or separately, as in the case of ASL and some form of English). For example, it has been reported that deaf children of Spanish parents are exposed to both spoken Spanish and some form of English-based signing (Luetke-Stahlman, 1982).

As to input, we can conclude that because most children in the United States have English-speaking parents, they are exposed to English, most likely in some form of English-based signing (Gallaudet Research Institute, 1985; Jordan & Karchmer, 1986). Therefore, the culture of most hearing-impaired children resembles that of their English-speaking parents.

Only deaf parents with severely to profoundly hearing-impaired children are most likely to use ASL. About 3 percent of these children have two deaf parents, and an additional 6 percent have at least one deaf parent. Not all deaf parents, however, use ASL with their children. Some parents use a form of English-based signing, some use ASL and some form of English (Brasel & Quigley, 1977; Collins-Ahlgren, 1974; Schlesinger & Meadow, 1972), and some speak only English to their children (Corson, 1973).

Despite this exposure to English in the home, we can assume that most severely to profoundly hearing-impaired children do not have an adequate command of spoken or signed English when they begin their formal education. It is clear from the results of secondary language assessments that this low level of achievement persists throughout their school years. As discussed in detail in Chapter 8, the results of national surveys consistently reveal that the majority of 18-to-19-year-old students who are severely to profoundly hearing-impaired graduate from high school programs able to read and write no better than average hearing students of 9 to 10 years (Allen, 1986; Quigley & Paul, 1986, 1989).

In sum, most students are unsuccessful in learning English as a first language or even at all. Some students, however, do come to school knowing ASL as a first language. For these students, at least, English should be taught as a second language using techniques found to be effective in bilingual or second-language learning programs.

A Case for ASL/ESL

The case for ASL/ESL can be argued from two general perspectives: (1) linguistic and cultural considerations, and (2) the effectiveness of current methods and programs (Paul, 1987; Quigley & Paul, 1984b, 1987). A third perspective, the incompatibility between using a contrived signed system and spoken English simultaneously, is discussed in the next chapter.

There is no doubt that some students know ASL as a first language. It is also probable that *most* severely to profoundly hearing-impaired students will learn ASL either by the time they complete their formal education or during their adulthood (Maxwell, 1983; Stewart, 1985; Supalla, 1986). Unlike most other students, ASL-using students are equipped with well-developed cognitive and linguistic foundations (in relation to ASL). In addition, like other first-language learners, they have used hypothesis-testing phenomena such as **underextensions** and **overextensions** (e.g., signing CHAIR for only one particular type of chair or ORANGE JUICE for all juices). These and other strategies of learning a first language should make it possible for them to acquire a second language in a bilingual or second-language education program. Like members of other minority-language groups, these students should be considered **linguistically different,** not **linguistically deficient.**

Most of these students are or will become members of a unique minority culture group—the Deaf culture—and thus culturally different. Many features of this culture are related to the use of ASL, but other important values, attitudes, and traditions are also evident (Padden, 1980). Most of these students are assimilated into Deaf culture. They are not born into it as are hearing minority children from non-English-speaking families. Membership in the Deaf culture is contingent mainly on communicative competence in ASL.

Another argument for the consideration of bilingual, or ESL, programs stems from the ineffectiveness of current programs and methods. As discussed in Chapter 7, since the 1970s, most hearing-impaired students have been educated in Total Communication programs in which signing and speech are used simultaneously (Gallaudet Research Institute, 1985; Jordan & Karchmer, 1986). Despite improvement in the construction of assessments and the implementation of early intervention, or preschool, programs, most severely to profoundly hearing-impaired students are still functionally illiterate when they graduate from high school.

Many educators have not accepted ASL as part of the philosophy of Total Communication. Therefore, the use of ASL as an instructional tool to teach English has not been extensively documented. In the few existing studies, the emphasis was on **grammatical acceptability** or grammatical **unacceptability** in ASL and English (Crutchfield, 1972; Jones, 1979). For example, in a recent study, elementary school students were taught to translate grammatical features of ASL into written English (Marbury & Mackinson-Smyth, 1986). After viewing a signed story in ASL, teachers and students discussed the main characters and events. The students were directed to focus their attention on ASL features in the signed story and to incorporate these into their translations. Teachers and students created a final draft of the story in English. There is a need for more studies as well as a greater emphasis on using more recent instructional approaches found to be effective in second-language learning programs (Paul, 1985; Paul & Quigley, 1987b).

If it is clear that ASL is a bona fide language separate from English and English-based signing and that most severely to profoundly hearing-impaired students are likely to have a range of competency in ASL, then it is proposed that these students be educated in a bilingual education program so that we can better understand the effects of ASL on the development of English. Curricular and instructional activities should be based on the prevailing findings in the research on literacy and on hearing minority-language students. Because this is likely to become one of the most important issues in the education of deaf students, we discuss at length the rationale and basic tenets of our proposed program and provide some examples of instructional activities.

BILINGUAL EDUCATION PROGRAM

On the basis of a synthesis of research studies on hearing minority-language students (Cummins, 1984; Quigley & Paul, 1984a), it is proposed that ASL-using deaf students be educated in a bilingual minority-language **immersion program.** In an immersion program, the emphasis is on developing and maintaining communicative competence in the native, or first, language, which in this case is ASL. Eventually, equal treatment is given to teaching English literacy, educational, and cultural concepts.

This kind of program, also called the **native language approach,** has these general principles:

1. Instruction in the early grades is in the first language (L1) only.
2. Reading and writing are introduced and developed in L1.
3. During grade 3, instruction is conducted in L1 and the second, or target, language (L2).
4. Reading and writing are introduced and developed in L2.

It is possible to implement only 1, 3, and 4 because ASL does not have a written component. Nevertheless, the use and study of ASL in a bilingual education setting should offer insights regarding the acquisition of a spoken language whose *form,* as well as grammar, is different from that of a sign language. Specifically, educators and researchers can investigate how ASL-using deaf students learn to read and write in English when they have little or no access to the phonological code of that language.

Instruction in ASL

From preschool to about the third grade, all instruction is conducted by immersion in ASL. It is important to develop students' understanding of the grammar and use of ASL and to help them perform cognitive tasks necessary for the later development of literacy, such as following directions, answering questions, solving problems, organizing ideas, and making inferences (Bowen, Madsen, & Hilferty, 1985). In addition, students should acquire a wide range of information or real-world knowledge about Deaf culture and the majority culture of the United States.

To develop **grammatical** and communicative **competence,** students need to use ASL in a variety of situations and topics that are meaningful and interesting. They can participate by sharing their experiences in activities such as show-and-tell, seeking and giving information, learning to make or do something, discussing hobbies and leisure interests, and solving problems. These tasks should be constructed so that they appeal to young students in the primary grades.

Reading-Related Activities

In bilingual minority-language immersion programs, literacy is typically introduced and established in the native language after students have achieved proficiency in the primary form (e.g., speech) of that language. American Sign Language does not have a written form, but there are still many activities that can be developed to help facilitate the later acquisition of literacy skills in English. These include classification tasks such as recognizing and using synonyms, antonyms, and **semantic maps** (i.e., connecting a word or phrase with related words expressing attributes or characteristics). These vocabulary/language activities are important for ". . . building bridges between the new and unknown in the minds of learners'' (Johnson & Pearson, 1984, p. 37).

Students must develop other high-level skills critical for reading comprehension—for example, applying **prior knowledge** and experiences, thinking about what they know or how they think (metacognitive ability), and answering different levels of questions. As is discussed in Chapter 8, research has demonstrated convincingly that comprehension is markedly influenced by prior knowledge or previously acquired experiences that learners bring to the task, especially in reading (Anderson, 1985; Anderson & Pearson, 1984). To construct meaning, learners must apply their prior or world knowledge—that is, they must understand new information by relating it to what they already know. Consequently, reading or reading-related instruction should focus on enriching the background knowledge of students and on teaching them ways to use it.

The foregoing discussion also applies to comprehension of stories presented in a primary mode, such as signing in ASL. Consider the following story, either signed or on videotape, as an example (Paul & Gramly, 1986):

Story

It is a beautiful Saturday morning. Jerry thinks it's a good day to read a book. However, he can't decide where to go. Should he go to the library? Should he read at the lake? The river? Well, since he wanted to be outside, Jerry decided to walk down to the river. He knew a perfect spot. When Jerry arrived at the river, he saw a huge tree with long branches hanging over part of the river bank. A great place to sit and read! (p. 14)

To activate and enrich the students' real-world knowledge, the following questions can be asked (signed) before viewing the story:

What do you like to do on a beautiful Saturday morning?
Does anyone like to read a book?
Do you have a favorite book?
Where do you like to read your book?
Have you ever read a book outside? Where?
Have you ever read a book by the lake or river?
Where did you sit? Why did you decide to sit there?

Students should think about the questions and answers as they view the story. They should also be told why they are being asked these questions. At the end of the story, the teacher can ask some students to retell the story to the rest of the class. In addition, questions that are related specifically to the story can be discussed, for example:

What day was it?
What did Jerry decide to do?
Where did he go?

Does Jerry like to read books?
Do you like to read books?
What else do you like to read?

Keep in mind that students may need to view a story several times if they are to answer questions from memory. As an alternative, they can view the story repeatedly as they search for the answers to the signed questions.

Instruction in ASL and English

Beginning with grade 3, instructional activities are introduced through English by signing (with speech as an option). The selection of a specific English-based signed system to use in this program is problematic and complex. It is recommended that the signing resemble that used by members of the Deaf community/culture when they communicate with signers who are not competent in ASL (Paul & Quigley, 1987b). Initially, ASL remains the predominant medium of instruction. Eventually, a bilingual and bicultural environment is established and maintained, and the two languages are used more or less equally throughout the school day. The major objective is to develop grammatical and communicative competence in English.

As in first-language teaching, there is no one best way to teach a second language. Approaches vary with teaching and learning styles, as is borne out by the limited research on language development and deafness (McAnally, Rose, & Quigley, 1987; Quigley & Paul, 1984a). Therefore, a panorama of natural and structural techniques should be implemented.

During the third grade, speech, speech reading, and auditory training activities can be implemented in the classroom. This is a controversial issue. It should be remembered, however, that hearing minority-language students in other minority-language immersion programs may not have received spoken input in the target language until the middle elementary grades. Research documents that this has very little or no long-lasting subsequent effects on the educational achievement or literacy level of these students (Cummins, 1984).

Reading and writing in English can be implemented during the third grade along with instruction in the other content areas. Literacy should be viewed as an **interactive** process in which students need to understand grammatical rules and engage in high-level thinking skills (King & Quigley, 1985). This interactive perspective should guide the development of all curricular and instructional activities and approaches.

Using ASL may be helpful in explaining difficult aspects of the written language of English; however, *it cannot or should not supplant the text*. Students also need structured lessons in dealing with certain grammar problems. Because these students are not competent in English, it would be most beneficial to present written information (e.g., vocabulary, syntax) in a spiraling or cyclical fashion. This means proceeding from simple to complex ideas and reinforcing (presenting) them repeatedly (King & Quigley, 1985; Quigley & King, 1981, 1982, 1983, 1984). Students need numerous opportunities to read and write and to share language experiences that develop comprehension and problem-solving strategies.

Evaluation

Can severely to profoundly hearing-impaired students learn to read and write in English through ASL only? As discussed in Chapter 8 on secondary language development, there are many important factors to consider in the comprehension of print. It should be obvious that the use of ASL is not sufficient. There is adequate documentation, however, to justify the establishment of a bilingual education program for some students. A case can be made also for other students for whom ASL is not a first language or for those who might not have a first, or native, language.

It is important, however, that such a program be evaluated experimentally—that is, the effects of ASL on academic achievement must be assessed. To accomplish this objective, there is a need to develop an adequate assessment of both ASL and English-based signing. The evaluation of a bilingual minority-language program should consider, but not be limited to, the following areas (Paul & Quigley, 1987b):

1. Identification of deaf students for placement in a bilingual program.
2. Assessment of grammatical and communication competency in ASL.
3. Evaluation of achievement in academic subjects presented via ASL.
4. Assessment of grammatical and communicative competency in English.
5. Evaluation of achievement in academic subjects presented via English.
6. Evaluation of psychosocial aspects (e.g., attitude, motivation). (p. 163)

In relation to evaluation, Quigley and Paul (1984a) have aptly stated that:

> Given the large body of research and practice with minority hearing children to draw from in establishing ASL/ESL programs and the probable willingness of deaf *and hearing* [words and emphasis added] parents to have their deaf children involved in such programs, it should be possible to initiate the programs carefully, evaluate them experimentally, and establish a data base on their effectiveness. (p. 197)

SUMMARY

The major objective of this chapter was to describe American Sign Language and to discuss its effects on severely to profoundly hearing-impaired students' educational achievement and development of English literacy skills. The chapter presented recent thinking on the linguistic, psycholinguistic, and neurolinguistic aspects of ASL and demonstrated how it is different from English and the English-based signed systems. In discussing the effects of ASL on the development of English, tentative answers were provided to two of the most important questions facing educators of hearing-impaired students: (1) What is the first, or primary, language of the students, and (2) Is it possible for the students to learn a spoken language through the use of a sign language? It was argued that the solutions to these queries were based on very limited data. To better assess the acquisition of English by ASL-using students, it was proposed that some, perhaps most, severely to profoundly hearing-impaired students be educated in a bilingual minority-language immersion program. The curricular and instructional practices of this program should adhere to the prevailing thinking in the research on hearing minority-language students and on reading and writing. Finally, it was argued that bilingual education programs should be evaluated experimentally, and guidelines for such an evaluation were suggested.

The scientific study of ASL began with the seminal work of Stokoe, and descriptions of its grammar appeared during the late 1970s. It is widely accepted that ASL is a bona fide language governed by rules pertaining to the major components of a language: phonology, syntax, semantics, and pragmatics. For example, there are phonological rules to follow for executing a sign just as there are phonological rules for speaking a word. It was emphasized that a complete description of a sign includes both manual and nonmanual movements. The latter group has caused considerable problems for educators in understanding the signing of hearing-impaired students.

Psycholinguistic and neurolinguistic research on ASL have focused on the perception, production, and acquisition of signs. Parallels in processing and in developmental stages have been observed between ASL signers and speakers of English, one of the most important of which is that the relation between a sign and its referent is arbitrary and thus must be learned. This has provided further support for the notion that sign languages are in fact bona fide linguistic systems. There is still considerable debate on whether signs are learned earlier than words, and whether ASL is predominantly processed in the left or right hemisphere of the brain.

In the education of hearing-impaired students, the major thrust of future research on ASL should concentrate on its effects on the development of English literacy skills, and subsequently, educational achievement. ASL is a visual-gestural, spatially based language, whereas English is primarily an auditory-articulatory, sequentially based language. Thus, ASL differs from English and from the English-based signed systems in grammar and form. In our view, the most important difference is that of *form,* and more research is needed to determine whether a spoken language can be adequately represented and acquired through the use of a manual form.

That there are very limited data on the effects of ASL on the development of English was discussed. We suggested that this issue might best be investigated within the context of a bilingual minority-language immersion program. Most severely to profoundly hearing-impaired students begin school with no knowledge of any language. If students come to school knowing a language, it is most likely to be ASL. A case for using ASL/ESL with these students, and perhaps with other students as well, can be made in relation to language and culture considerations and to the verified limited results of other language-teaching approaches.

The chapter described at length the principles of our proposed bilingual education program and presented some examples of instructional practices because we feel that bilingual education will soon become one of the most important issues facing educators of hearing-impaired students. The major goals of the program during the first few elementary years are to develop and maintain grammatical and communicative competence in ASL. English literacy and English-based signing activities for communication and instruction, as well as training in speech, speech reading, and the use of audition, are introduced during grade 3. As the students' knowledge of English increases, both ASL and English eventually can be used more or less equally throughout the school day. Proficiency in English is dependent in part on providing adequate, meaningful, systematic exposure to signed and written English in the classroom. Because there is no *best* language-teaching method, a wide variety of approaches were recommended. It is important to develop grammatical and communicative competence in English literacy. Finally, it was emphasized that any bilingual program must be experimentally evaluated.

COMPREHENSION

1. TRUE or FALSE?
   a. Historically, much of what is known about language acquisition and development has come from the study of both spoken and sign languages.
   b. Sign languages, like signed systems, are derived from spoken languages.
2. List and describe the four major linguistic components of a language.
3. American Sign Language is (select all that apply)
   a. A rule-governed language.
   b. Derived from American English.
   c. A visual-gestural language.
   d. Influenced by English in the United States.
   e. Typically executed simultaneously with spoken English.
4. The sign order of ASL syntax is (select applicable items)
   a. Verb-subject-object.
   b. Subject-verb-object.
   c. Subject-object-verb.
   d. Object-verb-subject.
   e. All of the above.
5. List and describe the four cherological (i.e., phonological) parameters of a sign.
6. TRUE or FALSE? Raising the eyebrows is a nonmanual aspect of signing.
7. Raising the eyebrows in ASL signals (select applicable items)
   a. A wh- question.
   b. A yes/no question.
   c. A negative statement.
   d. A positive statement.
   e. All of the above.
8. What does it mean to state that psycholinguistic development in sign languages may be similar to that of spoken languages? Use *negation* as an example.
9. TRUE or FALSE? The relation between a sign and its referent is pictorial, or ideographic. That is, individuals with no prior knowledge of a sign language can easily guess the meanings of most signs in that language.
10. TRUE or FALSE? Deaf children acquire a sign language at an earlier age than hearing children acquire a spoken language.
11. Neurolinguistic research has shown conclusively that ASL is processed (select applicable items)
   a. In the left hemisphere of the brain only.
   b. In the right hemisphere of the brain only.
   c. In both hemispheres.
   d. The processing of ASL is still not clear.
   e. None of the above.
12. Name and discuss two major ways in which ASL is different from English.
13. Which of the following statements is/are TRUE concerning the research on ASL and the development of English?

    a. The effects of ASL have been systematically studied since 1950.

    b. Early studies showed that deaf children of deaf parents perform better than deaf children of hearing parents.

    c. All deaf parents sign to their deaf children and only those children who have been exposed to signing perform well academically.

    d. Later studies showed that kind and use of communication mode are important for English language development.

    e. It is now clear that ASL is better than the English-based signed systems in developing English.

14. The case for ASL/ESL can be argued from two general perspectives. Briefly describe them.

15. Which of the following statements is/are TRUE about the bilingual education program proposed by the authors?

    a. It is a bilingual minority-language immersion program.

    b. Both ASL and English are used during the first three grades.

    c. Speech and auditory training skills are taught in the first grade.

    d. Instruction in the early grades is in ASL only.

    e. Reading and writing in English is introduced after communicative competency is achieved in ASL.

SUGGESTED ACTIVITIES

1. Ask someone who knows ASL to show you several animal and food signs. Can you guess the meaning of any of the signs?

2. You will need the following book: Humphries, T., Padden, C., & O'Rourke, T. J. (1980). *A basic course in American Sign Language*. Silver Spring, MD: National Association of the Deaf.

Describe how the following English words and sentences are signed in ASL.

    a. Words: boy, boys, woman, women, tree, trees, forest, sit, chair.

    b. Sentences:

        The girl gave the book to the boy.

        Open the window, please.

        Do you want some coffee?

        I don't want to see the movie.

        What's up!?!

3. Find out the following information:

    a. Is ASL taught as a course in your college or university?

        If so, is the instructor *certified* to teach it?

    b. Is ASL accepted as a foreign language requirement (similar to French, Spanish)? If not, why not?

FURTHER READINGS

Baker, C., & Padden, C. (1978). *American Sign Language: A look at its history, structure, and community*. Silver Spring, MD: T.J. Publishers.

Hoemann, H. (1978). *Communicating with deaf people: A resource manual for teachers and students of American Sign Language*. Baltimore, MD: University Park Press.

Markowicz, H. (1977). *American Sign Language: Fact and fancy*. Washington, DC: Gallaudet University Press.

Schlesinger, I., & Namir, L. (1978). *Sign Language of the Deaf: Psychological, linguistic, and sociological perspectives*. New York: Academic Press.

Siple, P. (Ed.). (1978). *Understanding language through sign language research*. New York: Academic Press.

Stokoe, W. (1972). *Semiotics and human sign languages*. The Hague: Mouton.

Stokoe, W. (1973). *Bilingual research program*. Washington, DC: Gallaudet University Press.

van Uden, A. (1986). *Sign languages of deaf people and psycholinguistics: A critical evaluation*. Lisse, Netherlands: Swets & Zeitlinger.

CHAPTER 7

Signed Systems

MAJOR POINTS TO CONSIDER

The three major categories of language/communication approaches

Some differences between a signed system and a sign language

Characteristics of English-based signed systems

Effectiveness of signed systems in developing English

The nature and extent of the signing of hearing-impaired students, their parents, and teachers

Relationship between knowing a signed system and developing English literacy skills

Typically, most hearing children acquire a spoken language with little difficulty. These children have internalized a number of grammatical rules by the time they begin their school years. That is, they have an intuitive idea of how their language works. Hearing children learn a language through exposure and use, but severely to profoundly hearing-impaired children who are not exposed to a comprehensive, complete, and consistent language or system have to be taught their first language. Most educators know that teaching a spoken language such as English to these students is not an easy task.

One of the most controversial debates in education about deafness is the type of signed system that should be used by teachers and parents/caretakers with hearing-impaired children (Quigley & Kretschmer, 1982; Quigley & Paul, 1984a). Previously, we have discussed two other language communication approaches: oral English and American Sign Language (ASL). In this chapter, we focus on the various English-based signed systems that have been developed for educational purposes. After describing the basic tenets of several systems, we show the relationship of these approaches to the structure of English. Then, we present a synthesis of research findings regarding the use and effects of each signed system on the development of English. Given that most of the systems have been in use for at least 15 years, we can discuss whether English as a spoken language can be represented adequately in a signed mode. Finally, we present some tentative conclusions that are based on the available data and the implications of them for further research efforts.

MANUALLY CODED ENGLISH

For the unsophisticated observer or even a teacher of hearing-impaired students, the process of learning to sign has become a complicated matter. There is the problem of what to learn given the variety of signed systems with names such as the Rochester Method, **Seeing Essential English, Signing Exact English, Manual English, Linguistics of Visual English, Signed English, Pidgin Sign English,** and the **Paget-Gorman Sign System.** In general, practitioners often make three assumptions about the various signed systems: (1) These are all English sign languages, (2) it is permissible to borrow *signs* from different systems to communicate concepts because all systems are based on one language, English, and (3) long-term exposure and use of the systems should result in competency in English (Quigley & Paul, 1984a; Wilbur, 1987).

The first assumption can be refuted by a clear understanding of the differences between a *language* and a *system* or *code*. Briefly, a language is a naturally developed **conventional system of arbitrary signals** decided on by the users of a language community to represent and communicate their ideas in a variety of home and social situations (Bloom & Lahey, 1978; de Villiers & de Villiers, 1978). As rule-governed symbol systems, languages are generative and are capable of evolving over time. By *generative,* we mean that native users have an intuitive knowledge of linguistic rules that they are able to understand and produce an infinite number of utterances, including those to which they have not been exposed. Because of extensive, long-term use of a language by many users in a variety of communicative settings, changes have occurred in pronunciation, spelling, and meanings of words. In addition, new words and concepts are often added to suit the needs of the language community.

It is true that a language is transmitted or expressed by a system or code, that is, conventional symbols agreed on by the users. Spoken languages are manifested by speech codes, whereas sign languages are executed with signed codes. Linguistic codes are natural, agreed-on representations of their respective languages and have evolved over time through use. Speakers or signers have little or no problems with variations of the codes such as **dialects** or styles. To understand and produce an utterance, a speaker or signer must have knowledge of the grammatical and pragmatic rules of a language and how these are represented in the code.

Signed systems are forms of English-based signing because they attempt to reflect the grammar of English manually. From this perspective, we can say that the systems are codes for transmitting English and can be considered as Manually Coded English. There are several problems with this viewpoint. First, all codes have been contrived or invented by a small group of persons. Second, they are not widely used outside of a specific educational environment (Gallaudet Research Institute, 1985; Jordan & Karchmer, 1986). Thus, the codes are artificially created for esoteric purposes, and their evolutionary changes are dependent on those that occur naturally in the speech or written codes of English. A particular signed system functions like the Morse code, in which dots and dashes are used to represent the alphabet of a language. Because signed systems do not evolve naturally, do not have separate linguistic components (e.g., syntax or semantics), and are dependent on the spoken languages that they represent, they cannot be considered as *sign languages*.

Another major difficulty with the signed codes can be seen in their relationship to the English language. Although they are all based on the structure of written, standard English, the rules for representing the grammar of English varies across the signed systems. One reason for differences in rules is obvious: The best way to represent English manually is still debatable.

One of the problems, however, is that many practitioners use signs from various systems to suit their needs. It is important to emphasize that these signs have been formed using different sets of rules. The rules for creating and using signs in one system are different from those for signs in another system. Borrowing signs from two or more systems makes it difficult for hearing-impaired children to receive consistent input so that they can form reliable hypotheses about the language they are trying to learn. With limited, and for the most part, unambiguous input, learners intuitively discover underlying, unspoken regularities or rules. Hearing-impaired children may be exposed to difficult rules in a haphazard or ambiguous manner, and thus they cannot internalize the grammatical aspects of English.

Probably the best argument for the unreliable, inconsistent relationship between the various systems and their representation of English can be seen in the limited results in achievement. Despite 15 or more years of use for most of the commonly used systems and their variations, there is little evidence of pervasive effects on English literacy or levels of educational achievement. The data on most of the approaches, however, should be interpreted with caution because practitioners do not always adhere to the rules of a particular system while signing. In fact, most teachers or practitioners do not follow a particular system but sign and speak in some simultaneous fashion (Jordan & Karchmer, 1986).

DESCRIPTION OF SIGNED SYSTEMS

Despite the great number of signed systems, their conception and use are not new. The first formal system was created in France by the Abbé de l'Epée who wanted to teach the grammar of French to his deaf students. He constructed Signed French by modifying the signs of the French Sign Language of the Deaf community and adding new, contrived signs (Lane, 1984; McAnally, Rose, & Quigley, 1987). In England, Sir Richard Paget developed the first English-based signing system, naming it A New Sign Language. After his death, the system underwent revisions and became A Systematic Sign Language, and finally, the Paget-Gorman Sign System.

David Anthony is credited with producing the first signed system in the United

States. It was done as his masters thesis at Eastern Michigan University (Anthony, 1966). Subsequently, Anthony's system, eventually named Seeing Essential English (SEE I), spawned the creation of others in America. Many of these signed systems have adopted some of the basic principles of SEE I.

A close inspection of the basics of the various signed systems reveals that they are all based on two languages, American Sign Language and English. Like the earlier work of de l'Epée, the creators attempted to modify the sign language of the Deaf community, ASL, and add new signs for the purpose of teaching the grammar of the majority language, in this case, English. In short, all systems adhere to an English word order. Another point in common is that the signed systems are supposed to be used with speech. That is, educators typically sign and speak simultaneously to hearing-impaired children in the classroom. As is discussed later, this has caused some problems with the use of the more cumbersome systems, that is, those that require several signs to represent the components of a single English word. In addition, speech, which provides important linguistic information, may not be readily accessible to severely to profoundly hearing-impaired students.

Some of the major differences between the English-based signed systems and ASL were described in Chapter 6. One of the crucial objectives of the various systems is to represent English in a manual mode as unambiguously as possible (Gustason, Pfetzing, & Zawolkow, 1972, 1980). The differences among the systems are a result of the many arbitrary decisions that have been made regarding certain grammatical aspects of English. For example, the creators contended with such issues as how to represent the various aspects of plurality (e.g., *boy* to *boys, man* to *men, ox* to *oxen*) and past tense (e.g., *walk* to *walked, run* to *ran, learn* to *learned*). Although all systems follow an English word order, they have different rules for the formation and use of signs. As is discussed later, one of the most important differences among the commonly used signed systems is their treatment of what constitutes a **root,** or **base, word** in English.

Rochester Method

In the Rochester Method (RM), finger spelling and speech are used simultaneously. This system was named after the Rochester School for the Deaf where it originated in the late 19th century (Scouten, 1984). In the Soviet Union, this method is called Neo-oralism, indicating that initially finger spelling was used to supplement oral approaches in teaching deaf children (Moores, 1987).

Finger spelling (dactylology) is a means of representing the alphabet and number system. In the United States, there are 26 distinct handshapes that correspond to the letters of the alphabet (see Figure 7.1). Finger spelling in the United States, France, Italy, and other European countries is executed with one hand. England, Australia, and other present and former members of the British Empire use a two-handed alphabet.

Finger spelling is a code for the written language system of English. Like the other signed systems, it is also similar to the Morse code. The major differences between finger spelling and writing can be seen in the areas of representation, presentation, and processing. Writing is a secondary form that represents speech, which is the primary mode of a spoken language, whereas finger spelling is a manual representation of the secondary form, or writing. Thus, the sender and receiver must know English, its al-

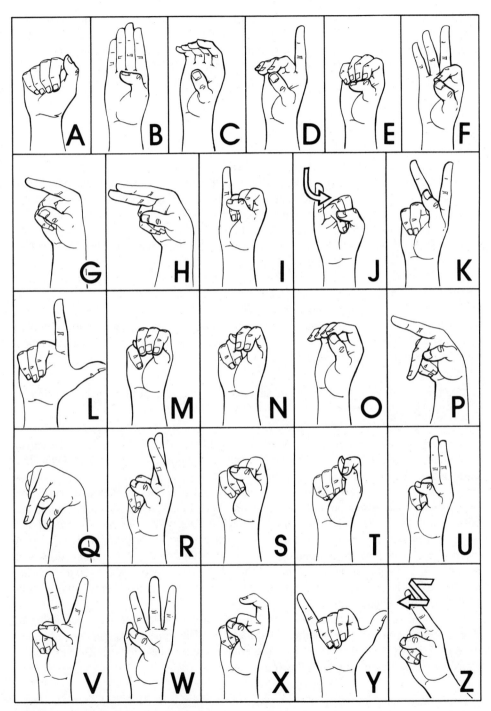

Figure 7.1. The alphabet of finger spelling.
T. Humphries, C. Padden, and T. J. O'Rourke, *A Basic Course in American Sign Language.* Silver Spring, MD: T. J. Publishers, 1980. Reprinted by permission.

phabet system, and the relationship between finger spelling and the alphabet. Writing is more or less permanent in that readers can proceed at their own pace and reread whenever necessary, but finger spelling is similar to speech in that it is transitory and serial. Finger spelling is processed differently from writing. There is some evidence to suggest that native ASL signers process finger spelling differently from nonnative signers (Padden & Le Master, 1985).

Seeing Essential English

The precursor of Seeing Essential English (SEE I) was the work of David Anthony in 1962 in Lapeer, Michigan (Bornstein, 1973). Anthony tried to create a manual system that would improve the English language skills of severely to profoundly hearing-impaired students. This work continued throughout the 1960s and was completed as his masters thesis. As stated previously, the thesis was the origin of Anthony's signed system, Seeing Essential English. The thesis has never been published; however, copies of it have been widely disseminated.

In 1969, Anthony became part of a formal group consisting of deaf adults, teachers, parents, and interpreters. This group met in Hollywood, California, to discuss further the idea of developing signs to represent English (Gustason, 1983; Gustason et al., 1980). In a matter of a few months, the group created a name, Seeing Essential English, and developed guidelines for the formation and use of signs. Two of the ten tenets agreed on by the members were (Gustason, 1983):

> 1) Any specific sign should mean one thing, and one thing only, and 2) English should be signed as it is spoken. This is especially true of idioms. (p. 41)

Seeing Essential English, a two-volume set, appeared in 1971. In SEE I, English words are categorized into three groups: basic, **compound,** and **complex.** Typically, basic words may be whole or complete words, as in *girl* and *the,* or bound roots as *hospice* in *hospital* or *gene* in *genetic, general,* and *generous.* Compound words are two or more basic words put together, as *butterfly* and *understand.* Complex words are basic words with **inflections** (e.g., *-ing*) and affixes (e.g., *un-, -ness*), as in *talked* and *girls.* In general, one sign is used to represent a base word. Additional signs or sign markers correspond to the morphological aspects of the words, that is, inflections and affixes. For example, in the word *slowly,* the root, or base, word is *slow* and *-ly* is the **suffix** marker. In SEE I, one sign represents *slow* and a sign marker represents *-ly* as in SLOW LY (see Figure 7.2).

The signs used to form a word are based on a two-out-of-three rule pertaining to three criteria: pronunciation, spelling, and meaning. The same sign is produced for two or more English words if two of the three criteria are the same for the affected words. Consider the word *right* in the following sentences:

1. John make a *right* turn.
2. That answer is *right.*
3. You have a *right* to do that.

SLOW

Palms–down, right hand moves slowly up back of horizontal left hand

–LY

(ALT. 1)

Palm-out I–L hand shakes downward

–LY

(ALT. 2)

Form L and then Y

Figure 7.2. Sign and sign markers for SLOWLY.
G. Gustason, D. Pfetzing, and E. Zawolkow, *Signing Exact English*. Los Alamitos, CA: Modern Signs Press, 1980. Reprinted by permission.
Note: Signing Exact English is SEE II.There is much overlap between SEE I and SEE II.

The same sign should be used to express the word *right* in each sentence because two criteria, pronunciation and spelling, are the same.

Signing Exact English

Some members of the group that met with Anthony in California did not agree with some of the sign formation rules of SEE I. Subsequently, one group led by Gustason et al. (1972) developed Signing Exact English (SEE II). There is much overlap between SEE I and SEE II, especially in the lexicon (about 75 percent of the signs) and the use of affixes (Bornstein, 1973). In addition, both systems follow the two-out-of-three rule described previously. The only exception to the rule is that inflected basic words (i.e., complex words) are not considered to be new words. For example, a past tense marker (irregular form) is added to the sign SEE to produce the word *saw*. This is not the same sign for either the noun *saw* or the verb in *to saw* (past tense is *sawed*).

The major difference between SEE I and SEE II centers on the concept of what constitutes a root word. This affects the manner in which compound and complex words are signed. It was demonstrated previously that the English words, *butterfly* and *understand,* are treated as two basic words in SEE I, and thus two signs are used to represent each word, BUTTER FLY and UNDER STAND. In SEE II, however, "If the meaning of the words separately is consistent with the meaning of the words together, then and only then are they signed as the component words" (Gustason et al., 1980, p. XIII). The word *butterfly* has no apparent relation to the meanings of the words *butter* and *fly,* and *understand* has no relation to the meanings of the words *under* and *stand.* Therefore, the words *butterfly* and *understand* require only one sign each. On the other hand, a word like *underline* would be signed UNDER LINE. Owing to the different concept of a base, or root, word, SEE I has more affix sign markers than SEE II.

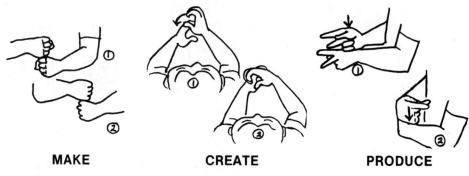

MAKE	CREATE	PRODUCE
Side of S touches on side of S; both twist to palm–in and touch again	Right C on left, twist to palm–in; rest right on left again	Touch right P on left, twist hands to palm–in and touch again

Figure 7.3. Signs for MAKE, CREATE, and PRODUCE.
G. Gustason, D. Pfetzing, and E. Zawolkow, *Signing Exact English.* Los Alamitos, CA: Modern Signs Press, 1980. Reprinted by permission.

Another difference between the two signed systems is in the use of ASL signs. As much as possible, SEE II incorporates an ASL sign if it translates into only one English word. This principle applies to words in any of the three groups, that is, basic, compound, or complex. Thus, ASL signs are used to represent words such as *baseball, misunderstand, can't,* and *careless.* There are some exceptions: for example, *basement* requires two signs. The sign vocabulary of SEE II is about 61 percent ASL-like signs, 18 percent modified ASL-like signs, and 21 percent newly invented signs. Modified signs include what is called **initialized signs.** For example, the handshapes for the ASL sign MAKE are changed (initialized) to C for CREATE and P for PRODUCE (see Figure 7.3).

Linguistics of Visual English

Another split in the group that met in California occurred in debate on the manner in which a sign should be illustrated in print. Most members favor pictures and written descriptions whereas one member, Dennis Wampler, wanted to use Stokoe's notational system (described in Chapter 6). Wampler (1972) published a booklet called *Linguistics of Visual English* (LVE or LOVE).

Similar to SEE I and II, LVE adheres to a two-out-of-three rule for forming signs. LVE signs, however, try to represent English morphemes, smallest grammatical unit with meaning, not word roots or affixes. The morphemic representation in LVE signs parallels the rhythm of speech. For example, a three-syllable word is represented by a three-movement sign. Because this system is not widely used, it is difficult to describe clearly how it differs from the SEE systems. Bornstein (1973) notes that "It might be more accurate to regard the basic elements of the LVE system as a sound representation of a morpheme rather than a morpheme per se" (p. 460). Bornstein also reported that LVE does not incorporate as many ASL signs as do the SEE systems.

Manual English

Personnel at the Washington State School for the Deaf (1972) developed Manual English (ME). This signed system combines grammatical principles from SEE II (e.g., plurals) and ASL (e.g., auxiliary verbs) as well as develops some of its own (e.g., options for forming past tense of verbs). Manual English has many signs in common with SEE II, but these are adapted to reflect local usage (Gustason, 1983). This signed system also contains a number of initialized signs. Many ASL signs are also part of ME. In particular, separate ASL signs for the various meanings of **multimeaning words** are used. Manual English also uses more finger spelling than do SEE II and ASL.

As for sign formation, ME signs tend to follow ASL concepts rather than English words. Most of the principles, however, are related to SEE II or some alterations of SEE II. For instance, nearly all the pronoun signs in ME and SEE II are similar. Differences between the two systems can be seen in the representation of verbs and affixes. Unlike SEE II, ME distinguishes between regular *(walk, walked)* and irregular *(run, ran)* verbs. ME does not contain as many affixes as SEE II and represents some affixes differently. For example, SEE II uses one form for the suffix *-er.* ME, on the other hand, has three *-er* sign markers. One sign marker refers to a person: It is called the agent marker, and it is similar to that used in ASL. A second marker reflects the comparative as in strong*er* and wis*er.* A third one refers to "everything else" (Wilbur, 1987, p. 264) such as *homer* (home run) or *painter* (cougar). The example of the *-er* suffix also illustrates the way ME combines rules from ASL and SEE II. An in-depth treatment of the Manual English signed system can be found in Wilbur (1987).

Signed English

Harry Bornstein and his associates (Bornstein, Saulnier, & Hamilton, 1983) developed Signed English (SE) at Gallaudet University in Washington, DC. This system is designed to present syntax and vocabulary to hearing-impaired children from 1 to 6 years old. The major focus of Signed English is to provide a typical English language environment resembling that given to hearing children.

Signed English consists of signs representing English words and sign markers for the most common inflectional aspects found in the language of young hearing children. There are 2,500 sign words in the SE lexicon. Most of the signs are ASL-like signs; the remaining ones are either contrived or borrowed from other signed systems. The signs appear to follow a dictionary entry rule. That is, each sign corresponds to one boldface lexical entry for an English word regardless of the type or number of meanings associated with that entry. For example, if the word *run* has about 100 boldface entries, then strictly speaking, there should be 100 SE signs. (There is, however, only one SE sign for *run.*) The 14 sign markers represent such morphological aspects as plurality, **possession, verb tense** and **verb agreement,** negation, **comparison,** and common suffixes such as *-y, -ly,* and *-er* (agent sign) (see Figure 7.4). Signed English has the fewest morphological markers of all the signed systems. Owing to the limited number of English words represented by the combination of signs and sign markers, finger spelling is used to present other words as needed.

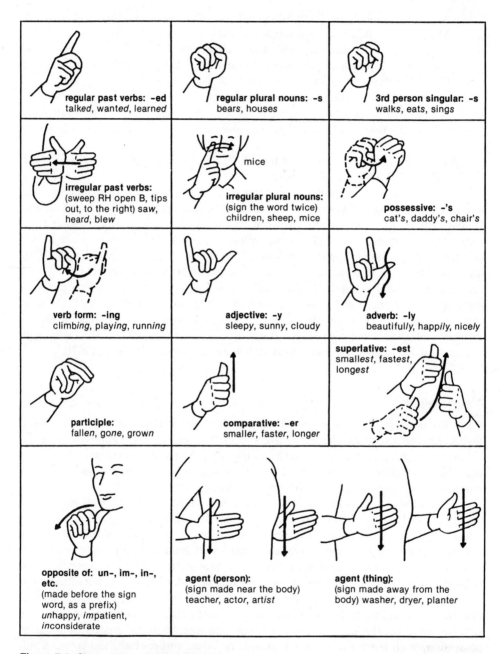

Figure 7.4. Sign markers of *Signed English*.
From *The Comprehensive Signed English Dictionary* by Karen Saulnier and Harry Bornstein, 1983, Washington, DC: Gallaudet University Press. Copyright© 1983 by Gallaudet University. Reprinted by permission.

Pidgin Sign English (English-like Signing)

Pidgin Sign English (PSE) has been referred to as signed English, sign English (Siglish), **American Sign English** (Ameslish), **manual English,** simultaneous communication, and Total Communication (Bragg, 1973; Quigley & Paul, 1987). Strictly speaking, PSE is not a contrived signed system similar to the ones discussed previously. In essence, PSE is related to the **pidginization** of American Sign Language and English, although it is argued that it cannot be called a pidgin in the true sense of the word. It might be better to label this form as **English-like signing.**

A pidgin is a communication form that develops naturally when two speakers or signers are unfamiliar with each other's language (Cokely, 1983). Typically, two languages are involved—two *spoken* languages or two *sign* languages. The resultant pidgin combines features (e.g., vocabulary, structures) from the two languages and generally adheres to the word order of the majority-culture language. It is difficult to define the structure of a particular pidgin because it varies with the competence of the speakers or signers in the two languages. In general, many of the linguistic aspects of pidgin users tend to reflect the grammar of their native language.

Pidgins are used mostly to communicate in context, primarily because they are reduced representations of either of the two languages. Although pidgin is a form of communication, not a language, a pidgin can become a language for a second generation of users.

At first glance, it appears that PSE is a pidginization of ASL and English. A closer inspection reveals difficulties. Is PSE a blend of ASL and *spoken* English? It is not clear how pidginization can occur when the forms of the two languages are not the same. For example, in a given sentence, a pidgin user could execute one or more signs, speak one or more words, and produce an utterance that could be half word/half sign (i.e., for the word *baseball, base* would be spoken, *ball* signed). One could say that PSE is a blend of ASL and English-like signing. What is English-like signing? Is it SEE I, SEE II, Manual English, or Signed English? Even if we agree on one of the signed systems, we still would not have a pidgin. As argued earlier, a signed *system* is not considered a sign *language*. A pidgin by definition borrows from two languages; the only language in our example here would be ASL.

Probably the most common characteristic of Pidgin Sign English is the use of ASL as much as possible in an English word order without contrived English-based grammatical markers. It should be clear that this type of signing is no longer ASL, just as speaking French in an English word order is no longer French. Nevertheless, this form of signing is likely to be understood by ASL-using deaf adults if most of the signed structures reflect the grammar of ASL. Consider the following sentence as an example:

The man is giving the woman the book.

One way to express this sentence in PSE is:

MAN GIVE-GIVE [ASL sign reflecting progressive movement] WOMAN BOOK.

Pidgin Sign English does not refer to the reduced abbreviated use of the various signed systems that results from the inconsistent execution of some of the principles— for example, leaving out signs or sign markers. In short, PSE might be the most widely used of all forms of signing; however, it is also the least well defined.

SIGNED SYSTEMS AND ENGLISH

Before discussing the instructional use and research effects of the signed systems, it is important to make some general remarks about the relationship of the systems to ASL and to English, summarizing some major points. First, the signed systems use only a few actual signs from the lexicon of ASL. Most of the signs are invented or contrived to represent the morphological structure of English. Second, the rest of the signs are altered forms of ASL signs. These signs have different handshapes or movements, some of which are not allowed by the grammar of ASL. Third, many signs in the systems are assigned grammatical functions (e.g., noun or verb) and meanings that are different from their uses in ASL. Finally, the signs are presented in an English word order, not the order in which they occur in ASL.

The signed systems try to model the vocabulary and syntax of English for the purpose of teaching English to hearing-impaired students. Using the previous descriptions of the basic rules of the systems, they can be placed on a continuum ranging from least representative to most representative of the structure of English. To illustrate this point, the following English word in the sentence below is translated into some of the signed systems.

English: That is *indescribable*
Rochester Method: Each letter is represented by a finger spelled handshape.

I-N-D-E-S-C-R-I-B-A-B-L-E

Signing Exact English: Two sign markers and an initialized ASL sign meaning *explain, describe* are used.

IN- DESCRIBE -ABLE

Signed English: The ASL sign for negation is used along with the initialized sign for *describe* (same as SEE II).

NOT DESCRIBE

Pidgin Sign English: One way to express this word is to use two ASL signs.

CAN'T EXPLAIN

In the context of the sentence, "can't explain" is what the signer means.

On the basis of a manual representation of an English word, we can conclude that the Rochester Method (RM) is most representative of the structure of English and PSE (i.e., English-like signing) is least representative. The other systems fall between these two extremes (see Figure 7.5). There is little relationship between representation of English and educational achievement for *most* severely to profoundly hearing-impaired students (Paul & Quigley, 1987a; Quigley & Paul, 1984a; cf., Luetke-Stahlman, 1988a).

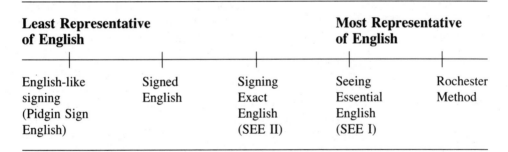

Figure 7.5. Relationship of the signed systems to standard English.

INSTRUCTIONAL AND FAMILIAL USE
OF THE SIGNED SYSTEMS

There have been several surveys on the extent and patterns of sign use in the school and home environments (Gallaudet Research Institute, 1985; Jordan, Gustason, & Rosen, 1979). Most of the data, however, reflect the presence or absence of sign communication use by students, parents, and teachers. It is difficult to make inferences regarding the nature or quality of signing even though they are important for understanding the development of language in hearing-impaired students. Because of the number of signed systems, there is considerable variation in the use of signing in schools and homes. Few signed systems are used in their entirety in a large number of settings. That is, a majority of signers do not adhere to a particular system but use a number of signs from various systems in conjunction with speech or lip movements (Strong & Charlson, 1987; Woodward, Allen, & Schildroth, 1985).

Students and Families

Most of the information here is based on data provided by the 1982–1983 Annual Survey by Gallaudet University Research Institute (Gallaudet Research Institute, 1985; Jordan & Karchmer, 1986). The results, however, are consistent with previous findings that have been reported since the mid-1970s. In general, nearly 70 percent of hearing-impaired students engage in some form of signing and attend schools in which signing is the major mode of communication and instruction. Only about 35 percent of the families of these students, however, use sign communication in the home.

The incidence of sign communication by hearing-impaired students is related to several important factors: (1) degree of hearing impairment, (2) age at onset, and (3) kind of educational program. The extent of sign usage may also be influenced by the student's age, speech intelligibility, ethnic status, and the hearing status of their parents/caretakers. Most students who sign have unaided severe to profound hearing losses and acquired their hearing impairment before they were 3 years of age. In addition, they are most likely to have poor speech ability. Most of these signing students are enrolled in full-time special education programs such as residential or day schools or self-contained classrooms in public schools. Very few students enrolled in only regular public school classrooms are signers, and most of these students have less-than-severe hearing impairments.

The single most important variable for the prevalence and extent of sign usage by hearing-impaired students is the educational program in which they are enrolled. This also affects the use of sign communication by the students' parents/caretakers. Thus, any variation in usage across the factors discussed earlier occurs with students in mainstreamed educational settings, that is, in classrooms with hearing classmates. For example, older hearing-impaired students are more likely to use signing than are the younger ones, and minority students with less-than-severe to severe losses engage in signing more often than white students with comparable losses. Minority students are also less likely to be enrolled in mainstreamed settings.

It is surprising that not much is known regarding the quality and nature of sign usage by students, parents/caretakers, and teachers. A clear understanding would provide more insights regarding cognitive and language development, including the acquisition of reading and written language by severely to profoundly hearing-impaired students. Most of the comments here are inferred from the limited data on the use of certain signed systems or of simultaneous communication in educational and home settings.

It is logical to assume that most severely to profoundly hearing-impaired students are exposed to English-based signing in the home and school. As discussed previously, English-based signing means *simultaneous communication;* that is, it involves the use of signs (and speech) from several systems, not the use of *one* signed system exclusively. Inferring from the results of secondary language assessments, we can say that most severely to profoundly hearing-impaired students have not acquired an adequate command of the rules of *any* of the signed systems or any combination of them (see discussion in Chapter 8). Although more research is needed, many severely to profoundly hearing-impaired students are most likely to have or acquire grammatical and communicative competence only in American Sign Language by the time they complete their formal education. In addition, given a choice between ASL and other forms of signing, many of these students prefer to use ASL in a variety of formal and informal situations.

Evidence suggests that sign usage in the home and school has a more positive effect on academic achievement than sign usage in school only (Babb, 1979). It is debatable whether type of signing (i.e., using a particular signed system) or quality of signing (i.e., consistent or systematic use) are critical for English language development (for another perspective see Luetke-Stahlman, 1988a, 1988b). In relation to quality of signing, it has been shown that it is possible to use some signed systems (particularly SEE II) in a systematic and consistent manner (Luetke-Stahlman, 1988a, 1988b). A number of parents and teachers, however, experience difficulty in adhering to the principles of formation and use of the signed systems. As a result, many sign users tend to omit certain signs, sign markers, or finger-spelled letters while communicating to severely to profoundly hearing-impaired students. It may be incompatible to use speech and some contrived signed systems simultaneously. Thus, many students may be exposed to an impoverished manual representation of English (Kluwin, 1981a; Marmor & Pettito, 1979; Reich & Bick, 1977; Strong & Charlson, 1987) or no representation at all.

To illustrate the difficulty teachers and parents/caretakers may have in using some of the contrived signed systems *consistently* most of the time, consider the following English sentence: *I also read the newspaper yesterday.* In Signing Exact English (SEE II), for example, this is signed as: I AL- SO READ plus PAST TENSE THE NEW-S PAPER YESTERDAY. A person having difficulty speaking and signing SEE II simultaneously might sign: I (say the word, *also,* but no sign) READ (no sign for past tense) NEW (no sign for *-s*) PAPER YESTERDAY. The signed translation of this execution reads, *I read* [present tense] *newpaper yesterday.* In another example, this same sentence is finger spelled in the Rochester Method (speaking and finger spelling simultaneously), as

I A-L-S-O R-E-A-D T-H-E N-E-W-S-P-A-P-E-R Y-E-S-T-E-R-D-A-Y.

A practitioner might omit letters and finger spell the sentence in the following manner

I A-L-S-O R-E-D T-H-E N-W-S-P-P-E-R Y-S-T-E-R-D-Y.

For the unskilled reader of finger spelling, the translation is *I also red the nwspper ysterdy.*

Instruction and Manually Coded English

During the 1970s, the philosophy of Total Communication became dominant in the education of hearing-impaired students, resulting in the use of simultaneous communication in most special programs (Moores, 1987; Wilbur, 1987). Most of the signed systems, therefore, have been in use for at least 15 years. The Rochester Method in particular has been used as an instructional approach since the late 19th century (Scouten, 1967). Despite the widespread use of the signed systems, there are few research data on their effects on the development of the primary and/or secondary forms of English. The merits of several contrived systems are presented in the order of their placement on a continuum from most representative to least representative of the structure of English (see Figure 7.5).

Rochester Method.   As discussed previously, the Rochester Method is the simultaneous use of speech and finger spelling. During the 1950s and 1960s, this system was widely used in special education programs for hearing-impaired students (Quigley, 1969). By the late 1970s, however, it was present in only a few programs, particularly at the secondary educational level (Jordan et al., 1979). It is suspected that this is the case today.

The important components of the Rochester Method are speech and finger spelling. Not much is known regarding severely to profoundly hearing-impaired children's acquisition of these skills when they are presented simultaneously. Some information is available, however, on children's receptive and expressive abilities with finger spelling (Akamatsu, 1982). There is also some speculation that the acquisition of finger spelling is similar to the acquisition of writing. It has been argued, however, that finger spelling is acquired independently of the orthographic (spelling-to-sound rules) and morphologic (word structure) systems of English (Padden & Le Master, 1985).

The ability to finger spell requires a much greater degree of motor coordination and dexterity than does signing. Young children experience difficulty in learning this system because it requires the ability to spell. In most cases, children move their fingers in a manner that *imitates* finger spelling. In this sense, only one or two letters may be articulated or distinctly recognized with the overall form of the finger movements approximating that of adult finger spelling.

By age 3, young hearing-impaired children are able to finger spell letters in a sequential manner. Later, they begin to observe the relationship between finger spelling and print. A skilled finger speller eventually forms words as units (i.e., as *movement envelopes*), not as sequences of letters (Wilbur, 1987). Typically, the finger speller may omit some finger-spelled handshapes. As a rule, the experienced finger speller can still understand the message because of familiarity of the context *and an adequate knowledge of English grammar.* Competence in English is necessary for comprehension and production of advanced finger spelling (Stuckless & Pollard, 1977). Nevertheless, Wilbur (1987, p. 217) has argued that ". . . the learning of fingerspelling should not be viewed as a normal language learning situation" because the learning of finger spelling requires much effort and formal training, and that the learning of language is not dependent on formal training.

Most of the research on the effectiveness of the Rochester Method has been conducted on students in residential or special schools and classrooms. Researchers compared the academic performance of students exposed to this method with that of students exposed to other methods. In general, more favorable results have been reported for the Rochester Method.

Quigley (1969), for example, studied students from nine residential schools. In a **longitudinal survey,** students exposed to the Rochester Method performed better than those exposed to simultaneous communication on various language-related subtests (e.g., vocabulary, reading) of the Stanford Achievement Test (SAT). It was reported, however, that the reading level of average 18-year-old hearing-impaired students was approximately seven grades below that of their hearing peers. In an **experimental study,** Quigley (1969) focused on young preschool children. Students taught with the Rochester Method perform better in reading (as measured by the SAT) and measures of written language (assessing writing ability) than students taught with oral methods. Moores, Weiss, and Goodwin (1978) also reported that students in preschool programs using the Rochester Method performed better than those in either oral or Total Communication (i.e., simultaneous method) programs.

Finger spelling has been shown to be an effective aid in teaching certain morphological structures of English, for example, past tense inflectional suffixes such as -*ed* or -*en* (Looney & Rose, 1979). To obtain the desired benefits, however, it appears that hearing-impaired students need to have some understanding of **basic English sentence patterns** such as *The boy is happy* and *The girl walked down the hall.* That is, they should be able to comprehend and express these sentences through writing and finger spelling. In addition, instruction in the use of English morphology should be systematic and consistent over time.

In sum, the Rochester Method, particularly the use of finger spelling, may be helpful in teaching some students certain grammatical aspects of English such as inflectional suffixes. When good oral techniques for teaching speech and speech reading are used in conjunction with the Rochester Method, the oral communication skills of hearing-impaired students do not deteriorate. When used with caution, finger spelling is effective as an instructional approach with some children as young as $3\frac{1}{2}$ years old. It can also be used to represent English words that have no sign equivalents in any of the signed systems. Despite the versatility of finger spelling in the Rochester Method, it should be remembered that it is not a cure-all (Quigley, 1969).

Seeing Essential English.   The effects of using Seeing Essential English (SEE I) to teach English language skills have been reported in a few studies involving hearing-impaired students from only a handful of educational programs (Raffin, 1976; Washburn, 1983). The findings of the earlier studies indicated that students acquire certain grammatical aspects of English in the same manner as do younger hearing children. For example, in learning about past tense markers and plurality, hearing-impaired students proceed through developmental stages similar to those of younger hearing children. Even the errors in production (e.g., *she goed; the mans*) are similar in nature for both groups of students. The rate of development for hearing-impaired students, however, was reported to be considerably slower, indicating a two- to six-year delay in some areas when compared to hearing peers.

The similar but slower development of English by hearing-impaired children exposed to SEE I has been documented by Schlesinger and Meadow (1972) and more intensively by Raffin and his associates (Gilman, Davis, & Raffin, 1980; Raffin, 1976; Raffin, Davis, & Gilman, 1978). The focus was on vocabulary and syntactic development, particularly on some of the most common English morphemes—for example, past tense, *-ed* as in *walked;* **present progressive,** *-ing* as in *is walking;* and plural, *-s* on nouns as in *boys.* The acquisition of the common English morphemes by hearing-impaired children, ranging in age from 6 to 12 years, was compared to that of young hearing children by Brown (1973).

One of the most important findings of these studies was that the acquisition and use of the SEE I markers (e.g., signs for *-ed, -e, -er*) were related to the consistency of teachers' production of the markers. If teachers use SEE I signs and markers in a consistent, systematic manner to represent English sentences, students are likely to develop an intuitive understanding of the rules of English grammar. Language learners need to receive input that is *reasonably* consistent and accurate so that they can figure out how their language works. Competent users of a language should be able to make judgments about accepted grammar and produce grammatical sentences that they have not heard, seen, or read before.

The most impressive results on the effects of SEE I have been reported in a more recent article by Washburn (1983), who described the growth of this signed system from its inception in Lapeer, Michigan, to its present use. Specifically, the focus was on the educational achievement results of students in three public school districts: Greeley, Colorado, Davenport, Iowa, and Richardson, Texas. It was argued that the use of SEE I in these schools contributed to the students' receptive understanding of English on two tests, the Stanford Achievement Test (SAT) and the Peabody Picture Vocabulary Test (PPVT). For example, the average reading grade levels of students in the Richardson, Texas, program were marked higher (one to two grade levels) than those of their hearing-impaired peers in other Texas programs on the basis of a longitudinal study of results from 1977 to 1981. The most impressive finding was that the hearing-impaired students in grades 11 and 12 scored in the top 20 percent of all *hearing* high school students taking the reading comprehension subset of the SAT. Experimental research, however, is needed to determine if the use of SEE I *caused* the difference in scores between students exposed to this method and those exposed to other methods. In addition, the effects of SEE I on the development of English literacy skills—that is, the ability to read and write, still needs to be investigated. It appears that Seeing Essential English may be an effective tool for teaching English to deaf students. "However, the use of SEE [I] is not a panacea, not 'the answer' to the vexing problem of providing English for the deaf youngster" (Washburn, 1983, p. 29).

Signing Exact English.   The signs from the lexicon of Signing Exact English (SEE II) have been reported to be the most widely used of all signed systems (Jordan et al., 1979). Educational materials are also available on the use of SEE II (Gustason, 1983). Despite the widespread use of its *signs,* the prevalence of the use of SEE II *as a signed system or educational tool* in schools has not been documented (Jordan & Karchmer, 1986).

Babb (1979) studied profoundly hearing-impaired students who had been exposed to SEE II. Half of the students were taught by SEE II in the school only. The other half were exposed to this system in the home and also at school. Babb compared the performance of the two groups on subtests of an achievement test, on a test of receptive knowledge of certain syntactic structures, and measures of written language (i.e., assessing their ability to write). In addition, the results of these groups were compared to those of the groups in the Brasel and Quigley (1977) study (discussed in Chapter 6) and to the scores from a national survey of academic achievement of hearing-impaired students (DiFrancesca, 1972).

Deaf students exposed to Signing Exact English in the home and school environments performed significantly better than did those students exposed to SEE II only in school. This seems to support the importance of the home environment for educational achievement. In addition, the achievement scores of the home-plus-school group were higher than those of a national sample of hearing-impaired students.

It is interesting that the home-plus-school group performed as well as the best group in the Brasel and Quigley study, probably exposed to Pidgin Sign English (PSE). Signing Exact English appears to be more representative of the structure of English than is Pidgin Sign English. It follows, then, that students exposed to SEE II should perform better than those students exposed to PSE on English-based achievement and diagnostic tests. Why this was not the case in the study by Babb is not clear. It is possible that the parents and teachers using Signing Exact English had problems adhering to the principles of the system in forming and producing signs. As discussed previously, practitioners sometimes omit signs or sign markers because of the cumbersome nature of some signed systems or the difficulty in signing and speaking simultaneously (Marmor & Pettito, 1979; Strong & Charlson, 1987). As a result, students may receive a representation of English that resembles that of Pidgin Sign English as used in the Brasel and Quigley study (1977).

More recently, it has been shown that some teachers can use SEE II consistently and systematically (Luetke-Stahlman, 1988b), and that students exposed to this system and others that are considered to encode completely a language perform well on literacy measures (Luetke-Stahlman, 1988a). For example, Luetke-Stahlman (1988a) examined the performance of hearing-impaired students, age 5 to 12 years, who were enrolled in public, private, and residential schools. Several variables were statistically controlled—for example, age, aided and unaided hearing acuity. Hearing-impaired students in one group had been exposed to oral English (OE), cued speech (CS), Seeing Essential English (SEE I), Signing Exact English (SEE II), and American Sign Language (ASL). The other group had been exposed to Signed/Manual English and PSE (or English-like signing). The literacy battery consisted of tests involving passage comprehension (using a cloze procedure), vocabulary, and syntax. In general, the results indicated that students exposed to OE, CS, SEE I, SEE II, and ASL performed significantly better than the other group on six of the seven measures used. Luetke-Stahlman (1988a) stated that the:

> Results of the study indicate that students exposed to instructional inputs that are either languages (English or ASL) or systems that attempt to completely encode spoken English tend to score higher on selected tests of achievement than do students exposed to input that does not correspond as highly to English. (p. 359)

Signed English.   Several studies have been conducted on the effects of Signed English (SE) on the development of English language skills. Bornstein, the creator of SE, and his associates have explored the effects of Signed English on primary language development in English (Bornstein, Saulnier, & Hamilton, 1980; Bornstein & Saulnier, 1981). They conducted a longitudinal study of 18 severely to profoundly hearing-impaired students enrolled in residential and day schools.

After four years, the researchers reported the growth in receptive and expressive skills of vocabulary and syntax. Similar to the findings of previous studies, the results show that hearing-impaired students proceed through developmental stages similar to those of younger hearing children. As expected, the rate of development of the hearing-impaired students was markedly slower. For example, it was reported that the vocabulary growth was half of that observed in the average hearing student. Specifically, the English language expressive abilities of the 9-year-old hearing-impaired students were found to be equivalent to those of 3- to 4-year-old hearing children.

In a follow-up investigation one year later, Bornstein and Saulnier (1981) focused on the students' use of the 14 Signed English markers. Compared to SEE I and SEE II, Signed English has very few morphological markers. The results, however, showed that most students do not use the markers consistently or systematically. In fact, even after five years of exposure, the students were using only half of the 14 SE sign markers.

The findings of Bornstein and his collaborators seem to question whether English morphological structures can be represented manually with contrived signs. It may also be that the students understand the concepts of past tense (as in *walked*) or present progressive (as in *I am running*) but are expressing these concepts in other ways. For example, the students may prefer to express their understanding of a sentence, question, or story by using ASL or ASL-like signs (Maxwell, 1983; Stewart, 1985; Supalla, 1986). It appears that many students have not learned the rules of English morphology. Thus, they are not able to express these rules by using *symbols* that represent them.

Not much is known about the effects of Signed English on the reading and writing abilities of severely to profoundly hearing-impaired students. Robbins (1983) examined the effects of some signs on reading. The results indicated that the reading comprehension ability of students usually improved when ASL-like signs were placed above the English words in the text. As discussed previously, Luetke-Stahlman (1988a) indicated that students exposed to this method do not perform as well as students exposed to systems that are considered to encode English in a more complete manner.

Pidgin Sign English.   The nature of teachers' signing that occurs in most Total Communication classrooms for hearing-impaired students can best be described as some form of Pidgin Sign English, or English-like signing (Woodward, 1986). For a number of reasons, most educational programs have not adopted a particular signed system. Some teachers may find it difficult to adhere to the principles of the more rigorous systems. In addition, they may not like certain signs for given English words. Thus, they search for or use signs from the other systems. Other teachers may borrow from various systems because of training, lack of knowledge, or to find a sign for an English word. Finally, some educators feel that it is not important, and may be limiting, to use signs from only one particular signed system, and for them the most important matter is to communicate adequately to hearing-impaired students in any way possible. This, in fact, is one of the basic tenets of the philosophy of Total Communication (Baker & Cokely, 1980; Gannon, 1981). Owing to the TC philosophy and the nature of PSE signing, a wide variety of signing occurs across teachers and across classrooms, even within the same school.

Given this conceptual framework, it is difficult to assess the effects of Pidgin Sign English, or English-like signing, on the development of English language skills. The nature of PSE is influenced in part by the grammatical competence of its users in the two languages involved—ASL and English. The range of language competence, however, is not reported in most studies. Much of what is reported is the achievement of hearing-impaired students in a simultaneous communication environment.

Some of the most interesting and contradictory findings are those of the effects of Pidgin Sign English on the development of secondary language. Recall that in the Brasel and Quigley (1977) study (discussed in Chapter 6) the PSE group performed better than the other three groups on measures of syntax and reading achievement. In addition, the PSE group performed as well as the SEE II group in the Babb (1979) study; but Luetke-Stahlman (1988a) reported that students exposed to PSE do not perform as well as students exposed to systems such as SEE I and SEE II.

In sum, there is some evidence that simultaneous communication has a positive effect on communication skills and academic achievement levels of many severely and profoundly hearing-impaired students (Delaney, Stuckless, & Walter, 1984). It must be emphasized that the effects are not due solely to the use of signing in a Total Communication program. Other important factors are the teachers' knowledge and skills, the curricula, the involvement of parents/caretakers and school personnel, and the development of *oral-communication skills.*

SUMMARY

This chapter discussed the basic rules of some of the major signed systems that are supposedly used in educational and home settings with hearing-impaired students. It also illustrated how each system tries to represent the grammatical structure of English. Finally, the chapter synthesized the limited research findings available on (1) the use of the systems by students, educators, and parents/caretakers, and (2) the effects of the signed systems on the development of English language skills.

Several signed systems are available. Those described here were the Rochester Method, Seeing Essential English, Signing Exact English, Manual English, Signed English, and Pidgin Sign English (English-like signing). We argued that these systems are not languages but codes or representations of one language—English. Thus, although the signs of ASL are *borrowed,* ASL signers are not likely to understand any of the other signed systems unless they have an adequate knowledge of English grammar *and* of the rules for producing signs in a particular system.

The English-based signed systems were arbitrarily contrived to teach English in educational settings. Unlike the growth of languages, they have not evolved naturally over time in a variety of communication situations. We also emphasized that the systems do not have their own linguistic components such as morphology, syntax, and semantics. The rule-governed grammar of the signed systems is based on that of standard English.

The inventors attempted to develop signed systems that would enable severely to profoundly hearing-impaired students to see English. Thus, they wanted to represent the grammatical structure of English in a manual way. It is important to remember that there are differences among the systems. There are variations in sign formation rules for representing certain aspects of English grammar such as plurality and verb tenses. One of the major differences is the way each system defines a root, or base, word in English.

On the basis of a manual representation of an English word, it is possible to place the various signed systems on a continuum ranging from most representative to least representative of the structure of English. The Rochester Method, in which finger spelling and speech are produced simultaneously, can be considered most representative of the grammar of English. Pidgin Sign English is least representative because it contains few contrived English-based sign markers. The other systems can be placed on the continuum between the Rochester Method and Pidgin Sign English.

The theoretical relationships of the signed systems to the structure of English may be questioned in light of what is known about the actual use of signing by many students, educators, and parents/caretakers. There is considerable variation in the use of signing in the home and school, and there might be several reasons for this phenomenon. Some practitioners find it difficult to adhere to the principles of sign formation, especially when they attempt to speak and sign simultaneously, which results in the omission of signs and sign markers. In addition, they borrow signs from among the systems because a particular system does not seem to meet their instructional needs. The inconsistent use of signing by hearing-impaired students may be mainly a result of their inadequate command of the grammar of English and of the rules of the systems.

More investigation is needed into the effects of the various signed systems on the development of English literacy skills. Most of the systems, in some form or another, have been used in most education programs with hearing-impaired students since the mid-1970s. It has been assumed that many students would develop the ability to read and write at a mature, adult level. Presently, there is only a little evidence to support this contention.

There may be several explanations for these limited results, assuming that parents and teachers can express themselves adequately in a signed system. It is possible that students have problems remembering all aspects of a signed utterance or do not understand how these aspects are connected grammatically. For example, in

THE BOY WHO QUICK + -LY KISS + -ED THE GIRL RECEIVE + -ED A
BEAUTIFUL PUNCH IN THE MOUTH.

students could have difficulty knowing (1) that the boy is the one who got punched, or (2) the sign marker -LY provides grammatical information about the sign-concept QUICK. Obviously, this situation is related to an understanding of English grammar. As discussed in Chapter 4, however, knowledge of English is also dependent on memory for at least sequential, hierarchical information. We are not suggesting that severely to profoundly hearing-impaired students have memory deficits per se. Rather, many students who are linked to the world of vision and have limited use of their residual hearing may not be able to memorize adequately information that represents the structures of spoken languages such as that of the signed systems. In this sense, there appears to be an overload of their memory processes (Quigley & Paul, 1984a; Wilbur, 1987). This may also explain why for some students sign languages are easier to learn than signed systems.

One other point should be considered. There is no doubt that many students understand the *concepts* underlying some of the signs. For example, it is possible that they understand the concept of *start* or *begin* as in the ASL sign START/BEGIN. This may not be enough, however, to help them *remember* that this concept can be read or written as *s-t-a-r-t* or *b-e-g-i-n*. This problem is still evident in the signed systems even if initialized handshapes are used—such as *S* for START or *B* for BEGIN or *I* for INITI-ATE. Thus, students have an adequate knowledge of concepts, but they may lack the necessary skills to read or write what it is that they *know*. This, of course, could explain in part the low literacy levels discussed in detail in Chapter 8.

With early intervention and well-developed curricular and instructional methods, it is possible to teach certain grammatical aspects of English. Many Total Communication programs do not emphasize the development of speech, speech reading, and auditory training as well as they should. The programs seem to overlook the contributions of these oral components to the development of reading and writing skills in hearing-impaired students, as has been reported in some oral and other successful TC programs. Finally, we emphasize that teaching English to severely to profoundly hearing-impaired students is an extremely complex process. Focusing on only the kind and use of a particular signed system is obviously not sufficient. There are many other important factors, one of the most important being: Teachers need to have a well-developed knowledge of the structure of the English language and of theory-based instructional methods.

COMPREHENSION

1. TRUE or FALSE? The three categories of language/communication approaches are Oral English, Pidgin Sign English, and American Sign Language.
2. The following statements is/are TRUE about signed systems in the United States.
   a. They attempt to reflect the grammar of English in a manual way.
   b. They are widely used outside educational environments.
   c. They have their own linguistic components (e.g., syntax) because they evolve naturally like other languages.
   d. They are the same as sign languages.
   e. All systems use the same rules in representing the structure of English.
3. What is the name of the first signed system created in the United States?
4. In the United States, the signed systems are based on two languages. What are they?
5. TRUE or FALSE? There were no signed systems before the 1960s.
6. Finger spelling and speaking simultaneously are known as (select all that apply)
   a. The Rochester Method.
   b. Signing Exact English.
   c. Neo-Oralism.
   d. Seeing Essential English.
   e. Finger spelling Exact English.
7. What is one of the most important differences between SEE I and SEE II?
8. Describe the two-out-of-three rule of SEE I and SEE II.
9. Which of the manual systems is considered most representative of the grammar of English? Least representative?
10. Why is it difficult to describe Pidgin Sign English?
11. The most widely used signed system in educational programs for hearing-impaired students is one of the following:
   a. American Sign Language
   b. Signed English
   c. Signing Exact English
   d. Seeing Essential English
   e. None of the above.
12. The *single, most important variable* for the prevalence and extent of sign usage by hearing-impaired students is one of the following:
   a. Degree of impairment
   b. Age at onset
   c. Etiology
   d. Type of education program
   e. Hearing status of parents
13. TRUE or FALSE? We have adequate knowledge about the nature of the signing abilities of students and their parents.
14. Which of the following statements is/are TRUE about the research on signed systems?
   a. All the 14 sign markers of Signed English are learned by the time hearing-impaired students are 15 years of age.

   b. Brasel and Quigley showed that their PSE group performed as well as the best SEE II
   in Babb's study.
   c. Luetke-Stahlman reported that the PSE group performed better than the SEE groups.
   d. Quigley stated that finger spelling is a panacea.
   e. Delaney, Stuckless, and Walter concluded that simultaneous communication may have
   some positive effects on the academic achievement levels of severely to profoundly
   hearing-impaired students.
15. Most researchers seem to agree that the use of signing only is not sufficient for developing
   English literacy skills. What are some other important factors?

SUGGESTED ACTIVITIES

1. Obtain the following books: Bornstein, H., Saulnier, K., & Hamilton, L. (1983). *The com-
   prehensive Signed English dictionary.* Washington, DC: Gallaudet University; Gustason, G.,
   Pfetzing, D., & Zawolkow, E. (1980). *Signing exact English.* Los Alamitos, CA: Modern
   Signs.
   Describe the signs in the two books for the following English words and sentences.
   a. Words:
   right, saw (past tense of *see*), *general, forest, men.*
   b. Sentences:
   I got the picture. (i.e., I understood.)
   The trucks ran over the books.
   The women are really beautiful.
   There is a run in my stocking.
   The man gave the ring to the woman.
2. Interview several teachers who sign to their hearing-impaired students (try to include a hearing-impaired teacher in your interview) to learn the following:
   a. The number of college or university courses in signing they had taken
   b. The type of signing (or signed system) that is required or used in their schools
   c. Their personal descriptions of their signing (i.e., ASL, PSE, other)
3. Videotape the signing of several teachers for about two to three minutes (include hearing-
   impaired teachers). See if you (or someone else) can describe the nature of the signing. That
   is, is it ASL, PSE, or some combination of several signed systems?
4. Videotape several hearing-impaired students and analyze their signing in the same manner.

FURTHER READINGS

Bornstein, H., Saulnier, K., & Hamilton, L. (1973–1984). *The Signed English series.* Washington, DC: Gallaudet University Press.

Blasdell, R., & Caccamise, F. (1976). *Factors influencing the reception of fingerspelling.* Houston, TX: American Speech and Hearing Association.

Caccamise, F., Hatfield, N., & Brewer, L. (1978). Manual/simultaneous communication (M/SC)
research: Results and implications. *American Annals of the Deaf, 123,* 803–823.

Evans, L. (1982). *Total communication: Structure and strategy.* Washington, DC: Gallaudet University Press.

O'Rourke, T. J. (1972). *Psycholinguistics and total communication: The state of the art*. Silver Spring, MD: American Annals of the Deaf.

Woodward, J. (1973). Some characteristics of pidgin sign English. *Sign Language Studies, 3,* 39–46.

CHAPTER 8

Development of English Literacy Skills

MAJOR POINTS TO CONSIDER

Definition of functional literacy

The major theoretical models of the reading process

The reading difficulties of severely to profoundly hearing-impaired students

Relationship between reading and writing

The written language productions of severely to profoundly hearing-impaired students

Instruction and assessment of literacy

Spoken forms of languages have existed for about 100,000 years. Written language, on the other hand, is a relatively young phenomenon, only about 5,000 years old (Just & Carpenter, 1987). In the early centuries of written language, the few individuals who had the ability to read and write were highly respected. Today, however, it is forgotten that literacy is such an intellectual feat because there are many people who can read and write effortlessly. Learning to read and write is as complex as learning to play the piano or a game of chess. Not everyone can play the piano or even play it well. The same is true for reading and writing.

Despite differences of opinion in relation to language/communication approaches, curricula, and instructional methods, most educators agree that it is critical for hearing-impaired students to develop adequate literacy skills. It is difficult to define literacy; however, with some qualification, we agree with a widely used definition proposed by Gray (1956):

A person is **functionally literate** when he has acquired the knowledge and skills in reading and writing which enable him to engage effectively in all those activities in which literacy is normally assumed in his culture or group *and in the majority culture of society* [emphasis added]. (p. 19)

In our view, literacy is or should be the primary goal in the education of hearing-impaired students. In most instances, the ability to read and write is a requisite for educational and vocational success, especially in a literate society such as the United States.

This chapter illustrates the impact of deafness on the development of English literacy skills. It presents achievement data on **reading comprehension** and written language abilities, and it discusses these areas in light of recent theories and research. In addition, current instructional practices in the teaching of reading and writing are examined. We argue that there needs to be a closer interrelationship among theory, assessment, curriculum, and practice. Finally, we provide suggestions for university preservice training programs and for further research efforts.

READING

Psychologists, philosophers, linguists, and reading researchers have tried to understand the process of reading. As Huey (1908/1968) said, these efforts

. . . to completely analyze what we do when we read would almost be the acme of a psychologist's dream for it would be to describe very many of the most intricate workings of the human mind, as well as to unravel the tangled story of the most remarkable specific performance that civilization has learned in all its history. (p. 8)

Although complete explanations of the reading comprehension process are not available, it is possible to present information on *theory-based* effective instructional strategies and practices for the development of reading skills (Anderson, Hiebert, Scott, & Wilkinson, 1985; Pearson, Barr, Kamil, & Mosenthal, 1984). Researchers, practitioners, and policymakers should be aware of the emerging views of the reading process.

Theoretical Models

Reading models can be grouped into three broad areas: text-based, reader- or knowledge-based, and interactive (Pearson et al., 1984; Singer & Ruddell, 1985). Proponents of text-based **(bottom-up)** models assume that the text itself has the most pervasive influence on readers' comprehension. Proponents of reader-based **(top-down)** models argue that the knowledge and skills readers bring to the text are more important than the actual information in the text itself. Interactive theorists believe that the reading comprehension process depends on the simultaneous use of text-based and knowledge-based information. These three models form the basis for instructional and curricular approaches.

Bottom-up Approaches.   In the bottom-up approaches, reading begins with the decoding of words and eventually culminates in meaning. Emphasis is placed on simple letter identification, **letter clusters,** and **sound-letter correspondences.** It is argued that readers must put sounds together to make words and sentences. Thus, they must match the **graphemes** of printed language with the corresponding phonemes of spoken language to understand the meaning of the text.

Consider the printed form of the word cat, which contains three phonemes and can be decoded as /kat/. If readers have semantic meaning for this spoken word, they should be able to relate that meaning to its printed equivalent. In this sense, readers are reading or can read only what they already know. Another important assumption of this model is that good readers mediate (think, solve problems) in a predominant speech-based code to assess meaning from print.

Top-down Approaches.   Proponents of top-down approaches assert that reading begins with what is already in the reader's head, not with what is on the printed page. It is assumed that readers use their prior or world knowledge (called *nonvisual information* by F. Smith, 1981) to figure out letters, words, and sentences. In this view, reading is not a precise process in which the reader must fixate on every letter of every word. Rather, reading comprehension is said to be similar to the comprehension of spoken language. Goodman (1970) refers to reading as a *psycholinguistic guessing game;* that is, readers make more accurate guesses about meaning based on a sample of the text. The more knowledge readers have about grammar and the more world experiences they have had, the less time they spend focusing on letter and sequence correspondence, and this in turn increases their skill and speed in reading.

Consider the following sentence as an example: *John went to the s   to buy bread.* From a top-down perspective, it is important for readers to know where *bread* can be bought. This information, along with their knowledge of language (particularly context clues), enables them to predict or hypothesize that *s   refers to *store.* From this perspective, knowledge in the reader's mind is more important than knowledge about letter-sound relationships.

Interactive Approaches.   The major tenet of interactive approaches is that good readers integrate information from the text with their own knowledge to construct meaning—an active, complex process requiring the development and coordination of both bottom-up and top-down skills. Good readers need to know about letter-sound and letter-sequence correspondences as well as other aspects of the grammar of the language in which they are reading. They also need to use their prior knowledge and certain cognitive processes (e.g., inferencing and predicting) to check and recheck their understanding of text-based features such as vocabulary and syntax and the content of the passage.

Some proponents of interactive approaches argue that reading comprehension is pervasively affected by previously acquired knowledge or experiences that readers bring to the text. Prior knowledge directs interpretation of the passage. To construct meaning, however, readers need to apply their prior knowledge. They come to understand new information by relating it to what they already know. A well-developed supply of prior or world knowledge facilitates reading comprehension whereas a limited stock of prior experiences hinders comprehension. In some instances, prior knowledge can get in the way of understanding the writer's message. For example, some readers may have such a strong belief in their knowledge of something that they force this interpretation on the text, regardless of the information presented. Thus, they can misconstrue what the writer is really trying to convey. In addition, readers with poor bottom-up skills do not always attend to text-based features, tending to overrely on their prior knowledge. This also can result in a misinterpretation of the passage.

In short, readers' knowledge and skills are stored in long-term memory (see Chapter 4) in a fairly systematic fashion and usually as summaries of past experiences. Readers abstract and generalize from their experiences to make sense of spoken and written language. As stated by Devine (1986):

> . . . comprehension begins as readers use the information that writers have put into their printed texts in order to create for themselves their own personal texts, texts they construct in their minds. (p. 10)

Because of their **explanatory power,** interactive theories have had a profound effect on reading research and instructional practices. After charting the reading achievement levels of severely to profoundly hearing-impaired students, we discuss their reading difficulties in relation to an interactive theoretical framework.

READING ACHIEVEMENT

In general, the reading achievement levels of hearing-impaired students have been based on the reading subtest scores of general achievement batteries such as the Metropolitan Achievement Test and the Stanford Achievement Test. Before the 1970s, tests standardized on nonhearing-impaired student populations were used to evaluate achievement of the hearing-impaired. The accuracy of the results have been questioned because hearing-impaired students were not part of the norming sample (i.e., they were not used as subjects in the development of test items and directions).

From the late 1960s to the mid-1980s an adapted version of the Stanford Achievement Test (SAT) has been developed, administered to, and normed on national samples of hearing-impaired students (Allen, 1986; DiFrancesca, 1972; Trybus & Karchmer, 1977). The score of a hearing-impaired student can be compared to that of other hearing-impaired or to hearing students of similar ages or grade levels. The Stanford Achievement Test—Hearing Impaired Version is the most commonly used standardized assessment in special educational programs for hearing-impaired students.

It is well documented that most severely to profoundly hearing-impaired students do not read as well as do their hearing counterparts (Allen, 1986; King & Quigley, 1985; Quigley & Paul, 1986, 1989). Despite special adaptations of the SAT, the reading grade levels of these students are not much different from those observed on nonadapted instruments. The results consistently reveal that average 18- to 19-year-old severely to profoundly hearing-impaired students are reading no better than average 9- to 10-year-old hearing students. In addition, the tests show an annual growth rate of only 0.3 reading grade level per year with a leveling off or plateau occurring at the third- or fourth-grade reading level. Even more distressing, general achievement batteries have been shown to overestimate the reading ability of hearing-impaired students (Davey, LaSasso, & Macready, 1983; Moores, 1987). Thus, the true reading achievement levels of most hearing-impaired students in special education programs may be even lower than the levels reported.

Notice that there are subgroups within the hearing-impaired student population who read as well as or better than their hearing peers. Some of these students, who are deaf by our definition, may be in highly structured comprehensive oral programs such as the Central Institute for the Deaf (Ogden, 1979), integrated in regular education programs (Ross, Brackett, & Maxon, 1982), or in well-developed Total Communication programs (Delaney, Stuckless, & Walter, 1984; Luetke-Stahlman, 1988a). Some common elements across these programs, which contain oral or signing students, are (1) parents are interested and involved with the education of their children, (2) curricular and instructional programs are well developed, and (3) perhaps the most important factor, students have well-established primary (i.e., speech and/or sign) language abilities.

A PERSPECTIVE ON READING DIFFICULTY

The low reading achievement levels of hearing-impaired students can be discussed within the framework of interactive theories of reading considered previously. It is convenient to illustrate students' problems in relation to certain text-based and reader-based variables that affect reading comprehension ability. Text-based variables include vocabulary, syntax, and **figurative language** such as idioms *(It's raining cats and dogs)* and metaphorical expressions *(John ran into a friend)*. Reader-based variables include prior or background knowledge, inferencing ability (e.g., answering questions, using context clues, making predictions), and internal coding strategies (e.g., using speech-based or sign-based structures to access meaning from print).

Research on Text-Based Variables

Vocabulary.   One of the most important components of reading comprehension is knowledge of word meanings (Anderson & Freebody, 1985; Paul, in press; Paul & O'Rourke, 1988). As expected, hearing-impaired students' vocabulary knowledge is inferior to that of their hearing counterparts. In addition, they acquire new words at a slower rate than do hearing students (Cooper & Rosenstein, 1966; LaSasso & Davey, 1987; Paul, 1984). One reason for this is that the students have difficulty learning meanings of words through reading alone. They may have poor strategies for word identification. For example, they may not be able to use context clues to figure out the meaning of a word. As discussed in Chapter 7, another reason could be the nature of the signed input of practitioners, which may not provide enough exposure to specific language structures such as morphology (i.e., words and word parts).

Additional insights into the low vocabulary levels can be gathered from the research on words with multiple meanings. There is no doubt that good readers know many words; that is, they know at least one meaning of many different words. Good readers, however, also know several meanings and other related associations, nuances, and concepts of many words (Dale & O'Rourke, 1986; Johnson & Pearson, 1984). A study of first basal word lists found that almost 90 percent of the words have several meanings (Searls & Klesius, 1984). In addition, more than two-thirds of words that appear most frequently in the spoken and written language of young children are multi-meaning words (Johnson, Moe, & Baumann, 1983). The importance of having an in-depth knowledge of words has been emphasized by Carroll (cited in Becker, 1977):

> . . . much of the failure of individuals to understand speech or writing beyond an elementary level is due to deficiency in vocabulary knowledge. It is not merely the knowledge of single words and their meanings that is important, but also the knowledge of the multiple meanings of words and their grammatical functions. (p. 535)

Research has shown that many severely to profoundly hearing-impaired students and other poor readers have difficulty with the fact that a word may have several meanings (Paul, 1984; Paul & O'Rourke, 1988; Pearson, 1985). For example, consider the following sentences:

1. The girl put her money in the *bank*.
2. The girl sat on the *bank* of the river.

If poor readers know any meaning for *bank*, it is likely to be the one expressed in sentence 1. Comprehension problems can surface when secondary or less common meanings of words, such as the meaning for *bank* in sentence 2, are used in stories. Poor readers may not be able to use sentence context clues to derive the meanings of words.

Syntax.   Knowledge of syntax has also been shown to be important for reading comprehension. Syntax has received considerable research attention (Quigley & Paul, 1984a; Wilbur, Power, Montanelli, & Steinkamp, 1976; Wilbur, 1987). For example, Quigley and his associates developed and administered the Test of Syntactic Abilities (TSA) to a national sample of deaf (i.e., profoundly hearing-impaired) students in the United States. They assessed students' knowledge of nine major structures as well as the presence of the structures in commonly used basal reading series:

Structures	**Examples**
Negation	The girl will not read the book.
	The boy did not catch the whale.
Conjunction	I like baseball and football.
	She caught and hit the dog.
Disjunction and	I read the book but he did not.
Alternation	He is sick or tired.
Determiners	one egg; the car; a book; some people; all of the girls.
Question Formation	Do you want this car?
	Where is my pipe?
	John ate the cake, didn't he?

Verb Processes   Jill will cook lunch and Jack will wash the dishes.
                               The boy was kissed by the girl.
Pronominalization   Since Sally was dirty, Mother washed her.
                               Mary bought herself a dress.
Relativization   The boy who kissed the girl ran away.
                               I saw the boy whom the girl hit.
Complementation   That he was late made me mad.
                               I like for you to drive my car.*

Similar to the findings on reading achievement tests, the results of this longitudinal project indicated that most 18- to 19-year-old deaf students performed inferior to the 8- to 9-year-old hearing students on all structures assessed. It was also found, however, that deaf students learn the structures in a manner similar to that of younger hearing students (see also Wilbur, 1977, and Wilbur & Goodhart, 1985). The order of difficulty of the various syntactic structures for deaf students is illustrated in Table 8.1. Even when acquiring the substructures within a particular structure, deaf students appear to proceed through developmental stages similar to those reported for hearing students. For example, three **question forms** are *yes/no* (e.g., *Do you want a glass of wine?*, **wh-** (e.g., *Where do you live?*), and *tag* (e.g., *You want to marry me, don't you?*). In general, *yes/no* questions were found to be easier to comprehend than *wh-* questions, which were easier than *tag* questions.

Wilbur and her coresearchers (Wilbur, 1977; Wilbur & Goodhart, 1985; Wilbur, Goodhart, & Fuller, 1989) argued that much of hearing-impaired students' problems with syntax is related to instructional practices. For example, teachers try to teach syntax on a sentential level, often neglecting to consider semantics and pragmatics. Acquisition of syntax depends on semantics and pragmatics as well as knowledge of syntax. As stated by Wilbur et al. (1989) in their study on English modals:

> Learning the syntactic rule provides a user of English with information about where in the sentence to put the modal, how to make a question when modals are present, and how to make a negative when modals are present. To approach an adequate account of the English modals, much more than transformational rules are needed. In the last decade, the case has been made for the importance of including proper pragmatic and semantic considerations, both in the classroom and in testing situations. (p. 16)

Quigley and his associates (Quigley et al., 1976) also reported a huge discrepancy between deaf students' comprehension of syntactic structures and the frequency of appearance of these structures in reading materials. The discrepancy was so great that they argued that modifications of existing reading materials would be of limited value. The work of these investigators provided the research base for the development of two reading series specifically designed for deaf students (Quigley & King, 1981–1984; Quigley, Paul, McAnally, Rose, & Payne, in press). These series may be useful for other language-impaired populations (e.g., those with a **learning disability** or mental retar-

---

*For a more detailed description of the various structures and additional examples, see Quigley et al., (1976), and Quigley, Steinkamp, Power, and Jones (1978).

TABLE 8.1. Summary of Performance on the TSA for Deaf Students

Structures	Across Ages	Age 10	Age 18	Gain
Negation				
be	79%	60%	86%	26%
modals	78	58	87	29
have	74	57	78	21
do	71	53	82	28
means	*76*	*57*	*83*	*26*
Conjunction				
deletion	74	59	86	27
conjoining	72	56	86	30
Disjunction and				
Alternation	36	22	59	37
Question Formation				
yes/no	74	48	90	42
wh-	66	44	80	36
tag	57	46	63	17
means	*66*	*46*	*78*	*32*
Verb Processes				
tense sequencing	63	54	72	18
auxiliaries	54	52	71	19
means	58	53	71	18
Pronominalization				
backward	70	49	85	36
personal	67	51	88	37
possessive adjectives	65	42	82	40
reflexivization	50	21	73	52
possessive pronouns	48	34	64	30
means	*60*	*39*	*78*	*39*
Relativization				
processing	68	59	76	17
embedding	53	51	59	8
referents	42	27	56	29
means	*54*	*46*	*63*	*18*
Complementation				
infinitives and				
gerunds	55	50	63	13

NOTE: For a more detailed description of the various structures and additional examples, see Quigley et al. (1976), and Quigley et al. (1978). SOURCE: Based on Quigley et al. (1976).

dation) who have been shown to have similar problems with reading comprehension (Paul, in press; Paul, 1985; Paul & O'Rourke, 1988).

Figurative Language. One of the most complex and colorful qualities of language is the use of figurative expressions. The reader may encounter many figurative elements such as figures of speech and **idiomatic** expressions. Examples of figures of speech include **simile** *(He is sly like a fox)*, **metaphor** *(He is a fox)*, and **onomatopoeia** *(The tap-tap-tap of the raindrops)*. Common idiomatic expressions are *It's raining cats and dogs,* John *ran into* a friend, and Mary is *going out of her mind.* Even multimeaning words can be used in figurative phrases as in The *head* of the class, The *eye* of the needle, and The *foot* of the mountain.

Systematic research on figurative language is in its infancy. The psychological study of this area proceeds with much difficulty because figurative language entails the interactions of grammar (vocabulary, syntax), meaning (semantics), and function (pragmatics).

Severely to profoundly hearing-impaired students have difficulty with many aspects of figurative language (Conley, 1976; Giorcelli, 1982; Payne & Quigley, 1987). Some researchers argue that students can understand certain metaphorical expressions if they understand the vocabulary and syntax used to express them (Iran-Nejad, Ortony, & Rittenhouse, 1981). Knowledge of some figurative elements, however, requires more than knowledge of the grammar, as can be seen in examples such as *He kicked the bucket, This book is over my head,* and *She looked up the number.* Like their knowledge of multimeaning words, hearing-impaired students' knowledge of figurative expressions is related to their levels of reading achievement (Fruchter, Wilbur, & Fraser, 1984). Thus, good readers know more about text-based features than do poor readers, and they also have skills to figure out some unknown features in the context of stories.

Research on Reader-Based Variables

Research on hearing students has established that reading comprehension is affected pervasively by certain reader-based variables such as prior or background knowledge, inferencing, and metacognition (i.e., thinking about your thinking processes while reading texts) (Pearson, 1984, 1985; Pearson et al., 1984). Little is known about the extent of the reader-based skills of severely to profoundly hearing-impaired students or the way they use these skills (King & Quigley, 1985; Quigley & Paul, 1989). Other reader-based variables that affect hearing-impaired students are modes of communication (i.e., oral, signed systems, and ASL) and internal coding systems (i.e., speech-based, sign-based, print-based, or multiple combinations). As is discussed later, it may be that modes of communication and internal mediating systems are not mutually exclusive. These variables are also affected by students' degree of hearing impairment (e.g., slight, mild, severe, or profound) and the socioeconomic status (e.g., income level, education level) of their parents/caretakers.

Prior Knowledge.   There is some evidence that severely to profoundly hearing-impaired students can use their background knowledge to comprehend aspects of the text (Kluwin, Getson, & Kluwin, 1980). Because the students are presumed to lack bottom-up skills (e.g., use of phonics) or to have only poor ones, most of the limited data seem to indicate that they use a top-down schematic (stored prior knowledge) approach during the reading process (Ewoldt, 1981, 1982). It has been emphasized, however, that the students' reading difficulties should be viewed and studied from an interactive theoretical perspective in which both bottom-up and top-down processes are critical. Prior knowledge is extremely important for the development of bottom-up skills and other reader-based skills such as inferencing and metacognition. More research is needed on the effects of prior knowledge on the reading comprehension ability of hearing-impaired students.

Metacognition.   In general, metacognitive skills are knowledge of strategies or pro-cesses used to comprehend the text (Baker & Brown, 1984; Brown, Armbruster, & Baker, 1986). These comprehension strategies also have important applications for teaching study skills to students. It is becoming apparent that metacognitive skills (i.e., being aware of and applying comprehension strategies) are important in reading for compre-hension or meaning and reading for remembering. Good readers constantly engage in checking, monitoring, evaluating, and summarizing their understanding of the text. Es-sentially, they are trying to figure out what it is that they know or do not know by relating and comparing aspects of the text with their own knowledge. Knowing how to comprehend means that they use appropriate strategies to remedy their difficulties with comprehension.

Most of the research on the reading metacognitive abilities of hearing-impaired students has been limited to judgments of grammaticality for single sentences (Kretsch-mer, 1976; Quigley et al., 1976). For example, students are instructed to read sentences and determine if the sentences are acceptable (i.e., feels right) or unacceptable (i.e., does not feel right). Inferring from the evidence on reading achievement levels, it can be surmised that most severely to profoundly hearing-impaired students lack effective metacognitive strategies for reading.

Inferencing.   Good readers use their prior knowledge and metacognitive skills to make inferences about the text (Gordon & Pearson, 1983; Mason & Au, 1986). They try to infer the meanings of words, certain syntactic structures, and other text-based features. Good readers also are able to draw conclusions, make predictions, and answer **infer-ential questions**—that is, questions that require them to connect various portions of the text and to use their background knowledge. Inferencing skills are important for all stages of the reading process, from beginning (grades 1 to 3) to advanced (above grade 3) reading.

Although research on inferencing and deafness is limited, it may be that many students have poor inferential skills (Wilson, 1979) (see discussion in King & Quigley, 1985). For example, an inspection of students' performance on achievement and diag-nostic reading tests reveals their difficulty in answering nonliteral questions.

Consider the following short passage:

The Four Food Groups

The best way to get the nutrients we need is to choose our meals from the four food groups. They are milk, breads and cereals, meats, and fruits and vegetables. Can you name foods in each of the four food groups? Ice cream and cheese are part of the milk group. Ham, nuts, and hamburger are all from the meat group. There are many fruits and vegetables.

An example of an inferential question is: What are the names of the four food groups? To answer this question, students need to infer that the clue is the word *They* in the second sentence. *They* refers to the food groups. Thus, students need to integrate two parts of the text to answer this question. Another example of an inferential question, and one that requires the students to apply their prior knowledge, is: What are names of some foods in the vegetable group? The answer to this question is not explicitly stated in the passage. The question is motivated by the text, but the answer comes from the student's prior knowledge about nutrition, especially about food groups and the foods in them.

It is possible that severely to profoundly hearing-impaired students' poorly developed inferential abilities influence their use of inappropriate strategies (e.g., word association, copying, or visual matching) in answering multiple-choice or **free-response** questions on vocabulary and reading tests (Davey & LaSasso, 1983; LaSasso, 1986; Wolk & Schildroth, 1984). Typically, students focus on one or more words in questions (and/or alternatives). Then they search for words or phrases that are similar or nearly similar in form or meaning in the passage. Their answers are based on these strategies.

The following is an example of a visual matching strategy from LaSasso (1986):

> In order to overcome this difficulty, the Indians have devised a very ingenious method of disarming the fish. Horses are driven into the ponds and the *eels* expend their electrical charge on the horses. *Then the fish are easily harpooned and caught.* It is only after long rest and food that they are again able to build up their ability to shock their enemies.
>
> Question: How do Indians catch eels?
> Response: Then the fish are easily harpooned and caught. (p. 232)

Other poor readers as well as hearing-impaired students also use inappropriate strategies in answering inferential questions. Thus, it is important to teach students to become better at drawing inferences in order to improve their reading comprehension ability.

Internal Coding Systems and Reading.   The general cognitive functioning of severely to profoundly hearing-impaired students was described in Chapter 4. One of the issues discussed was the manner in which adolescents and adults process information in short-term (i.e., working) and long-term (i.e., higher-level) memory. This section describes briefly the relationship between internal coding processes in short-term memory and in reading ability (Baddeley, 1979).

To proceed from print to meaning, readers engage in linguistic mediating that is based on the morphophonemic (morphology and phonology) structure of the language in which they are reading (Ehri & Wilce, 1985). It is hypothesized that the mediating system of good readers is predominantly speech-based—that is, it is an internal representation of the spoken language to which hearing readers are exposed. It is thought that hearing readers convert (i.e., recode) printed words into their phonological equivalents in order to access meanings (Gough, 1985). In addition, a speech-based internal mediating system may be critically important for processing syntactic structures and for developing inferential and metacognitive skills for connected reading.

On the basis of short-term memory studies, we can conclude that most severely to profoundly hearing-impaired students use predominantly a combination of nonspeech-based mediating codes such as sign (most commonly used), finger spelling, or print. Some students, however, do predominantly use a speech-based code, and they are better readers than students who primarily use nonspeech codes (Conrad, 1979; Hanson, 1985; Lichtenstein, 1984, 1985, n.d.; Rodda & Grove, 1987). It appears that speech recoders are able to hold more spoken-language information such as words and syntax in their short-term, or working, memories. This more efficient representation of spoken-language stimuli in working memory enables speech-recoder readers to comprehend the meaning of sentences, particularly the underlying semantic relationships between the words in sentences. Thus, speech-recoders are better than nonspeech-based recoders in comprehending sentences that contain literal word-order structures such as *The boy went to the store* and nonliteral, or hierarchical, structures such as the passive voice (e.g., *The dog was hit by the girl*) and relative clauses (e.g., *The boy who kissed the girl ran away*).

The speech-recoding ability of most severely to profoundly hearing-impaired students may not be as efficient as that of hearing students (Lichtenstein, 1984, n.d.). Hearing-impaired readers are selective in their recoding of English grammar. They recode only the more semantically important information, and they frequently omit features such as function words (e.g., *of, for*) and suffixes (e.g., *-ed, -ly*). Thus, most hearing-impaired readers are not developing a complete internal representation of the grammatical structure of English.

From one perspective, the selective speech-recoding process of students is argued to be an adaptive strategy related to their limited working-memory capacity. Hearing-impaired students are storing as much information as they can in their working memory, but the amount of information is less than that stored in the working memory of their hearing peers. This explains in part why most hearing-impaired speech-recoders do not read as well as their hearing counterparts. It may also be that the nature and use of the internal coding strategies, particularly speech-based coding, is related to the nature and use of the mode of communication (i.e., oral, ASL, or sign systems) to which hearing-impaired students have been exposed (Quigley & Paul, 1989). As discussed in Chapter 7, most students are probably not exposed to a consistent, reliable model of English grammar. Therefore, they are unable to develop and internalize adequate principles on how English works.

In sum, there is little doubt that speech-recoding capacity is important for reading comprehension. We agree with Hanson (1985) that "The question of what the nature of the speech-based representation used by deaf students is and how this representation is developed remains" (p. 110).

Other Factors.   Two other important characteristics of speech-based decoders should be discussed: degree of hearing impairment and socioeconomic status. These two factors are considered *fixed factors*—that is, they are not affected directly by educational intervention (Trybus, 1978). It has been documented repeatedly that degree of hearing impairment and socioeconomic status (SES) are strongly related to the level of reading ability and to the rate of reading growth (Allen, 1986; Quigley & Paul, 1986). In addition, both factors have been shown to affect other areas such as speech intelligibility, use of hearing aids, and amount of time spent in preschool.

There is no question that degree of hearing impairment and SES affect reading ability. The more interesting question, however, is *Do they cause low levels of reading achievement?* The evidence is very strong for degree of hearing impairment (King & Quigley, 1985; Moores, 1987; Quigley & Paul, 1984a). If severely to profoundly hearing-impaired children are linked predominantly to the world of vision, then there may be limits to the development of advanced reading skills because such skills seem to require internalized auditory-language experiences. This is true despite early intervention and adequate amplification systems. As we have stated elsewhere, "It might . . . signify that means other than reading should be sought for imparting information to some types of deaf children" (Quigley & Paul, 1984a, p. 50).

Socioeconomic status is possibly a related rather than a causative factor in reading development. Certain conditions *associated* with low SES, such as mismatches between the languages (also dialects) and cultures of the home and school, do affect reading achievement. Research on hearing children (Alexander, 1979), however, indicates that the effects of these conditions may be minimized in homes where reading and writing are highly valued activities. In these homes, parents/caregivers are literate and spend time reading to their children, and they encourage their children to read to them. Schools must also be committed to developing literacy by implementing effective instructional and curricular activities.

WRITING

What is writing? How do children learn to write? In the 1980s there has been a flurry of research studies that have attempted to answer these questions (Hillocks, 1986; Mosenthal, Tamor, & Walmsley, 1983; Rubin & Hansen, 1986). Traditionally, the focus has been on grammar, punctuation, spelling, penmanship, and other mechanical aspects of writing. More recently, researchers have studied writing as a process and have explored idea development, sentence generation, and paragraph organization. This new emphasis has attempted to show (Raimes, 1983):

> . . . that writing means writing a connected text and not just single sentences, that writers write for a purpose and a reader, and that the process of writing is a valuable learning tool for all. (p. 11)

Despite this shift from an emphasis on the product of composition to the process of composition, we still do not have adequate answers to how children learn to write. As argued by Mosenthal (1983), the major reason for the lack of understanding is because most research studies have been conducted in the absence of well-established, prevailing theories about the acquisition of written language in the classroom setting. It is difficult to define writing and "classroom writing competence" (Mosenthal, 1983, p. 27). The emphasis on the process of writing, however, has provided some insights to how writing can be defined. Perhaps the best way to understand writing is to consider it as similar to the process of reading.

Comprehension and Composition

Until recently, educators and researchers tried to demonstrate ways in which reading and writing were different from each other. Evidence suggests that the two areas are interrelated and encompass similar processes (Rubin & Hansen, 1986; Tierney & Leys, 1984). When students perform activities in reading, they often engage in activities in writing, and vice versa. Even students' writing styles have been reported to be affected by what they read. Good writers are often said to be good readers. Composition, however, does involve more than reading because good readers are not always good writers.

It is permissible to consider that reading, like writing, is composition (Pearson, 1984; Tierney & Pearson, 1983). Writing can be viewed from the standpoint of interactive theories of reading. Both writing and reading involve interactions between the student and the text in which the student is trying to construct meaning. Readers construct meaning from texts in existence; writers construct meaning by producing texts. In this sense, both processes resemble the act of composing.

The act of writing requires *planning, composing,* and *revising.* During the planning or prewriting stage, students use their prior knowledge to choose a topic, generate ideas, identify their audience, and devise a tentative organizational plan (Whitt, Paul, & Reynolds, 1988). The students begin writing during the composing or drafting stage. Drafting can be described as tentative writing. Revisions occur during and after composition. Writers attempt to polish, alter, expand, and clarify their manuscripts. These are not necessarily discrete stages. Writers can revise their plans or plan their revisions (Tierney & Pearson, 1983).

Reading also involves planning, composing, and revising. Planning is similar to prereading activities that deal with enriching and activating the prior knowledge of the readers. During reading, readers attempt to construct a tentative model of what the text means. They may revise their models of meaning as they gain additional insights by relating information in the text to what they already know. Revisions, even expansions or new perspectives, can also occur after reading when both teacher and reader discuss the story. As aptly stated by Tierney and Pearson (1983):

> . . . what drives reading and writing is this desire to make sense of what is happening—to make things cohere. A writer achieves that fit by deciding what information to include and what to withhold. The reader accomplishes that fit by filling in gaps . . . or making uncued connections. All readers, like all writers, ought to strive for this fit between the whole and the parts and among the parts. (p. 572)

In sum, writing develops as a result of, and in conjunction with, reading. Good writers develop higher-level thinking skills such as organization, intent, and purpose. This does not mean, however, that the **lower-level mechanical skills** such as grammar and punctuation are not important. Just as fluent reading requires that lower-level word identification skills become automatic, proficiency in writing requires that lower-level mechanical skills become automatic. This is important to remember in light of the recent research and instructional attention on the process of writing rather than the product.

WRITING AND DEAFNESS

Like the studies on hearing students, the research on writing and deafness has focused mostly on the product rather than on the process of writing (Quigley & Paul, 1989; *Volta Review,* 1985). Whether the emphasis is on product or process, we are inclined to agree with Moores (1987) that ''The evidence suggests that the problems deaf children face in mastering written English are more formidable than those they face in developing reading skills'' (p. 281). This is true if writing encompasses more than just reading skills.

If poor readers are invariably poor writers, then it is not surprising that research on the written language production of severely to profoundly hearing-impaired students reveals the same low levels of achievement as that of their reading ability. Similar to learning to read, most hearing-impaired writers are struggling with both low-level (e.g., mechanical) and high-level (e.g., organizational) skills. Most hearing children can increase their reading levels through writing activities and improve their writing skills through reading activities. This situation is different for most severely to profoundly hearing-impaired students, mainly because of our recurring theme: Most of the students have not developed an internal representation of English. Many students cannot even express their thoughts in English in a primary mode—that is, either through speech and/or signing. It is also highly unlikely that they can express themselves adequately through writing. The ability to write is generally contingent on the ability to read, which is affected by a primary language form on which both processes are based (for another viewpoint, see Conway, 1985).

To illustrate the written language problems of severely to profoundly hearing-impaired students, it is convenient to discuss research in relation to the manner in which the writing products (i.e., form) have been analyzed. Most of the studies have been motivated by the prevailing linguistic theories of the time, namely, **traditional/structural** and **transformational generative grammar.** In comparing the written production of hearing-impaired students with that of hearing students, researchers provided insights into productivity or amount, complexity of sentences, parts of speech, and types of errors (Quigley & Paul, 1984a, 1989; Yoshinaga-Itano & Snyder, 1985). Much of the available information concerns analyses of *sentences.* A few recent studies have used analyses beyond the sentence level (Yoshinaga-Itano & Snyder, 1985), examined writing as a process approach (Ewoldt, 1985; Gormley & Sarachan-Deily, 1987), or suggested that writing and reading should be taught as a whole language process—that is, as a literacy process, not as a process that should be separated into components (Taylor, 1983).

Analyses of Sentences: Traditional/Structural

Early studies analyzed single sentences within a traditional or structural framework. From a traditional perspective, the emphasis is on prescription, that is, the *correct* way to use words in sentences. Structural analyses focus on *describing* the surface or text features of written sentences. Both of these viewpoints were influenced by theories of behaviorism that described language development in terms of environmental influences. Not much attention was given to the process or manner in which students learn to speak/sign or write.

Most of the analyses were conducted on a sample of hearing-impaired students' written productions on free response tasks. Typically, students were exposed to visual stimuli such as pictures, picture sequences, or short films, and were required to write their reactions. Their writings were analyzed and compared with those of hearing peers.

As to productivity, or the amount of writing, the levels of written language of hearing-impaired students of high school age were reported to be equal or inferior to those of the average 10-year-old hearing student (Heider & Heider, 1940; Myklebust, 1964; Simmons, 1963; Stuckless & Marks, 1966). For example, the average sentence length of 17-year-old hearing-impaired students was equivalent to that produced by 8-year-old hearing students. No differences between the two groups, however, were observed for the total number of words in the sentences or passages.

In relation to sentence complexity, the written language productions of severely to profoundly hearing-impaired students can be described as rigid, or stereotypic. That is, researchers have reported that a number of recurring, redundant phrases or sentences appear frequently such as *They had an idea, I see a*   , and *There is a*   . The students also did not produce many compound (e.g., *Mary went to the movies and the store*) or complex (e.g., *John was happy because he won the game*) sentences. They tended to use less variety of parts of speech than did hearing students. Certain parts of speech such as **determiners** *(a, an, the)*, nouns *(house, boy)*, and verbs *(run, see)* were used more often than adverbs *(slowly, beautifully)* and **conjunctions** *(and, or, but)*. The written compositions also contained a number of errors that were categorized as additions (putting in unnecessary words), omissions (omitting necessary words), substitutions (using inappropriate words in place of other words), and word-order deviations (inappropriate order of words in the sentences). In relation to sentence complexity, errors, or use of parts of speech, the major emphasis was on describing them, not on providing explanations on how or why students produced them.

Analyses of Sentences: Transformational Generative Grammar

With the advent of theories of transformational generative grammar, the emphasis on subsequent analyses of written compositions shifted from descriptive to explanatory. From this perspective, language is considered generative; that is, its users have an intuitive knowledge of the rule system, or how their language works (Chomsky, 1957, 1965). Thus, they are able to produce and comprehend an infinite number of sentences, including some they have never heard or read previously. By analyzing the user's sentences, it is possible to describe the rule-governed system under which the user is operating.

Written language samples of severely to profoundly hearing-impaired students have been elicited from both free-response (e.g., students react to visual stimuli) and **controlled-response** (e.g., multiple-choice) tasks (Hunt, 1965; Marshall & Quigley, 1970; Powers & Wilgus, 1983; Quigley et al., 1976; Taylor, 1969). Two statements can be made: (1) Most students have not internalized rules for producing or comprehending English, and (2) Although students do not know English as well as hearing students, they are still learning it in the same developmental manner.

The errors in the writings were described and explained in relation to rule categories established by generative grammar—for example, morphological and **transformational rules.** Morphology concerns the use of inflectional (e.g., *-ing*) and derivational (e.g., *-ness*) rules. Transformation refers to the production and comprehension of structures such as conjunctions (e.g., *and, but*), relative clauses (e.g., clauses starting with *that, who, which*), and passive voice (e.g., The boy *was hit* by the girl).

In following morphological rules, hearing-impaired students had the most difficulty with verb inflections, as in *She fly* instead of *she flies* (present tense omitted) or *The table broked* instead of *The table broke* (redundant use of past tense marker). In general, the students either omitted, overgeneralized, or used the inflections inappropriately. Next in order of difficulty were the use of plurals (*sheeps* for *sheep,* or *Six boy* instead of *Six boys*) and the possessive (such as *'s* and *s'*. The patterns of error were similar to those found in the writing of much younger hearing children.

It was difficult to describe the rule violations in the students' use of transformations, mainly because very few of these structures were found in their writings. The most frequently appearing structure was the conjunction which students omitted *(A ant see a tree or bird),* location *(The dove got out of the tree and took a leaf threw it down),* and deletion rules *(The ant threw a ball on the ground and put in his room).* Finally, there was a similarity between the students' use of certain syntactic structures and their comprehension of the same structures on diagnostic tests such as the Test of Syntactic Abilities (Quigley et al., 1978).

Severely to profoundly hearing-impaired students have mastered many simple, active declarative sentence structures, especially those expressed in a subject-verb-object format as in *The boy went to the store.* Nevertheless, they still make numerous errors in applying morphological, and in some cases, transformational rules. In addition, they rarely produce sentences that contain complex transformations.

Perhaps the strongest evidence for the students' lack of understanding of English can be found in the studies using tasks of grammaticality (Kretschmer, 1976; O'Neill, 1973; Quigley et al., 1976). The students were required to judge whether sentences were *right* or *wrong.* In general, hearing-impaired students were more likely to accept ungrammatical sentences than were hearing students. Most of the ungrammatical sentences contained errors that had been observed in their written compositions. It has been suggested that many hearing-impaired students operate under a rule-governed system that is not standard English. A comprehensive review of much of this work is in Quigley and Paul (1984a) and in McAnally, Rose, and Quigley (1987).

Beyond the Sentence Level

Analyses of written compositions at an intersentential level and of writing as a process have been motivated by pragmatic theories of language acquisition (Gleason, 1985; Lucas, 1980; Yokoyama, 1986). As defined earlier, pragmatics is the study of language development in relation to function and use. According to some theorists and researchers, intersentential analyses permit a better understanding of the relationship between form (e.g., morphology, syntax) and meaning (i.e., semantics). It is argued that studying the interaction between semantics and syntax on an intersentential level may provide insights into the low literacy levels of severely to profoundly hearing-impaired students. In addition, improvement in the writing of students is more likely to result from an emphasis on writing as a communicative process, particularly with the focus on planning, composing, and revising.

A reanalysis of the data of Quigley et al. (1976) revealed that deaf students committed more syntactic errors on an intersentential level than on a sentential level (Wilbur, 1977). It was thought that deaf students were receiving instruction that focused too heavily on producing correct single sentences. This resulted in stilted written compositions without many imaginative or metaphorical expressions. It was concluded that deaf students need instruction to help them construct meaningful paragraphs or passages that emphasize organization and content.

Research on writing as a process approach with a focus on both meaning (semantics) and form (syntax) in deaf children's writings is in its infancy (Gormley & Sarachan-Deily, 1987; Sarachan-Deily, 1982, 1985). Gormley and Sarachan-Deily's study (1987) is illustrative of the paradigm shift in research on writing. They analyzed the written language samples of high-school students with severe to profound hearing impairments.

The students were placed in two groups: good writers and poor writers. Placement was based on judgments and general impression ratings of teachers and one of the investigators. Then, the investigators conducted in-depth analyses of the writings of the two groups. They provided data in relation to three categories: content, linguistic aspects, and surface mechanics. *Content* referred to such items as introduction, supporting statements, summary, conclusion, and identifying an audience. Content involves the higher-level skills of writing. *Linguistic aspects* included word order, omission of parts of speech, and violation of semantic relations. *Surface mechanics* pertained to spelling, punctuation, capitalization, legibility, and minor grammatical errors such as **articles** and possessives. Linguistic aspects and surface mechanics are usually considered lower-level skills.

Results showed that both poor and good writers produced a number of errors in surface mechanics and linguistics. There were no significant differences, however, between the groups on surface mechanics and on some of the linguistic aspects. As for content, the compositions of good writers were significantly more developed, cohesive, and appropriate than those of poor writers. Good writers focus on making their compositions clear and readable. In short, the major differences between good and poor writers were in the use of higher-level writing skills. These differences were evident through analyses on an intersentential level and consideration of the higher-level skills of writing. The researchers maintained that instruction in writing should emphasize the communicative process. In particular, they noted that there is a need to encourage hearing-impaired writers to reread and revise their manuscripts. They also suggested that improvements in surface mechanics and linguistic aspects may occur if the students engage in the rereading and revision processes of writing.

It may not be enough, however, only to encourage severely to profoundly hearing-impaired students to reread and revise their compositions. From an interactive theoretical perspective, it is important for writers to develop both lower-level and higher-level skills. In many instances, poor writers, like poor readers, may need comprehensive instruction in both areas. To become proficient writers, students must develop their skills in lower-level writing until it becomes automatic so that they can spend most of their time on organization, intent, and other higher-level skills during the writing process.

INSTRUCTION AND ASSESSMENT

There should be a close interrelationship among theory, instruction, and assessment for reading and writing. In general, instructional and assessment practices and procedures have not adhered to the salient principles of the emergent views of reading and writing as constructive processes (Nystrand & Knapp, 1987; Pearson & Valencia, 1986; Valencia & Pearson, 1987). In addition, the idea that comprehension and composition are remarkably similar is often neglected. Finally, in attempts to maintain objectivity, teachers are not always as involved in the construction of assessments as they should be.

Instruction and Reading

Not much is known about the effectiveness of reading instructional methods and materials in teaching reading. Although a variety of methods has been promoted, very little research has been or is being conducted to assess their merits (Clarke, Rogers, & Booth, 1982; King & Quigley, 1985). Much of what is known has come from survey studies in which respondents provide information by answering questions (i.e., on questionnaires). In essence, "The current state of instructional methodology is one of confused eclecticism" due to "the remarkable lack of empirical data in this critical area" (Clarke et al., 1982, p. 65).

Many teachers of hearing-impaired students may not be adequately trained to teach reading. For example, it was reported that 20 percent of teachers responsible for teaching reading had had only one or no courses in reading at the college or university level (Coley & Bockmiller, 1980). This percentage might have been higher had the sample included all teachers of hearing-impaired students.

Another perspective on teacher preparation can be seen in a survey that reported teachers to be divided on using bottom-up or top-down approaches in the teaching of reading, and that most teachers prefer **meaning-emphasis** rather than **code-emphasis** approaches (Lanfrey, cited in King & Quigley, 1985, pp. 76–77). This is also the case for many reading teachers of hearing students. It is important to mention that the information we have provided on teachers of hearing-impaired students has come from surveys of teachers in residential schools. Thus, the findings may not be representative of all programs. Nevertheless, these either-or viewpoints run counter to the emerging framework of reading as an interactive process in which readers use bottom-up and top-down skills to construct a model of what the text means. An excellent treatment of these and other instructional issues can be found in Chapter 4 of King and Quigley (1985) and in Pearson (1984, 1985).

Instructional methods and materials used with hearing-impaired students have been reported in three national surveys covering residential and day programs (Hasenstab & McKenzie, 1981; LaSasso, 1978, 1987a). The general findings of the most recent survey are reported here (LaSasso, 1987a). Areas covered include the extent of basal reader and **language-experience approaches** (LEA), types of **basal readers** used, and some reasons for the use of special basal reading programs. On the survey questionnaire, the respondents could select more than one answer in some categories of questions.

Most education programs responding to the survey used either basal readers (83 percent of residential schools, 80 percent of day class/programs) or the language-experience approach (79 percent of residential schools, 74 percent of day programs). The basal reader is the more commonly used technique at the elementary and intermediate levels. It was also reported that many secondary (i.e., high schools) programs are using basal readers. Basal readers and language-experiences were used mainly because teachers believed that their particular preference represented the best way to teach reading.

Generally, in the LEA, "students dictate stories to the teacher, who records the stories and uses that printed material to develop students' vocabularies, specific reading skills, and comprehension abilities" (LaSasso, 1987a, p. 86). Teachers play a predominant role in determining what and how to teach reading skill. The main problem, however, is that programs lack comprehensiveness or continuity in their use of the LEA. Many education programs have no policy or depend on informal communication among teachers for coordination of their reading programs. Finally, although teacher participation in the reading program is commendable, the effectiveness of this participation must be questioned, given what is known about the preparation of teachers.

Presently, more than 20 basal readers are being used by the education programs for hearing-impaired students. The four most commonly used series are *Reading Milestones* (published by Dormac), *Reading Systems and Systems Unlimited* (published by Scott, Foresman), *Ginn 360* and *Ginn 720* (published by Ginn & Co.), and *Houghton Mifflin Readers* (published by Houghton Mifflin). Respondents were asked to rate these series on several variables such as vocabulary, syntax, figurative language, and content. *Reading Milestones* (RM) was rated higher than the other series in all areas except interest level and diagnostic materials. In general, RM was selected because it was specifically developed for hearing-impaired students. More than half of the programs that reported using basal series were using RM, apparently with satisfaction.

The effects of special or adapted materials on the reading comprehension of hearing-impaired students have not been extensively studied. Some positive support can be found in a study by Heine (1981) on the use of RM. The comprehension of **literal questions** by hearing-impaired students was reported to be equal to or better than was that of a comparison group of hearing students. It was argued earlier that special or adapted materials may be necessary because of the huge mismatch between the language and content of typical reading materials and severely to profoundly hearing-impaired students' understanding. It is recognized, however, that more research is needed to assess the merits of all instructional methods and materials.

A Model of Reading Instruction

We do not intend to present a comprehensive model of reading instruction. A more detailed description of this issue can be found in Anderson et al. (1985). It is important, however, to highlight some areas that need improvement. Specifically, we refer to instruction of vocabulary and comprehension skills, and the role of the teacher in the reading program.

Vocabulary.   There is no question that readers' knowledge of the topic of a passage, including key vocabulary included in the passage, is a better predictor of comprehension than is any other measure of reading achievement (Johnston, 1984; Johnston & Pearson,

1982). Vocabulary instruction needs to move away from what can be termed the definition-and-sentence approach to a conceptual or classification approach (Paul, in press; Paul & O'Rourke, 1988). Typically, the focus has been on what a word means and how it is used in a sentence. Attention should be given to the entire conceptual framework elicited by the word. Teachers should help students acquire new words and concepts and a deeper knowledge of old words and concepts by bridging the unknown and known information. Techniques for helping students relate what they know about words to what they do not know are semantic mapping, **semantic feature analyses,** and other forms of **semantic elaboration.** For a description of these approaches, see Heimlich and Pittelman (1986). As stated by Pearson (1984, p. 16), instead of asking, ''What is it the children do not know and how can I get that into their heads?'' we should ask, ''What is it that the children *do* know that is enough like the new concepts so that I can use it as an anchor point?''

Comprehension.   Comprehension is or should be the most important goal of reading. No text is ever completely explicit; that is, no text specifies all relationships among characters, events, and things, or explains everything in detail. In short, no text defines comprehension. Thus, the reader needs to play an active constructive role and build a model of what the text means, typically inferring a great deal of information during reading. Comprehension results from the interaction of the reader and the text. This interaction is affected by the prior knowledge, strategies, and other reader-based factors, and by the demands of the reading task.

The crux is that teachers should be aware of text-based and reader-based factors that could affect comprehension. Reader-based factors, especially the application of prior knowledge, metacognitive, and inferential skills, are extremely important. Thus, teachers may need to develop prereading questions that build background for story comprehension. These questions should require students to make inferences and predictions and to understand what they know or do not know about specific topics. Much of the postreading activities should also focus on inferential questions. Readers should also be asked comparison questions; they should be asked to apply what they have read to other situations, and even other stories.

The Role of the Teacher.   Teachers should play an active role in providing instruction in reading. This role involves more than following the guidelines and instructions in the teacher's guide. It involves more than directing students to read the story, asking and providing answers to questions, and then requiring students to do workbook activities for reinforcement. Like the student's text, the teacher's guide is not and cannot be explicit. Teachers should read the story and build *their* models of what the text means to provide the basis for the construction of important prereading questions and activities to enrich and activate the prior knowledge of the students. By being active participants, teachers may understand what is needed to help students develop metacognitive and inferential abilities. Teachers may need to *teach* students such skills as how to make inferences, where to find an answer to a question, and how to find out what they do know and how to apply it to what they do not know. In short, teachers should teach, model, and provide feedback on comprehension skills. This may require a substantial amount of time to be spent on the construction of prereading and postreading activities. Nevertheless, the end result is that many students will eventually become better readers.

Instruction and Writing

In the education of hearing-impaired students, written language instruction and language development practices have been tightly interwoven (McAnally, Rose, & Quigley, 1987; Moores, 1987; Quigley & Paul, 1984a). Teachers often used written language to teach English, especially if they favored a structural instructional approach or a combined approach involving both structural and natural methods.

The natural approach attempts to elicit and develop English in a holistic manner. By exposing hearing-impaired students to a typical language environment, it is expected that they will discover principles and rules about how the English language works in the same manner as do hearing children. In this view, language is not taught to, but is acquired by, hearing-impaired students in natural, meaningful, communicative situations. The natural instructional method does not advocate the use of specific symbol systems to represent certain English grammatical structures such as question-words (e.g., *who, what, where*), parts of speech (e.g., nouns, verbs, adjectives), and syntactic structures (e.g., noun phrases).

In the structural approach to the teaching of language, symbol systems are highly important. Students are expected to acquire English in an analytical manner. Specifically, they are required to understand the important grammatical aspects of a language within the constraints of a strictly sequenced curriculum. One of the ways students demonstrate their understanding is through writing sentences, using patterns that have been taught.

In a recent national survey, it was reported that most educational programs for hearing-impaired students use a combined approach in language instruction (King, 1984). Combined approaches may entail natural and structural methods or structural and eclectic (i.e., the use of various methods at the discretion of teacher) methods. More than half of the programs use writing to teach English, and most programs employ some type of symbol system. The percentage of programs using symbol systems has increased across instructional levels, from more than 50 percent at the preschool level to nearly 98 percent at the high school level. Many programs also use more than one symbol system. We can conclude that written language instruction in these programs is primarily structural and focuses on the product of writing rather than on the process (*Volta Review*, 1985).

There is little empirical evidence on the effectiveness of the various methods and materials for written language instruction. The superiority of natural or structural approaches or some combination of them has not been documented. As noted by King (1984), there is a great need for research to assess the merits of the various symbol systems that are used to teach English. It is important to assess written language instruction regardless of whether programs are using a product or process approach or some combination.

A Model of Writing Instruction

It is likely that the teaching of writing will emphasize comprehension and other higher-level skills as well as the composition of passages rather than single sentences or paragraphs (Nystrand & Knapp, 1987; Reynolds, 1985; Whitt, Paul, & Reynolds, 1988). Lower-level skills such as mechanics, however, should not be neglected. Our intent is to present some salient principles of writing as a process, principles that we have briefly discussed previously.

Many students can learn to write by writing. Many writers, however, also need to learn strategies that lead them through the complex stages of the writing process. The teacher needs to be actively involved with the students to help them develop, apply, and adapt strategies as they engage in the composing process. The three broad steps in composition are *planning* (or prewriting), *composing,* and *revising.*

Planning, or Prewriting.   Planning, or prewriting, activities are similar to prereading activities. The teacher should enrich and activate the prior knowledge of students to prepare them for developing their compositions. Through the use of questions and semantic elaboration techniques (e.g., semantic maps), the teacher can help students choose a topic, generate and organize ideas, identify an audience, and establish a purpose for writing.

Composing.   During this stage, students write the first draft of their composition, using their outlines or semantic maps to guide the organization and content of their papers. Teachers can also prompt students with questions and comments. For example, the teacher may inquire, ''What did your dad's car look like?'' or comment, ''You did a good job supporting your views.'' Students also may receive additional support and insights from their peers.

Revising.   During the revising stage, the writer again takes on the role of a reader. Through rereading, writers attempt to polish, alter, expand, and clarify their manuscripts. At this time, the teacher may decide that some students need more specific instructions in lower-level skills such as grammar, spelling, capitalization, and punctuation. Depending on the extent of the problem, instruction can begin here and continue at another appropriate time. Instruction may be necessary and meaningful because students are having difficulty rewriting or combining sentences or selecting more appropriate words. The goal is to help students master lower-level skills so that they can spend more time on the higher-level skills that are important for becoming proficient in writing.

Issues in Assessment

There are many types of tests for assessing reading and writing, including standardized **norm-referenced** tests, **criterion-referenced** tests, tests that accompany reading or writing programs, teacher-made tests, classroom observations, samples of student's work, and a record of the interactions between students and teacher (Farr & Carey, 1986; Valencia & Pearson, 1987). The test tasks may require free (e.g., recall of events in stories) and/

or controlled (e.g., multiple-choice questions) choices. Each test type has advantages and disadvantages. The selection of a good test or tests depends on the questions that need to be answered. For example, if a student's score is to be compared with other students of similar ages or ability, a standardized norm-referenced test, selected for its match with district curricula, may provide adequate data. If the goal is to pinpoint a student's weaknesses and strengths in a particular domain such as math or reading, then a diagnostic criterion-referenced test may be appropriate. A more detailed discussion of this issue can be found elsewhere (King & Quigley, 1985; Quigley & Paul, 1986).

Tests on reading and writing are usually related to theoretical views of the nature of reading and/or writing. There is a growing body of evidence, however, that assessment has not kept pace with the emerging views of reading and writing (Nystrand & Knapp, 1987; Pearson & Valencia, 1986). The tests used often represent contradictory views. For example, in relation to reading tests, Pearson and Valencia (1986) stated:

> Prior knowledge is a major determinant of reading comprehension, yet we mask any relation between knowledge and comprehension on tests by using many short passages about unfamiliar, sometimes obscure, topics.
>
> To accomplish the goals of reading, readers must orchestrate many so-called skills, yet many of our reading assessment schemes fragment the process into discrete skills, as if each was important in its own right. (p. 4)

Pearson and Valencia also listed other shortcomings—for example, that current tests with their short, contrived passages do not assess inferential thinking and reading strategies.

The problems associated with short, contrived passages have been documented in a review of several prominent reading and writing tests by a panel of experts (Nystrand & Knapp, 1987). It was argued that tests should use samples of actual discourse because of the inadequate context of short passages for testing certain skills. To improve the quality of standardized tests, several recommendations were made:

1. Test writers should provide adequate context for testing the skills which they seek to measure.
2. Tests and sections of tests should require students actually to do what they say they test.
3. Tests of genitive skills, such as writing, should reveal and identify the actual errors of the test taker.
4. Tests should use actual, not contrived texts, i.e., texts specially composed for the tests.
5. In reading, tests should use a range of prose and text types.
6. In writing, tests should elicit more than one type of writing sample, on different topics in different genres. (pp. 5–6)

In relation to hearing-impaired students, there are other important issues to consider. For example, it has been suggested that the students' performances on achievement tests may vary according to the tasks required, whether students can look back or not, and types of questions asked (e.g., LaSasso, 1986, 1987b). It is also important to know if hearing-impaired students were a part of the sample used to develop norms, or standards. Although current measures for assessing reading and writing abilities in hearing-impaired students need to be improved, we can still conclude that the average severely to profoundly hearing-impaired high school graduate is reading and writing no better than the average 8- or 9-year-old hearing student. These and other issues related to achievement are discussed in Chapter 9.

SUMMARY

This chapter described the reading and writing abilities of severely to profoundly hearing-impaired students and discussed difficulties in relation to emerging theoretical views. It was reported that the overwhelming majority of the students cannot read or write above a third or fourth grade level. Results of achievement tests show that these students' advancement in reading proceeds at less than one-half grade level per year.

Within an interactive theoretical framework, hearing-impaired students' reading problems were illustrated in two categories: text-based and reader-based variables. Text-based variables refer to aspects of the text such as vocabulary, syntax, and figurative language. Some reader-based variables are prior knowledge, inferencing, and metacognitive skills. It was found that students acquired certain text-based structures at a much slower rate than did their hearing peers; however, both groups proceed through similar developmental stages. Not much is known regarding the reader-based variables of hearing-impaired students because most research studies have focused on text-based factors. Thus, there is a need for future studies on strategies of reading, especially inferencing and metacognitive skills to provide additional insights on the test-taking strategies of severely to profoundly hearing-impaired students.

Given the fact that the processes of comprehension and composition are similar, it is no surprise that hearing-impaired students also demonstrated low levels of writing ability. Much of the research on writing has also been on the product or text-based variables, especially on a sentential level. That is, researchers have typically analyzed certain textual features such as vocabulary and syntax in samples of written language. As expected, severely to profoundly hearing-impaired students do not have an adequate command of the numerous rules of standard English grammar. On the basis of error analyses, it was concluded that most students operate under a system which is not that of standard English. In the few studies about writing as a process approach, it was found that many hearing-impaired writers have problems with the higher-level skills of organization, intent, and cohesion. Although more investigations are needed on writing as a process and on writing connected discourse, it was argued that hearing-impaired students still need instruction in lower-level skills such as mechanics and grammar as well as in the higher-level skills.

Research on internal coding strategies has provided additional insights regarding low literacy levels. Much of the research concerns the nature of short-term memory and the relationship of STM to reading ability. It was reported that most severely to profoundly hearing-impaired readers mediate in a combination of nonspeech-based codes such as signing, finger spelling, and print in order to access meaning from print. Readers who mediate *primarily* with a speech-based code, however, were reported to be better readers than those who mediate primarily through nonspeech codes. The higher reading levels of the speech recoders were attributed to their ability to hold more spoken language information in short-term memory. Spoken language information, specifically, temporal-sequential linguistic units, may be necessary for comprehending hierarchical structures such as relative clauses and the passive voice. Research on short-term memory processes highlights the importance of the development of cognition and primary language to the development of reading and writing. It can be argued that the development of secondary language in English is highly dependent on the presence of spoken language structures (i.e., auditory-oral experiences) in the internalized primary language system of students.

More research is needed to determine the relationship of coding strategies to the development of literacy. Most reading and writing approaches assume the existence of an auditory-based primary language form that is lacking or extremely limited in most severely to profoundly hearing-impaired students. Because most of these students use predominantly nonspeech-based codes, it is important to understand how reading and writing can be taught to them.

Knowledge about the effectiveness of instructional practices and materials has not kept pace with that about the processes of reading and writing. Very little is known regarding instruction and deafness, and there appears to be little ongoing research in this area. Thus, most instructional practices are not based on empirical data but on philosophical arguments.

It was reported that many teachers may be inadequately prepared to teach reading. Teachers are divided on ways to teach reading, whether to use bottom-up or top-down methods. Both bottom-up and top-down skills are important within an interactive theoretical framework. The results of a recent national survey revealed that basal readers and the language experience approach are the most commonly used instructional programs. Of the basal readers examined, *Reading Milestones,* which was specifically developed for deaf students, was found to be the most commonly used series.

Instruction in written language development has been influenced by the two general approaches used to teach language: natural and structural. Most educational programs use a combination of the two. In addition, many programs use reading, written language, and certain symbol systems to teach the structure of English. The superiority of the general approaches or the merits of the various symbol systems in the teaching of English has not been empirically established. It is also possible that many teachers of hearing-impaired students are ill-prepared to teach writing, especially writing as a process.

The role of the teacher in the teaching of reading and writing should not be underestimated. Teachers need to be well grounded in the current theoretical views of literacy. Specifically, teachers should know as much about reading and writing as a physics teacher knows about physics. They should also be aware of instructional practices that are *theory-based.* The chapter presented salient aspects of instructional models for the teaching of both reading and writing. It was emphasized that teachers need to be active participants in the teaching of lower-level and higher-level skills of comprehension and composition.

Finally, the chapter argued for improvements in the construction of tests for assessing literacy skills. In general, current tests have not adhered to the emerging views of reading and writing processes. There needs to be a closer interrelationship among theory, assessment, and practice. It is also important for teachers to receive training in assessment so that they can evaluate the merits of their instructional practices and materials.

COMPREHENSION

1. What is functional literacy?
2. What are the three major theoretical models for understanding the process of reading?
3. Which theory states that reading is a psycholinguistic-guessing or hypothesis-testing game?
4. Which theory states that the letter mediates the word? In other words, a predominant amount of emphasis is placed on simple letter identification, letter clusters, and sound-letter correspondences.
5. According to interactive theory, reading is
   a. An active search for meaning.
   b. A constructive process.
   c. A strategic process.
   d. None of the above.
   e. Items *a, b,* and *c.*
6. Most 17-to-18-year-old severely to profoundly hearing-impaired students read:
   a. As well as their hearing peers.
   b. At about the eighth-grade level.
   c. At about the third- or fourth-grade level.
   d. None of the above.
   e. Items *a, b,* and *c.*
7. TRUE or FALSE? According to the authors, the reading difficulties of deaf students can and should be discussed within the framework of top-down theories of reading.
8. Name two text-based variables and two reader-based variables.
9. For both hearing and hearing-impaired students, which question form is the easiest to comprehend in reading materials?
   a. wh- questions
   b. yes/no questions
   c. tag questions
   d. none of the above
   e. Items *a, b,* and *c*
10. TRUE or FALSE? More knowledge is available on hearing-impaired students' comprehension of text-based factors rather than of reader-based factors.
11. On the basis of short-term memory studies, it can be concluded that most severely to profoundly hearing-impaired students use predominantly
   a. Speech-based mediating code.
   b. Nonspeech-based mediating code.
   c. Graphemic code only.
   d. A finger spelled code only.
   e. None of the above.
12. How are reading and writing related?
13. TRUE or FALSE?
   a. Grammar and spelling are lower-level skills of writing.
   b. Not much is known on the effectiveness of reading instructional methods and materials.
14. To improve reading and writing assessments, it is necessary to
   a. Construct short passages about unfamiliar topics.

    b. Construct passages that assess inferential thinking and strategies.
    c. Use a range of prose and text types.
    d. Items *b* and *c* only.
    e. Items *a* and *c* only.

SUGGESTED ACTIVITIES

1. Obtain teacher's manuals for several basal reading series. Describe the prereading and post-reading activities associated with some stories in each series. Can you tell if the manuals espouse a particular theory of reading?

2. Reread the section on *Theoretical Models* from page 178 to page 180 in this chapter (read it only once!). Allow yourself about 10 minutes to write a one-page summary. Then, reread the section. This time, make an outline of some important points under each heading, for example, *Bottom-Up Approaches, Top-Down Approaches,* and *Interactive Approaches.* Use this outline to write another one-page summary. Each heading should comprise one paragraph. Was the second time around easier? Why or why not?

3. The following passage demonstrates the effects of prior knowledge on reading comprehension. (Taken from Anderson, R., Reynolds, R., Schallert, D., & Goetz, E. (1977). Frameworks for comprehending discourse. *American Educational Research Journal, 14,* 367–381.)

> Rocky slowly got up from the mat, planning his escape. He hesitated a moment and thought. Things were not going well. What bothered him most was being held, especially since the charge against him had been weak. He considered his present situation. The lock that held him was strong but he thought he could break it. He knew, however, that his timing would have to be perfect. Rocky was aware that it was because of his early roughness that he had been penalized so severely—much too severely from his point of view. The situation was becoming frustrating; the pressure had been grinding on him for too long. He was being ridden unmercifully. Rocky was getting angry now. He felt he was ready to make his move. He knew that his success or failure would depend on what he did in the next few seconds.

> What do you think this passage is about? There are at least two interpretations!

FURTHER READINGS

Chall, J. (1983). *Stages of reading development.* New York, NY: McGraw-Hill.

Hirsch, E. (1987). *Cultural literacy.* Boston, MA: Houghton Mifflin.

Huck, C. (1987). *Children's literature in the elementary school* (4th ed.). New York, NY: Holt, Rinehart, & Winston.

Jensen, J. (Ed.). (1984). *Composing and comprehending.* Urbana, IL: National Conference on Research in English.

Kozol, J. (1985). *Illiterate America.* New York, NY: Doubleday.

McNeil, J. (1987). *Reading comprehension.* Glenview, IL: Scott, Foresman.

Reading and the hearing-impaired individual. (1982). *Volta Review, 84,* (5), September, R.E. Kretschmer (Ed.). Special Issue.

CHAPTER 9

Academic Placement, Assessment, and Achievement

MAJOR POINTS TO CONSIDER

Educational placements

Instruction and curriculum

Types of assessment

Preschool, early intervention, and achievement

Research on elementary and secondary educational programs

Effects of placement on educational achievement

Postsecondary education

In this chapter, the major issues we discuss are placement, assessment, achievement, and their interrelationships. We give data on types of educational placement and the percentages and characteristics of students in the various programs. We also discuss issues related to placement: the training of teachers, the use of regular education or specially designed curricula, the concept of the **Individualized Educational Plan (IEP),** and the use of educational interpreters. In relation to assessment, we present some perspectives on the major types and the need to develop more tests normed on hearing-impaired students. Much of the chapter focuses on the academic achievement of severely to profoundly hearing-impaired students in preschool, elementary and secondary, and postsecondary educational programs. There is sufficient information to provide some conclusions regarding the achievement of these students, especially those leaving secondary education programs.

PLACEMENT

Academic placement has been a major issue in educating hearing-impaired students. As discussed in Chapter 1, placement has been related to language and communication. Historically, residential school environments have been identified with the use of simultaneous communication methods of teaching. On the other hand, day programs, that is, day schools and day classes, were identified with oral-communication approaches. In the 1980s, school placement has become the center of attention again with the emphasis on mainstreaming, or the placement of hearing-impaired students in public-school classrooms.

With the proliferation of simultaneous communication teaching methods, the distinction between educational environments that was based on the language/communication issue is no longer evident. Consequently, the debate has shifted from residential versus day school placement to the relative merits of the various available placement options and their effects on academic achievement and psychosocial development. In Chapter 1, several placement options for hearing-impaired students were delineated: residential schools, day schools, day classes, resource rooms, and itinerant programs. The placement programs and the students who attend them are described briefly here.

Special Schools

Historically, most hearing-impaired students have attended special schools such as residential and day schools (Moores & Kluwin, 1986; Quigley & Frisina, 1961). Residential schools, public or private, provide both educational and housing facilities for students. Provision for some hearing-impaired students to integrate educationally with hearing students has been made. Day schools are typically located in large metropolitan centers and are self-contained units for hearing-impaired students only who commute to them daily. No housing facilities are provided.

At present, about one-third of hearing-impaired students attend residential schools with about 10 percent being in day schools. About 40 percent of residential students commute to their schools. Most of the students in special schools have unaided severe to profound hearing impairments. There is some speculation also that residential schools have been receiving an increasing number of multihandicapped hearing-impaired students (Schildroth, 1986).

Day Classes

Most hearing-impaired students attend day classes, which are located in one or more schools in which most of the students are normally hearing. Instruction of the hearing impaired may occur in self-contained classrooms where the students stay for the whole day, or it may occur in regular classrooms where they spend part or most of their time.

Additional kinds of programs have been established to meet individualized needs. For example, there are resource rooms that hearing-impaired students attend to receive specialized help in content areas such as English, mathematics, and reading. There are also itinerant programs. Hearing-impaired students who attend regular education classes full time receive special help from support personnel such as **speech pathologists,** audiologists, and teachers who travel to several schools to provide individualized instruction and to consult with regular education teachers.

Day Students in Regular Classrooms.   There is considerable variation in estimates on the number of hearing-impaired students attending integrated, or mainstreamed, public school classes. For example, Karchmer (1984) reported that slightly less than 50 percent of all hearing-impaired students were academically integrated at least part time in regular classrooms. Libbey and Pronovost (1980) observed that 27 percent of hearing-impaired adolescents were not academically integrated and that an additional 18 percent attended only one regular mainstreamed class. According to Wolk, Karchmer, and Schildroth (1982), 6.2 percent of hearing-impaired students in part-time special education programs and 62 percent of students in full-time special education programs did not attend regular mainstreamed public school classes.

A strong relationship exists between degree of hearing impairment and integration—that is, the decision to integrate and the nature and extent of integration. For example, there is agreement that most students in integrated settings have better hearing, namely, an unaided hearing loss that averages less than 90 dB (Allen & Osborn, 1984; Wolk et al., 1982). In addition, most of these students have a postlinguistic hearing impairment. This group has language and communication problems that are pervasively different from those of students who are prelinguistically hearing impaired, especially those with severe to profound impairments (the main focus of this book).

A number of researchers and educators have argued that the placement of hearing-impaired students in mainstreamed classrooms is dependent on several important factors such as academic achievement (especially reading achievement), communication ability, and psychosocial development (Moores & Kluwin, 1986; Nix, 1976; Northcott, 1973; Pflaster, 1980). After conducting an in-depth investigation, one researcher concluded "that highly developed oral skills are required for the successful integration of hearing-impaired children" (Pflaster, 1980, p. 80). The importance of highly developed oral skills (e.g., speech, speech reading, and the use of residual hearing) for literacy and other academic subjects is highlighted in a later discussion on the academic achievement of select severely to profoundly hearing-impaired students.

INSTRUCTION

There are a few available studies regarding the preparation of teachers of hearing-impaired students in elementary- and secondary-level education programs. Traditionally, academic training in the communication areas such as language, speech, speech reading, and the use of residual hearing has dominated university teacher-training programs. Thus, many teachers are not adequately prepared to teach content subjects such as reading, mathematics, social studies, and science (King & Quigley, 1985; Lang, 1989). This is true also for many teachers of hearing students, especially in the areas of mathematics and science (Lang, 1989).

As discussed in Chapter 8, approximately 20 percent of teachers of hearing-impaired students have had only one or no courses in reading (Bockmiller & Coley, 1981; Coley & Bockmiller, 1980). The respondents were teachers who were primarily responsible for the teaching of reading. It was also noted that teachers with more training used a wider variety of instructional techniques than those teachers with less training.

Poor preparation of teachers has been observed in science instruction. Many teachers of hearing-impaired students are assigned to teach classes for which they are not qualified. This was one of the major findings by a hearing-impaired scientist who visited 20 K–12 educational programs for hearing-impaired students in the United States (Redden, 1979). More recently, Lang and Propp (1982) conducted a national survey on about 500 science teachers of hearing-impaired students. About 35 percent of the respondents taught science in residential schools; the remaining 65 percent were in day programs, that is, public day schools and classes. The researchers reported that approximately 74 percent of the respondents had *no* degree in science education. Half of this latter group stated that they had not taken *any* science education courses. In addition, few science teachers in this survey had formal training leading to degrees in the physical sciences. About 90 percent of the respondents had obtained degrees in the education of hearing-impaired students.

Similar findings were reported for teachers of mathematics. Johnson (1977) conducted a survey of mathematics programs, materials, and methods in schools for hearing-impaired students. As a result, Johnson advocated better training of teachers. This advocacy was supported in a later review by Broadbent and Daniele (1982) who, as have others (e.g., Lang, 1989; Moores, 1985a), concluded that so much emphasis has been placed on the teaching of communication skills that (1) very little research has been done on the development and evaluation of instructional approaches and materials in mathematics, and (2) very little instructional time has been devoted to the teaching of mathematics in the classroom. There is some evidence that the amount of time spent has a positive effect on the achievement level of the students, particularly in computation (Culbertson, 1974; Suppes, Fletcher, & Zanotti, 1976). Finally, teachers of hearing-impaired students with little training in mathematics tend not to use methods that have been found to be effective with hearing students, at least as a starting point.

Ethnic Minority Groups

According to the annual surveys by CADS, more than 30 percent of hearing-impaired students are African American, Hispanic American, Asian American, and Native American children. African American students account for about 18 percent and Hispanic American students about 12 percent of the ethnic minority student population. Similar to the research on minority hearing students, minority hearing-impaired students do not perform as well as other hearing-impaired students on achievement tests. Some educators believe that educational services for these students are inferior because their unique cultural needs and backgrounds are not taken into account (Delgado, 1984; Fischgrund, Cohen, & Clarkson, 1987), as is also true for hearing students who are members of minority groups.

Not much is known about the most effective instructional methods and procedures for use with various minority groups. Many teachers have not received training in working with students from a wide range of cultural backgrounds. An example of the need for cultural sensitivity is provided by Fischgrund et al. (1987):

The Hispanic family generally has a pronounced sexual division of labor. The father is considered the main source of authority and the final arbiter; the mother is the chief executive, conducting the daily business of running the family. As the primary broker of services to the family, she conducts relations with institutions, including the school. A parent specialist who wishes to discuss either a problem or special programs with a parent must usually deal with the mother. However, any major decision requires the father's approval. To communicate with the family, a professional must understand this subtle distinction. (p. 60)

There is also an underrepresentation of minorities among teachers of hearing-impaired students. For example, nonwhite teachers account for only 5 percent of the sample in a national survey (Corbett & Jensema, 1981).

CURRICULUM

Crandall (1984) conducted a national survey on curricular issues in schools for hearing-impaired students. Analyzing the returns from administrators and teachers, it was found that day schools (i.e., programs and classes) used state or district curricula as sources for their programs. In other words, day schools used the curricula of students in regular education programs in their districts or states. On the other hand, residential schools were most likely to develop their own curricula—that is, special curricula designed specifically to meet the needs of hearing-impaired students. Only 5 percent of residential schools used either state or district curricula as reference.

Curricula include course outlines, descriptions, education goals, and education materials. The decision to use regular education or specially developed materials in the curriculum is extremely complex and influenced by whether the developmental patterns of hearing-impaired students are similar to or different from those of the general student population. Much of the evidence on language development suggests that severely to profoundly hearing-impaired adolescents proceed through similar developmental stages, make the same type and variety of errors, and employ learning strategies similar to those the general student population uses at a younger age (Quigley & King, 1981–1984, 1982; Quigley & Paul, 1984a; Quigley et al., in press). Thus, when constructing special materials, it is important to keep in mind the developmental patterns of hearing students. For example, effective science curricula for hearing students are those that emphasize self-initiated discovery and exploratory experiences. These science curricula, however, are used in only a few programs for hearing-impaired students (Lang & Propp, 1982).

Although the use of special materials and curricula is controversial, the ultimate goal should be to enable hearing-impaired students to use the regular materials of the general population at some particular milestone. As stated by King and Quigley (1985), there has been little research conducted on the effectiveness of using special reading materials. Crandall (1984) reported that administrators do not employ formal objective methods of evaluating the strengths and weaknesses of their curricula. Typically, evaluations of curricula are based on subjective measures such as informal observation and teacher feedback. Formal evaluation is important for ensuring that there are strong interrelations among curricula, instruction, and assessments. These interrelations are necessary in order to know accurate levels of academic achievement of hearing-impaired students. We discuss this later in greater detail.

Individualized Educational Plan (IEP)

Whether teachers of hearing-impaired students use regular or special curricula, they are mandated by law (PL 94–142) to develop an Individualized Educational Plan (IEP) for each student. The IEP is designed not only to individualize instruction but also to meet the unique needs of students who require special education services. Only a few basics of the IEP are presented here. A more detailed treatment of this complex topic and related issues can be found elsewhere (Heward & Orlansky, 1988; Kirk & Gallagher, 1986; Sabatino & Mann, 1982).

The IEP consists of input from a multidisciplinary team that includes appropriate education personnel who provide services to the student. For hearing-impaired students, the personnel involved can be speech pathologists, audiologists, school psychologists, medical specialists, **social workers,** and the student's teachers in regular and special education programs. The development of the IEP should be undertaken with the input and consent of the parents/caregivers and, if possible, the student for whom the IEP is being written.

From one perspective, the IEP is an individualized curriculum for a specific student. Typically, it includes goals and objectives that pertain to the student's academic, vocational, social, and personal needs. Based on formal and informal assessments, the planned program should include the following (Sabatino, 1982):

1. A statement of the present level of the student's educational performance.
2. A statement of the annual goals, including short-term objectives.
3. A statement of the specific educational services to be provided and the extent to which the student will be able to participate in regular programs.
4. The projected dates for initiation of such services and their anticipated duration.
5. Appropriate objective criteria, evaluative procedures, and schedules for determining whether instructional objectives have been met. (p. 31)

In sum, it is important to individualize instruction in order to meet the needs of each hearing-impaired student. To determine its effectiveness, the IEP, like any other curriculum, should be subjected to formal evaluations. As stated previously, there need to be close interrelations among instruction, assessments, and IEPs so that accurate achievement levels of hearing-impaired students can be reported.

EDUCATIONAL INTERPRETERS

Interpreting as a profession began with the establishment of a national organization of interpreters in 1964, the National Registry of Professional Interpreters and Translators for the Deaf (Cokely, 1980). In 1965 the organization was renamed the Registry of Interpreters for the Deaf (RID). Programs for training interpreters have been established in many states. Typically, such training programs are associated with 2-year community or technical postsecondary institutions. Since the 1960s, educational interpreting has made it possible for many hearing-impaired students to enroll in regular postsecondary institutions (Zawolkow & DeFiore, 1986). ''The documented success of so many post-secondary school programs for the deaf may be attributed in part to the establishment of effective interpreter services'' (Moores, 1985a, p. 18).

With the passage of Public Law 94–142 in 1975, there has been a growing need for educational interpreting for mainstreamed hearing-impaired students in elementary and secondary programs. In a national survey in which responses were received from 74% of the interpreter training programs (42 programs), Gustason (1985) found that about 37 percent of the trainees planned to obtain employment in public school settings. Many of the respondents also indicated that there is a strong need for clarification of roles and responsibilities, training, and evaluation of interpreters who work in these settings (Zawolkow & DeFiore, 1986).

The roles and responsibilities of educational interpreters are considerably different from those of **freelance interpreters,** who interpret for deaf adults in medical and legal situations. Although educational interpreting differs from school to school, interpreters often perform such tasks as tutoring, assisting regular education teachers and teachers of hearing-impaired students, keeping records, and supervising hearing-impaired students (Zawolkow & DeFiore, 1986).

Florida was the first state to address the issue of role, responsibility, and certification for educational interpreters (*Technical Assistance Paper,* 1986). In conjunction with several interpreting associations within the state, the Bureau of Education for Exceptional Students (Division of Public Schools) developed a certification process and a separate Code of Ethics that pertain to interpreting in the classroom. The main intent was to demonstrate that educational interpreting is different from other forms of professional interpreting.

The most important need is for national guidelines regarding the training and evaluation of educational interpreters in elementary and secondary education (Gustason, 1985; Moores, 1985a, 1987; Zawolkow & DeFiore, 1986). Several matters should be addressed. For example, should educational interpreters be required to take course work in education of hearing-impaired students, tutoring, psychology, and other education-related fields? In which language/communication system should interpreters be required to demonstrate competency? As discussed in Chapter 7, this is a complex issue that affects also the training and evaluation of the sign-communication skills of teachers of hearing-impaired students. Finally, should oral interpreting standards and guidelines be established? In oral interpreting situations, the interpreter uses speech instead of signs to convey the spoken message of the teacher (see Northcott, 1984). The hearing-impaired student speech reads the interpreter rather than the classroom teacher.

There is a need to determine how educational interpreting can be more effective in contributing to the improvement of levels of academic achievement of hearing-impaired students. Much of the research on interpreting has focused on psychological aspects such as time lag between the spoken message and the interpreted message . There is a related discussion in Strong and Rudser (1985). Research on interpreting will have little effect until more is known about the sign-communication skills of hearing-impaired students.

ASSESSMENT

A test can be defined as ". . . a means of measuring the knowledge, skill, feeling, intelligence, or aptitude of an individual or group" (Gay, 1981, p. 109). Test scores can identify, classify, and evaluate test takers. Many different kinds of tests are available and many different ways to classify them. The three broad categories are norm-referenced, criterion-referenced, and **informal tests** and/or procedures (Anastasi, 1982; Gronlund, 1981; Salvia & Ysseldyke, 1985). Much of what is known about the educational achievement of severely to profoundly hearing-impaired students has come from the use of norm-referenced and criterion-referenced tests (Quigley & Paul, 1986). It is important to understand the basic principles of these tests.

Standardized Norm-Referenced Tests

The main purpose of standardized norm-referenced tests is to indicate what students have learned in comparison with other similar students at the same grade (or age level). The tests are administered to large numbers of representative students across several grade levels. A sufficient number of students are tested so that a table of norms (i.e., standards) can be established. The average grade level scores that have been computed represent overall achievement rather than a particular ability.

The grade equivalent score compares the performance of a student to the average performance of groups of students across various grades. The number expresses a level of achievement in grades and tenths of a grade. A score of 5.9 is the score that would be earned by the average fifth grader near the end of the school year (i.e., nine-tenths of the school year). Grade equivalent scores are not recommended for comparing the performances of students or for making decisions about instruction. Grade equivalent scores are discussed here to give the reader an idea of the academic achievement levels of severely to profoundly hearing-impaired students as compared to their hearing counterparts. In-depth discussion of the use of grade equivalent scores and other issues such as strengths and weaknesses of norm-referenced tests can be found elsewhere (Salvia & Ysseldyke, 1985).

Several achievement test batteries have typically been administered to hearing-impaired students—for example, the California Achievement Test (CAT), the Metropolitan Achievement Test (MAT), and the Stanford Achievement Test (SAT). These tests include reading, mathematics, science, and social studies. Some subjects—reading, for example, may have various subtests. The overall achievement is the combination of the subtest scores.

Perhaps the most widely used achievement test with hearing-impaired students is the SAT (Allen, 1986; Gentile & DiFrancesca, 1969). An adapted version of this test has been developed by the Center for Assessment and Demographic Studies (CADS) (formerly the Office of Demographic Studies) at Gallaudet University. The adapted SAT version has been standardized on hearing-impaired students, considering their special needs. Despite some changes in test administration and the elimination of a few inappropriate subtests, the performance of hearing-impaired students can be compared with the norms established for their hearing counterparts (Allen, 1986; Allen, White, & Karchmer, 1983).

The effectiveness of norm-referenced tests is dependent on an adequate standardization process. That is, standardization implies uniformity of procedures, directions, and scoring. Just as important is a sufficient evaluation of national course content within the selected academic areas (Anastasi, 1982; Salvia & Ysseldyke, 1985). Participating schools should find that the content and skills assessed by the achievement test are similar to those in their curricula.

Criterion-Referenced Tests

Criterion-referenced tests focus on performance in a particular domain such as mathematics, reading, or language. The test score reflects the extent to which the student has mastered the information. The student's score relates to a specific predetermined objective (criterion) or set of objectives. The number of items answered correctly is compared with some *absolute* standard. Unlike norm-referenced tests, criterion-referenced tests do not compare the test taker with anyone else. Thus, these tests are often used for diagnostic purposes in education to reveal a student's strengths and weaknesses in a particular area. Examples of criterion-referenced tests include placement tests and end-of-level tests in reading and mathematics. Even teacher-made tests can be considered a form of criterion testing. Adequate criterion-referenced tests can help teachers and educators in planning and developing appropriate educational programs for students (Berk, 1980).

One of the most important concepts of criterion-referenced testing is *minimum competency*. A competency is a behaviorally stated objective that specifies the performance of a test taker. For example, in mathematics, a competency could include the ability to add two-digit numbers or to solve word problems. Competencies deal with observable behavior and are *minimum measures* of performance. In a typical reading series, it may be recommended that a student obtain a score of at least 85 percent before moving on to the next skill level. The minimum criterion levels are abitrarily defined by the test makers.

It is important to remember that criterion-referenced tests are constructed according to a set of concepts or skills that relate to a particular theory on the nature of the subject. For example, the Test of Syntactic Abilities (TSA) (Quigley, Steinkamp, Power, & Jones, 1978) is supposed to test knowledge of the major syntactic structures of English according to a linguistic theory termed *transformational generative grammar* (Chomsky, 1957, 1965). Thus, students' scores on a specific syntactic structure reflect the extent of their knowledge of it.

Achievement and Diagnostic Functions

The content of norm-referenced and criterion-referenced tests can be and often is quite similar. Even test item formats are often identical. Some achievement instruments are designed to permit analyses of students' weaknesses and strengths and to compare an individual score with the norms. The same is true for tests that are primarily diagnostic in nature. For example, the TSA's norms permit comparisons of hearing-impaired students' scores with those of a national sample of hearing-impaired students.

Because test scores are likely to be overused and misused, we recommend that the reader seek additional information elsewhere about other important issues such as interpretation of test results, reliability, and validity (Anastasi, 1982; Gay, 1981; Gronlund, 1981; Salvia & Ysseldyke, 1985). Most tests used with severely to profoundly hearing-impaired students have been standardized on hearing students (Quigley & Paul, 1986). There is a need to develop additional norm-referenced and criterion-referenced tests for hearing-impaired students.

PRESCHOOL AND EARLY INTERVENTION

Many educators and researchers would agree with the statement by Ross et al. (1982): "The necessity for the early detection of a hearing impairment now appears beyond dispute" (p. 5). There is consensus that early identification, and possibly amplification, are important for the development of a fluent, intelligible communication system between children and their parents/caregivers, and also for the development of literacy skills. Although many preschool and early intervention programs involve hearing-impaired students from age 3 to 5 years, the Commission on Education of the Deaf (1988) has recommended to the Congress of the United States the establishment of programs for infants from birth to 3 years old. This would necessitate at least an improvement in identification procedures. Early intervention programs, as well as other programs for hearing-impaired children, require a wider range of services than those for children in regular education—training in speech, audition, language, and communication methods. Such programs should also include counseling for family and parents because success is considered to be dependent on the involvement of family members.

Despite the purported importance of preschool and early intervention programs, there are few studies demonstrating the effectiveness of such programs for hearing-impaired students (Goppold, 1988; Moores, 1985b, 1987). Most of the literature contains descriptions of programs and methods and polemic arguments for effectiveness by the developers of the programs. Some exemplary oral and Total Communication early intervention programs have been described (Ling, 1984a, 1984b).

Evaluation of early intervention programs may be difficult because deafness is a low-incidence condition. Some early studies focused mainly on assessing the effects of communication methods on preschool deaf students (Quigley, 1969). Moores (1987) argued that the lack of data may be due to the continuing debate over the use of specific communication methods, that is, oral or Total Communication methods. The persistence of this debate is evident in a recent review of early intervention studies (Goppold, 1988). The controversy surrounding the language/communication issue is still so strong that one can arrive at two different interpretations for the same results of studies in the literature (Ling, 1984a, 1984b). There is a need for more objective experiments.

Some Early Studies

During the 1960s, public early intervention programs became available to a number of hearing-impaired children. Much of the data concerns programs in residential and day schools. Some of the early studies reported little or no beneficial effects of the programs. For example, both Phillips (1963) and Craig (1964) compared students who received preschool training with those who received no training. Phillips reported no differences between the two groups in language arts, mathematics, and socialization skills, and Craig found no differences for reading and speech reading (lip reading) skills.

These surprising trends were supported by several studies conducted during the late 1960s in the United States. For example, Vernon and Koh (1970) compared children who received an oral preschool education at the John Tracy Clinic in California with other children who received no preschool training. They reported no differences between the groups on speech and speech reading (lip reading) skills.

Even more surprising findings were documented by McCroskey (1967, 1968), who reported differences in favor of students who received *no* early training when compared to those who received training in a program that placed a strong emphasis on the development of auditory skills. McCroskey argued, however, that students who received early training could have had more severe problems because they were identified at an earlier age.

Some of the earliest successes of early intervention programs have been documented by a number of studies conducted in the Soviet Union on the use of the neo-oral approach (Moores, 1972; Morkovin, 1960; Quigley, 1969). Neo-oralism is the use of oral methods and finger spelling simultaneously. It is similar to the Rochester Method used in the United States. Finger spelling was used with Russian students as young as 2 to 3 years old; they learned to finger spell in less than a year. Neo-oralism, particularly the use of finger spelling, has been reported to increase vocabulary growth and speech reading ability.

The most representative study on the use of finger spelling, especially with young hearing-impaired students in the United States, has been the work of Quigley (1969). Quigley compared the language comprehension ability of 16 young students of above-average IQ (ages 3.5 to 4.5 years) who were exposed to the Rochester Method with matched students who were exposed to an oral method in residential schools. Students exposed to the Rochester Method performed significantly better than the other students in reading (SAT scores) and written language. As stated in Chapter 7, Quigley concluded that the Rochester Method is a valuable educational tool but that it is not a panacea.

Later Studies

The work of Moores and his associates is representative of the more recent studies on the effectiveness of early intervention programs (Moores, 1985b; Moores, Weiss, & Goodwin, 1978). They followed children between the ages of 2 to 4 years old (mean = 3 years) for 4 years in seven early intervention programs, ranging in communication method (i.e., oral and Total Communication), educational setting (i.e., residential and day), and placement (i.e., self-contained and integrated). Moores and his collaborators reported the findings of their longitudinal project in several areas. Of interest here are the findings on academic achievement.

On the basis of the results of the Metropolitan Achievement Test (MAT) Primer Battery, it was reported that the hearing-impaired children were performing as well as their hearing counterparts in reading but below hearing peers in mathematics. The researchers hypothesized that more instructional time and much more emphasis were placed on reading than on mathematics in these programs, and also that the growth in reading would be slower as hearing-impaired students became older because of their difficulty in understanding complex English syntax. In comparing the performance of students in the various early intervention programs, Moores reported that students exposed to the Rochester Method had significantly higher scores than those exposed to other methods in reading, mathematics, and academic achievement.

More recently, Goppold (1988) analyzed the published longitudinal results of early intervention studies conducted since the middle 1960s. Goppold was interested in the enduring theme of the effects of communication mode, oral or Total Communication, on the academic achievement of preschool severely to profoundly hearing-impaired students from birth to 5 years old. His review, which included studies discussed in Chapter 4 on mother-child dyads, such as that of Greenberg (1983), indicated that students in Total Communication programs had higher academic achievement than did their counterparts in oral education programs. As with integration and communication mode, it should be emphasized that early intervention is not an all-encompassing factor. Other factors of importance are the quality of instruction and curricula, and involved parents/caregivers. Success can be documented in well-established programs of either kind (Ling, 1984a, 1984b). Additional longitudinal studies on the effects of early intervention are needed, particularly to delineate the myriad of factors that contribute to and ensure the educational success of students.

ELEMENTARY AND SECONDARY EDUCATION

Most of the early studies of the academic performance of hearing-impaired students at the elementary and secondary levels focused on language comprehension abilities. The work of Pintner and his associates is representative (Pintner, 1918, 1927; Pintner & Paterson, 1916, 1917). Using the Trabue Language Completion Tests, they investigated students in oral and manual classrooms in residential schools. Two prominent enduring trends were observed: (1) The abilities of most students were either below or at the fourth-grade level as compared to hearing peers, and (2) There was very little gain in language comprehension ability (about 2 to 3 years) despite 12 years of instruction. The test results are given in Table 9.1.

Similar results were reported later in a national study by Pintner (1927) using the Pintner Educational Survey. Pintner based this educational achievement test on items from standardized educational tests used with hearing students. He studied the performances of the students in reading, mathematics, and other academic areas. His sample included nearly all hearing-impaired students from age 12 and up in all special schools in the United States at that time. He reported that the average 15-year-old hearing-impaired student with 12 to 13 years of education was performing at an academic level commensurate with that of the average 9-year-old hearing student.

Achievement Tests Other than the SAT

The findings reported by Pintner and his associates have been confirmed by later studies using achievement tests normed on hearing students. There is little disagreement in the findings of these investigations, especially about reading achievement (Balow, Fulton,

TABLE 9.1. Students' Performance on the Trabue Language Completion Test

Years of Instruction	Type of Program		
	Oral	Manual	Combined
2	−2.0	−2.0	−2.0
3	−2.0	—	−2.0
4	−2.0	−2.0	−2.0
5	2.8	2.3	2.6
6	3.2	2.3	2.8
7	3.3	2.8	3.1
8	3.8	3.3	3.6
9	3.7	3.2	3.5
10	4.3	3.2	3.8
11	4.5	3.8	4.2
12	4.5	3.6	4.1

NOTES: Scores interpreted in grade norms for hearing students. Scores rounded to the nearest tenth. −2.0 = below second grade.
Combined = average score of oral and manual students.
SOURCE: Based on Pintner and Paterson (1916).

& Peploe, 1971; Myklebust, 1964; Pugh, 1946; Wrightstone, Aronow, & Moskowitz, 1963). For example, the low mean reading grade and the slow gain in overall achievement were documented in a national study that also attempted to establish special reading norms for hearing-impaired students (Wrightstone et al., 1963). The researchers studied students from age 10 years to about 17 years old. The results revealed that a small percentage of this group reached a 4.9 grade level or higher. In addition, the mean reading grade levels for the students increased at a rate of less than one grade level in 5 years, from 2.7 grades for the youngest group to 3.5 grades for the oldest group.

Many researchers reported the language and reading achievement of hearing-impaired students on tests such as the Metropolitan Achievement Test, the Columbia Vocabulary Test, and the New Developmental Reading Tests. It was assumed that academic achievement is heavily influenced by performance on subtests dealing with language and reading variables. This has been shown in investigations that documented high intercorrelations among the scores of various subtests of the SAT (Allen, 1986; Babbini & Quigley, 1970; Quigley, 1969).

Stanford Achievement Test—Unadapted Version

Before the early 1970s, educators and researchers examined the academic achievement of hearing-impaired students using an SAT battery that was normed on hearing children. The work of Goetzinger and Rousey (1959) is representative. Focusing on residential students between the ages of 14 and 21 years and with 12 or more years of education, the researchers reported that the mean reading grade level of the students was 4.5 years and that the mean grade level for arithmetic computation and reasoning was about 7.0 years when compared to hearing counterparts. Like Pintner and others, Goetzinger and Rousey observed that the achievement gap between hearing and hearing-impaired stu-

TABLE 9.2. Grade Equivalent Means for Reading, Language, and Arithmetic on the Stanford Achievement Test

Subtest	Years					Gain
	1	2	3	4	5	
Combined Reading	3.3	3.6	4.0	4.3	4.6	1.3
Language	3.9	4.5	5.0	5.7	6.2	2.9
Combined Arithmetic	4.1	4.6	5.0	5.5	6.1	2.1

SOURCE: Based on Babbini and Quigley (1970).

dents widens as students become older, especially in higher-level language skills. This led them to conclude that "Perhaps, . . . there can never be complete compensation for the lack of auditory experiences with respect to the average child who has suffered early severe deafness'' (p. 229).

Another representative study was the work of Babbini and Quigley (1970), who reexamined the data reported by Quigley (1969) on students from six residential schools. Specifically, they analyzed the students' scores on the language, reading, and arithmetic (computation and reasoning) subsets of the SAT. They also analyzed samples of written language. As expected, the findings revealed low levels of academic achievement and slow growth patterns. For example, the researchers reported that students advanced at the rate of about one-third grade per year on language and reading subtests. Advancement in mathematics was not much better—only one-half grade per year (see Table 9.2). After completing 12 to 13 years of education, the average reading grade level of the hearing-impaired students was about seven grades below that of their hearing peers. Their overall educational achievement was nearly six grades lower.

Babbini and Quigley also found high intercorrelations for all subtests of the SAT that were administered. They deduced that the SAT was primarily assessing only one major ability—that is, English language competence—not academic achievement. To obtain a more accurate assessment of achievement, the researchers recommended the development and use of instruments normed on hearing-impaired students. During the 1970s, this issue was addressed with the construction of two tests, the Test of Syntactic Abilities (TSA) (Quigley et al., 1978) and an adapted version of the Stanford Achievement Test (Allen, 1986).

Research on the TSA

As discussed in Chapter 8, Quigley and his collaborators (Quigley et al., 1976; Quigley & Paul, 1984a) investigated the syntactic abilities of a national sample of profoundly hearing-impaired students between the ages of 10 and 19 years, using the TSA. They studied students' comprehension of nine of the major English syntactic structures— determiners, question formation, relativization, conjunction, complementation, **nominalization,** pronominalization, negation, and the verb system.

Quigley and his associates also collected and analyzed academic achievement scores. They repeated findings documented by previous investigators. The average reading grade level of 19-year-old deaf students was less than fourth grade. The average mathematics

TABLE 9.3. Grade Equivalent Means on the Stanford Achievement Test Across a Nine-Year Period

Subtests	Student's Age 10–12	13–15	16–18	Gain
Language	3.4	4.6	5.2	1.8
Total Reading	2.6	3.1	3.7	1.1
Total Arithmetic	3.7	4.6	6.2	2.5

SOURCE: Based on Quigley et al. (1978).

grade level was slightly higher than sixth grade. From the youngest age group (10 years old) to the oldest group (19 years old), growth in language was less than 2 years (grade levels), growth in reading was slightly higher than 1 year, and growth in arithmetic was about $2\frac{1}{2}$ years (see Table 9.3).

SAT—Adapted Version

Since the late 1960s, the Center for Assessment and Demographic Studies (CADS) has conducted several investigations on the educational achievement of a national sample of hearing-impaired students in the United States. Analyses of items and administration procedures of their earlier achievement studies aided in the construction of an adapted version of the Stanford Achievement Test. The adapted version contained norms for hearing-impaired students, and it still permitted comparisons of the performance of hearing-impaired students with that of their hearing counterparts. CADS also collected information on other characteristics of the students and examined their effects on educational achievement. The characteristics included degree of hearing impairment, age at onset, type of educational program, and socioeconomic status. Despite special adaptations to create a better assessment of achievement, the CADS findings corroborated those of earlier studies using achievement tests normed on hearing students. Indeed, the findings are not much different from the results of Pintner and his collaborators.

In the first national survey, approximately 12,000 hearing-impaired students between the ages of 7 and 19 years in special education programs and classes were tested (Gentile & DiFrancesca, 1969). Results were presented for all students and for those with an unaided loss of 60 dB or greater in the better ear. Of interest here are the results of the latter group, particularly those students taking the top-level batteries such as the Intermediate Battery II and the Advanced Battery. Table 9.4 shows the means for students ages 16 to 19 years old on the subtests of spelling, language, science, social studies, total reading, and total arithmetic. For the advanced battery, paragraph meaning is used instead of total reading.

Nearly 82 percent of all students taking the SAT were reading at a grade level of 4.5 or lower. The arithmetic scores of this group were at a grade level of 5.5 or lower. Considering the percentages associated with paragraph meaning, language, and total arithmetic as an index of total educational achievement, slightly more than half of the students performed between grade levels of 5.5 and 5.9 or below, levels similar to those reported by Babbini and Quigley (1970) on the students in their study.

TABLE 9.4. Grade Equivalent Means for 16- to 19-Year-Old Students on the Intermediate II Battery and the Advanced Battery of the Stanford Achievement Test

	Age of Students					
	16		**17**		**18**	**19**
Subtests	**Intermediate Battery II**	**Advanced Battery**	**Intermediate II**	**Advanced**	**Advanced**	**Advanced**
Spelling	6.08	7.38	5.64	7.60	7.93	7.87
Language	4.57	5.82	4.40	6.02	6.15	6.00
Science	4.24	6.03	4.05	6.00	5.84	5.85
Social Studies	4.87	5.89	4.72	5.92	5.87	5.79
Total Reading	4.17	—	4.02	—	—	—
Paragraph Meaning	—	5.77	—	5.90	5.79	5.68
Total Arithmetic	5.41	7.00	5.34	7.24	7.42	7.19

SOURCE: Based on Gentile and DiFrancesca (1969).

In the second national survey, about 17,000 hearing-impaired students between the ages of 6 and 21 years took the achievement batteries (DiFrancesca, 1972). The mean scores of this group were lower than those reported in the first survey. The scores of the latter survey, however, were considered to be more accurate because of improvements in the screening procedures (i.e., in assigning a specific test battery level such as primary and intermediate to students). In general, most severely to profoundly hearing-impaired students were reading at about a fourth-grade level or lower. The mathematics grade level of this group was about the fifth grade or lower. For the total sample, the average growth in reading was 0.2 grade level per year. Table 9.5 depicts mean scores for the subtests of paragraph meaning and total arithmetic for students between the ages of 16 to 19 years on the Advanced Battery (i.e., the highest group).

In 1974 the first special edition of the Stanford Achievement Test was administered to approximately 7,000 hearing-impaired students, with results nearly similar to those of the two earlier national surveys (Trybus & Karchmer, 1977). For example, the median grade level for the total sample was 4.5, and it was reported that only 10 percent of the students in the best reading group were reading at or above the eighth grade level. Considering the results across 3 years, the overall growth in reading achievement

TABLE 9.5. Mean Scores of 16- to 19-year-old Students on Paragraph Reading and Total Arithmetic on the Advanced Battery of the Stanford Achievement Test

	Age of Students in Years			
Subtests	**16**	**17**	**18**	**19**
Paragraph Reading	7.4	7.5	7.6	6.9
Total Arithmetic	8.3	8.5	8.8	8.5

SOURCE: Based on DiFrancesca (1972).

was reported to be about a grade level of 0.8, or slightly less than 0.3 grade level per year.

The findings of the most recent national survey were documented by the Gallaudet Research Institute (1985) and discussed in detail by Allen (1986). The two common themes were repeated: low achievement levels and the slow growth in reading. For the oldest group of students (i.e., from 16 to 18 years old), the median grade level range for arithmetic computation was from 7.0 to 7.5 grades. The median grade level range for reading comprehension was from 2.9 to 3.2 grades. Allen (1986) stated that the median reading scores for the 1983 sample were significantly higher than those for the 1974 sample at every age range compared (i.e., based on the results of statistical conversion methods that permit comparisons to be made). Although these results are encouraging, most severely to profoundly hearing-impaired students in the latest survey were still reading at or below a fourth-grade level. The median reading achievement level of hearing students has improved since 1974, however. Thus, the performance of the hearing-impaired students has lagged further behind that of hearing students.

The CADS surveys indicated that most severely to profoundly hearing-impaired students performed better on subtests on mechanical skills such as spelling and capitalization than on subtests that involve reading comprehension such as paragraph meaning. A similar pattern emerged for mathematics. Subtests involving computation were easier than those involving the understanding and application of mathematical concepts. This pattern has been supported by other earlier studies on the mathematics problem-solving abilities of hearing-impaired students (Pendergrass & Hodges, 1976). Thus, the educational achievement of students is influenced pervasively by their language and reading comprehension ability. It can be argued that the adapted version of the SAT, like other achievement tests, is still measuring the English language competency of severely to profoundly hearing-impaired students rather than overall academic achievement (Moores, 1987; Quigley & Paul, 1986). Finally, as discussed in Chapter 8, the national surveys have confirmed that two complex factors significantly affect academic achievement: degree of hearing impairment and socioeconomic status. These two factors are associated with other important factors such as speech intelligibility, preschool experience, and the use of residual hearing of the students.

Select Hearing-Impaired Students

The findings of national surveys should be interpreted with caution. These investigations tend to obscure the educational achievement of certain subgroups within the hearing-impaired student population. For example, students in some well-established comprehensive Total Communication programs performed better than the national norms (for hearing-impaired students) (Luetke-Stahlman, 1988a; Delaney, Stuckless, & Walter, 1984). In addition, the surveys do not include severely to profoundly hearing-impaired students in comprehensive oral programs such as the Central Institute for the Deaf (Lane, 1976a, 1976b; Lane & Baker, 1974) or those in integrated classrooms (Messerly & Aram, 1980; Pflaster, 1980; Geers & Moog, 1989).

A large number of these students performed on grade level when compared with hearing counterparts, but it should be remembered that this was a select group of students. (See Geers & Moog, 1989). For example, the mean IQ score of the former CID students in the Lane and Baker study was 115, which is considerably higher than the national average of 96.6 reported in national surveys (Jensema, 1977). In addition, this select group of students had involved parents, adequate preschool experiences, and well-developed oral communication skills that were thought to be the results of adequate training in speech, speech reading, and the use of residual hearing (Calvert, 1986; Connor, 1986; Ling, 1984a; Ross, 1977, 1986a, 1986b).

Placement and Achievement

As discussed previously, another enduring debate in the education of hearing-impaired students has been the effects of academic placement on educational achievement. Like language/communication, academic placement alone is not or should not be considered an all-important factor. Other factors also affect achievement, such as the quality of instruction and curricula. It was argued previously that comparing the achievement of students in various educational settings requires at least agreement that the comparisons be of groups of students with similar characteristics. For example, the educational achievement of profoundly hearing-impaired students in residential settings can be compared with that of other profoundly hearing-impaired students in regular public school classrooms. Other important variables, such as age at onset of impairment, parental status, and intelligence, should also be considered. If these critical factors are not taken into account, then comparisons are being made between two *dissimilar* populations (Quigley & Kretschmer, 1982).

Several investigators compared the psychoeducational performances of students attending residential schools as day students with those of students who attended the same schools as residential students (Karchmer & Petersen, 1980; Quigley & Frisina, 1961). No significant differences in educational achievement were found between the two groups. It was observed, however, that day students in residential schools had more intelligible speech than residential students in the same schools.

Other earlier studies indicated that the academic achievement, speech intelligibility, speech reading, and psychosocial adjustment of day school students were higher than those of residential students (Pintner, 1927; Upshall, 1929). The later works of Myklebust (1964) and Quigley et al. (1976) revealed that the language abilities of day school students (and day residential students) were superior to those of residential school students.

Comparisons have also been made between residential students and students in regular public school classes. Like the comparisons between day school and residential school students, the results are difficult to interpret. Farrugia and Austin (1980) reported that severely hearing-impaired students in public school settings showed lower levels of self-esteem and social, emotional, and mature behaviors than did their hearing-impaired counterparts in residential settings. The findings of Farrugia and Austin were not confirmed in a later study by Cartledge, Paul, Jackson, and Drumm (1988). In this study, no significant differences were found between groups of severely to profoundly hearing-impaired students in the two settings as determined by the ratings of the teachers.

As discussed previously, most students who are mainstreamed in regular public school classes have postlinguistically hearing impairments and few additional handicapping conditions. In addition, the students in integrated settings have a better unaided ear average of less than 90 dB (Allen & Osborn, 1984; Wolk, Karchmer, & Schildroth, 1982). Very few studies have compared groups of similar students in both integrated and nonintegrated settings or have statistically controlled for dissimilar factors (Kluwin & Moores, 1985; Moores, Kluwin, & Mertens, 1985; Wolk et al., 1982).

In general, results revealed that integrated students had higher levels of academic achievement than did their nonintegrated counterparts. Wolk et al. (1982) argued, however, that the differences between the groups could not be due totally to integration. Kluwin and Moores (1985) maintained that the differences found in their study resulted from instructional variables. For example, regular education teachers in integrated classrooms had better training in certain content areas such as mathematics, had higher levels of expectation of success, and exposed their students to a greater amount of demanding materials than did teachers of hearing-impaired students in self-contained classrooms.

It is difficult to compare the performance of students in different educational settings; however, there is a need for additional studies using this paradigm. Quigley and Kretschmer (1982) stated that the most valid and reliable data can be obtained on students within the same schools and/or settings such as day students and residential students in residential schools. For example, residential living seems to have a negative effect on the development of skills such as speech intelligibility and speech reading. According to Quigley and Frisina (1961), this effect could be due to the greater emphasis on and additional opportunities for day students to develop these skills. Indeed, recent evidence indicates that there is a much greater emphasis on oral-communication skills in oral programs than in Total Communication programs (Ross & Calvert, 1984), leading to better spoken language skills for students in oral-communication programs.

POSTSECONDARY EDUCATION

Postsecondary education refers to formal education programs that serve individuals who have completed secondary education programs (i.e., twelve grades) or who are beyond the age of compulsory school attendance. Examples include research institutions, 4-year colleges, 2-year community colleges and technical schools, and schools for specialties such as law, medicine, and art. Much of what is available in the published literature about deafness is descriptions of postsecondary education opportunities and services (DeCaro, Karchmer, & Rawlings, 1987; Frisina, 1978; Rawlings & King, 1986). Few studies document academic achievement levels, including the levels of reading achievement, of prelinguistically severely to profoundly hearing-impaired students.

Historical Perspectives—1864 to 1960

In 1864 Gallaudet College (now Gallaudet University) was founded to provide hearing-impaired students with an opportunity for postsecondary education in the liberal arts. Gallaudet remains the only liberal arts college for hearing-impaired individuals in the world, although it does admit hearing students. From 1864 to about 1960, it was the only *special* postsecondary institution (Rawlings & King, 1986; Saur & Stinson, 1986). Hearing-impaired students either had to attend Gallaudet or try to enroll and succeed in a typical regular college, university, or technical school that usually did not have special support services. In addition, there were no special vocational or technical programs. Gallaudet College was not fully accredited until 1955. Thus, before then it was difficult for students to gain admittance to graduate education at other institutions because the other schools did not accept their undergraduate credits from Gallaudet (Moores, 1987).

The 1960s to the Present

During the 1960s, 18 postsecondary programs were established, notably, the National Technical Institute for the Deaf in Rochester, New York, which was founded in 1965. One of the major aims of NTID is to provide "technical education and training of deaf youth and adults in order to prepare them for successful employment and community participation" (Frisina, 1978, p. 488). Postsecondary education programs continued to be established during the 1970s and 1980s. The programs provide a continuum of services ranging from special programs for hearing-impaired students such as that at Gallaudet or NTID at one end to programs that provide regular education with no support services at the other end. The availability of services is related to the size of student enrollments in the programs (DeCaro et al., 1987).

Student Enrollment, Characteristics, and Achievement

At present there are more than 140 special programs, enrolling more than 5,500 hearing-impaired students in the United States and Canada. An additional 3,000 to 5,000 students attend regular postsecondary institutions. About 8,000 to 11,000 individuals with hearing losses, then, are enrolled at institutions of higher learning (DeCaro et al., 1987; Lang & Conner, 1988; Rawlings & King, 1986; Wulfsberg & Petersen, 1979). Hearing-impaired students are also more likely to attend postsecondary programs full time than are their hearing counterparts (DeCaro et al., 1987). There are more male students than female students, and white students are more likely than minority students to continue their education after high school.

Hearing-impaired students enroll in postsecondary programs at rates similar to or higher than those of hearing students (Kerstetter, 1985). Estimates range from 30 percent to slightly more than 50 percent of all hearing-impaired students graduating from special education secondary programs. The percentage of prelinguistically severely to profoundly hearing-impaired students entering postsecondary programs is probably much lower (Moores, 1987; Quigley, Jenne, & Phillips, 1969). At special schools such as NTID and Gallaudet, however, most students are prelinguistically severely to profoundly hearing-impaired (Lang & Conner, 1988). Students with less severe hearing impairments typically attend regional, state, and local programs for deaf students or programs not specifically designed for deaf students.

It has been reported that hearing-impaired students (regardless of degree of impairment and age at onset) at postsecondary institutions have average or above average reading skills when compared to their hearing counterparts (Kerstetter, 1985). These students are most likely to do well and to receive a 4-year degree (Saur & Stinson, 1986). Considering prelinguistically severely to profoundly hearing-impaired students only, the average grade level of reading comprehension of students beginning postsecondary training is probably about grade 8 (Thyan, 1979). As discussed previously, test construction for this group is extremely difficult (Willingham, Ragosta, Bennett, Braun, Rock, & Powers, 1988). From another perspective, the findings of a project conducted by Educational Testing Service researchers on the Scholastic Aptitude Test and the Graduate Record Examinations General Test indicated that (Willingham et al., 1988):

> Test scores underpredicted the college performance of students with hearing impairments, but only those in special programs for deaf students; predictions based on test scores plus high school average did not misrepresent performance in mainstream college programs. Admissions tests in standard English may not be useful for deaf students who are taught with a manual language throughout the school and college years. (p. xv)

Although evidence is limited, we can still present some estimates of the levels of academic achievement of severely to profoundly hearing-impaired students at federally supported institutions such as Gallaudet University and NTID. For example, Hall (1929) analyzed the academic achievement scores on the SAT Advanced Battery of 62 deaf students in preparatory and freshman classes at Gallaudet College and reported that the median general achievement performance of the preparatory class was slightly below the ninth grade level, with a range from sixth to above the eleventh grade level. The median score of the freshman group was slightly higher than the tenth grade level, with a range from seventh to above the twelfth grade level. The improvement from preparatory to freshman level was probably a result of attrition among the weaker students. Both groups, however, had low scores in reading achievement—the median grade level was about sixth or seventh grade.

In 1955, Fusfeld analyzed the SAT Advanced Battery scores of two successive classes of preparatory students at Gallaudet College. At the end of the first year, the median achievement level was reported to be about 9.2 grades. At the end of the second year, the median level was 8.9 grades. The range for both years was from fifth to twelfth grade level. Low reading and writing scores were also noted by Fusfeld (1955) who remarked that "Examples from English composition papers of pupils . . . manifested marked failings in written discourse, and in particular a marked lack of grammatical sense in application" (p. 69).

It has been reported that students entering the National Technical Institute for the Deaf have an eighth-grade reading level (average), based on scores from various standardized achievement tests (Thyan, 1979). While they are at NTID, however, many students improve their level of reading comprehension. Notable gains have also been observed in other areas such as speech and writing abilities. For reading comprehension, the average growth rate is slightly more than one grade per year. As noted by Thyan (1979): "At NTID . . . we are finding that they not only can improve in these skills, but in some areas they improve at a faster rate than was evidenced during their public school training" (p. 65).

In a more recent study, Reynolds (1986) assessed the reading performance of Gallaudet University students on a criterion-referenced reading test. The age range of the students was 18 to 30 years, and their academic standings ranged from freshmen to seniors. The degree of hearing impairment extended from 27 to 120 dB, with a mean of 93 dB in the better unaided ear. As discussed previously, most of the students at Gallaudet, and in this study, were prelinguistically severely to profoundly hearing-impaired. The results indicated that the performance of the postlinguistically hearing-impaired students was significantly higher than those of the prelinguistically impaired students. The criterion-referenced test also provided norms for hearing students at various grade levels. It was reported that "The mean score for the deaf sample (i.e., *all hearing-impaired students in this sample*) (emphasis added) falls between the means of the ninth- and tenth-grade distributions for hearing norms, and is almost the same as the average readability level of many introductory college texts" (p. 363).

There is a need for more research on hearing-impaired students in postsecondary institutions, especially students with prelinguistically severe to profound hearing losses. Although enrollment at postsecondary educational programs has increased dramatically, very few severely to profoundly hearing-impaired students receive bachelor's degrees from 4-year institutions (Ouellette, 1985). Most students complete programs that award degrees or certificates at or below the associate-of-art level (Ouellette, 1985; Rawlings & King, 1986). Moores (1987) stated that ". . . although deaf students today may have equal access to higher education in general, relatively few receive the support necessary to complete the requirement for a full four-year bachelor's degree" (p. 323). It may also be that many of these students simply do not have adequately developed literacy skills to enable them to graduate.

SUMMARY

This chapter discussed some of the major issues and concerns related to placement, assessment, and achievement of severely to profoundly hearing-impaired students from preschool to postsecondary institutions. The primary focus was on academic achievement and its interrelationships with assessment, instruction, and curriculum. A better understanding of this issue should lead to an improvement in academic achievement.

As we have previously said, placement has a long, contentious history. Traditionally, it has been associated with the language/communication issue. That is, residential schools have used simultaneous communication whereas day schools and programs have employed oral communication. This trend has changed with the proliferation of Total Communication programs. At present, most programs employ simultaneous communication; thus, the distinction between residential and day schools and day programs is no longer evident.

Several placement options were described, for example, residential programs, day classes, and the more recent programs that use resource rooms and itinerant personnel. Nearly one-third of hearing-impaired students attend residential programs. Most of these students have prelinguistically severe to profound hearing losses. In addition, about 40 percent of this group are day students—that is, they commute to residential schools. There is some speculation that residential schools have been receiving an increasing number of hearing-impaired students with additional handicaps.

There is considerable variation in estimates of the percentage of hearing-impaired students who are enrolled or mainstreamed in academic or nonacademic regular-education classes. It is thought that hearing-impaired students with losses ranging from slight to moderate make up the largest group of mainstreamed students and that most of these students have acquired their impairments postlinguistically. Very few students with profound, especially prelinguistic, impairments attend regular education classes. Students in mainstreamed academic classes have been reported to have adequate achievement levels in reading, communication ability, and psychosocial development.

Many teachers are inadequately prepared to teach academic subjects such as reading, mathematics, and science. In addition, not enough emphasis is placed on multicultural education, that is, education of ethnic and other minority groups. Most programs that prepare teachers have emphasized communication, language, speech, speech reading, and auditory-training/learning skills. This does not mean, however, that teachers attain a high level of competence in these areas.

Teachers' knowledge of academic subjects reflects their lack of using and evaluating curricular materials that have been proven effective with hearing students. The use of special materials is necessary and beneficial; however, the main goal should be to enable hearing-impaired students to use the materials of mainstreamed society. Individualized instruction through the IEP is also important, but this should be subjected to formal evaluation to determine its effectiveness. There need to be close interrelations among instruction, curriculum, and assessment so that accurate levels of achievement of hearing-impaired students can be reported.

Also having had an impact on instruction and assessment is educational interpreting. Much work needs to be done in delineating the roles, responsibilities, and qualifications of interpreters in classroom situations. It was suggested that educational interpreting is different from other forms of professional interpreting. Advancement of knowledge in interpreting is dependent in part on a better understanding of the execution and reception of the various signed systems and American Sign Language.

A portion of the chapter was devoted to discussing assessment. It is important for teachers and other professionals to understand the main tenets of testing. Two broad types of tests were described: norm-referenced and criterion-referenced tests. Most tests used with hearing-impaired students have been standardized on hearing students. Thus, there is a need to develop additional norm-referenced and criterion-referenced tests for hearing-impaired students.

No general educational improvement in achievement in most students who are severely to profoundly hearing-impaired has been observed since the work of Pintner in the early years of the 20th century. The average student completing a secondary education program is still reading and writing at a level commensurate with the average 9- to 10-year-old hearing student. Achievement in mathematics is about one or two grades higher. Since the beginning of formal achievement testing, two enduring patterns have been reported: *low levels* and *small gains* in achievement despite 12 to 13 years of education.

These patterns have persisted despite preschool and early intervention and improvement in the construction of tests normed on hearing-impaired students. Examples of small gains in achievement include the results of the Test of Syntactic Abilities (TSA) (Quigley, Steinkamp, Power, & Jones, 1978; discussed in Chapter 8) and the results of the adapted version of the Stanford Achievement Test by the Center for Assessment and Demographic Studies. It cannot be argued that the findings are not representative of most severely to profoundly hearing-impaired students because high-achieving unidentified students are mainstreamed into regular education programs. Students in mainstreamed classes are more likely to have postlinguistic slight to moderate hearing impairments. In addition, it is highly unlikely that there are many severely to profoundly hearing-impaired students in regular education programs who have not been identified and evaluated.

The best overall achievement is found in students who are enrolled in comprehensive oral programs or integrated into regular education programs, which suggests a relationship between academic placement and achievement. Factors other than placement, however, may be important—for example, the quality of instruction and curricula. It should also be remembered that these successful students may represent a select group. That is, they have high IQs and well-established verbal language abilities, and their parents/caregivers are highly involved in their educational process.

Some information was also provided on students in postsecondary education programs—for example, enrollment figures, characteristics, and achievement. It was reported that hearing-impaired students are more likely to attend postsecondary programs full time than are their hearing counterparts. The number of postsecondary programs and the number of hearing-impaired students attending such programs have increased dramatically since the 1960s. Nevertheless, very few severely to profoundly hearing-impaired students receive bachelor's degrees from 4-year institutions. Although more research is needed, it can be concluded that many of these students do not have adequate literacy skills.

COMPREHENSION

1. Discuss the relationship between integration in regular educational classes and hearing impairment, particularly severity and age at onset of impairment.
2. TRUE or FALSE? Today, residential schools use simultaneous communication only whereas day programs use oral communication only.
3. There is some evidence that many teachers of hearing-impaired students (check all that apply)
   a. Have little university training in communication areas.
   b. Are not well prepared to teach subjects such as reading, mathematics, and science.
   c. With good training in content areas tend to use a wider variety of instructional techniques than those teachers with less training.
   d. Devote a greater amount of time to teaching mathematics than to teaching language.
   e. Have no specific degree in science education.
4. TRUE or FALSE? Contrary to the situation in regular education, members of minority groups are well represented among teachers of hearing-impaired students.
5. Designate the following descriptions as either *regular educational curriculum* or *specially designed curriculum:*
   a. Most likely to be used by residential schools.
   b. Most likely to be found in day programs.
   c. Used to meet the individual needs of hearing-impaired students.
   d. Beneficial if there is a huge mismatch between the language in texts and the language competence of students.
   e. Ultimate goal of instruction is to enable hearing-impaired students to use these materials at some particular milestone.

6. TRUE or FALSE? The IEP
   a. Is designed to meet the unique needs of students who require special educational services.
   b. Is not mandated by law but strongly encouraged for special education students.
   c. Consists mainly of input from the special education teacher only.
   d. Is also mandated for regular education students.
   e. Should be subjected to formal evaluations to determine its effectiveness.
7. What, according to several surveys, are the major needs of educational interpreters?
8. Label the following as *norm-referenced tests* and/or *criterion-referenced tests*.
   a. Indicate what students have learned in comparison with other similar students at the same grade (or age level).
   b. Test of Syntactic Abilities.
   c. Test scores reflect the extent to which students have mastered the information in a particular domain.
   d. Test scores represent overall achievement rather than a particular ability.
   e. One of the most important concepts is minimum competency.
   f. Tests are often used for diagnostic purposes.
   g. Stanford Achievement Test
9. Research on preschool and early intervention indicated that (check all that apply)
   a. There are very few empirical studies showing the effectiveness of such programs for hearing-impaired students.
   b. Most of the literature contains descriptions of programs and methods.
   c. It is clear that TC early intervention programs are more effective than oral early intervention programs.
   d. More instructional time and much more emphasis are placed on mathematics than on reading (Moores, 1985b; Moores, Weiss, & Goodwin, 1978).
   e. The Rochester Method is a panacea for educational problems of young hearing-impaired children (Quigley, 1969).
   f. Early intervention is not an all-encompassing factor.
10. TRUE or FALSE? The following statements concern the research on elementary and/or secondary educational hearing-impaired students:
   a. The general findings reported by Pintner and his associates have not been confirmed by later investigators.
   b. Results consistently revealed low mean reading grade levels and slow gains in overall achievement.
   c. The achievement gap between hearing and hearing-impaired students widened as students became older, especially in areas that involve higher-level language skills.
   d. Hearing-impaired students performed better on subtests involving reading comprehension than on those concerning spelling and capitalization.
   e. Mathematical computational problems were easier than the understanding and application of mathematical concepts.
   f. Educational achievement is influenced pervasively by language and reading comprehension ability.
   g. Reading achievement levels on the adapted SATs were considerably higher than those on the earlier unadapted SATs.
11. Why should the findings of national surveys be interpreted with caution?
12. Consider the following statement as true: ''Integrated hearing-impaired students have higher academic achievement levels than do their nonintegrated counterparts.'' Now discuss why the differences between these two groups may not be the result of *integration* only.
13. TRUE or FALSE? The following statements relate to postsecondary issues:

    a. Much of what is available in the published literature is descriptions of opportunities and services.

    b. In general, the percentage of hearing-impaired students enrolling in programs is lower than that of hearing students.

    c. Prelinguistic severely to profoundly hearing-impaired students are most likely to enroll at Gallaudet or NTID.

    d. Most prelinguistic severely to profoundly hearing-impaired students receive the bachelor degree from 4-year institutions other than Gallaudet or NTID.

    e. Most hearing-impaired students who begin their program at Gallaudet or NTID have a mean reading level of about the 11th grade.

SUGGESTED ACTIVITIES

1. Compare the Stanford Achievement Test for hearing students with the adapted SAT for hearing-impaired students.
    a. How do the tests differ?
    b. What are the levels of reliability and validity for both tests?
    c. Can the adapted SAT be used to plan a reading program for hearing-impaired students? How?

2. Select five hearing-impaired students in high school. Record their SAT scores in reading comprehension for the past 6 years. How much has each student improved over this time?

3. Administer two informal reading inventories to a hearing-impaired student. Record the student's strengths and weaknesses.

4. Interview several teachers of hearing-impaired students. Solicit their opinions regarding the following:
    a. The use of achievement tests
    b. The use of informal tests
    c. Minimum competency examinations for hearing-impaired students.

FURTHER READINGS

Allen T. (1986). *Understanding the scores: Hearing-impaired students and the Stanford Achievement Test* (7th Editon). Washington, DC: Gallaudet University Press.

Hammill, D. (Ed.). (1987). *Assessing the abilities and instructional needs of students.* Austin, TX: Pro-Ed.

Hoffmann, B. (1964). *The tyranny of testing.* New York: Collier Books.

Kretschmer, R., & Kretschmer, L. (Eds.). (1988). Communication assessment of hearing-impaired children: From conversation to classroom. *Journal of the Academy of Rehabilitative Audiology,* Monograph Supplement, *21.*

Noll, V., Scannell, D., & Craig, R. (Eds.). (1979). *Introduction to educational measurement* (4th ed.). Boston, MA: Houghton Mifflin.

Owen, D. (1985). *None of the above: Behind the myth of scholastic aptitude.* Boston, MA: Houghton Mifflin.

Quigley, S. (Ed.). (1965). *Interpreting for deaf people*. Washington, DC: U.S. Department of Health, Education, and Welfare, Social and Rehabilitation Service, Rehabilitation Services Administration.

The deaf student in college: Beyond the classroom. (1983). Washington, DC: Gallaudet University Press.

CHAPTER 10
Multihandicapped Students

MAJOR POINTS TO CONSIDER

Definitional concerns

Wide variations in estimates of incidence

Deafness and additional handicaps

Instruction and curriculum

Language and communication

Multihandicapped adults

This chapter focuses on severely to profoundly hearing-impaired students with additional handicapping conditions. It provides some perspectives on definitions and incidence figures, and it discusses the relationships among additional handicapping conditions and other important variables such as degree of hearing loss, sex, and etiology (i.e., cause of deafness). Also discussed are the effects of current classification procedures on the training of preservice teachers, curricula, and the selection of educational practices for some multihandicapped students such as deaf-blind students (i.e., students with **dual-sensory impairment**) students. Finally, a brief overview is presented on residential alternatives and employment for handicapped adults.

Much has been written in the literature about the coexistence of deafness and other educationally significant handicaps (Mencher & Gerber, 1983; Tweedie & Shroyer, 1982; Vernon, 1969b; Wolff & Harkins, 1986). As a result, there has been an increase in educational and other professional services. However, the available information provides little or no assistance to teachers and other personnel in meeting the educational needs of hearing-impaired students with additional handicaps (Schloss, Smith, Goldsmith, & Selinger, 1984).

The nature and extent of educational problems of hearing-impaired students with additional handicapping conditions have not been systematically investigated. Historically, this has been a very complicated task. For example, Stewart (1971) stated several problems in developing adequate programming that are still evident today: (1) incomplete descriptions of the population, (2) little use of effective training procedures such as behavior modification techniques (cf., Jones, 1984), and (3) lack of sufficient instructional and curricular materials. There is also a need for adequately trained professionals (Konar & Rice, 1982; Shroyer, 1982). The difficulty of providing adequate training and establishing effective programming cannot be overemphasized. As stated aptly by Mencher and Gerber (1983):

> The special nature of multiple handicaps is such that their effects are not simply additive, but rather they interact with each other in ways not thoroughly understood to create a complex array of secondary consequences. (p. 2)

Thus, multihandicapped hearing-impaired students complicate the tasks of identification, classification, assessment, selection of instructional and curricular activities, management, and educational goals.

No one questions that the existence of additional handicaps has a negative effect on language, communication, and the levels of academic achievement of students. For example, it has been reported that the achievement levels of a national sample of hearing-impaired students with additional handicaps are inferior to those of hearing-impaired students with no additional handicaps, and the performance of the multihandicapped group lags farther behind as the students become older (Ries, 1973). By the age of 17 years, there is a little more than one grade difference in reading comprehension and more than two grades difference in arithmetic computation between the two groups. The development of adequate English literacy skills may not be a realistic goal for most multihandicapped students. As discussed in Chapter 1, the primary goal of educating these hearing-impaired students is occupational self-sufficiency, which may best be achieved by the use of at least a functional curriculum rather than one that focuses on teaching literacy skills and academic subjects (Schloss et al., 1984).

DEFINITION

One of the most serious problems in programming, preservice training, and funding is the range of interpretations of educational definitions of students with multiple handicaps (Heward & Orlansky, 1988; Kirk & Gallagher, 1986; Michael & Paul, in press). Constructing definitions or descriptions is difficult because of numerous factors that must be considered, such as degree of hearing impairment and severity of additional handicapping conditions. Variations in definitions can also result from the perspectives of various professionals—medical, psychological, legal, or educational. For example, Snell (1978) defined students with multiple handicaps as:

1. All moderately, severely, and profoundly mentally retarded individuals.
2. All severely and profoundly emotionally disturbed individuals.
3. All moderately and profoundly retarded individuals who have at least one additional impairment (i.e., deafness, blindness, crippling condition). (p. 6)

This definition does not include individuals with multiple sensory problems such as deaf-blind students. In fact, deaf-blind, or dual-sensory impaired, individuals are not considered as part of the multihandicapped student population according to the definition in Public Law 94–142 (1975). Most educators of either hearing-impaired or visually impaired students would argue that the deaf-blind student is multihandicapped (Moores, 1987). There is general agreement, however, that definitions of multihandicaps or deaf-blindness refer to the existence of concomitant impairments resulting in educational difficulties that cannot be accommodated in programs designed solely for one of the impairments (*Federal Register,* 1973; Public Law 94–142, 1975; cf., Gentile & Mc-Carthy, 1973).

A wide variety of handicapping conditions have been reported in hearing-impaired students—mental retardation, learning disability, emotional or behavior disorders, visual impairment, brain damage or injury, epilepsy, orthopedic problems, cerebral palsy, and heart disorders (Schein, 1975; Vernon, 1969b, 1982; Wolff & Harkins, 1986). It may be that the association of some additional handicaps with deafness is caused by the use of unreliable assessments or is the result of inappropriate demands imposed by hearing parents and professionals on children and youth (Moores, 1987; Vernon, 1987a). As discussed in Chapter 4, another possible factor is the lack of a fluent and intelligible communication system between the students and significant others such as parents/caregivers and teachers.

The presence of additional handicapping conditions does not always lead to special treatment in another type of educational program. In some instances, the multihandicapped student remains in a classroom or program with other nonhandicapped hearing-impaired students. Gentile and McCarthy (1973) stated that the additional handicapping condition can be considered as ". . . any physical, mental, emotional or behavior disorder that significantly adds to the complexity of educating a hearing impaired student" (p. 2). This description is acceptable to most educators of hearing-impaired students who attempt to modify their instructional and curricular approaches to meet the individual needs of their students (Tweedie & Shroyer, 1982).

INCIDENCE

As can be expected, there is wide variation in incidence figures on multihandicapped hearing-impaired students reported in the literature. The discrepancies in the figures are influenced by definitions of educationally significant handicaps, methods of collecting data, and accuracy of the students' data available in the schools. Many researchers find that it is extremely difficult to obtain accurate information and reliable incidence figures on students with additional handicaps (Conrad, 1979; Moores, 1987; Rodda & Grove, 1987; Wolff & Harkins, 1986). For example, it is stated that the categories of emotional, behavioral, and brain problems are likely to contain inflated figures. Because of their difficulty in developing adequate sign communication skills, many teachers and other professionals are likely to misdiagnose hearing-impaired students. Mislabeling or misdiagnosis is considered one of the most serious problems (Moores, 1987; Rodda & Grove, 1987).

It is estimated that about 11 percent of all students in elementary and secondary education programs in the United States have educationally significant handicaps (U.S. Department of Education, 1983). There seems to be a higher incidence of additional handicaps in hearing-impaired students than that which has been reported for the general student population. One possible reason for this may be that some of the major causes of deafness result in a number of additional handicapping conditions such as brain damage, aphasic disorders, and mental retardation (Vernon, 1969b, 1982, 1987a). In addition, some multihandicapped individuals are likely to have health-related problems. For example, individuals deafened by congenital rubella syndrome (CRS) have a greater risk of developing abnormalities such as diabetes or other abnormalities of glucose metabolism (Shaver, Boughman, & Nance, 1985). A review of the literature revealed that estimates of hearing-impaired students with one or more additional handicapping conditions ranges from 11 to 54 percent.

Vernon (1969b) analyzed the data on about 420 moderately to profoundly hearing-impaired students in one residential school. The researcher was interested in determining the relationship between the cause of deafness and the presence of additional handicaps. Student information was obtained from school records that included the results of psychological tests and teachers' ratings. About 49 percent of the students had one or more additional handicaps. The high percentage was probably due to the inclusion of only those students for whom data on cause of deafness was available. As discussed in Chapter 2, a large percentage (estimates range from 25 to about 40 percent) of deafness in children is due to unknown causes [Brown, 1986]). It is suspected that many of these students became hearing-impaired as a result of heredity. Among genetically deafened students, the incidence of additional handicaps has been found to be much lower than that observed among students with other causes of deafness (Vernon, 1969b, 1987a; Moores, 1987; Wolff & Harkins, 1986). Thus, Vernon's percentage could have been much lower if these students had been included in the study.

Conrad (1979) analyzed the results of teachers' interviews concerning the prevalence of additional handicaps in about 470 hearing-impaired adolescents in schools and programs for deaf students in England and Wales and reported that 11 percent of his sample of hearing-impaired students had one or more educationally significant additional handicaps. This percentage is markedly lower than the 49 percent reported by Vernon (1969b) and the 54 percent reported by England's Department of Education and Science in 1972 (Conrad, 1979). The latter percentage was derived from the results of interviews with children conducted by medical personnel as well as from school reports. Conrad, however, did not include the data on students with mental retardation and visual impairments in his analysis. It is estimated that about 13 percent of hearing-impaired students are also mentally retarded, visually impaired, or both (Wolff & Harkins, 1986). The inclusion of these students could have inflated Conrad's figure to about 24 percent.

The most consistent data on incidence of multihandicapped hearing-impaired students have been provided by the annual surveys conducted by the Center for Assessment and Demographic Studies at Gallaudet University. As discussed in Chapter 9, the students in the CADS survey are representative of most severely to profoundly hearing-impaired students in special education programs and classes in the United States. Students with lesser degrees of hearing impairment and enrolled in regular education programs or in special private schools have not been included in the national investigations.

The percentage of students with one or more additional handicapping conditions has remained fairly constant from the results of the first annual survey in 1968–1969 (Rawlings & Gentile, 1970) to those of the 1982–1983 survey (Wolff & Harkins, 1986). This is true despite the change in definitions and the number of categories associated with the various handicapping conditions. For example, Rawlings and Gentile (1970) reported that about 31 percent of the more than 21,000 students in the 1968–1969 survey had one or more handicapping conditions. Analyzing the results of annual surveys from 1969 to 1972, Gentile and McCarthy (1973) stated that the incidence of students with additional handicaps ranged from about 31 percent to about 33 percent. The two most recent surveys (Karchmer, 1985; Wolff & Harkins, 1986) reported that approximately 30 percent of hearing-impaired students have one or more additional handicaps, a percentage that is also similar to that reported on students in special programs and schools in Canada (Karchmer, Allen, Petersen, & Quaynor, 1982; Mencher, 1983). In addition, it is estimated that about 21 percent of these students (in the United States) have only one additional handicapping condition (Wolff & Harkins, 1986). The four most common disabilities reported are mental retardation, learning disability, emotional or behavior problems, and visual impairment (including blindness and uncorrected visual problems).

The findings of the most recent survey available (Wolff & Harkins, 1986) can be compared to those reported for the general population of students in 1982. As stated earlier, the incidence of multihandicaps among the general student population is about 11 percent (U.S. Department of Education, 1983). Additional handicapping conditions are about three times more prevalent in hearing-impaired students. As observed by Wolff and Harkins (1986):

> . . . each of the specific handicaps listed by the U.S. Department of Education was more common in hearing-impaired children . . . than in the general population. Cognitive-behavioral handicaps (mental retardation, learning disability, and severe emotional disturbances) were much more common in the general population than were physical disabilities, a finding that parallels those of the Annual Survey. (p. 66)

RELATIONSHIP OF DEAFNESS AND ADDITIONAL HANDICAPS

As discussed previously and in Chapter 2, a higher incidence of additional handicaps has been associated with certain causes of hearing impairment such as rubella, trauma, the Rh factor, and prematurity (Brown, 1986). On the other hand, genetically caused deafness results in the lowest incidence of additional handicapping conditions (Vernon, 1969b, 1982, 1987a). In national surveys, it has been reported that mildly to moderately impaired students have higher percentages of one or more additional handicapping conditions than do severely to profoundly hearing-impaired students, probably as a result of the underrepresentation of students with lesser degrees of impairment in the surveys.

The results of the most recent national survey (Wolff & Harkins, 1986) indicated relationships between the incidence of additional handicaps and (1) sex, and (2) ethnic background (specifically, African American students). These patterns parallel those reported for the general population of students (U.S. Department of Education, 1983). Male students were more likely to be multihandicapped than were female students, and a higher percentage of African American hearing-impaired students (about 37 percent) have been reported to have additional handicaps, especially mental retardation. This overrepresentation of African American hearing-impaired students with multihandicaps led Wolff and Harkins (1986) to conclude, "These findings suggest that bias in evaluation procedures is still a problem" (p. 68). Finally, because of the rubella epidemic of the 1960s, many hearing-impaired students at the secondary education level in the annual surveys are reported to be multihandicapped. This pattern is likely to change as the students graduate or leave programs (Karchmer, 1985).

Mental Retardation

The field of mental retardation is replete with debates on what constitutes the condition of mental retardation. Discussions have centered on factors such as intelligence, adaptive behavior, etiology, and type of education or training program (Heward & Orlansky, 1988; Kirk, 1962). Mentally retarded students, like other students with a need for special education, are members of a heterogeneous group. Some current research is attempting to establish homogeneous subgroups with general characteristics (Kamhi & Johnston, 1982). It is argued that advances in knowledge are limited until the interrelationships among learning, intelligence, and development are clearly understood (Scott, 1978). At present, the most widely used definition is that proposed by the American Association of Mental Deficiency (Grossman, 1973):

> Mental retardation refers to significantly subaverage general intellectual functioning existing concurrently with deficits in adaptive behavior, and manifested during the developmental period. (p. 11)

Subaverage intellectual functioning means that an individual scored below the IQ norm for her age group (in statistical jargon, this is referred to as being at least two standard deviations below the norm), although numbers may vary according to the norms of certain standardized tests. Table 10.1 illustrates approximate levels of intelligence (Heward & Orlansky, 1988; Ingalls, 1978; Kirk & Gallagher, 1986). Adaptive behavior may be assessed by tests such as the Vineland Social Maturity Scale or the Adaptive Behavior Scale.

The American Association on Mental Deficiency has identified and categoried some causes of mental retardation: infection and intoxication, traumas, metabolism disorders, brain diseases, unknown parental influences, chromosomal abnormalities, gestational disorders, and environmental influences (Grossman, 1977). One of the most common genetic disorders is *Down's syndrome,* in which individuals have 47 chromosomes instead of the typical 46. Down's syndrome results in mild to moderate mental retardation and can be accompanied by a variety of other health-related conditions such as hearing impairments and heart problems. Retardation from infection and intoxication includes

TABLE 10.1. Levels of Intelligence According to Two IQ Tests

Level	IQ Range	
	Stanford-Binet	WISC–R
Borderline (slow learner)	68–83	70–84
Mild retardation (educable)	52–67	55–69
Moderate retardation (trainable)	36–51	40–54
Severe retardation	20–35	25–39
Profound retardation	19–	24–

NOTE: Each level of intelligence corresponds to one standard deviation below what is considered normal. The average range for the Stanford-Binet is 84 to 116, and the average range for the WISC–R is 85 to 115. Based on Gillespie and Johnson (1974) and Heward and Orlansky (1988). These sources can be consulted for further information.

fetal alcohol syndrome, lead poisoning, and congenital rubella disease. One of the most difficult conditions to explain is the relationship between mental retardation and certain environmental factors such as low socioeconomic status. It has been argued that children of low socioeconomic status are more susceptible to a number of health-related conditions (Gillespie & Johnson, 1974; Heward & Orlansky, 1988; Kirk & Gallagher, 1986; Robinson & Robinson, 1965).

Deafness and Mental Retardation.   Estimates of the percentage of hearing-impaired students with mental retardation vary considerably. Weir (1963) stated that 11 percent of students in residential and day schools also had some degree of mental retardation. The CADS annual surveys during the 1970s and 1980s reported a range of 6 to 8.5 percent. Other estimates of the prevalence of hearing-impaired mentally retarded children and adults in residential institutions and public schools that serve mentally retarded individuals ranged from 10 to 15 percent (Brannan, 1982; Healey & Karp-Nortman, 1975).

The recent percentages reported by CADS on hearing-impaired students are still higher than estimates of mentally retarded students in the general school population (Heward & Orlansky, 1988; Kirk & Gallagher, 1986). As discussed previously, the discrepancies may be a result of the use of inappropriate tests or the poor sign communication skills of the examiners. It may also be that certain causes of deafness produce a higher incidence of mental retardation as well as other handicapping conditions.

Debate as to the most appropriate placement of hearing-impaired students with mental retardation is widespread. Some educators believe that some students can receive the most appropriate education in traditional educational programs for mentally retarded students (discussed by Naiman, 1982). Others believe that the students have more specialized needs that cannot be met in traditional programs for either mentally retarded or hearing-impaired students (Kirk & Gallahger, 1986). It is probably best to emphasize that not all educational needs of hearing-impaired students with mental retardation can be met in one setting or with one curriculum. A range of educational placements and curricular activities should be available.

Learning Disability

Hammill, Leigh, McNutt, and Larsen (1981) stated that:

> Learning disabilities is a generic term that refers to a heterogeneous group of disorders
> manifested by significant difficulties in the acquisition and use of listening, speaking,
> reading, writing, reasoning or mathematical abilities. These disorders are intrinsic to the
> individual and presumed to be due to central nervous system dysfunction. Even though
> a learning disability may occur concomitantly with other handicapping conditions (e.g.,
> sensory impairment, mental retardation, social and emotional disturbance) or environ-
> mental influences (e.g., cultural differences, insufficient/inappropriate instruction, psy-
> chogenic factors), it is not the direct result of those conditions or influences. (p. 336)

The foregoing definition implies that there is an intrinsic psychological or neurological
factor that has interfered with the development of the cognitive and linguistic abilities
of students.

The term *learning disability* was introduced by Samuel Kirk at a conference in
1963 for parents of students who had perceptual handicaps (Gerber, 1981). Since that
time, two general models for describing learning disability have dominated the field: the
medical model and the behavioral model. From a medical perspective, learning disability is viewed as an organic etiology. Terms used to describe this condition include, but
are not limited to, the following: organic brain disease or dysfunction, minimal brain
damage, and minimal brain dysfunction syndrome. Terms from a behavioral perspective
include hyperkinetic syndrome, dyslexia, specific reading disability, perceptual handicaps, and specific learning disability (Gerber, 1981; Wong, 1979a, 1979b).

In many states, students are labeled as having learning disabilities if their scores in
academic subjects on standardized tests are at least two grades below those of their
nondisabled peers. It should be emphasized, however, that not all students, particularly
those with at least average intelligence, who have this degree of discrepancy have learning disabilities. In addition, some educators of hearing-impaired students, for example,
Moores (1987), argue that "terms such as 'emotional disorder,' 'behavioral disorder,'
and 'learning disorder' have not been differentiated sufficiently. . . . (p. 120). In-depth
discussions on the nature and extent of learning disabilities can be found elsewhere
Gerber & Bryen, 1981; Heward & Orlansky, 1988; Kirk & Gallagher, 1986; D. Smith,
1981).

Severe neurological impairments can sometimes accompany hearing impairment
and produce various types of learning disabilities. Deafness and learning disability
can result from trauma, complications of pregnancy, and serious infections (Shroyer,
1982; Vernon, 1969b; Wolff & Harkins, 1986). Subsequent problems with cognitive
functioning such as aphasic disorders (Vernon, 1969b), motor control (Auxter, 1971),
and visual-spatial and other perceptual difficulties (Shroyer, 1982) can occur.

Deafness and Learning Disability.   As with other handicapping conditions, there is
wide variation in the incidence of deafness accompanied by learning disabilities (LD).
Estimates of incidence range from 1 percent to more than 35 percent, with a majority
of the estimates between 3 percent and 16 percent. The results of a recent survey (Pow-

ers, Elliott, & Funderburg, 1987) indicated an estimated incidence of 6.7 percent. The findings of the 1982–1983 CADS survey revealed a figure of 8.1 percent, second only to that of mental retardation (Wolff & Harkins, 1986). The wide variation in the incidence of learning-disabled hearing-impaired students could be a result of several factors such as difficulties in the use of appropriate assessments and the lack of clearly defined criteria for identification. Whatever the estimates, Funderburg (1982) argued that this group of students is likely to be one of the most misdiagnosed and unserved groups of handicapped students.

Auxter (1971) conducted one of the first investigations on the presence of learning disabilities in hearing-impaired students, trying to ascertain perceptual motor characteristics that account for differences in the academic performance of hearing-impaired students of similar ages and levels of intelligence. Results indicated differences between groups on tasks such as muscular strength, motor speed, motor planning, and the integration of neuromuscular control. The impact of these differences on the academic performance of the students, however, has been questioned (Vockell, Hirshoren, & Vockell, 1972).

Recent studies have documented the existence of visual-spatial and other perceptual deficiencies in hearing-impaired students (Ratner, 1985; Shroyer, 1982). For example, it has been shown that deficits in spatial relationship have a negative impact on communicative, social, and academic development. From another perspective, several investigators have examined the cognitive styles of groups of hearing-impaired students and their effects on academic performance (LaSasso, 1986; McDaniel, 1980). The discussion of the test-taking strategies of hearing-impaired students on reading tasks in Chapter 8 is an example of this line of research. There is variation in cognitive styles; however, as stated by Wolff and Harkins (1986):

> What is unclear is the extent to which the diagnosis of learning disabilities may at times represent not a true disability, but rather a case of pronounced difference from the hearing norm in cognitive style. (p.76)

Two recent surveys documented a need for dealing with the identification, assessment, and programming of hearing-impaired students with learning disabilities (Elliott & Powers, 1988; Powers et al., 1987). For example, Powers et al. (1987) analyzed the responses of directors of 63 programs with about 11,000 hearing-impaired students. The respondents indicated that about 6.7 percent, or 736 hearing-impaired students, had a learning disability. The percentages of LD hearing-impaired students at each school level was as follows: preschool—3.6 percent; elementary—6.5 percent; middle/junior high—8 percent; and high school—6.9 percent.

The respondents were also asked to list characteristics of LD hearing-impaired students that differentiated them from typical hearing-impaired students. The two highest categories were achievement discrepancy (23 responses) and perceptual problems (20 responses). Not far behind were behavior (15 responses), attention problems (14 responses), and learning styles (14 responses). Other categories included language problems, memory difficulty, inconsistent performance, and poor organization skills. This variety of behaviors led Moores (1987) to argue that there is little research that demonstrates differentiation among the various handicapping conditions. Indeed, Powers et al. (1987) stated:

> Some confusion is likely in determining whether a hearing-impaired student with one or more additional handicaps is learning disabled, emotionally disturbed, or mentally retarded. Many behaviors and academic performance problems may be common to all three categories of special education students. (p. 104)

The researchers concluded that their survey results documented the existence of a group of hearing-impaired students whose academic performances are different from those of typical hearing-impaired students. They added, however, that it is not clear whether these differences can be characterized as learning disabilities. Despite problems with definition and identification, it has been reported that many teacher educators believe there is a need for more specialized training within current university-level teacher preparation programs that focuses on hearing-impaired students with additional learning problems (Elliott & Powers, 1988).

Emotional/Behavioral Problems

Emotional/behavioral problems refer to the degree and duration of age-inappropriate behaviors in students that cause psychological, social, and educational difficulties (Heward & Orlansky, 1988; Kirk & Gallagher, 1986; Paul & Epanchin, 1982; Wood & Lakin, 1982). Classification of behavior problems can be influenced by medical or educational perspectives. From another viewpoint, Quay and Werry (1979) reported attempts to discover patterns of interrelated behaviors through analyses of check lists and rating scales. Four categories of deviant behaviors were delineated: conduct disorder, anxiety/withdrawal, immaturity, and socialized aggression. Other methods of identifying behavior problems include tests such as the Rorschach Ink Blot, Minnesota Multiphasic Personality Inventory *(MMPI)*, and the Vineland Social Maturity Scale.

An occasional display of age-inappropriate behavior is not sufficient to categorize a student as having emotional/behavioral problems. Rather, it is the degree and duration of such behavior. The perspective of the professional is another important factor that contributes to the labeling of students. Disagreements among educators and researchers have resulted in variations in incidence figures. For example, Rubin and Balow (1978) analyzed the results of teacher ratings on about 1,600 students in kindergarten through sixth grade in regular education classes. About 60 percent of the students in school for six years were considered to exhibit a behavior problem by at least one teacher. In the general school population, incidence estimates range from about 2 percent to as high as 25 percent. The U.S. Department of Education (1983), however, reported an estimate of less than 1 percent of the total school population with deviant behavior. As discussed previously, these figures are influenced by difficulties with assessment and identification procedures. It should also be remembered that several studies require teachers to rate students' behavior at a specific time. This procedure could have inflated figures because many students exhibit some deviant behavior occasionally. It is likely that some of the estimates could have been lower if the emphasis had been on the *degree and duration of the inappropriate behavior.*

Deafness and Behavior Problems. A familiar theme is repeated here regarding the incidence of deafness and behavior problems. In earlier studies, the prevalence rates for deviant behaviors in hearing-impaired students varied from 8 percent to as high as 33 percent (Jensema & Trybus, 1975; Meadow, 1980). More recently, it has been reported that about 6 percent of the national sample of hearing-impaired students have behavior problems (Wolff & Harkins, 1986). All these estimates are higher than that reported by the U.S. Department of Education (1983).

   Wolff and Harkins (1986) stated:

> The same organic insults implicated as causes in learning disabilities are also known causative factors in some childhood behavioral syndromes, most notably attention deficit disorder, both with and without hyperactivity. This may, to some extent, explain the comparatively high prevalence of behavioral problems among deaf students. . . . (p. 76)

Other researchers also support the notion of some overlapping in behaviors and problems associated with learning disability and behavior disturbances (Heward & Orlansky, 1988; Kirk & Gallagher, 1986).

   Wolff and Harkins (1986) and others (Conrad, 1979; Moores, 1987; Rodda & Grove, 1987), argued that there might be additional non-physiological causes of behavior problems in hearing-impaired students, for example, poor family and peer relations and communication problems. In Chapter 4, it was suggested that many conflicts in the classroom might be reflective of behavior adjustment or communication problems, rather than examples of severe psychological/behavior conditions. Both Conrad (1979) and Cohen (1980) have shown that incidence estimates of hearing-impaired students exhibiting deviant behaviors are inflated by about 20 to 25 percent owing to inadequate classification procedures used by teachers. This seems to support the notion that teachers' judgments result in unusually high estimates (Rubin & Balow, 1978).

   In general, most surveys indicate that hearing-impaired students have more behavior problems than the general population of students. It is not clear, however, how these results should be interpreted. As discussed in Chapter 4, there is a need for the development of more accurate tests and for more qualified mental-health professionals to work with hearing-impaired individuals.

Deaf-Blind Students

Typically, individuals with deaf-blindness (i.e., dual-sensory impairments) are classified as severely handicapped (D'Zamko & Hampton, 1985). Most state agencies follow the federal definition of deaf-blind as stated in Public Law 94–142 (Federal Register, 1973):

> Deaf-blind means concomitant hearing and visual impairment the combination of which causes such severe communication and other developmental and educational problems that they cannot be accommodated in special educational programs solely for the hearing handicapped child or the visually handicapped child. (p. 196)

In the early 1960s, only individuals who had incurred severe hearing and visual impairments from spinal meningitis or other diseases were considered deaf-blind (Michael & Paul, in press). Because of the rubella epidemic during the 1960s, the characteristics of this population have changed to include sensory impairments accompanied by other handicapping conditions such as mental retardation. It has been reported that about 60 percent of students with dual-sensory impairments also are severely to profoundly retarded (Jensema, 1979a, 1979b). Students categorized as deaf-blind may have (1) dual-sensory impairments only, (2) additional cognitive disabilities, (3) central-processing problems, and (4) *Ushers syndrome,* that is, progressive sensory impairment (Konar & Rice, 1982).

Recently, a number of educators and researchers have argued for a functional classification system of deaf-blindness (Dunlap, 1985; Konar & Rice, 1982). The main tenet of this notion is to classify students based on ability rather than on primary handicapping condition. For example, Dunlap (1985) found that groups of deaf-blind students could be differentiated more effectively on variables such as gross motor ability, language, and socialization rather than on measures of vision and audition only.

Until the late 1960s, the education of deaf-blind students was confined to expensive private residential schools. There were few efforts to identify and educate these students. The rubella epidemic brought increased attention to deaf-blindness as well as to other multihandicapping conditions. This resulted in the establishment of regional and multistate centers that provide services for students with dual-sensory impairments.

The most recent CADS survey revealed that about 2 percent of a national sample of hearing-impaired students in special education programs and classes are legally blind, and that another 4 percent have uncorrected visual problems (Wolff & Harkins, 1986). The high incidence of deaf-blindness and additional handicaps has led to the placement of many students in multihandicapped programs rather than in classrooms with qualified teachers who can serve students with severe handicaps. Because about 94 percent of these students have residual hearing and/or residual vision (Fredericks & Baldwin, 1987), it is possible that many of them in multihandicapped programs are not receiving appropriate intervention, such as training in the development of vision and audition (Michael & Paul, in press). In addition, many teachers of hearing-impaired students with dual-sensory or other multihandicapping impairments may not be adequately prepared to work with these students.

PREPARATION OF TEACHERS

There is little disagreement that many teachers in the education of hearing-impaired students have had little formal university-level training in dealing with multiple or severe handicapping conditions. Anderson and Stevens (1969) examined the qualifications of 150 teachers of hearing-impaired students with mental retardation in residential schools for deaf students. They reported that more than 75 percent of the teachers were placed in their present position as a result of administrative decisions rather than their own preferences, and 86 percent of the teachers stated a need for additional training.

More recently, Jones and Johnson (1985) conducted a survey of 119 programs serving multihandicapped hearing-impaired students. They reported that only 8 percent of the teachers had formal training in working with the multihandicapped students. Most of the teachers had training in the education of hearing-impaired students, and some of them had also received academic training in another special education area.

Most teachers apparently receive on-the-job training or upgrade their skills through inservice training that may not be efficient (D'Zamko & Hampton, 1985; Powers et al., 1987). One problem is that there are few university-level training programs. D'Zamko and Hampton (1985) reported that only one university—Gallaudet—offers a teacher-preparation program in the area of multihandicapped hearing-impaired students. It is difficult to develop programs that deal with the numerous needs of a heterogeneous population (Baldwin, 1986; Covert & Fredericks, 1987). Training for working with the deaf or with the mentally retarded students may not be sufficient for working with mentally retarded hearing-impaired students. Preservice training for certification in multihandicaps or severe handicaps may not offer important information about vision or audition for students with dual-sensory impairments. In short, it has been argued that the certification requirements in many states are so generic that training programs do not provide the skills for working effectively with these hearing-impaired students (Curtis & Tweedie, 1985; D'Zamko & Hampton, 1985).

Teachers may also need further training in classroom management techniques that have been found to be effective with special education students, such as the use of **behavior modification procedures** (Belcastro, 1979; Jones, 1984; Shroyer, 1982). It has been suggested that many of the techniques used with typical hearing-impaired students can also be effectively used with multihandicapped hearing-impaired students (Shroyer, 1982). It may be necessary, however, for teachers to become more familiar with other variations of behavior modification procedures and learn more effective ways to structure their classrooms for meeting the needs of their students. A recent review revealed that there has been an increase in the use of behavior modification techniques with multihandicapped hearing-impaired students for teaching academic and socialization skills; however, further research on the effectiveness of the procedures is needed (Jones, 1984).

CURRICULUM

Two models have influenced the construction and use of curricular activities and materials with multihandicapped students, as well as with nonhandicapped students: *developmental* and *functional* (Bailey, Jens, & Johnson, 1983; Filler, 1983). The **developmental model** has produced two approaches. The milestone approach espouses activities based on the developmental stages of typical nondisabled children. It does not consider the age-appropriateness of the activities. Children must acquire skills of one stage before proceeding to the next one. Examples include the Bayley Scales of Infant Development and the Vineland Social Maturity Scale. Another approach, based on the work of Piaget (1952), emphasizes the development of cognitive, linguistic, and social aspects. It provides little information on other development areas.

The **functional model** is based on the work of several behavioral and social-learning theorists (Bandura & Walters, 1963; Skinner, 1953; Watson, 1913). The functional curriculum emphasizes the development of acceptable behaviors rather than developmental milestones. Schloss et al. (1984) stated:

> A functional curriculum may be defined as a curriculum that facilitates the development of skills most likely to be maintained and reinforced in subsequent educational and independent living environments. From a student perspective, the hallmarks of functional curriculum objectives are relevance and currency. . . . Using tools, for example, is a relevant objective for a student expected to enter a building trades profession. . . . Personal hygiene skills may be described as current because they are practiced daily. (pp. 370–371)

Typically, descriptions of students' behaviors are recorded on behavior checklists. Acceptable social behavior and academic skills are taught by the use of behavior modification techniques such as operant conditioning (see discussion in Chapter 2) and task analysis.

Descriptions and use of these methods (and their combinations) with multihandicapped hearing-impaired students can be found in the literature (Mavilya, 1982; Naiman, 1979, 1982; Powers et al., 1987; Stewart, 1982). Nevertheless, the merits of many curricular materials and techniques, based on either of the two models, have not been empirically evaluated (Bailey et al., 1983). In addition, there may be little consistency across programs. For example, in the Jones and Johnson (1985) survey discussed previously, it was reported that 65 curricula were used in the 119 educational programs that served multihandicapped hearing-impaired students. Only six of these curricula were implemented in four or more programs. About one-sixth of the programs surveyed developed their own curricula.

EARLY INTERVENTION

The importance of early intervention for children with handicapping conditions has been widely documented (Reynolds & Birch, 1977). The theoretical models that have influenced the development of curricula have also influenced the development of early intervention programs (Michael & Paul, in press). Provence (1974) argued that all early intervention programs should have some basic guidelines: (1) evaluation of parental skills, (2) partnership between parents/caregivers and other parents/caregivers, (3) development of a prescriptive home program, and (4) establishment of a network of interdisciplinary professionals.

Early intervention programs for deaf-blind students should be eclectic and use techniques that foster the development of motor and sensory skills across a variety of settings (Fredericks & Baldwin, 1987). Michael and Paul (in press) and others (Fredericks & Baldwin, 1987; Goetz & Gee, 1987) held that communication and mobility skills of deaf-blind students should improve if a sufficient amount of training is given to the use of residual hearing and residual sight.

The most effective early intervention programs seem to be those that are implemented as early as possible. As discussed in Chapter 9, the Commission on Education of the Deaf (1988) has recommended an improvement in identification procedures in order to provide early and intensive education to hearing-impaired students from birth to 3 years of age. With children who are deaf-blind, or dual-sensory impaired, this type of early intervention program is even more critical. The major objectives of these programs are to help parents/caregivers ensure the progress of their babies and understand the implications of the disabilities. If parents/caregivers confront their children's disabilities with a challenging, positive attitude, then the children are more likely to develop to their fullest potential.

LANGUAGE/COMMUNICATION ISSUES

The language/communication system that should be used with multihandicapped hearing-impaired students is as complex and controversial a subject as it is with hearing-impaired students with no additional handicaps. Here we provide a brief overview of some of the systems that can be implemented in programs for multihandicapped students. The goals of language/communication vary with the members of the population (Lloyd, 1976; Lloyd & Karlan, 1984; Moores, 1982). Achieving a high level of competence in a language may be a realistic goal for only a few students. It is likely that the objective is to enable individuals to express their basic *wants* and *needs*. Whatever the goals, teachers should have a competent knowledge of language development, particularly of the preverbal or prelinguistic stage, and they should be aware of strategies for developing communicative interactions.

It should be emphasized that the various language/communication systems have been considered as augmentative/alternative communication systems. In some cases, the systems are used instead of speech. There have been instances where the use of manual communication led to increased speech production as well as increased socialization behaviors. An excellent treatment of this issue has been discussed by Fristoe and Lloyd (1979), who listed 16 factors to explain the effectiveness of sign communication, including: (1) removal of pressure for speech, (2) functional vocabulary, and (3) visual representation. Some of these factors may also be applicable to other nonverbal communication systems such as graphic and **Bliss symbols** (Bliss, 1965). Most school-age children with deaf-blindness communicate primarily through nonspeech modes (Curtis & Donlon, 1984).

Manual Communication

Manual communication has been used extensively with nondeaf severely handicapped populations (Schiefelbusch, 1980). Ironically, one of the problems confronting practitioners is what signed system to use. As discussed in Chapter 7, this is a confusing and complex issue, and it can lead to other problems if practitioners do not adhere to the rules of one system. The decision to implement a particular signed system also depends on the sophistication of the students. The more cumbersome systems can present problems of cognitive processing as well as motor problems.

The use of American Sign Language and other forms of manual communication has been reported in a survey of programs for multihandicapped hearing-impaired students that has been discussed previously (Jones & Johnson, 1985). Nearly all the respondents indicated the use of some form of manual communication, and about one-fifth stated that they implemented ASL. There seems to be a higher use of ASL in multihandicapped programs than in other programs for hearing-impaired students with no additional handicaps. It is possible, however, that the respondents meant that the sign vocabulary of ASL, rather than the full-blown language, is predominantly used with multihandicapped students (Woodward, 1986).

Other Nonspeech Communication Systems

Other nonspeech communication systems that can be used with multihandicapped hearing-impaired students include graphic communication systems such as print (Mc-Donald & Schultz, 1973), and symbol systems such as language boards, a **Rebus** (Lloyd, 1976), Bliss symbols (Bliss, 1965), and **Non-Slip** (i.e., Non-Speech Language Initiation Program) (Carrier, 1974; Carrier & Peak, 1975). Vanderheiden and Grilley (1976) discussed some important aspects of effective communication systems. First, the systems should have physical aspects that indicate or transmit the message. Second, there should be a set of symbols that can be manipulated to represent concepts and ideas. Finally, there should be rules and procedures for combining and presenting the symbols. A more detailed treatment of these issues can be found in Lloyd (1976), Mathy-Laikko, Ratcliff, Villarruel, and Yoder (1988), and Schiefelbusch (1980).

Both the Rebus and Bliss symbols are ideographic, or concept-based in nature. The Rebus symbols are more likely to influence beginning reading behaviors such as pre-reading skills (e.g., recognition of the alphabet and so on). The Bliss symbol system, however, may be more widely used.

The development of the Non-Slip system was based on the work of Premack (1970, 1971), who attempted to teach chimpanzees to communicate by a symbol system in which users select and arrange plastic chips in order to convey messages. Unlike the Rebus and Bliss symbols, the Non-Slip symbols do not resemble or represent objects.

Although the use of nonspeech communication systems is effective in helping multihandicapped students to develop expressive and receptive communication skills, progress is extremely slow and laborious. In many cases, these communication systems may be the students' only means of expressing wants and needs.

MULTIHANDICAPPED ADULTS

Although the primary focus of this book is on education, it is appropriate to discuss briefly issues such as residential alternatives and employment for multihandicapped hearing-impaired adults. Much has been written on these issues in relation to mentally retarded adults and normalization—that is, permitting adults to reside in areas that provide opportunities to engage in various activities similar to those of typical adults such as shopping and eating out in restaurants (Wolfensberger, 1972). Recently, there has been an increase in the development of community-based residential alternatives for multihandicapped and severely handicapped adults (Heward & Orlansky, 1988). Living arrangements range from residing in institutions to independent living. Three common types of alternatives are **foster-family** homes, group homes, and apartments. The following discussion of these arrangements is based on the discussion in Heward and Orlansky (1988).

Residential Alternatives

Foster-family homes provide temporary residence for a specific period. Traditionally, families have taken in children. Recently, handicapped adults have become part of the family; that is, they participate in daily activities and develop close interpersonal relationships. This arrangement offers a number of opportunities for handicapped adults to interact with other members of the community. Families who take in these individuals receive financial reimbursement.

Group homes provide a residential setting for *groups* of handicapped adults. The number of handicapped adults who live together can range from 2 to about 20. The homes are staffed by trained personnel called *houseparents*. Most group homes are operated by agencies at the local and state level. A few are owned by private individuals who still must adhere to state regulations. The nature of the homes varies. Some are permanent residential arrangements for the handicapped adults. In group homes, the houseparents and their assistants develop programs to teach the residents self-care and other important personal and social skills. Other homes serve as *half-way houses*—that is, an intermediate step before independent living in an apartment.

Group homes are the most widely used residential alternative for handicapped adults, certainly for mentally retarded adults (Heward & Orlansky, 1988). Wolfensberger (1972) maintained that the homes should be in residential neighborhoods, not in commercial areas, and that they should look like typical homes in the same area to avoid being conspicuous.

For handicapped adults, apartment living is the epitome of independent living. This alternative offers them the greatest number of opportunities to participate in typical everyday activities (Heward & Orlansky, 1988). Three apartment arrangements are **cluster, coresidence,** and **maximum independence.** In the cluster arrangement, handicapped adults live in several neighboring apartments and the supervisory personnel live nearby in another apartment. Both a handicapped and a nonhandicapped person live in a coresidence apartment. Coresidence can be a permanent arrangement or an intermediate step toward more independent living. In the maximum independence situation, two to four handicapped adults live together. They are primarily responsible for their day-to-day affairs. A staff person usually visits weekly to help residents resolve difficult problems.

Employment

A major rehabilitation goal is to help handicapped adults obtain and hold jobs. As discussed in Chapter 4, many typical severely to profoundly hearing-impaired individuals are underemployed. Vernon and Hyatt (1981) stated that about 25 percent of deaf individuals comprise a hard-core unemployed group. Describing members of this group, Vernon (1987b) stated:

> Many are young and from urban areas. A disproportionate number are Black or Hispanic. Many receive SSI, welfare, and other forms of government assistance such as Aid to Dependent Children. Crime is high in this group, as are prison costs. Many of these individuals read at a second or third grade level. (p. 191)

Some multihandicapped hearing-impaired adults are also members of the group described by Vernon. Occupational choices are limited because many members of this group do not have skills that would make them employable.

Traditionally, training programs and facilities have been provided by state rehabilitation agencies. Recently, there has been an increase in vocational services for multihandicapped and severely handicapped adults. Some major types of training and services provided by rehabilitation centers and sheltered workshops are work evaluation, work adjustment, training in vocational skills, and on-the-job training programs (Bigge & O'Donnell, 1976). The purpose of work evaluation tasks is to determine the client's strengths and weaknesses and to establish vocational goals. Work adjustment deals mainly with developing positive work attitudes, whereas training in vocational skills focuses on specific skills needed for the job. On-the-job training occurs where the handicapped adult is planning to be employed. There is some evidence that specific training in these areas can reduce unemployment among low-achieving hearing-impaired adults (Hurwitz, cited in Moores, 1987). More research is needed on multihandicapped hearing-impaired adults, especially those who were part of the rubella epidemic in the 1960s.

The most common type of employment and training occurs in a sheltered workshop. Some workshops provide transitional activities to train their clients for outside jobs. Extended sheltered workshops provide extended or long-term employment and operate in the same way as any other business. That is, they secure contracts from other businesses in order to provide work for their clients.

There are also work activity centers, a form of sheltered workshop, which are primarily for handicapped individuals who cannot engage in long-term work tasks. Typically, work activities are interspersed with other activities such as self-care, social activities, and recreation.

SUMMARY

This chapter presented a brief introduction to some of the major issues facing educators, researchers, and other professionals who work with hearing-impaired individuals with additional handicapping conditions. Little research has been done with multihandicapped individuals, although there has been a proliferation of professional services. One reason for the dearth of investigations is that it is extremely difficult to describe this population. The effects of multihandicaps are not simply additive. The interactions of the handicaps have complicated the tasks of identification, classification, assessment, instruction, and curricular activities.

A number of handicapping conditions have been associated with deafness, including mental retardation, learning disability, behavior disorders, visual impairment, brain damage, epilepsy, orthopedic problems, cerebral palsy, and heart disorders. There is a wide variation in incidence figures on multihandicapped students. Most of the figures are higher than those reported for the general population. From one perspective, it has been suggested that the variety and higher incidence of additional handicaps in hearing-impaired individuals are a result of certain causes of hearing impairment such as rubella, trauma, and prematurity. Some researchers argued, however, that the figures are inflated because of several factors such as inadequate records, the use of unreliable assessments, the perspectives of professionals, and poor classroom management situations. Another factor may be the lack of a fluent and intelligible communication system between the handicapped individuals and significant others (i.e., parents/caregivers, relatives, professionals).

The most consistent data on the incidence of multihandicapped hearing-impaired students have been provided by the annual surveys conducted by the Center for Assessment and Demographic Studies at Gallaudet University. Since the inception of the project, it has been reported that about one-third of hearing-impaired students in special education programs and classes have additional handicaps. Most of these students have only one additional handicapping condition. The CADS surveys also presented some insights into the relationships between incidence of additional handicaps and other important variables such as degree of impairment, sex, and ethnic groups. It was reported that the patterns associated with sex and minority groups paralleled those documented for the general population of students.

The four most common disabilities associated with deafness are mental retardation, learning disability, emotional or behavioral problems, and visual impairment (including blindness and uncorrected visual problems). The chapter provided some background information on each area separately, including problems with identification, assessment, and instruction. It was noted that not much is known in relation to deafness and each of these additional handicaps. For example, in a survey study on the presence of learning-disabled hearing-impaired students, researchers concluded that their results documented the existence of a group of hearing-impaired students whose behaviors are different from those of typical hearing-impaired students. It was not clear, however, whether these differences could be characterized as learning disabilities.

There is little doubt that teachers of hearing-impaired students are not well trained to work with multihandicapped hearing-impaired students. Many teachers receive on-the-job training and are apt to use a variety of untested instructional and curricular activities. Even teachers in early intervention programs may not provide appropriate services. One reason for these phenomena is that there are very few university-level training programs. It is difficult to develop adequate training programs and establish certification requirements because of the heterogeneity of students with additional handicaps.

In relation to language and communication, it was noted that some issues in this area parallel those of typical hearing-impaired students discussed in Chapter 7. A wide variety of communication systems have been used, including manual communication, graphic communication, and symbol systems such as language boards, Rebus symbols, Bliss symbols, and Non-Slip symbols. It was emphasized that the use of nonspeech communication systems has been shown to be effective in helping multihandicapped hearing-impaired students develop some receptive and expressive skills.

The last section of the chapter dealt briefly with two of the major issues of multihandicapped adults, namely, residential alternatives and employment. There has been an increase in community-based living arrangements and employment opportunities for adults with multiple and severe handicaps. Some common types of residential and employment options were described. These conditions have made it possible for handicapped adults to become more involved in typical everyday interactions in the mainstream of society.

COMPREHENSION

1. Which of the following statements is/are TRUE?
   a. The effects of multiple handicaps are simply additive.
   b. Multihandicapped students complicate the tasks of identification, classification, assessment, instruction, and curriculum.
   c. Definitions of multihandicapped students are not affected by perspectives of professionals.
   d. Deaf-blind students are considered part of the multihandicapped student population.
   e. Multihandicaps refer to concomitant impairments that result in educational difficulties that cannot be accommodated in programs designed solely for one of the impairments.
2. TRUE or FALSE? The presence of additional handicapping conditions does not always lead to special treatment in another educational program.
3. What are some factors that may account for the wide variations in estimates of incidence? According to the latest national survey, what percentage of the hearing-impaired student population has one or more additional handicaps?
4. A cause of deafness that results in the lowest incidence of additional handicapping conditions is:
   a. Heredity
   b. Rubella
   c. Trauma
   d. Rh factor
   e. Prematurity
5. TRUE or FALSE? The results of the most recent national survey indicated that
   a. Female students are more likely to be multihandicapped than male students.
   b. A high percentage of African American hearing-impaired students (about 37 percent) has been reported to have additional handicaps.
   c. Bias in evaluation procedures is no longer a problem.
6. What are the two major factors that are part of the definition of mental retardation?
7. Discuss briefly the debate on the most appropriate placement of hearing-impaired students with mental retardation.
8. Label the following as *medical model* or *behavior model* of learning disability (LD):
   a. Dyslexia
   b. Specific learning disability
   c. Organic etiology
   d. Samuel Kirk
   e. Minimal brain damage
9. TRUE or FALSE? In many states, students are labeled as learning disabled if their achievement scores are at least one grade below those of their nondisabled peers.
10. According to the latest national survey, the most common additional handicap of hearing-impaired students is:
    a. Learning disability

b. Mental retardation
c. Emotional/behavioral problems
d. Blindness
e. Cerebral palsy

11. What, according to one recent survey, are the two major characteristics of LD hearing-impaired students that differentiate them from typical hearing-impaired students?

12. TRUE or FALSE?
  a. In diagnosing students with emotional/behavioral problems, the existence of age-inappropriate behaviors alone are sufficient.
  b. Although most surveys indicate that hearing-impaired students have more behavioral problems than the general population of students, it is not clear how these results should be interpreted.

13. Describe briefly the meaning of a functional classification system of deaf-blindness.

14. Why may it be educationally inappropriate to place deaf-blind students in multihandicapped programs?

15. Discuss some major characteristics of teachers who work with multihandicapped hearing-impaired students. The discussion has been started for you.

    Many teachers in the education of hearing-impaired students have had little formal university-level training in the area of multihandicapping or severe handicapping conditions. . . .

16. Label the following descriptions as either *developmental curriculum* or *functional curriculum:*
  a. Based on the work of behavioral and social-learning theories.
  b. Emphasizes the development of acceptable behaviors.
  c. Espouses activities based on learning stages of typical nondisabled students.
  d. Requires children to acquire skills of one stage before proceeding to the next one.
  e. Records descriptions of student's behaviors on behavior checklists.
  f. Does not consider the age-appropriateness of the activities.

17. According to Provence (1974), what are some basic guidelines of early intervention programs?

18. Name the three major categories of nonspeech communication systems that have been used with multihandicapped hearing-impaired students.

19. Define the following terms:
  a. Normalization
  b. Group homes
  c. Maximum independence
  d. Sheltered workshop

SUGGESTED ACTIVITIES

1. For this activity, you will need one or more communication boards such as Rebus, Bliss, and Non-Slip (see references in chapter).
  a. Use the board(s) to communicate the following sentences:
     I want a glass of water.
     My mother is climbing the walls.
     There is a fly in my soup.
     Can anyone tell me where my pipe is?
     I can't find this word in the dictionary.

It is raining cats and dogs today.

I ran into a good friend yesterday.

b. Which board is easier and faster for you to use?

c. Find out which communication board is most commonly used in your school district.

2. Interview several teachers of multihandicapped hearing-impaired students. Find out the following:

a. Their academic training for this position.

b. Their opinions regarding methods of communicating with their students (i.e., ASL, communication boards, etc.).

c. What they have written on the IEPs for their students.

d. The additional handicaps of the hearing-impaired students in the classrooms.

3. Place cotton and ear plugs in your ears and blindfolds on your eyes to simulate deaf-blindness. Engage in the following activities and record your observations:

a. Turn on the TV or radio.

b. Converse with friends and relatives (yes, you can speak!)

c. Walk around inside and outside your house or apartment.

d. Make a sandwich or pour a glass of water.

e. Compare these experiences with those you had earlier when you were "deaf" only.

f. Repeat this experiment as only a "blind" person by removing the cotton and ear plugs.

FURTHER READINGS

Berdine, W., & Blackhurst, A. (Eds.). (1985). *An introduction to special education* (2nd ed.). Boston, MA: Little, Brown.

Bullis, M. (Ed.). (1989). *Research on the communication development of young children with deaf-blindness*. Monmouth, OR: Oregon State System of Higher Education, Communication Skills Center for Young Children with Deaf-Blindness, Teaching Research Division.

Bullis, M., & Fielding, G. (Eds.). (1988). *Communication development in young children with deaf-blindness: Literature review*. Monmouth, OR: Oregon State System of Higher Education, Communication Skills Center for Young Children with Deaf-Blindness, Teaching Research Division.

Campbell, B., & Baldwin, V. (Eds.). (1982). *Severely handicapped hearing impaired students*. Baltimore, MD: Brookes.

Cherow, E., Trybus, R., & Matkin, N. (Eds.). (1985). *Hearing-impaired children and youth with developmental disabilities: An interdisciplinary foundation for service*. Washington, DC: Gallaudet University Press.

Kavale, K., & Forness, S. (1985). *The science of learning disabilities*. San Diego, CA: College-Hill.

CHAPTER 11

Reflections and Directions

MAJOR POINTS TO CONSIDER

Academic placement and achievement

Literacy

Language and communication

This chapter provides some reflections and directions based on previous discussions. The three interrelated central areas are academic placement and achievement, literacy, and language/communication. Within each major area, the intent is to present in capsule form the general conclusions drawn from the relevant chapters of this book as *reflections*. Related to the *reflections* are *directions,* which include trends and suggestions for further research in order to improve the education of hearing-impaired students.

REFLECTIONS

Placement and Achievement

Several educational placement options are available for hearing-impaired students—residential schools, day schools, day classes in public schools, resource services, and itinerant services. Historically, many students have attended residential and day schools, with the majority in residential schools. From the 1960s to the present, however, there has been an increase in the number of students attending day classes, particularly in public school programs. As a result, most hearing-impaired students are enrolled in public schools and are mainstreamed in regular education classes for varying parts of the school day. Only about one-third of the hearing-impaired student population attends residential programs.

One of the most enduring and controversial debates in the education of hearing-impaired students has been the effects of placement on achievement. Much of what is known in this area concerns students in elementary and secondary education programs. The academic achievement level of most severely to profoundly hearing-impaired students completing a secondary education program is about six to seven grades lower than that of their hearing counterparts. In fact, low achievement levels and slow academic growth have been consistent patterns since the beginning of the formal testing movement.

Exceptions to these patterns have been observed for many students in comprehensive oral education programs and those integrated into regular education classes, including hard-of-hearing students. Eventually, most students in comprehensive oral programs attend regular education classes. This seems to indicate that integration is an important factor contributing to high academic achievement. Integration, however, is not an all-encompassing factor, and it may not even be a critical one. Other factors such as well-established aural/oral skills, English language competence, curricular and instructional practices, and the qualifications of teachers need to be considered.

Literacy

Numerous studies and surveys have indicated repeatedly that average 18-to-19-year-old severely to profoundly hearing-impaired students are reading and writing on a level commensurate with average 9-to-10-year-old hearing students. The annual growth rate in reading is less than one-half grade, plateauing at about the third- or fourth-grade level after 12 to 13 years of school. As with academic achievement, exceptions have been noted for students in comprehensive oral programs or integrated into public school classes. These students are more likely to develop higher literacy skills than other hearing-impaired counterparts in general. It should be remembered that many of these successful students are more select in socioeconomic status and intelligence, factors that interact with others of importance such as early education, the use of residual hearing, and parental involvement.

The literacy difficulties of severely to profoundly hearing-impaired students should be considered from an interactive theoretical framework in which both lower-level skills (e.g., word identification, punctuation) and higher-level skills (e.g., metacognitive ability, organization) are used to construct meaning. Several factors contribute to the development of literacy, and one of the most important of them is the use of a speech-based code by students to mediate between print and meaning. Students who rely predominantly on a speech-based code have been reported to read better than those who predominantly use a nonspeech-based code. The superiority of speech-based recoders has been attributed to their ability to hold more spoken-language stimuli in short-term memory, which enables them to decode and interpret complex structures while reading.

Language/Communication

A synthesis of the data reveals no clear evidence for the superiority of any of the various language/communication systems for all or even most severely to profoundly hearing-impaired students. The effects of American Sign Language on the development of English has not been systematically studied in the 20th century. Such study is merited and needed. Thus far, the most promising educational results have been observed with multisensory comprehensive oral approaches and with some signed systems such as English-like signing, Seeing Essential English, and Signing Exact English. Like many orally trained students, a number of successful students exposed to the signed systems also have fairly adequate oral-communication abilities (e.g., speech reading and use of residual hearing), which may have contributed to their high development of English literacy skills.

DIRECTIONS

Placement and Achievement

It is probable that special schools—residential and day schools—will not substantially increase their enrollment for the remainder of this century, partly because of the effects of Public Law 94–142 and partly because of societal attitudes toward special schools. The greatest impact may be felt by day schools, which will lose more students to public classes, especially hard-of-hearing students with mild to moderate losses.

Although public schools will continue to enroll most of the hearing-impaired student population, it is likely that residential schools will receive and serve the greater number of severely to profoundly hearing-impaired students with additional handicaps. Because multihandicapped deafness is such a low-incidence and severe condition, these students are better served in residential schools, which are more likely to have a comprehensive range of support services and trained staff than are local public school systems.

Literacy

Owing to its effects on success in school and, subsequently, in society, there will be more emphasis placed on improving the English literacy level of hearing-impaired students. Increased research will probably be conducted within current theoretical frameworks, focusing on critical areas such as prior knowledge, metacognition, and certain language variables—vocabulary, syntax, and figurative language. Similar research is likely with the writing process because of the emerging viewpoint that both reading and writing share basic underlying properties. Eventually, this perspective should lead to improvements in instruction, curriculum, and assessment, and a closer interrelationship among these three areas in the schools.

Improvements in the English literacy skills of the severely to profoundly hearing-impaired will also require a better understanding of the relations between literacy and the student's internal coding strategies. Specifically, it is important to study further the effects of speech-based and nonspeech-based coding strategies on comprehending and composing texts. The results will have a pervasive impact on instructional and curricular practices and even on educational philosophies. Current thinking on the relation between internal codes and reading suggest that the development of literacy may not be a realistic goal for many prelinguistically severely to profoundly hearing-impaired students who rely predominantly on a nonspeech-based code. Many of these students may need to receive educational information from videotapes and other media.

Language/Communication

More investigations are needed on the effects of the major approaches—Total Communication, oralism, and American Sign Language—on the development of English language skills. Support for the study of how and if ASL can be used to teach English literacy will result from persistent low achievement levels of students and advocacy by members of the Deaf culture. In relation to the TC approaches, there is a need to increase what is known about the execution and reception of the various signed systems without accompanying speech by students and teachers. For example, researchers should address (1) whether English, or any other spoken language, can be represented completely and clearly by a signed system, (2) the relationship between the representation of English by a signed system and the memory processes of the receiver, (3) the use of signing with multihandicapped hearing-impaired students, and (4) the ability of practitioners to speak and sign simultaneously within a particular system. A better understanding of sign communication systems is important for the development of cognition, language, and literacy.

COMPREHENSION

1. State the authors' major conclusions (i.e., reflections) regarding most severely to profoundly hearing-impaired students and the following:
   a. Educational achievement
   b. Integration
   c. Literacy level
   d. The superiority of any of the various language/communication systems
2. What does the following statement mean?
   The literacy difficulties of severely to profoundly hearing-impaired students should be considered from an interactive theoretical framework.
3. What do the authors recommend (i.e., directions) for further research concerning the following:
   a. literacy
   b. the Total Communication approaches
4. What does the following statement mean?
   A better understanding of sign communication systems is important for the development of cognition, language, and literacy.

SUGGESTED ACTIVITIES

1. Compare the authors' major conclusions (i.e., reflections) with those of other authors on education and deafness.
2. Reread the authors' recommendations for further research. Propose additional topics that need further investigation.

FURTHER READINGS

Highet, G. (1976). *The immortal profession: The joys of teaching and learning*. New York: Weybright & Talley.

Richardson-Koehler, V., Berliner, D., Casanova, U., Clark, C., Hersh, R., & Shulman, L. (Eds.). (1987). *Educators' handbook: A research perspective*. White Plains, NY: Longman.

Sutherland, M. (1988). *Theory of education*. White Plains, NY: Longman.

Organizations and Centers*

Alexander Graham Bell Association for the Deaf, Inc.
3417 Volta Place, NW
Washington, DC 20007
Voice/TDD: (202) 337–5220

American Deafness and Rehabilitation Association
P.O. Box 55369
Little Rock, AR 72225
Voice/TDD: (501) 375–6643

American Speech-Language-Hearing Association
10801 Rockville Pike
Rockville, MD 20852
Voice/TDD: (301) 897–5700
            (301) 897–8682
            (800) 638–8255

Conference of Educational Administrators Serving the Deaf
Gallaudet University
800 Florida Avenue, NE
Washington, DC 20002
Voice/TDD: (202) 651–5015

Convention of American Instructors of the Deaf
P.O. Box 2163
Columbia, MD 21045
Voice/TDD: (301) 461–9988

Deafpride, Inc.
1350 Potomac Avenue, SE
Washington, DC 20003
Voice/TDD: (202) 675–6700

Helen Keller National Center for Deaf-Blind Youths and Adults
111 Middle Neck Road
Sands Point, New York 11050
Voice/TDD: (516) 944–8900

John Tracy Clinic
806 West Adams Blvd.
Los Angeles, CA 90007
Voice: (213) 748–5481
TDD: (213) 747–2924
        (800) 522–4582

National Association of the Deaf
814 Thayer Avenue
Silver Spring, MD 20910
Voice/TDD: (301) 587–1788

---

*National Information Center on Deafness
 Gallaudet University
 800 Florida Avenue, NE

National Center for Law and the Deaf
Gallaudet University
800 Florida Avenue, NE
Washington, DC 20002
Voice/TDD: (202) 651–5373

National Cued Speech Association
P.O. Box 31345
Raleigh, NC 27622
Voice/TDD: (919) 828–1218

National Information Center on Deafness
Gallaudet University
800 Florida Avenue, NE
Washington, DC 20002
Voice: (202) 651–5051
TDD: (202) 651–5052
Voice/TDD: (800) 672–6720

Self Help for Hard of Hearing People, Inc.
7800 Wisconsin Avenue
Bethesda, MD 20814
Voice: (301) 657–2248
TDD: (301) 657–2249

Glossary

Academic achievement. The performance of students on standardized, or norm-referenced, tests. Students' scores are compared to other students of similar ages or in similar grades. Also known as educational achievement.

Academic placement. The type of educational program in which a student is enrolled. Also known as educational placement.

Adjective. A word used to describe or identify persons, places, things, or ideas. Examples: *little* boy, *that* boy, *wonderful* plan.

Adverb. A word that describes or modifies an adjective, a verb (e.g., *see, do, walk*), or another adverb (e.g., slowly). Examples: *very* smart (adjective) woman, walked (verb) *fast, very* fast (adverb).

Affixes. Word part (i.e., morpheme) that are added to a word (i.e., base or root word), either at the beginning (prefix), at the end (suffix), or in the middle (infix). The affix changes or alters the meaning of the word. Examples: advance*ment, ir*responsible.

Affricates. Two consonantal sounds in English *(ch, j)*. Bursts of air are sustained for a short time to produce the sounds.

Age at onset. The age at which a hearing loss is sustained.

Air conduction. A process by which sound reaches the inner ear by means of the air in the outer ear and the motion of the middle-ear structures.

American Sign English. Another name for Pidgin Sign English. In general, the use of American Sign Language signs in an English word order, with few or no contrived sign markers for affixes such as *-ing* or *ir-*.

American Sign Language (ASL) A bona fide language with its own grammar. ASL uses manual (hand) and nonmanual (eye brows, shoulders) signals to express concepts and ideas.

Amplification systems. Assistive devices such as individual hearing aids, group hearing aids (e.g., radio frequency systems), visual aids, and tactile aids used to develop the hearing skills of hearing-impaired individuals.

Articles.   Words (e.g., *a, an, the*) used before names of persons, places, things, or ideas to limit or provide definiteness.

Articulation.   The act or manner of producing sounds, particularly consonants and vowels.

At-risk.   Individuals who are highly susceptible to mental and physical disabilities, diseases, or illnesses.

Attitudinal deafness.   A quality of individuals who identify with and are accepted by members of the Deaf culture. Characteristic of a person who supports values and goals of the Deaf culture.

Audiogram.   A graph for recording and displaying the results of a hearing evaluation.

Audiology.   The science or study of hearing. Practitioners are called audiologists.

Audiometry.   An instrument used to measure hearing acuity.

Auditory-articulatory.   Internalization of or exposure to speech and hearing stimuli.

Auditory cortex.   The section of the brain that receives and processes information about sounds.

Auditory management.   Use of early intervention and amplification and/or other procedures to maximize the development and conservation of hearing and to facilitate adjustment to the environment.

Auditory sensory deprivation.   Being deprived of or prevented from hearing sounds during the early stages of life.

Auditory training/learning.   The use of procedures and techniques such as early intervention, amplification, and the structuring of the environment to facilitate development of sound perception and production.

Basal readers.   Reading textbooks that contain passages arranged in sequential order of difficulty, typically from readiness (before first grade) to about the eighth-grade level.

Base word.   The main part of a word or a word that can be used independently with meaning. Examples: in*complete, cat, girl*s. Also known as a free morpheme. See also **Morphemes.**

Basic English sentence patterns.   Simple sentences containing no complex structures. Examples: *The boy hit the ball, The girl went to the theater.*

Behaviorism.   A learning theory that emphasizes the influence of the environment. Behaviors are described as connections between stimuli and responses.

Behavior modification procedures.   The application of conditioning or other learning techniques to change or shape behavior: based on the theory of behaviorism.

Behavior observation audiometry.   Audiometric techniques used with young children. A passive type of testing in which children's reactions, rather than responses, to sounds are observed.

Bicultural.   Being exposed to or growing up in two cultures—that is, customs, science, literature, and language associated with a group of individuals that distinguish them from those of another group.

Bilingual.   Communicating or being able to communicate in two languages, either in the primary (i.e., spoken, sign) and/or secondary (reading and writing) modes.

Bliss symbols.   Ideographic or concept-based nonspeech communication symbols for representing objects and ideas.

Bone conduction.   The process by which sound reaches the inner ear via the cranial bones, bypassing the outer- and middle-ear structures.

Bottom-up.   A text-based model of reading comprehension that emphasizes decoding of words by letters, combinations of letters, and the correspondences between letters and sounds.

Breathiness.   Improper control of the breath during the production of speech, which affects voice pitch and quality.

Captioned films.   Motion pictures that contain subtitles that reflect the remarks of the characters.

Center for Assessment and Demographic Studies (CADS).   A research center located at Gallaudet University in Washington, DC. The Center attempts to collect and analyze (1) the performances of individuals on tests and (2) information related to demography (e.g., size, distribution, hearing loss, and other human characteristics).

Central (hearing losses).   Hearing losses resulting from disorders of the central auditory function in the brain, generally located beyond the peripheral hearing system (outer, middle, and inner ear).

Classical conditioning audiometry.   Audiometric procedures based on classical conditioning principles of behaviorism.

Classifiers.   Pronoun-signs that include information such as size, shape, and function of the referent (i.e., people, objects, events, ideas). See also **Pronouns.**

Clearinghouses.   Central agencies or place that collect, classify, and disseminate information related to a particular area.

Clinical (model).   A philosophical position that focuses on correcting, curing, or preventing disabling conditions such as deafness and blindness. Also known as the medical, or pathological, model.

Cluster (arrangement).   A type of apartment arrangement in which handicapped individuals live in several apartments and the supervisory personnel lives nearby in another apartment.

Code-emphasis.   An approach in teaching beginning reading that emphasizes the use of decoding skills, particularly phonics.

Cognition.   The acquisition, organization, and application of knowledge.

Cognitive.   Processes or structures that concern forms of knowing, specifically perceiving, imagining, reasoning, and evaluating.

Cognitive-dominant.   Relating to a learning theory that states that language development is dependent on the development of cognition. Cognition dominates language.

Cognitive process.   The activity responsible for the acquisition and representation of knowledge.

Cognitive structure.   Knowledge; something acquired and represented.

Commission on Education of the Deaf.   A national advisory group established by the Congress of the United States to study the present status of education of hearing-impaired individuals in this country.

Comparison.   Adjectives and adverbs that indicate a greater amount of a quality or characteristic. Example: *slower* is the comparative of *slow, more rapidly* is the comparative of *rapidly*.

Complementation.   A complex sentence that contains one of the complementizers such as *for-to*, or *that*. Examples: It is important *for Mary to read the book;* It appears *that she is going to Chicago*.

Complex (words).   Words that contain a base or root word (i.e., free morpheme) and a word part (i.e., bound morpheme) that does not occur alone. Examples: *cat* (root word) + *s* (bound morpheme) = *cats; bi + annual* = biannual. Also words that contain a combination of word parts that do not appear in isolation. Examples: *beautiful, glorification*.

Compound (words).   Two words that can appear together or separately; however, the meaning is related to the two parts as a whole. Examples: *riverbank, bubble gum, White House,* and *blueprint*.

Comprehensive oral programs.   Programs that offer and emphasize a well-established comprehensive array or oral-education components such as speech, speech reading, and auditory training/learning.

Concrete operation. The third of Jean Piaget's four stages of cognitive development in which children are able to use rules based on concrete instances but still cannot deal with abstract qualities.

Conductive (hearing losses). Relating to hearing losses due to the inefficient transfer of sound energy to the inner ear. Typically, the abnormality or problem occurs in the outer or middle ear.

Conjunctions. Words (e.g., *and, but, or, until*) that join together sentences or parts of a sentence. Examples: Put the book *and* the paper on the desk, Do you want coffee *or* tea? I am going to town, *but* he is staying at home.

Consonantal blends and clusters. A blend of consonants in words such as *bl*ue and *cl*ip; a cluster of consonants in words such as *str*ing and *spl*ash.

Controlled response. Relating to a forced-choice test in which the respondent must select one or more of the alternatives for the answer. Examples: True/False, Multiple-choice.

Conventional behavior audiometry. Traditional audiometric procedures that require an individual to respond to a sound stimulus by raising a finger or pushing a button.

Conventional system of arbitrary signals. The symbols (oral or sign) of a language that are rule-governed and decided on (intuitively) by the users.

Coresidence (apartment). An apartment in which both a handicapped and a nonhandicapped person live. This arrangement can be permanent or an intermediate step toward independent living.

Criterion-referenced. Relating to tests that compare a student's performance to an absolute standard within a specific domain or area. Students' strengths and weaknesses can be described.

Cultural model. A philosophical position that perceives the attributes of members of the minority culture or group as different rather than deviant from those of majority culture norms.

Day programs. Educational programs in which hearing-impaired students attend classes during the day and return home after school.

Day school. A special regional school for hearing-impaired students in large metropolitan areas. The students commute to school.

Deaf-blindness. Condition of a person with severe hearing and visual impairments such that their educational needs cannot be met by programs focusing on one or the other impairment. Also known as **Dual-sensory impairment.**

Deaf community. A heterogeneous group of hearing-impaired individuals concerned with values, rights, and other issues related to hearing impairment. This term and *Deaf culture* are often used interchangeably. In reality, some, but not all, deaf individuals may be members of the Deaf culture. See also **Deaf culture.**

Deaf culture. A closed group of individuals with its own organization, values, customs, social structures, attitudes, and language (American Sign Language). See also **Deaf community.**

Deafness. Condition of a person with a severe to profound hearing impairment in the better unaided ear who is dependent on vision for language and communication, even with the use of amplification systems. See also **Degree of hearing impairment.**

Decibels (dB). Units for measuring the intensity or loudness of sounds.

Decoding. Pertaining to the identification of words and meanings by letter-sound correspondences or word parts.

Degree of hearing impairment. The five categories of hearing impairment are as follows: slight (27 to 40 dB), mild (41 to 55 db), moderate (56 to 70 db), severe (71 to 90 db), and extreme or profound (91 db and greater).

Determiners.   Words occurring before a noun (name of person, place, thing, or idea) that *determine* some quality of that noun. Examples include articles *(a, an, the)* and demonstratives *(this, that)*.

Developmental model.   The theory that all individuals proceed through a similar series of milestones or stages in cognitive and language development. Skills at one developmental stage must be acquired before proceeding to the next one.

Diagnostic assessments.   Tests that attempt to specify individual's strengths and weaknesses. See also **Criterion-referenced.**

Dialects.   Regional varieties of language use, specifically related to the use of vocabulary, grammar, and pronunciation. Examples: the pronunciations of the vowels in words such as *either, neither,* and *potato.*

Directionality.   Movement of a sign that provides certain syntactic information such as the subject and object of the signed utterance.

Direct objects.   The objects of verbs. Examples: I gave *the pen* to Mary; She saw *the flying saucer.*

Dual-sensory impairment.   See **deaf-blindness.**

Early amplification.   The use of amplification or the establishment of an auditory management program for hearing-impaired children as early as possible, particularly during the first two or three years of life.

Early identification.   The identification of individuals with hearing impairments as early as possible, preferably at birth or during the first year of life.

Early intervention.   The identification and establishment of programs for at-risk children to foster cognitive, communicative, social, and emotional development.

Educational interpreters.   Interpreters who work in classroom settings. See also **Interpreters.**

Emotional and behavioral problems.   The degree and duration of age-inappropriate behaviors in students that cause psychological, social, and educational difficulties.

English-based signed systems.   Any of the various signed systems based on the morphosyntactic structure of written English—for example, Pidgin Sign English (English-like signing), Signed English, Manual English, Signing Exact English, Seeing Essential English, and Linguistics of Visual English.

English-like signing.   The use of ASL signs in an English word order. Few sign markers (i.e., signs for *-er, -ing*) are used. Also known as American Sign English, sign English, and Pidgin Sign English.

Ethnic status.   Races or large groups of individuals classified according to common traits, customs, and characteristics.

Etiology.   Cause of a disease or abnormal condition.

Experiential.   Derived from or related to experience.

Experimental study.   A research study conducted under controlled conditions to test a hypothesis.

Explanatory power.   The ability of a theory to explain and predict phenomena.

External locus of control.   Characteristic of individuals who react passively to the world, not taking responsibility for their actions. Such individuals feel that they have no control over their lives.

Figurative language.   The expression of ideas analogously using words and phrases typically used with other concepts. Also known as metaphorical usage. Examples include figures of speech such as simile *(cheeks like roses)* and the use of idioms *(it's raining cats and dogs).*

Finger spelling. The use of handshapes to represent the letters of the alphabet.

Formal operation. The last Piagetian (Jean Piaget) stage of cognitive development characterized by logical and abstract thinking and conceptualization.

Foster family. A family providing parental care and residence for individuals who are not blood or legally related.

Freelance interpreters. In general, interpreters who are not under long-term contractual agreement. See also **Interpreting.**

Free response. Relating to tasks on which individuals can make open-ended responses to stimuli or items.

Frequencies. The number of sound waves per second produced by a vibrating body.

Fricatives. Sounds produced by the random turbulence of air as it is forced through a narrow opening.

Functionally literate. Relating to the ability to read and write at a mature level in the general language of the majority culture of society.

Functional model. A theory that emphasizes the development of acceptable age-appropriate behaviors. A functional curriculum is based on a functional model.

Gallaudet University. Located in Washington, DC in the United States, this is the only liberal arts university in the world for hearing-impaired students, although it does admit hearing students.

Grammar. The rules or principles governing the structure and use of a language.

Grammatical acceptability. The acceptance (i.e., feels right or correct) of certain linguistic utterances as judged by native or competent users of the language.

Grammatical competence. The skill of an individual who has an intuitive understanding of the rules or principles of the grammar of the language.

Grammatical unacceptability. The unacceptability (i.e., feels wrong or is inappropriate) of certain linguistic utterances as judged by native or competent users of the language.

Graphemes. The written symbols or representations of phonemes (sounds) expressed by letters of an alphabet.

Group aids. Group or classroom hearing amplification systems that use, for example, radio-frequency transmission or infrared light.

Hard-of-hearing. Traditionally, the description of an individual with a hearing loss ranging from slight up to and including the moderate level. See also **Degree of hearing impairment.**

Hearing. Relating to an individual with normal hearing ability.

Hearing aids. Personal, or individual, hearing aids.

Hearing impairment. A generic term that refers to all degrees of hearing losses. See also **Degree of hearing impairment.**

Hearing status. The hearing acuity of an individual, that is, whether a person is normally hearing or has a hearing loss.

Hearing threshold. The level expressed in decibels at which an individual hears a pure tone 50 percent of the time.

Higher-level skills. Important complex cognitive skills such as memory, inferencing, reasoning, and problem solving.

Hypothesis testing. Evaluating tentative assumptions or explanations intuitively, specifically in the areas of language and reading.

Idiomatic. Pertaining to idioms and other metaphorical usages. See **Figurative language.**

Immersion program. Bilingual or second-language education program in which instruction and assessment are conducted in a language and culture that are not the native or first language and culture of students in the classroom.

Indirect (objects). Objects of verbs that receive the action or intention. Example: Mary gave *John* the book.

Individualized Educational Plan (IEP). An individualized curriculum for each special education student that is mandated by law. The plan is based on the student's needs and academic achievement.

Individualized instruction. Instruction geared to the specific needs of the child, typically in a special education classroom. The content of instruction is based on the individualized educational plan.

Inferencing. To arrive at a conclusion or discover relationships by reasoning from facts and premises.

Inferential questions. Questions whose answers are not explicitly stated, that is, the answers must be inferred from the information given.

Inflections. Word endings that change the shape of the root word and provide syntactic information. Meaning of the root word is not affected. Examples: *boy* to *boys, walk* to *walking, slow* to *slowly*.

Informal tests. Checklists, informal inventories, and records of observations used to assess the performances of students.

Information processing. A stage-of-processing model of cognitive development on which interactive theories of reading are based. The model asserts that meaning during reading is accessed by stages.

Initialized signs. The modification of ASL signs by changing one handshape to resemble a finger-spelled letter that corresponds to the first letter of the English word.

Inservice. Relating to individuals who are certified or qualified to render professional services— for example, teachers, doctors, and lawyers.

Intelligence. The capacity of individuals to acquire and apply information or knowledge.

Intensity. The magnitude of force or energy; perceived as loudness in relation to sound.

Interactive. Relating to a theory of reading which states that there is an interaction between the reader and the text. Specifically, the reader must integrate prior knowledge with the information in the text in order to construct a model of what the text means.

Internal mediating system. The mediating system that readers use to proceed from print to meaning. Also known as internal coding strategy.

Internalized language. A rule-governed language that is used for thought and communication. Also known as inner language.

Interpreting. To translate information from one language or form to another. The interpreted message may be signed or presented orally (i.e., via lip movements without the use of voice).

Intonation. The rise and fall of pitch during speech production.

IQ tests. Instruments used to measure the relative mental capacity of individuals.

Itinerant programs. Programs in which teachers and other professionals travel to various schools to provide individualized services to students.

Kinesthetic. Pertaining to sensory experiences derived from the movements of end organs in muscles and joints of the body. In conjunction with the static sense of the inner ear, kinesthetic experience provides information about the positions of body structures in space.

Language and communication.   The oral or manual language/communication system used by and with students for developing receptive and expressive skills.

Language competence.   See **Grammatical competence.**

Language-dominant.   Relating to a learning theory which states that cognitive development is dependent on language. Language dominates or determines thought.

Language-experience approaches.   Reading approaches that advocate the use of stories that students provide to teachers as a starting point for reading instruction. Eventually, students write their own reading materials.

Larynx.   The upper part of the windpipe that houses the vocal cords or folds.

Learned helplessness.   See also **External locus of control.**

Learning disability.   A condition based on a discrepancy of one or more years between the mental capacity and academic achievement of students.

Least restrictive environment.   An educational placement that is most conducive to meeting the individual learning needs of a special education student.

Letter clusters.   A string or group of letters such as consonant blends (e.g., *sl, bl*), consonant clusters (e.g., *str, spl*), consonant and vowel digraphs (e.g., *sh, oa*), and pronunciation patterns such as consonant-vowel-consonant (e.g., *cat*).

Linguistically deficient.   Condition of individuals who do not have competence in the language of the majority culture of society.

Linguistically different.   Condition of individuals whose competence is in a language that is not the one used by members of the majority culture of society.

Linguistics of Visual English.   A signed system designed to represent English manually by the rhythm of speech. Thus, a two-syllable English word is represented by a two-movement sign.

Lip reading.   The process of comprehending the speaker's message by observing the lips and surrounding areas.

Literal questions.   Questions whose answers are stated explicitly in the text; little or no inference is required.

Longitudinal survey.   A scientific study that focuses on changes in individuals over a period of time or development.

Long-term memory (LTM).   According to a stage-of-processing cognitive development model, this is a permanent place for the representation and storage of information.

Lower level.   In reading, skills such as decoding and structural analyses; in writing, skills such as punctuation, capitalization, and spelling.

Majority culture.   The mainstream culture of society based on and transmitted by the speaking/using language of the majority.

Majority language.   The language of the majority or ruling culture of society. The main language that is expressed by the majority of newspapers, magazines, books, and other media.

Manual alphabet.   Representation of letters by handshapes. See also **Finger spelling.**

Manual (communication).   Relating to visual-gestural communication systems such as sign languages and signed systems. See also **American Sign Language** and **Signed systems.**

Manual English.   A contrived signed system that combines principles of ASL and Signing Exact English. Developed at the Washington State School for the Deaf.

Manual English.   Synonymous with Pidgin Sign English (i.e., English-like signing). The use of ASL signs in an English word order.

Manually coded English.   The categorical term for all contrived signed systems in the United States (Pidgin Sign English is not included).

Maximum independence.   One type of apartment arrangement in which two or more handicapped adults live together. It is considered the epitome of an independent living situation for most handicapped adults.

Mean.   In general, the sum of the scores divided by the total number of scores.

Meaning-emphasis.   Relating to the use of meaning approaches in the teaching of vocabulary (e.g., whole word) and other reading-related activities.

Mechanical skills.   The lower-level skills of the writing process—for example, spelling, punctuation, and capitalization. See also **Lower level.**

Mentally retarded.   Condition of individuals who are educationally and vocationally retarded (i.e., developmentally delayed) because of subnormal intelligence and maladaptive behavior.

Metacognition.   Awareness of thought processes. In reading, the awareness of thinking and use of strategies in attempting to comprehend the text.

Metalinguistic.   Thinking about language and language processes. See also **Metacognition.**

Metaphor.   Figurative language. Also, a figure of speech. Example: *The night is a blanket.*

Minority language.   A language that is not the language of mainstream society.

Mixed (hearing losses).   A combination of conductive and sensorineural disorders, specifically middle and inner ear losses. Peripheral hearing impairments involving outer, middle, and inner ear.

Modulation.   A change in the form of a sign, via rate and movement, that adds to the meaning of the sign.

Morphemes.   The smallest units of meaning. For example, the word *cats* has two morphemes, *cat* and *-s.*

Morphology.   The study or description of morphemes, the smallest unit of grammatical structure and meaning.

Multimeaning words.   Words that have more than one meaning; polysemy. Most words in the English language are multimeaning words.

Multisensory.   Involving more than one of the senses: audition, vision, olfaction (smell), taction (touch), and gustation (taste).

Nasal (cavity).   The nose passage through which air flows for the production of nasal speech sounds, *m, n,* and *ng.*

Nasality.   Characteristics of sounds that are normally produced through the nose with the mouth passage occluded. In relation to speech problems, nasality refers to the atypical production of other sounds in this manner.

Native language approach.   An approach that advocates the use of the native or home language of students for instruction during the first few years of school before introducing and using the second, or majority, language of society.

Natural (approach).   Approach according to which language should not be taught; rather the child should acquire it in natural meaningful situations.

Negation.   The use of a negative element such as *no, not, never, un-,* and *ir-* in sentences or clauses.

Neo-oralism.   A term used by educators in the Soviet Union during the 1950s to refer to the instructional use of finger spelling and speech simultaneously. See also **Rochester Method.**

Neurolinguistics.   The study of linguistic development from a neurological (i.e., nervous system) perspective, including brain function and structure related to language.

Nominalization.   The production of nouns and noun phrases from other form classes, or parts of speech, such as adjectives and verbs. Examples: The adjective *real* can become *reality,* the verb *discuss* can become *discussion.*

Non-Slip system.   A nonspeech communication system that uses abstract symbols that do not resemble or represent objects. Initially used to teach chimpanzees to communicate.

Nonspeech-based.   Relating to the use of sign, finger spelling, print (grapheme), and other codes that are not phonological based to mediate in order to proceed from print to meaning.

Norm-referenced.   Relating to tests in which norms are available so that students' performances can be compared with other students of similar ages or in similar grades.

Norms.   Values that describe the performances of groups of students of similar ages or in similar grades.

Note taking.   The recording of class notes for a hearing-impaired person who needs to watch (e.g., to lip read or receive signs) the teacher or an interpreter in order to receive information.

Nouns.   Names of persons, places, things, or ideas.

One-word stage.   A stage of linguistic development from about 10 months to about 2 years of age in which the child communicates primarily through the use of single words.

Onomatopoeia.   A figure of speech in which words suggest the sense. Example: *The tap-tap-tap of the raindrops on the roof.*

Operant conditioning audiometry.   Audiometric procedures based on the theory of behaviorism, particularly in the area of operant conditioning. Two versions include the use of tangible reinforcement and play audiometry.

Oral (cavity).   The mouth area, extending from the lips to the pharynx (throat).

Oral communication.   Referring to components such as speech, speech reading, and the development of residual hearing.

Oral English.   Reception and expression of spoken English.

Oral-manual controversy.   The debate surrounding the relative benefits of an oral or manual communication system in developing the educational potential of hearing-impaired students, particularly in English and English literacy skills.

Overextensions.   The use of words to represent not only the intended objects or persons but also other similar-looking objects or persons. Example: The use of *doggie* to refer to the family dog as well as to other dogs and other animals such as cows, pigs, and horses.

Paget-Gorman Sign System.   One of the first English-based signed systems, developed in England.

Passive voice.   A verb form. The three types discussed are *nonreversible, reversible,* and *truncated.* Nonreversible means that the subject and object cannot be reversed; *The car was washed by the woman.* Reversible means that the subject and object can be reversed; *The man was kissed by the woman.* Truncated means that the subject (i.e., agent) is not explicitly stated: *The window was struck.*

Peripheral hearing system.   The anatomy and physiology of structures in the outer, middle, and inner ear.

Personality development.   The personal and social development of behaviors and emotions within individuals.

Pharyngeal cavity.   The throat passage extending from the back of the mouth to the esophagus (a muscular tube leading to the stomach).

Phonation.   The production of speech sounds.

Phonemes.   The smallest units of speech; for example, the word *cats* has four phonemes.

Phonology.   The study of or relating to speech sounds.

Pidginization.   The combination of two languages; typically, one language provides mostly vocabulary words whereas the other provides syntax.

Pidgin Sign English.   Signing that results from the combination of ASL and English-based signed systems. The basis for vocabulary items and grammatical structures depends on the grammatical competence of the signer. For example, a native user of ASL is likely to use a predominant amount of ASL grammatical structures.

Pitch.   Perception of frequency of sound waves; highness or lowness of certain sounds.

Play audiometry.   Audiometric procedures based on the operant conditioning of behaviorism. These procedures make audiological testing a game and are considered most reliable for evaluating young children. Also known as play conditioning audiometry.

Plurals.   More than one of something. Examples: *cows, horses, deer, oxen.*

Possession.   A word or group of words in the grammar of a language that show ownership or a condition analogous to ownership. Examples: *his* car, Mary'*s* purse, the hat *of the man.*

Postlinguistically.   Relating to hearing impairment that occurs after exposure to spoken language during a critical period after the age of two years. Also known as postlinguistic impairment.

Pragmatics.   The branch of linguistics that deals with the use of language in real-world meaningful situations and the way form is influenced by language function.

Prelinguistically.   Relating to hearing impairment that occurs before exposure to spoken language during a critical period before the age of two years. Also known as prelinguistic impairment.

Preoperation.   Pertaining to the second stage of Jean Piaget's theory of cognitive development, extending from about age 2 through age 7. The child learns to think symbolically and can encounter reality on a representational level.

Prepositions.   Words that connect nouns or pronouns with verbs, adjectives, or other nouns or pronouns by showing relationships. Examples: John walked *along* the road; She stood *beside* me. Other prepositions are *for, at, in.*

Present progressive.   A verb structure that expresses continuing action in the present tense. Examples: He *is going,* she *is watching,* they *are swimming.*

Preservice.   Relating to individuals who are in training for professional careers.

Primarily auditory.   An oral approach that focuses mainly on the development of residual hearing (i.e., remaining hearing acuity). The use of speech reading is minimized. Also known as aural-oral, aural, auditory, and auditory-global.

Primary language.   The language acquired initially by students, either in the home or school. Also refers to the form of a language acquired initially, that is, spoken or signed. (In this case, secondary language means reading and writing).

Prior knowledge.   The storehouse of previously acquired linguistic and cognitive experiences in long-term memory.

Pronominalization.   The substitution of a pronoun (e.g., *he, she, it*) for a noun or noun phrase.

Pronouns.   Words used in place of nouns to reduce redundancy. Example: Mary is a school teacher, and *she* teaches dance. See also **Pronominalization.**

Psycholinguistics.   The study of the relation between language use and psychological processes, and also the study of language development.

Psychological/behavioral problems.   See **Emotional and behavioral problems.**

Psychology of deafness. The notion that there are certain behavioral traits that are uniquely attributed to deafness, suggesting that the behavior and thinking processes of deaf persons are different from those of the general population.

Psychosocial. Relating to the cognitive, emotional, and social development of individuals. See also **Personality Development.**

Public Law 94–142. A law that gives handicapped students the right to receive the most appropriate education from which they can benefit or reach their maximum potential. Mandates that schools document the academic progress of these students through the Individualized Educational Plan (IEP).

Pure tone. Relating to a sound that has a discrete frequency level such as 1,000 or 2,000 Hz.

Pure-tone audiometry. A hearing evaluation based on the perception of pure tones at various frequency levels.

Pure-tone averages. The hearing acuity of an individual based on the average scores obtained across the speech frequencies—500, 1,000, and 2,000 Hz.

Qualitative. Pertaining to the manner of acquisition of cognitive and linguistic structures. The focus is on how individuals develop, what developmental stages they proceed through.

Quantitative. Pertaining to the amount or rate of acquiring cognitive and linguistic structures. The focus is on how much an individual has developed or acquired within a specified period.

Question forms. Forms such as *yes/no* (e.g., *Do you want to go?*), *wh-* (e.g., *Where is my pipe?*), and *tag* (e.g., *You ate the cookie, didn't you?* or *You didn't eat the cookie, did you?*). Also known as question formation.

Reading comprehension. The process of understanding the text and of constructing a model of what the text means.

Rebus. A nonspeech communication system that is based on ideographic or conceptual symbols and is considered to foster the development of beginning reading behaviors such as the recognition of the alphabet.

Reduplication. In general, a repeated movement of a sign that provides morphological information. For example: The sign for SIT-SIT = *chair*.

Regular education. Synonymous with public school education programs, as opposed to those of special schools.

Relative clauses. Clauses that contain one of the relative pronouns such as *that, who, whom,* or *which.* Examples: *who kissed the girl, to whom the letter was written,* and *that bit the cat.*

Residential schools. Special schools for hearing-impaired students only. Students can live in dorms or commute to the schools.

Residual hearing. The amount of usable hearing that remains after the onset of a hearing impairment.

Resonance. The quality of voiced sounds (e.g., intensification, enrichment) provided by the configurations of the nasal, oral, and pharyngeal cavities or passages.

Resource rooms. Special classrooms or rooms with support personnel such as teachers, speech pathologists, or tutors who provide additional or remedial services that meet the individual needs of hearing-impaired students.

Rhythm. The alternation of strong and weak aspects in the flow of silence and sound in speech, for example, stressed and unstressed syllables, and pauses.

Rochester Method. A manual communication method in which speech and finger spelling are executed simultaneously. See also **Finger spelling** and **Neo-oralism.**

Root word. See **Base word.**

Second language. A language acquired by individuals who already have competence in one language.

Secondary language. Reading and writing.

Seeing Essential English. The first contrived signed system developed in the United States, by David Anthony, who attempted to create a one-to-one correspondence between a sign and an English morpheme. Known as SEE I.

Segmental. Relating to speech sounds such as vowels and consonants.

Self-concept. The individual's evaluation of himself or herself.

Self-contained. Relating to special classes within public schools in which special education students spend varying portions of the school day.

Semantic elaboration. Any technique that emphasizes a network or cluster of relationships, particularly the conceptual framework surrounding words and concepts.

Semantic feature analyses. Elaboration techniques that use grids to show relationships between words and concepts.

Semantic maps. Diagrams or webs that illustrate the network of relationships among words and concepts and related words and concepts.

Semantics. A branch of linguistics that focuses on meanings of words.

Sensorimotor. The first stage of Jean Piaget's cognitive developmental model, extending from birth to about 2 years of age. Through movement as well as the senses, the child learns about objects, time, and space on a concrete basis.

Sensorineural. Hearing impairment due to problems with the sense organ and/or the auditory nerve.

Sensory registers. The first stage in the processing of information. Unanalyzed information is stored for a brief period.

Short-term memory. The second stage of the information processing model, which holds a limited amount of information for a short period before it is processed into long-term memory or is gone. Also known as working memory.

Sibilants. A group of speech sounds produced by frication, the forcing of air through a narrow opening. Examples: /s/, /z/, /ʃ/ (*sh*) or /tʃ/ or (*ch*), /dzh/, or (*j*).

Signed English. A contrived signed system designed by Harry Bornstein that uses only 14 inflectional sign markers. The system was developed for use with young hearing-impaired children.

signed English. Synonymous with Pidgin Sign English (English-like signing). See **Pidgin Sign English.**

Signed systems. Contrived sign communication systems that are based on the morphosyntactic structure of standard English. See also **English-based signed systems.**

Signing Exact English. A contrived signed system, known as SEE II, which was developed because of disagreements with the creator of Seeing Essential English (SEE I). One of the major differences between SEE I and SEE II is the definition of a base or root word. Like SEE I, SEE II attempts to create a one-to-one correspondence between a sign and an English morpheme.

Simile. A figure of speech using the words *like* or *as* to compare two unlike things. Example: *cheek like roses*. See also **Figurative language.**

Simultaneous communication. The use of manual communication and speech in a simultaneous manner.

Social workers. Personnel who engage in the field of social work, that is, in the study and treatment of economically underprivileged and socially maladjusted individuals.

Socioculture. The study of language development within a natural conversational context. See also **Pragmatics.**

Socioeconomic status. The relative position or status of an individual in society based on income, profession, and residence.

Socioemotional. See **Personality development** and **Psychosocial.**

Sound-letter correspondence. The correspondence between a grapheme (letter in print) and its associated sound or sounds. Also known as letter-sound correspondence.

Special education. Education program for students with special needs. Conditions of students include learning disability, mental retardation (developmentally handicapped), deaf-blind, and hearing impairment.

Special instructional and curricular materials. Language or reading materials that are controlled for certain variables such as vocabulary, syntax, figurative language, and concepts. The controlled variables are introduced and sequenced in a spiralling fashion, that is, proceeding from the easiest to the most difficult structures.

Special schools. Residential or day schools that enroll hearing-impaired students only.

Speech audiometry. Audiometric evaluation of an individual's capacity to detect, discriminate, and comprehend speech stimuli.

Speech-based code. A mediating code based on the phonological system of a language that enables the person to proceed from print to meaning.

Speech discrimination. The discrimination (observing differences) of speech sounds at a comfortable hearing level.

Speech frequencies. 500, 1,000, and 2,000 Hz.

Speech mechanisms. Structures that are important in the production of speech such as the lips, tongue, teeth, velum, and lungs.

Speech pathologists. Highly trained professionals who work with individuals exhibiting speech and language problems. A related term is speech therapists.

Speech perception. The perception or comprehension of speech.

Speech reading. Reading the speaker's lips and surrounding areas in order to comprehend the speaker's message. See also **Lip reading.**

Speech reception. The threshold level at which an individual understands speech stimuli 50 percent of the time.

Spoken language. Language that uses speech as the primary mode of communication. Examples include English, French, and Spanish.

Spontaneous language samples. Typically, samples of spoken language that are elicited by the use of pictures, movies, or other media forms.

Standard English. English that is uniform, acceptable, and well established through usage in informal and formal speech and writing of educated individuals.

Standardized tests. Norm-referenced tests. See **Norms** and **Norm-referenced.**

Structural (approaches). Approaches which assert that language must be taught, especially by the use of grammatical or structural categories pertaining to parts of speech or special classes such as nouns, verbs, or *wh-* forms.

Structural linguistics. A field of linguistics that was strongly influenced by behaviorism. Emphasis was placed on the structure of the language rather than on underlying competence rules of the user.

Stuttering. Repetitive speech due to psychological and/or physiological causes.

Subjects. Individuals who participate in a research study.

Subject-verb-object. The word order of a particular utterance. Specifically, the subject is first, followed by the verb, and then the object. Example: *John* (subject) *hit* (verb) *the ball* (object).

Suffix. An affix added to the end of a base or root word. See also **Affix** and **Morphemes.**

Support services. Ancillary services that meet the individual needs of hearing-impaired students in both mainstreamed and self-contained classrooms. Examples include audiologist, counselor, interpreter, note taker, speech pathologist, and tutor.

Suprasegmental. Pertaining to aspects of speech that have an influence on the adequate production of sounds; for example, respiration, rate, rhythm, stress pattern, and duration.

Syllable. A unit of spoken language that consists of one or more sounds or letters. Examples: *syl la ble; ob li ga tion; in cline.*

Symbol systems. The use of words or abstract symbols to represent categories for teaching the structure of language. See **Structural approaches.**

Syntax. Word order.

Tag question. A question form that ends with a positive or negative tag. Examples: *You don't want the apple pie, do you?; You do want the apple pie, don't you?*

Theory. A plausible or acceptable scientific law, principle, or rule that explains the relationships of a set of facts and events.

Top-down. Relating to processes such as the application of prior knowledge and metacognitive skills during reading. Also, a model of reading which asserts that the use of these skills is sufficient for understanding letters, words, and sentences. Knowledge in the readers' heads is considered more important than knowledge about letter-sound relationships.

Total Communication. An educational philosophy that supports the use of simultaneous communication approaches in instruction to meet the individual needs of hearing-impaired students. See also **Simultaneous communication.**

Traditional/structural. Pertaining to two earlier periods of linguistics. Traditional linguistics focused on prescribing the correct or appropriate grammar. Structural linguistics emphasized the descriptions of grammar based on surface structures.

Transduction. The conversion of sound energy from one form to another.

Transformational generative grammar. A linguistic theory or model which states that the surface structure of a sentence can be related to the deep structure by linguistic transformations. The emphasis is on the speaker's intuitive competence in the language rather than on performance.

Transformational rules. Rules such as deletion, insertion, and transposition that relate the deep structure to the surface structure (i.e., spoken utterances).

Unaided ear. The hearing threshold level or hearing acuity of the ear without the use of amplification systems.

Underextensions. Labels that are used in a narrow sense, that is, other appropriate examples of the label are not included. For example, the label *doggie* is used for the family dog and not for other dogs in the neighborhood.

Unisensory. Relating to the use of one sense; in oralism, a method designed to develop the sense of audition, or the use of residual hearing.

Unscientific. Characteristic of research that does not follow the scientific method and thus is considered invalid or unreliable.

Velum. The soft palate, a membranous covering or partition, in back of the oral cavity that plays a role in the production of speech sounds.

Verb.   Part of speech showing action or state of being. Examples: *eat, run, feel, is, was, think.*

Verb agreement.   An inflectional property of verbs that indicates agreement with the subject regarding number, person, case, or gender. Examples: The girls *are* happy; The girl *is* happy; I *am,* you *are,* he *is.*

Verb aspects.   The properties of verbs such as tense and agreement. See **Verb agreement** and **Verb tense.**

Verb tense.   Grammatical property that expresses the time of the verb, for example, past and nonpast.

Visual-gestural-spatial.   Relating to the medium in which sign languages are expressed and received—that is, by the use of vision, body movement, and space.

Vocal folds (vocal cords).   Two pairs of flaplike folds of mucous membrane located in the larynx, responsible for adding voice to speech sounds. Also known as vocal cords.

Vocal tract.   The passage for producing speech sounds, extending from the throat to the lips.

Voiced.   Relating to the presence of voiced sound (e.g., vibration of the vocal cords) in the production of speech. Examples: /b/, /m/, /d/.

Voiceless.   Pertaining to the absence of voiced sound (i.e., vibration of the vocal cords) in the production of speech. Examples: /p/, /t/, /k/.

Wh- questions.   Questions that begin with or include a *wh-* form. Examples: *Where is my pipe?; What is her name?*

Working memory.   See **Short-term memory.**

Written language.   The secondary language forms of reading and writing. Also, the writing or written productions of individuals.

Yes/no questions.   Questions that require a yes/no response or some variation. Examples: *Do you want some turkey? Yes; Did she want to marry him? Not really.*

References

Abraham, S., & Stoker, R. (1984). An evaluation of methods used to teach speech to the hearing-impaired using a simulation technique. *Volta Review, 86,* 325–335.

Acoustical Society of America. (1982). *Specification of hearing aid characteristics.* ANSI S3.22–1982. New York: Author.

Akamatsu, C. (1982). *The acquisition of fingerspelling in preschool children.* Unpublished doctoral dissertation, University of Rochester, New York.

Alexander, C. (1979). Black English dialect and the classroom teacher. *Reading Teacher, 33,* 571–577.

Allen, T. (1986). Patterns of academic achievement among hearing impaired students: 1974 and 1983. In A. Schildroth and M. Karchmer (Eds.), *Deaf children in America* (pp. 161–206). San Diego, CA: Little, Brown.

Allen, T., & Osborn, T. (1984). Academic integration of hearing-impaired students: Demographic, handicapping, and achievement factors. *American Annals of the Deaf, 129,* 100–113.

Allen, T., White, C., & Karchmer, M. (1983). Issues in the development of a special edition for hearing-impaired students of the seventh edition of the Stanford achievement test. *American Annals of the Deaf, 128,* 34–39.

Alpern, G., & Boll, T. (1972). *The developmental profile.* Indianapolis, IN: Psychological Development Publications.

Altshuler, K., Deming, W., Vollenweider, J., Rainer, J. & Tendler, R. (1976). Impulsivity and profound early deafness: A cross cultural inquiry. *American Annals of the Deaf, 121,* 331–345.

Anastasi, A. (1982). *Psychological testing* (5th ed.). New York: Macmillan.

Anderson, B. (1975). *Cognitive psychology: The study of knowing, learning, and thinking.* New York: Academic Press.

Anderson, M., Boren, N., Caniglia, J., Howard, W., & Krohn, E. (1980). *Apple Tree.* Beaverton, OR: Dormac.

Anderson, R. (1985). Role of the reader's schema in comprehension, learning, and memory. In H. Singer and R. Ruddell (Eds.), *Theoretical models and processes of reading* (3rd ed.) (pp. 372–384). Newark, DE: International Reading Association.

Anderson, R., Hiebert, E., Scott, J., & Wilkinson, I. (1985). *Becoming a nation of readers: The report of the commission on reading.* Washington, DC: U.S. Department of Education, The National Institute of Education.

Anderson, R., & Freebody, P. (1985). Vocabulary knowledge. In H. Singer & R. Ruddell (Eds.), *Theoretical models and processes of reading* (pp. 343–371). Newark, DE: International Reading Association.

Anderson, R., & Pearson, P. D. (1984). A schema-theoretic view of basic processes in reading comprehension. In P. D. Pearson, R. Barr, M. Kamil, & P. Mosenthal (Eds.), *Handbook of Reading Research* (pp. 255–291). White Plains, NY: Longman.

Anderson, R., & Stevens, G. (1969). Qualifications of teachers of mentally retarded deaf pupils in residential schools for the deaf. *Special Education in Canada, 43,* 23–32.

Anthony, D. (1966). *Seeing Essential English.* Unpublished master's thesis, Eastern Michigan University, Ypsilanti.

Antia, S. (1982). Social interaction of partially mainstreamed hearing impaired children. *American Annals of the Deaf, 127,* 18–25.

Antia, S., & Kreimeyer, K. (1987). The effects of social skill training on the peer interaction of preschool hearing-impaired children. *Journal of the Division of Early Childhood, 11,* 206–216.

Antia, S., & Kreimeyer, K. (1988). Maintenance of positive peer interaction in preschool hearing-impaired children. *Volta Review, 90,* 325–337.

Auxter, D. (1971). Learning disabilities among deaf populations. *Exceptional Children, 37,* 573–577.

Babb, R. (1979). *A study of the academic achievement and language acquisition levels of deaf children of hearing parents in an educational environment using Signing Exact English as the primary mode of manual communication.* Unpublished doctoral dissertation, University of Illinois, Urbana-Champaign.

Babbidge Committee Report. (1965). *Education of the deaf in the United States.* Report of the advisory committee on the education of the deaf. Washington, DC: U.S. Government Printing Office.

Babbini, B., & Quigley, S. (1970). *A study of the growth patterns in language, communication, and educational achievement in six residential schools for deaf students.* Urbana: University of Illinois, Institute for Research on Exceptional Children. (ERIC Document Reproduction Service ED 046 208).

Bachara, G., Raphael, J., & Phelan, W. (1980). Empathy development in deaf pre-adolescents. *American Annals of the Deaf, 125,* 38–41.

Baddeley, A. (1979). Working memory and reading. In H. Bouma (Ed.), *Processing of visible language* (Vol. 1) (pp. 355–370). New York: Plenum.

Bailey, D., Jens, K., & Johnson, N. (1983). Curricula for handicapped infants. In S. Garwood & R. Fewell's *Educating handicapped infants: Issues in development and intervention* (pp. 387–415). Rockville, MD: Aspen.

Baker, C., & Cokely, D. (1980). *American sign language: A teacher's resource text on grammar and culture.* Silver Spring, MD: T. J. Publishers.

Baker, L., & Brown, A. (1984). Metacognitive skills and reading. In P. D. Pearson, R. Barr, M. Kamil, & P. Mosenthal (Eds.), *Handbook of reading research* (pp. 353–394). White Plains, NY: Longman.

Baldwin, V. (1986). *Prevalence of students with deaf-blindness.* Final Project Report. Washington, DC: Office of Special Education and Rehabilitation, Special Education Programs.

Balow, B., Fulton, H., & Peploe, E. (1971). Reading comprehension skills among hearing-impaired adolescents. *Volta Review, 73,* 113–119.

Balow, I., & Brill, R. (1975). An evaluation of reading and academic achievement levels of 16 graduating classes of the California School for the Deaf, Riverside. *Volta Review, 77,* 255–266.

Bandura, A., & Walters, R. (1963). *Social learning and personality.* New York: Holt, Rinehart and Winston.

Bates, E., Benigni, L., Bretherton, I., Camaioni, L., & Volterra, V. (1979). *The emergence of symbols: Cognition and communication in infancy.* New York: Academic Press.

Beck, K., Beck, C., & Gironella, O. (1977). Rehearsal and recall strategies of deaf and hearing individuals. *American Annals of the Deaf, 122,* 544–552.

Becker, W. (1977). Teaching reading and language to the disadvantaged—What we have learned from field research. *Harvard Educational Review, 47,* 518–543.

Beebe, H., Pearson, H., & Koch, M. (1984). The Helen Beebe speech and hearing center. In D. Ling (Ed.), *Early intervention for hearing-impaired children: Oral options* (pp. 15–63). San Diego, CA: College-Hill.

Behling, J. (1975). *Research methods: Statistical concepts and research practicum.* Washington, DC: University Press of America.

Belcastro, F. (1979). Use of behavior modification with hearing-impaired subjects. *American Annals of the Deaf, 124,* 820–824.

Bellugi, U., Klima, E., & Siple, P. (1974). Remembering in signs. *Cognition, 3,* 93–125.

Bender, R. (1970). *The conquest of deafness: A history of the long struggle to make possible normal living to those handicapped by lack of normal hearing.* Cleveland, OH: Case Western Reserve University Press.

Berg, F., & Fletcher, S. (1970). *The hard of hearing child.* New York: Grune & Stratton.

Berger, K. (1972). *Speechreading: Principles and methods.* Baltimore, MD: National Educational Press.

Berk, R. (Ed.). (1980). *Criterion-referenced measurement: The state of the art.* Baltimore, MD: John Hopkins University Press.

Berlin, C. (Ed.). (1984). *Hearing science.* San Diego, CA: College-Hill.

Bess, F., Freeman, B., & Sinclair, J. (Eds.). (1981). *Amplification in education.* Washington, DC: Alexander Graham Bell Association for the Deaf.

Bess, F., & McConnell, F. (1981). *Audiology, education, and the hearing-impaired child.* St. Louis, MO: Mosby.

Best, B., & Roberts, G. (1976). Early cognitive development in hearing impaired children. *American Annals of the Deaf, 121,* 560–564.

Bigge, J., & O'Donnell, P. (Eds.). (1976). *Teaching individuals with physical and multiple disabilities.* Columbus, OH: Merrill.

Blackwell, P., Engen, E., Fischgrund, J., & Zarcadoolas, C. (1978). *Sentences and other systems: A language learning curriculum for hearing-impaired children.* Washington, DC: Alexander Graham Bell Association for the Deaf.

Blair, F. (1957). A study of the visual memory of deaf and hearing children. *American Annals of the Deaf, 102,* 254–263.

Blair, J., Peterson, M., & Viehweg, S. (1985). The effects of mild hearing loss on academic performance of young school-age children. *Volta Review, 87,* 87–93.

Bliss, C. (1965). *Semantography.* Sydney, Australia: Semantography Publications.

Bloom, L., & Lahey, M. (1978). *Language development and language disorders.* New York: Wiley.

Bloomquist, C. (1986). Minimum competency testing programs and hearing-impaired students. In A. Schildroth & M. Karchmer (Eds.), *Deaf children in America* (pp. 207–229). San Diego, CA: College-Hill.

Blumenthal, A. (1970). *Language and psychology: Historical aspects of psycholinguistics*. New York: Wiley.

Bockmiller, P., & Coley, J. (1981). A survey of methods, materials, and teacher preparation among teachers of reading to the hearing-impaired. *Reading Teacher, 34,* 526–529.

Boothroyd, A. (1984). Auditory perception of speech contrasts by subjects with sensorineural hearing loss. *Journal of Speech and Hearing Research, 27,* 134–144.

Boothroyd, A. (1986). *Speech acoustics and perception*. Austin, TX: Pro-Ed.

Borg, W., & Gall, M. (1963). *Educational research: An introduction* (2nd ed.). New York: McKay.

Borg, W., & Gall, M. (1979). *Educational Research* (3rd ed.). White Plains, NY: Longman.

Bornstein, H. (1973). A description of some current sign systems designed to represent English. *American Annals of the Deaf, 118,* 454–463.

Bornstein, H., & Saulnier, K. (1981). Signed English: A brief follow-up to the first evaluation. *American Annals of the Deaf, 126,* 69–72.

Bornstein, H., Saulnier, K., & Hamilton, L. (1980). Signed English: A first evaluation. *American Annals of the Deaf, 125,* 467–481.

Bornstein, H., Saulnier, K., & Hamilton, L. (1983). *The comprehensive Signed English dictionary*. Washington, DC: Gallaudet University Press.

Bowen, J., Madsen, H., & Hilferty, A. (1985). *TESOL: Techniques and procedures*. Rowley, MA: Newbury House.

Braden, J. (1987). An explanation of the superior performance IQs of deaf children of deaf parents. *American Annals of the Deaf, 132,* 263–266.

Bragg, B. (1973). Ameslish—Our American heritage: A testimony. *American Annals of the Deaf, 118,* 672–674.

Brannan, C. (1982). A survey of programs and services to hearing-impaired/mentally retarded children. In D. Tweedie & E. Shroyer (Eds.), *The multihandicapped hearing-impaired: Identification and instruction* (pp. 29–36). Washington, DC: Gallaudet University Press.

Brasel, K., & Quigley, S. (1977). The influence of certain language and communication environments in early childhood on the development of language in deaf individuals. *Journal of Speech and Hearing Research, 20,* 95–107.

Briccetti, K. (1987). Mental health services for deaf students in California. *American Annals of the Deaf, 132,* 280–282.

Broadbent, F., & Daniele, V. (1982). A review of research on mathematics and deafness. *Directions, 3*(11), 27–36.

Brown, A., Armbruster, B., & Baker, L. (1986). The role of metacognition in reading and studying. In J. Orasanu (Ed.), *Reading comprehension: From research to practice* (pp. 49–75). Hillsdale, NJ: Erlbaum.

Brown, R. (1973). *A first language: The early stages*. Cambridge, MA: Harvard University.

Brown, S. (1986). Etiological trends, characteristics, and distributions. In A. Schildroth & M. Karchmer (Eds.), *Deaf children in America* (pp. 33–54). San Diego, CA: College-Hill.

Byrne, D. (1983). Theoretical prescriptive approaches to selecting the gain and frequency response of a hearing aid. *Monographs in Contemporary Audiology, 4*(1), 1–40.

Calvert, D. (1986). Speech in perspective. In D. Luterman (Ed.), *Deafness in perspective* (pp. 167–191). San Diego, CA: College-Hill.

Calvert, D., & Silverman, S. (1975). *Speech and deafness*. Washington, DC: Alexander Graham Bell Association for the Deaf.

Calvert, D., & Silverman, S. (1983). *Speech and deafness* (2nd ed.). Washington, DC: Alexander Graham Bell Association for the Deaf.

Carrier, J. (1974). Application of functional analysis and a nonspeech response mode to teaching language. *American Speech and Hearing Association Monograph,* No. 18.

Carrier, J., & Peak, T. (1975). *Non-SLIP*. Lawrence, KA: H&H Enterprises.

Carroll, D. (1986). *Psychology of language*. Monterey, CA: Brooks/Cole.

Cartledge, G., Paul, P., Jackson, D., & Drumm, P. (1988). *Social skill assessment of deaf adolescents in public and residential school settings*. Paper presented at the American Educational Research Association (AERA) Annual Convention, New Orleans, LA, April.

Chaplin, J. (1975). *Dictionary of psychology*. (rev. ed.). New York: Dell.

Cheskin, A. (1982). The use of language by hearing mothers of deaf children. *Journal of Communication Disorders, 15*, 145–153.

Chilson, R. (1985). Effects of cued speech instruction on speechreading skills. *Cued Speech Annual, 1*, 60–68.

Chomsky, N. (1957). *Syntactic structures*. The Hague: Mouton.

Chomsky, N. (1965). *Aspects of the theory of syntax*. Cambridge, MA: Massachusetts Institute of Technology Press.

Chomsky, N. (1968). *Language and mind*. New York: Harcourt, Brace, & World.

Chomsky, N. (1975). *Reflections on language*. New York: Pantheon Books.

Clarke, B., Rogers, W., & Booth, J. (1982). How hearing impaired children learn to read: Theoretical and practical issues. *Volta Review, 84*, 57–69.

Clarke, M., & Ling, D. (1976). The effects of using cued speech: A follow-up study. *Volta Review, 78*, 23–35.

Clarke School for the Deaf. (1971). *Auditory training*. Northampton, MA: Author.

Cohen, B. (1980). Emotionally disturbed hearing-impaired children: A review of the literature. *American Annals of the Deaf, 125*, 1040–1048.

Cokely, D. (1980). Sign language: Teaching, interpreting, and educational policy. In C. Baker & R. Battison (Eds.), *Sign language and the Deaf community: Essays in honor of William C. Stokoe* (pp. 137–158). Silver Spring, MD: National Association of the Deaf.

Cokely, D. (1983). When is a pidgin not a pidgin? An alternate analysis of the ASL–English contact situation. *Sign Language Studies, 38*, 1–24.

Cole, E., & Gregory, H. (Eds.). (1986). Auditory learning. *Volta Review, 88*(5), September, 1986. [Special Issue].

Cole, N. (1988). From the dean's desk . . . In *College of Education Newsletter*, Winter (pp. 3–4). Urbana-Champaign, IL: University of Illinois.

Coley, J., & Bockmiller, P. (1980). Teaching reading to the deaf: An examination of teacher preparedness and practices. *American Annals of the Deaf, 125*, 909–915.

Collins-Ahlgren, M. (1974). Teaching English as a second language to young deaf children: A case study. *Journal of Speech and Hearing Disorders, 39*, 486–500.

Commission on Education of the Deaf. (1988). *Toward equality: Education of the deaf, a report to the President and the Congress of the United States, February*. Washington, DC: U.S. Government Printing Office.

Conley, J. (1976). Role of idiomatic expressions in the reading of deaf children. *American Annals of the Deaf, 121*, 381–385.

Connor, L. (1986). Oralism in perspective. In D. Luterman (Ed.), *Deafness in perspective* (pp. 117–129). San Diego, CA: College-Hill.

Conrad, R. (1979). *The deaf school child*. London, England: Harper & Row.

Conrad, R., & Weiskrantz, B. (1981). On the cognitive ability of deaf children with deaf parents. *American Annals of the Deaf, 126*, 995–1003.

Conway, D. (1985). Children (re)creating writing: A preliminary look at the purpose of free-choice writing of hearing-impaired kindergarteners. *Volta Review, 87*(5), 91–107.

Cooper, R., & Rosenstein, J. (1966). Language acquisition of deaf children. *Volta Review, 68*, 58–67.

Corbett, E., & Jensema, C. (1981). *Teachers of the hearing-impaired: Descriptive profiles.* Washington, DC: Gallaudet University Press.

Cornett, R. O. (1967). Cued speech. *American Annals of the Deaf, 112,* 3–13.

Cornett, R. O. (1984). Book review: Language and deafness. *Cued Speech News, 17*(3), p. 5.

Corson, H. (1973). *Comparing deaf children of oral deaf parents and deaf parents using manual communication with deaf children of hearing parents on academic, social, and communication functioning.* Unpublished doctoral dissertation, University of Cincinnati, Ohio.

Covert, A., & Fredericks, H. (1987). Introduction. In A. Covert & H. Fredericks (Eds.), *Transition for persons with deaf-blindness and other profound handicaps: State-of-the art* (pp. 1–3). Monmouth, OR: Teaching Research Publications.

Craig, W. (1964). Effects of preschool training on the development of reading and lipreading skills of deaf children. *American Annals of the Deaf, 109,* 280–296.

Craik, F., & Lockhart, R. (1972). Levels of processing: A framework for memory research. *Journal of Verbal Learning and Verbal Behavior, 11,* 671–684.

Crandall, K. (1984). *Curriculum process: A national survey of administrators and teachers in programs serving deaf students.* (Working Paper). SCOPE (Systematic Collaborative Outreach Project Effort), Pre-College Programs at Gallaudet College and the National Technical Institute for the Deaf, Rochester, New York.

Creaghead, N. (1985). Phonological development. In P. Newman, N. Creaghead, & W. Secord, *Assessment and remediation of articulatory and phonological disorders* (pp. 41–68). Columbus, OH: Merrill.

Creaghead, N., & Newman, P. (1985). Articulatory phonetics and phonology. In P. Newman, N. Creaghead, & W. Secord, *Assessment and remediation of articulatory and phonological disorders* (pp. 13–39). Columbus, OH: Merrill.

Cromer, R. (1976). The cognitive hypothesis of language acquisition and its implications for child language deficiency. In D. Morehead & A. Morehead (Eds.), *Normal and deficient child language* (pp. 283–333). Baltimore, MD: University Park Press.

Crutchfield, P. (1972). Prospects for teaching English Det + N structures to deaf students. *Sign Language Studies, 1,* 8–14.

Culbertson, L. (1974). CAI-Beneficial teaching tool at Texas School for the Deaf. *American Annals of the Deaf, 119,* 34–40.

Cumming, C., & Rodda, M. (1985). The effects of auditory deprivation on successive processing. *Canadian Journal of Behavioral Science, 17,* 232–245.

Cummins, J. (1984). *Bilingualism and special education: Issues in assessment and pedagogy.* San Diego, CA: College-Hill.

Curtis, W., & Donlon, E. (1984). A ten-year follow-up study of deaf-blind children. *Exceptional Children, 50,* 449–455.

Curtis, W., & Tweedie, D. (1985). Content and process in curriculum planning. In E. Cherow, N. Matkin, & R. Trybus (Eds.), *Hearing-impaired children and youth with developmental disabilities* (pp. 246–270). Washington, DC: Gallaudet University Press.

Dale, E., & O'Rourke, J. (1986). *Vocabulary building: A process approach.* Columbus, OH: Zaner-Bloser.

Davey, B., & LaSasso, C. (1983). An examination of hearing-impaired readers' test-taking abilities on reinspection tasks. *Volta Review, 85,* 279–284.

Davey, B., LaSasso, C., & Macready, G. (1983). Comparison of reading comprehension task performance for deaf and hearing readers. *Journal of Speech and Hearing Research, 26,* 622–628.

Davis, H. (1978). Anatomy and physiology of the auditory system. In H. Davis & S. R. Silverman, *Hearing and deafness* (4th ed.) (pp. 46–83). New York: Holt, Rinehart and Winston.

Davis, J. (Ed.). (1977). *Our forgotten children: Hard-of-hearing pupils in the schools.* Minneapolis, MN: Audio Visual Library Service.

Davis, J. (1986). Academic placement in perspective. In D. Luterman (Ed.), *Deafness in perspective* (pp. 205–224). San Diego, CA: College-Hill.

Davis, J., & Blasdell, R. (1975). Perceptual strategies employed by normal-hearing and hearing-impaired children in the comprehension of sentences containing relative clauses. *Journal of Speech and Hearing Research, 18,* 281–295.

Davis, J., Shepard, N., Stelmachowicz, P., & Gorga, M. (1981). Characteristics of hearing-impaired children in the public schools: Part II—Psychoeducational data. *Journal of Speech and Hearing Disorders, 46,* 130–137.

DeCaro, J., Karchmer, M., & Rawlings, B. (1987). Postsecondary programs for deaf students at the peak of the rubella bulge. *American Annals of the Deaf, 132,* 36–42.

Delaney, M., Stuckless, E. R., & Walter, G. (1984). Total communication effects—a longitudinal study of a school for the deaf in transition. *American Annals of the Deaf, 129,* 481–486.

Delgado, G. (Ed.). (1984). *The Hispanic deaf: Issues and challenges for bilingual special education.* Washington, DC: Gallaudet University Press.

Demerath, N., & Maxwell, G. (1976). *Sociology: Perspectives and applications.* New York: Harper & Row.

de Villiers, J., & de Villiers, P. (1978). *Language acquisition.* Cambridge, MA: Harvard University Press.

Devine, T. (1986). *Teaching reading comprehension: From theory to practice.* Boston, MA: Allyn & Bacon.

Di Carlo, L. (1964). *The deaf.* Englewood Cliffs, NJ: Prentice-Hall.

DiFrancesca, S. (1972). *Academic achievement test results of a national testing program for hearing-impaired students* (Series D, No. 9). Washington, DC: Gallaudet University, Center for Assessment and Demographic Studies.

Dodd, B. (1976). The phonological systems of deaf children. *Journal of Speech and Hearing Disorders, 41,* 185–198.

Doehring, D., Bonnycastle, D., & Ling, A. (1978). Rapid reading skills of integrated hearing-impaired children. *Volta Review, 80,* 399–409.

Doll, E. (1965). *Vineland social maturity scale: A condensed manual of directions.* Circle Pines, MN: American Guidance Service.

Dolman, D. (1983). A study of the relationship between syntactic development and concrete operations in deaf children. *American Annals of the Deaf, 128,* 813–819.

Dunlap, W. (1985). A functional classification system for the deaf-blind. *American Annals of the Deaf, 130,* 236–243.

D'Zamko, M., & Hampton, I. (1985). Personnel preparation for multihandicapped hearing-impaired students: A review of the literature. *American Annals of the Deaf, 130,* 9–14.

Eastman, G. (1974). *Sign me Alice: A play in Sign Language.* Washington, DC: Gallaudet University Press.

Edwards, A., & Jones, D. (1976). *Community and community development.* The Hague, Netherlands: Mouton.

Egan, J. (1948). Articulation testing methods. *Laryngoscope, 58,* 955–991.

Ehri, L., & Wilce, L. (1985). Movement into reading: Is the first stage of printed word learning visual or phonetic? *Reading Research Quarterly, 20,* 163–179.

Elliott, R., & Powers, A. (1988). Preparing teachers to serve the learning disabled hearing impaired. *Volta Review, 90,* 13–18.

Elliott, L., & Katz, D. (1980). *Development of a new children's test of speech discrimination.* St. Louis, MO: Auditec.

Erber, N. (1974). Visual perception of speech by deaf children: Recent developments and continuing needs. *Journal of Speech and Hearing Disorders, 39,* 178–185.

Erber, N. (1975). Auditory-visual perception of speech. *Journal of Speech and Hearing Disorders, 40,* 481–492.

Erber, N. (1982). *Auditory training.* Washington, DC: Alexander Graham Bell Association for the Deaf.

Ewoldt, C. (1981). A psycholinguistic description of selected deaf children reading in sign language. *Reading Research Quarterly, 13,* 58–89.

Ewoldt, C. (1982). Diagnostic approaches and procedures and the reading process. *Volta Review, 84,* 83–94.

Ewoldt, C. (1981). A psycholinguistic description of selected deaf children reading in sign language. *Reading Research Quarterly, 17,* 58–89.

Farr, R., & Carey, R. (1986). *Reading: What can be measured?* (2nd ed.). Newark, DE: International Reading Association.

Farrugia, D., & Austin, G. (1980). A study of socioemotional adjustment patterns of hearing-impaired students in different educational settings. *American Annals of the Deaf, 125,* 535–541.

Farwell, R. (1976). Speech reading: A research review. *American Annals of the Deaf, 121,* 13–30.

Federal Register. (1973). 38 (196), Part 121 C.37.

Filler, J. (1983). Service models for handicapped infants. In S. Garwood & R. Fewell (Eds.), *Educating handicapped infants: Issues in development and intervention* (pp. 132–156). Rockville, MD: Aspen.

Fischgrund, J., Cohen, O., & Clarkson, R. (1987). Hearing-impaired children in Black and Hispanic families. *Volta Review, 89*(5), 59–67.

Fitzgerald, E. (1929). *Straight language for the deaf.* Staunton, VA: McClure.

Flavell, J. (1977). *Cognitive development.* Englewood Cliffs, NJ: Prentice-Hall.

Fowler, C. (1985). Current perspectives on language and speech production: A critical overview. In R. Daniloff (Ed.), *Speech science* (pp. 193–278). San Diego, CA: College-Hill.

Fredericks, H., & Baldwin, V. (1987). Individuals with sensory impairments: Who are they? In L. Goetz, D. Guess, & K. Stremel-Campbell (Eds.), *Innovative program design for individuals with dual sensory impairments* (pp. 3–15). Baltimore, MD: Brookes.

Friedman, L. (Ed.). (1977). *On the other hand: New perspectives on American Sign Language.* New York: Academic Press.

Frisina, R. (1978). Postsecondary education. In H. Davis & S. R. Silverman, *Hearing and deafness* (4th ed.) (pp. 483–495). New York: Holt, Rinehart and Winston.

Fristoe, M., & Lloyd, L. (1979). Signs used in manual communication training with persons having severe communication impairment. *AAESPH Review, 4,* 364–373.

Fruchter, A., Wilbur, R., & Fraser, B. (1984). Comprehension of idioms by hearing-impaired students. *Volta Review, 86,* 7–18.

Funderburg, R. (1982). The role of the classroom teacher in the assessment of the learning-disabled hearing-impaired child. In D. Tweedie & E. Shroyer (Eds.), *The multihandicapped hearing-impaired: Identification and instruction* (pp. 61–74). Washington, DC: Gallaudet University Press.

Furth, H. (1964). Conservation of weight in deaf and hearing children. *Child Development, 35,* 143–150.

Furth, H. (1966). *Thinking without language: Psychological implications of deafness.* New York: Free Press.

Furth, H. (1971). Education for thinking. *Journal of Rehabilitation of the Deaf, 5*(1), 7–17.

Furth, H. (1973). *Deafness and learning: A psychosocial approach.* Belmont, CA: Wadsworth.

Fusfeld, I. (1955). The academic program of schools for the deaf: A cross section evaluation. *Volta Review, 57,* 63–70.

Gagné, R. (1977). *The conditions of learning* (3rd ed.). New York: Holt, Rinehart and Winston.

Gallaudet Research Institute. (1985). *Gallaudet Research Institute Newsletter.* J. Harkins, (Ed.). Washington, DC: Gallaudet University Press.

Gannon, J. (1981). *Deaf heritage: A narrative history of deaf America.* Silver Spring, MD: National Association of the Deaf.

Garrison, W., & Tesch, S. (1978). Self-concept and deafness: A review of the research literature. *Volta Review, 80,* 457–466.

Gay, L. (1981). *Educational research: Competencies for analysis and application* (2nd ed.). Columbus, OH: Merrill.

Geers, A., & Moog, J. (1989). Factors predictive of the development of literacy in profoundly hearing-impaired adolescents. *Volta Review, 91,* 69–86.

Geers, A., Moog, J., & Schick, B. (1984). Acquisition of spoken and signed English by profoundly deaf children. *Journal of Speech and Hearing Disorders, 49,* 378–388.

Gentile, A., & DiFrancesca, S. (1969). *Academic achievement test performance of hearing-impaired students. United States, Spring 1969.* (Series D, No. 1). Washington, DC: Gallaudet University, Center for Assessment and Demographic Studies.

Gentile, A., & McCarthy, B. (1973). *Additional handicapping conditions among hearing-impaired students—United States: 1971–1972* (Series D, No. 14). Washington, DC: Gallaudet University, Center for Assessment and Demographic Studies.

Gerber, A. (1981). Historical trends in the field of learning disabilities: An overview. In A. Gerber & D. Bryen, *Language and learning disabilities* (pp. 1–23). Baltimore, MD: University Park Press.

Gerber, A., & Bryen, D. (1981). *Language and learning disabilities.* Baltimore, MD: University Park Press.

Gillespie, P., & Johnson, L. (1974). *Teaching reading to the mildly retarded child.* Columbus, OH: Merrill.

Gilman, L., Davis, J., & Raffin, M. (1980). Use of common morphemes by hearing-impaired children exposed to a system of manual English. *Journal of Auditory Research, 20,* 57–69.

Giolas, T. (1986). *Aural rehabilitation.* Austin, TX: Pro-Ed.

Giorcelli, L. (1982). *The comprehension of some aspects of figurative language by deaf and hearing subjects.* Unpublished doctoral dissertation. Urbana-Champaign, IL: University of Illinois.

Gleason, J. (1985). *The development of language.* Columbus, OH: Merrill.

Goetz, L., & Gee, K. (1987). Functional vision programming. In L. Goetz, D. Guess, & K. Stremel-Campbell (Eds.), *Innovative program design for individuals with dual-sensory impairments* (pp. 76–97). Baltimore, MD: Brookes.

Goetzinger, C., & Rousey, C. (1959). Educational achievement of deaf children. *American Annals of the Deaf, 104,* 221–231.

Gold, T. (1980). Speech production in hearing-impaired children. *Journal of Communication Disorders, 13,* 397–418.

Goodman, K. (1970). Reading: A psycholinguistic guessing game. In H. Singer & R. Ruddell (Eds.), *Theoretical models and processes of reading* (pp. 259–272). Newark, DE: International Reading Association.

Goppold, L. (1988). Early intervention for preschool deaf children: The longitudinal academic effects relative to program methodology. *American Annals of the Deaf, 133,* 285–288.

Gordon, C., & Pearson, P. D. (1983). *The effects of instruction in metacomprehension and inferencing on children's comprehension abilities* (Tech. Rep. No. 277). Champaign, IL: University of Illinois, Center for the Study of Reading.

Gormley, K., & Sarachan-Deily, A. (1987). Evaluating hearing-impaired students' writing: A practical approach. *Volta Review, 89,* 157–170.

Gough, P. (1985). One second of reading. In H. Singer and R. Ruddell (Eds.), *Theoretical models and processes of reading* (3rd ed.) (pp. 661–686). Newark, DE: International Reading Association.

Gray, W. (1956). *The teaching of reading and writing.* Paris: UNESCO.

Greenberg, M. (1980a). Hearing families with deaf children: Stress and functioning as related to communication method. *American Annals of the Deaf, 125,* 1063–1071.

Greenberg, M. (1980b). Social interaction between deaf preschoolers and their mothers: The effects of communication method and communication competence. *Developmental Psychology, 16,* 465–474.

Greenberg, M. (1983). Family stress and child competence: The effects of early intervention for families with deaf infants. *American Annals of the Deaf, 128,* 407–417.

Greenberg, M., & Kusché, C. (1989). Cognitive, personal, and social development of deaf children and adolescents. In M. Wang, M. Reynolds, & H. Walberg (Eds.), *The handbook of special education: Research and practice* (Vol. 3) (pp. 95–129). Oxford, England: Pergamon.

Greenberg, M., Kusché, C., Calderon, R., Gustafson, R., & Coady, B. (1983). *The PATHS Curriculum* (2nd ed.). University of Washington, Department of Psychology, Seattle.

Greenberg, M., & Marvin, R. (1979). Attachment patterns in profoundly deaf preschool children. *Merrill-Palmer Quarterly, 25,* 265–279.

Gregory, J. (1987). An investigation of speechreading with and without cued speech. *American Annals of the Deaf, 132,* 393–398.

Gresham, F., & Elliott, S. (1987). *Social skills rating scale-teacher: Junior/senior high school form.* Baton Rouge, LA: Louisiana State University. [Unpublished Assessment].

Groht, M. (1933). Language as taught in the Lexington School. *American Annals of the Deaf, 78,* 280–281.

Groht, M. (1958). *Natural language for deaf children.* Washington, DC: Alexander Graham Bell Association for the Deaf.

Gronlund, N. (1981). *Measurement and evaluation in teaching* (4th ed.). New York: Macmillan.

Gross, B., & Gross, R. (1985). *The great school debate: Which way for American education?* New York: Simon & Schuster.

Grossman, H. (Ed.). (1973). *Manual on terminology and classification in mental retardation, 1973 revision.* Washington, DC: American Association on Mental Deficiency.

Grossman, H. (Ed.). (1977). *Manual on terminology and classification in mental retardation.* Washington, DC: American Association on Mental Deficiency.

Gustason, G. (1983). *Teaching and learning Signing Exact English.* Los Alamitos, CA: Modern Signs Press.

Gustason, G. (1985). Interpreters entering public school employment. *American Annals of the Deaf, 130,* 265–266.

Gustason, G., Pfetzing, & D., Zawolkow, E. (1972). *Signing exact English.* Los Alamitos, CA: Modern Signs Press.

Gustason, G., Pfetzing, & D., Zawolkow, E. (1980). *Signing exact English.* Los Alamitos, CA: Modern Signs Press.

Hack, Z., & Erber, N. (1982). Auditory, visual, and auditory-visual perception of vowels by hearing-impaired children. *Journal of Speech and Hearing Research, 25,* 100–107.

Hagborg, W. (1987). Hearing-impaired students and sociometric ratings: An exploratory study. *Volta Review, 89,* 221–228.

Hall, P. (1929). Results of recent tests at Gallaudet College. *American Annals of the Deaf, 74,* 389–395.

Hammill, D., Leigh, L., McNutt, G., & Larsen, S. (1981). A new definition of learning disabilities. *Learning Disability Quarterly, 4,* 336–342.

Hanson, V. (1985). Cognitive processes in reading: Where deaf readers succeed and where they have difficulty. In D. Martin (Ed.), *Cognition, education, and deafness: Directions for research and instruction* (pp. 108–110). Washington, DC: Gallaudet University Press.

Hanson, V., & Bellugi, U. (1982). On the role of sign order and morphological structure in memory for American Sign Language. *Journal of Verbal Learning and Verbal Behavior, 21,* 621–633.

Harris, J. (1986). *Anatomy and physiology of the peripheral auditory mechanism.* Austin, TX: Pro-Ed.

Hasenstab, M., & McKenzie, C. (1981). A survey of reading programs used with hearing-impaired students. *Volta Review, 83,* 383–388.

Haskins, H. (1949). *A phonetically balanced test of speech discrimination for children.* Unpublished master's thesis, Northwestern University, Illinois.

Hatfield, N., Caccamise, F., & Siple, P. (1978). Deaf students' language competency: A bilingual perspective. *American Annals of the Deaf, 123,* 847–851.

Haug, O., Baccaro, P., & Guilford, F. (1967). A pure-tone audiogram on the infant: The PIWI technique. *Archives of Otolaryngology, 86,* 435–440.

Healey, W., & Karp-Nortman, D. (1975). *The hearing-impaired, mentally retarded: Recommendations for action.* Washington, DC: American Speech and Hearing Association.

Heider, F., & Heider, G. (1940). A comparison of sentence structure of deaf and hearing children. *Psychological Monographs, 52,* 42–103.

Heidinger, V. (1984). *Analyzing syntax and semantics.* Washington, DC: Gallaudet University Press.

Heimlich, J., & Pittelman, S. (1986). *Semantic mapping: Classroom applications.* Newark, DE: International Reading Association.

Heine, M. (1981). *Comprehension of high and low level information in expository passages: A comparison of deaf and hearing readers.* Unpublished doctoral dissertation, University of Pittsburgh, Pennsylvania.

Henggeler, S., & Cooper, P. (1983). Deaf child–hearing mother interaction: Extensiveness and reciprocity. *Journal of Pediatric Psychology, 8,* 83–95.

Hester, M. (1969). Education of the deaf. In J. Griffith (Ed.), *Persons with hearing loss* (pp. 150–165). Springfield, IL: Thomas.

Heward, W., & Orlansky, M. (1988). *Exceptional children: An introductory survey to special education* (3rd ed.). Columbus, OH: Merrill.

Higgins, P. (1980). *Outsiders in a hearing world: A sociology of deafness.* Beverly Hills, CA: Sage.

Hillery, G. (1974). *Communal organizations.* Chicago, IL: University of Chicago Press.

Hillocks, G., (1986). *Research on written composition: New directions for teaching.* Urbana, IL: National Conference on Research in English.

Hirsh, I., Davis, H., Silverman, S. R., Reynolds, E., Eldert, E., & Benson, R. (1952). Development of materials for speech audiometry. *Journal of Speech and Hearing Disorders, 17,* 321–337.

Hiskey, M. (1966). *Hiskey–Nebraska test of learning aptitude: Manual.* Lincoln, NE: Union College Press.

Hodgson, W., & Skinner, P. (Eds.). (1981). *Hearing aid assessment and use in audiologic habilitation* (2nd ed.). Baltimore, MD: Williams & Wilkins.

Hoffmeister, R. (1985). Families with deaf parents: A functional perspective. In K. Thurman (Ed.), *Children of handicapped parents* (pp. 111–130). New York: Academic Press.

Hoffmeister, R., & Wilbur, R. (1980). The acquisition of sign language. In H. Lane and F. Grosjean (Eds.), *Recent perspectives on American Sign Language* (pp. 61–78). Hillsdale, NJ: Erlbaum.

Huey, E. (1908/1968). *The psychology and pedagogy of reading*. New York, NY: Macmillan. (Reprinted, Cambridge, MA: Massachusetts Institute of Technology).

Humphries, T., Padden, C., & O'Rourke, T. J. (1980). *A basic course in American Sign Language*. Silver Spring, MD: T. J. Publishers.

Hunt, K. (1965). *Grammatical structures written at three grade levels*. Champaign, IL: National Council of Teachers of English.

Huntington, A., & Watton, F. (1986). The spoken language of teachers and pupils in the education of hearing-impaired children. *Volta Review, 88,* 5–19.

Ingalls, R. (1978). *Mental retardation: The changing outlook*. New York: Wiley.

Iran-Nejad, A., Ortony, A., & Rittenhouse, R. (1981). The comprehension of metaphorical uses of English by deaf children. *Journal of Speech and Hearing Research, 24,* 551–556.

Jeffers, J., & Barley, M. (1971). *Speechreading (lipreading)*. Springfield, IL: Thomas.

Jensema, C. (1975). *The relationship between academic achievement and the demographic characteristics of hearing-impaired children and youth* (Series R, No. 2). Washington, DC: Gallaudet University, Center for Assessment and Demographic Studies.

Jensema, C. (1977). Letter to the editor. *Volta Review, 79,* p. 180.

Jensema, C. (1979a). A review of communication systems used by deaf-blind people: Part 1: *American Annals of the Deaf, 124,* 720–725.

Jensema, C. (1979b). A review of communication systems used by deaf-blind people: Part 2. *American Annals of the Deaf, 124,* 808–809.

Jensema, C., & Trybus, R. (1975). *Reported emotional/behavioral problems among hearing-impaired students in special education programs* (Series R, No. 1). Washington, DC: Gallaudet University, Center for Assessment and Demographic Studies.

Jerger, S. (1984). Speech audiometry. In J. Jerger (Ed.), *Pediatric audiology* (pp. 71–93). San Diego, CA: College-Hill.

Jerger, S., & Jerger, J. (1982). Pediatric speech intelligibility test: Performance-intensity characteristics. *Ear and Hearing, 3,* 325–334.

Jerger, S., Lewis, S., Hawkins, J., & Jerger, J. (1980). Pediatric speech intelligibility test. I. Generation of test materials. *International Journal of Pediatric Otorhinolaryngology, 2,* 217–230.

Johnson, D., Moe., A., & Baumann, J. (1983). *The Ginn word book for teachers: A basic lexicon*. Lexington, MA: Ginn.

Johnson, D., & Pearson, P. D. (1984). *Teaching reading vocabulary* (2nd ed.). New York: Holt, Rinehart and Winston.

Johnson, K. (1977). A survey of mathematics programs, materials, and methods in schools for the deaf. *American Annals of the Deaf, 122,* 19–25.

Johnston, P. (1984). Background knowledge and reading comprehension test bias. *Reading Research Quarterly, 19,* 219–239.

Johnston, P., & Pearson, P. D. (1982). *Prior knowledge connectivity and the assessment of reading comprehension* (Tech. Rep. No. 245). Urbana, IL: University of Illinois, Center for the Study of Reading.

Jones, P. (1979). Negative interference of signed language in written English. *Sign Language Studies, 24,* 273–279.

Jones, T. (1984). Behavior modification studies with hearing-impaired students: A review. *American Annals of the Deaf, 129,* 451–458.

Jones, T., & Johnson, J. (1985). *Characteristics of programs for multihandicapped hearing-impaired students*. Paper presented at the Convention of American Instructors of the Deaf, St. Augustine, Florida.

Jordan, I., Gustason, G., & Rosen, R. (1979). An update on communication trends at programs for the deaf. *American Annals of the Deaf, 124,* 350–357.

Jordan, I., & Karchmer, M. (1986). Patterns of sign use among hearing-impaired students. In A. Schildroth and M. Karchmer (Eds.), *Deaf children in America* (pp. 125–138). Boston, MA: Little, Brown.

Just, M., & Carpenter, P. (1987). *The psychology of reading and language comprehension.* Boston, MA: Allyn & Bacon.

Kamhi, A., & Johnston, J. (1982). Towards an understanding of retarded children's linguistic deficiencies. *Journal of Speech and Hearing Research, 25,* 435–445.

Kantor, R. (1980). The acquisition of classifiers in American Sign Language. *Sign Language Studies, 28,* 193–208.

Karchmer, M. (1984). Hearing impaired students and their education: Population perspectives. In W. Northcott (Ed.), *Introduction to oral interpreting: Principles and practices* (pp. 41–59). Baltimore, MD: University Park Press.

Karchmer, M. (1985). A demographic perspective. In E. Cherow, N. Watkin, & R. Trybus (Eds.), *Hearing-impaired children and youth with developmental disabilities* (pp. 36–56). Washington, DC: Gallaudet University Press.

Karchmer, M., Allen, T., Petersen, L., & Quaynor, A. (1982). Hearing-impaired children and youth in Canada: Student characteristics in relation to manual communication patterns in four special education settings. *American Annals of the Deaf, 127,* 89–104.

Karchmer, M., & Belmont, J. (1976). *On assessing and improving deaf performance in the cognitive laboratory.* Paper presented at the American Speech and Hearing Association, Houston, Texas.

Karchmer, M., Milone, M., & Wolk, S. (1979). Educational significance of hearing loss at three levels of severity. *American Annals of the Deaf, 124,* 97–109.

Karchmer, M., & Petersen, L. (1980). *Commuter students at residential schools for the deaf* (Series R, No. 7). Washington, DC: Gallaudet University, Center for Assessment and Demographic Studies.

Karmiloff-Smith, A. (1979). *A functional approach to child language: A study of determiners and reference.* New York: Cambridge University Press.

Kennedy, P., Northcott, W., McCauley, R., & Williams, S. (1976). Longitudinal sociometric and cross sectional data on mainstreamed hearing-impaired children: Implications for preschool planning. *Volta Review, 78,* 71–81.

Kerlinger, F. (1973). *Foundations of behavioral research* (2nd ed.). New York: Holt, Rinehart and Winston.

Kerstetter, P. (1985). *Demographic predictors of postsecondary program choice of hearing-impaired secondary school students.* Unpublished doctoral dissertation, Gallaudet University, Washington, DC.

King, C. (1981). *An investigation of similarities and differences in the syntactic abilities of deaf and hearing children learning English as a first or second language.* Unpublished doctoral dissertation, University of Illinois, Champaign-Urbana.

King, C. (1984). National survey of language methods used with hearing-impaired students in the United States. *American Annals of the Deaf, 129,* 311–316.

King, C., & Quigley, S. (1985). *Reading and deafness.* San Diego, CA: College-Hill.

Kirk, S. (1962). *Educating exceptional children.* Boston, MA: Houghton Mifflin.

Kirk, S., & Gallagher, J. (1986). *Educating exceptional children* (5th ed.). Boston, MA: Houghton Mifflin.

Klima, E., & Bellugi, U. (1979). *The signs of language.* Cambridge, MA: Harvard University Press.

Kluwin, T. (1981a). The grammaticality of manual representation of English in classroom settings. *American Annals of the Deaf, 126,* 417–421.

Kluwin, T. (1981b). A rationale for modifying classroom signing systems. *Sign Language Studies, 31,* 179–188.

Kluwin, T., Getson, P., & Kluwin, B. (1980). The effects on experience on the discourse comprehension of deaf and hearing adolescents. *Directions, 1*(3), 49.

Kluwin, T., & Moores, D. (1985). The effects of integration on the mathematics achievement of hearing-impaired adolescents. *Exceptional Children, 52,* 153–160.

Kodman, F. (1963). Educational status of hard-of-hearing children in the classroom. *Journal of Speech and Hearing Disorders, 28,* 297–299.

Konar, V., & Rice, D. (1982). *Strategies for serving deaf-blind clients.* Hot Springs, AR: Arkansas Research and Training in Vocational Rehabilitation.

Konigsmark, B., & Gorlin, R. (1976). *Genetic and metabolic deafness.* Philadelphia: Saunders.

Kool, V., Pathak, K., & Singh, S. (1983). Short-term recall of visually presented additive and nonadditive digital material by deaf and hearing subjects. *Journal of General Psychology, 108,* 19–25.

Kretschmer, R. E. (1976). *Judgments of grammaticality by 11, 14, and 17 year old hearing and hearing impaired youngsters.* Unpublished doctoral dissertation, University of Kansas, Lawrence.

Kusché, C. (1985). Information processing and reading achievement in the deaf population: Implications for learning and hemispheric lateralization. In D. Martin (Ed.), *Cognition, education, and deafness: Directions for research and instruction* (pp. 115–120). Washington, DC: Gallaudet University Press.

Kusché, C., & Greenberg, M. (1983). The development of evaluative understanding and role-taking in deaf and hearing children. *Children Development, 54,* 141–147.

Kusché, C., Greenberg, M., & Garfield, T. (1983). Nonverbal intelligence and verbal achievement in deaf adolescents: An examination of heredity and environment. *American Annals of the Deaf, 128,* 458–466.

Lane, H. (1976a). Thoughts on oral advocacy today . . . with memories of the society of oral advocates. *Volta Review, 78,* 136–140.

Lane, H. (1976b). The profoundly deaf: Has oral education succeeded? *Volta Review, 78,* 329–340.

Lane, H. (1980). A chronology of the oppression of sign language in France and the United States. In H. Lane & F. Grosjean (Eds.), *Recent perspectives on American Sign Language* (pp. 119–161). Hillsdale, NJ: Erlbaum.

Lane, H. (1984). *When the mind hears: A history of the deaf.* New York: Random House.

Lane, H., & Baker, D. (1974). Reading achievement of the deaf: Another look. *Volta Review, 76,* 489–499.

Lane, H., & Grosjean, F. (Eds.). (1980). *Recent perspectives on American Sign Language.* Hillsdale, NJ: Erlbaum.

Lang, H. (1989). Academic development and preparation for work. In M. Wang, M. Reynolds, & H. Walberg (Eds.), *The handbook of special education: Research and practice* (Vol. 3) (pp. 71–93). Oxford, England: Pergamon.

Lang, H., & Conner, K. (1988). Faculty development: Meeting the needs of postsecondary educators of deaf students. *American Annals of the Deaf, 133,* 26–29.

Lang, H., & Propp, G. (1982). Science education for hearing-impaired students: State-of-the-art. *American Annals of the Deaf, 127,* 860–869.

LaSasso, C. (1978). National survey of materials and procedures used to teach reading to hearing-impaired children. *American Annals of the Deaf, 123,* 22–30.

LaSasso, C. (1986). A comparison of visual matching test-taking strategies of comparably-aged normal-hearing and hearing-impaired subjects with comparable reading levels. *Volta Review, 88,* 231–238.

LaSasso, C. (1987a). Survey of reading instruction for hearing-impaired students in the United States. *Volta Review, 89,* 85–98.

LaSasso, C. (1987b). What parents of hearing-impaired need to know about student reading levels. *American Annals of the Deaf, 132,* 218–220.

LaSasso, C., & Davey, B. (1987). The relationship between lexical knowledge and reading comprehension for prelingually, profoundly hearing-impaired students. *Volta Review, 89,* 211–220.

Leiter, R. (1979). *Leiter international performance scale: Instruction manual.* Chicago, IL: Stoelting.

Levine, E. (1976). Psycho-cultural determinants in personality development. *Volta Review, 78,* 258–267.

Levine, E. (1981). *The ecology of early deafness: Guides to fashioning environments and psychological assessments.* New York: Columbia University Press.

Levitt, H. (1989). Speech and hearing in communication. In M. Wang, M. Reynolds, & H. Walberg (Eds.), *The handbook of special education: Research and practice* (Vol. 3) (pp. 23–45). Oxford, England: Pergamon.

Libbey, S., & Pronovost, W. (1980). Communication practices of mainstreamed hearing-impaired adolescents. *Volta Review, 82,* 197–213.

Liben, L. (Ed.). (1978). *Deaf children: Developmental perspectives.* New York: Academic Press.

Liben, L. (1984). The development and use of memory strategies by deaf children and adults. In D. Martin (Ed.), *International symposium on cognition, education, and deafness:* Working papers (Vol. 1) (pp. 239–256). Washington, DC: Gallaudet University Press.

Lichtenstein, E. (1984). Deaf working memory processes and English language skills. In D. Martin (Ed.), *International symposium on cognition, education, and deafness:* Working papers (Vol. 2) (pp. 331–360). Washington, DC: Gallaudet University Press.

Lichtenstein, E. (1985). Deaf working memory processes and English language skills. In D. Martin (Ed.), *Cognition, education, and deafness: Directions for research and instruction* (pp. 111–114). Washington, DC: Gallaudet University Press.

Lichtenstein, E. (n.d.). The relationships between reading processes and English skills of deaf college students: Parts I and II. [Unpublished manuscript].

Liddell, S. (1980). *American Sign Language syntax.* The Hague: Mouton.

Liden, G., & Kankkunen, A. (1969). Visual reinforcement audiometry. *Acta Otolaryngologica, 67,* 281–292.

Lindsay, P., & Norman, D. (1972). *Human information processing.* New York: Academic Press.

Ling, D. (1976). *Speech and the hearing impaired child: Theory and practice.* Washington, DC: Alexander Graham Bell Association for the Deaf.

Ling, D. (Ed.). (1984a). *Early intervention for hearing-impaired children: Oral options.* San Diego, CA: College-Hill.

Ling, D. (Ed.). (1984b). *Early intervention for hearing-impaired children: Total communication options.* San Diego, CA: College-Hill.

Ling, D. (1986). Devices and procedures for auditory learning. *Volta Review, 88*(5), 19–28.

Ling, D., & Clarke, B. (1975). Cued speech: An evaluative study. *American Annals of the Deaf, 120,* 480–488.

Ling, D., & Ling, A. (1978). *Aural habilitation: The foundations of verbal learning in hearing-impaired children.* Washington, DC: Alexander Graham Bell Association for the Deaf.

Livingston, S. (1983). Levels of development in the language of deaf children: ASL grammatical process, SE structures, and semantic features. *Sign Language Studies, 40,* 193–286.

Lloyd, L. (Ed.). (1976). *Communication assessment and intervention strategies.* Baltimore, MD: University Park Press.

Lloyd, L., & Karlan, G. (1984). Nonspeech communication symbols and systems: Where have we been and where are we going? *Journal of Speech and Hearing Disorders, 28,* 3–20.

Lloyd, L., Spradlin, J., & Reid, M. (1968). An operant audiometric procedure for difficult-to-test patients. *Journal of Speech and Hearing Disorders, 33,* 236–245.

Long, N., Fitzgerald, C., Sutton, K., & Rollins, J. (1983). The auditory-verbal approach: Ellison, a case study. *Volta Review, 85,* 27–30, 35.

Looney, P., & Rose, S. (1979). The acquisition of inflectional suffixes by deaf youngsters using written and fingerspelled modes. *American Annals of the Deaf, 124,* 765–769.

Lucas, E. (1980). *Semantic and pragmatic language disorders: Assessment and remediation.* Rockville, MD: Aspen Systems.

Luetke-Stahlman, B. (1982). A philosophy for assessing the language proficiency of hearing-impaired students to promote English literacy. *American Annals of the Deaf, 127,* 844–851.

Luetke-Stahlman, B. (1983). Using bilingual instructional models in teaching hearing-impaired students. *American Annals of the Deaf, 128,* 873–877.

Luetke-Stahlman, B. (1988a). The benefit of oral English-only as compared with signed input to hearing-impaired students. *Volta Review, 90,* 349–361.

Luetke-Stahlman, B. (1988b). Documenting syntactically and semantically incomplete bimodal input to hearing-impaired subjects. *American Annals of the Deaf, 133,* 230–234.

Luetke-Stahlman, B., & Weiner, F. (1982). Assessing language and/or system preferences of Spanish-deaf preschoolers. *American Annals of the Deaf, 127,* 789–796.

Luterman, D. (1984). *Counseling the communicatively disordered and their families.* Boston, MA: Little, Brown.

MacNamara, J. (1972). The cognitive basis of language learning in infants. *Psychological Review, 79,* 1–13.

MacNamara, J. (Ed.). (1977). *Language learning and thought.* New York: Academic Press.

Maestas y Moores, J. (1980). Early linguistic environment. *Sign Language Studies, 26,* 1–13.

Marbury, N., & Mackinson-Smyth, J. (1986). *ASL and English: A partnership.* Paper presented at the American Sign Language Research and Teaching Conference, Newark, California, April, 1986.

Markowicz, H. (1980). Myths about American Sign Language. In H. Lane and F. Grosjean (Eds.), *Recent perspectives on American Sign Language* (pp. 1–6). Hillsdale, NJ: Erlbaum.

Marmor, G., & Pettito, L. (1979). Simultaneous communication in the classroom: How well is English grammar represented? *Sign Language Studies, 23,* 99–136.

Marshall, W., & Quigley, S. (1970). *Quantitative and qualitative analysis of syntactic structure in the written language of deaf students.* Urbana, IL: University of Illinois, Institute for Research on Exceptional Children.

Martin, D. (Ed.). (1985). *Cognition, education, and deafness: Directions for research and instruction.* Washington, DC: Gallaudet University Press.

Martin, F. (1986a). Audiology in perspective. In D. Luterman (Ed.), *Deafness in perspective* (pp. 15–33). San Diego, CA: College-Hill.

Martin, F. (1986b). *Basic audiometry.* Austin, TX: Pro-Ed.

Martin, F. (1987). Speech tests with preschool children. In F. Martin (Ed.), *Hearing disorders in children: Pediatric audiology* (pp. 265–298). Austin, TX: Pro-Ed.

Mason, J., & Au, K. (1986). *Reading instruction for today.* Glenview, IL: Scott, Foresman.

Mathy-Laikko, P., Ratcliff, A., Villarruel, F., & Yoder, D. (1988). Augmentative communication systems. In M. Bullis & G. Fielding (Eds.), *Communication development in young children with deaf-blindness: Literature review* (pp. 225–261). Monmouth, OR: Oregon State System of Higher Education, Communication Skills Center for Young Children with Deaf-Blindness, Teaching Research Division.

Maxwell, M. (1983). Simultaneous communication in the classroom: What do deaf children learn? *Sign Language Studies, 39,* 95–112.

Maxwell, M. (1985a). Introduction: Ethnography and education of deaf children. *Sign Language Studies, 47,* 97–108.

Maxwell, M. (1985b). Sign language instruction and teacher preparation. *Sign Language Studies, 47,* 173–180.

Mavilya, M. (1982). Assessment, curriculum, and intervention strategies for hearing-impaired mentally retarded children. In D. Tweedie & E. Shroyer (Eds.), *The multihandicapped hearing-impaired: Identification and instruction* (pp. 113–123). Washington, DC: Gallaudet University Press.

McAnally, P., Rose, S., & Quigley, S. (1987). *Language learning practices with deaf children.* San Diego, CA: Little, Brown.

McCartney, B. (1986). An investigation of the factors contributing to the ability of hearing-impaired children to communicate orally as perceived by oral deaf adults and parents and teachers of the hearing impaired. *Volta Review, 88,* 133–143.

McClelland, K. (1978). Hearing mechanism. In P. Skinner & R. Shelton, *Speech, language, and hearing: Normal process and disorders* (pp. 102–121). Reading, MA: Addison-Wesley.

McClure, A. (1977). Academic achievement of mainstreamed hearing-impaired children with congenital rubella syndrome. *Volta Review, 79,* 379–384.

McClure, W. (1969). Historical perspectives in the education of the deaf. In J. Griffith (Ed.), *Persons with hearing loss* (pp. 3–30). Springfield, IL: Thomas.

McCrone, W. (1979). Learned helplessness and level of underachievement among deaf adolescents. *Psychology in the Schools, 16,* 430–434.

McCroskey, R. (1967). Early education of infants with severe auditory impairments. *Proceedings of the International Conference on Oral Education of the Deaf* (pp. 1891–1905). Washington, DC: Alexander Graham Bell Association for the Deaf.

McCroskey, R. (1968). *Final report of a four year home training program.* Paper presented at the Alexander Graham Bell National Convention, San Francisco, California.

McDaniel, E. (1980). Visual memory in the deaf. *American Annals of the Deaf, 125,* 17–20.

McDonald, E., & Schultz, A. (1973). Conversation boards for cerebral palsied children. *Journal of Speech and Hearing Disorders, 38,* 73–88.

McGarr, N., Head, J., Friedman, M., Behrman, A., & Youdelman, K. (1986). The use of visual and tactile sensory aids in speech production training: A preliminary report. *Journal of Rehabilitation Research and Development, 23,* 101–110.

McNew, S., & Bates, E. (1984). Pragmatic bases for language acquisition. In R. Naremore (Ed.), *Language science* (pp. 67–105). San Diego, CA: College-Hill.

Meadow, K. (1968). Early manual communication in relation to the deaf child's intellectual, social, and communicative functioning. *American Annals of the Deaf, 113,* 29–41.

Meadow, K. (1980). *Deafness and child development.* Berkeley, CA: University of California Press.

Meadow, K. (1983). An instrument for assessment of social-emotional adjustment in hearing-impaired preschoolers. *American Annals of the Deaf, 128,* 826–834.

Meadow, K., Greenberg, M., Erting, C., & Carmichael, H. (1981). Interactions of deaf mothers and deaf preschool children: Comparisons with three other groups of deaf and hearing dyads. *American Annals of the Deaf, 126,* 454–468.

Meadow, K., Karchmer, M., Petersen, L., & Rudner, L. (1980). *Meadow/Kendall social-emotional assessment inventory for deaf students: Manual.* Washington, DC: Gallaudet University, Pre-College Programs.

Mencher, G. (1983). Hearing loss and multiple handicaps: Occurrence and effects. In G. Mencher & S. Gerber (Eds.), *The multiply handicapped hearing-impaired child* (pp. 5–11). New York: Grune & Stratton.

Mencher, G., & Gerber, S. (Eds.). (1983). *The multiply handicapped hearing-impaired child.* New York: Grune & Stratton.

Messerly, C., & Aram, D. (1980). Academic achievement of hearing-impaired students of hearing parents and of hearing-impaired parents: Another look. *Volta Review, 82,* 25–32.

Meyerhoff, W. (1986). *Disorders of hearing.* Austin, TX: Pro-Ed.

Michael, M., & Paul, P. (in press). *Early intervention for infants with deaf-blindness.* Columbus, OH: Ohio State University, Department of Educational Services and Research. ERIC Document Reproduction Service.

Miller, J., Chapman, R., & Bedrosian, J. (1977). *Defining developmentally disabled subjects for research: The relationships between etiology, cognitive development, language and communicative performance.* Paper presented at the Second Annual Boston University Conference on Language Development, Boston, Massachusetts.

Miller, J., & Pfingst, B. (1984). Cochlear implants. In C. Berlin (Ed.), *Hearing science* (pp. 309–339). San Diego, CA: College-Hill.

Miles, D. (1976). *Gestures: Poetry in Sign Language.* Northridge, CA: Joyce Publishers.

Mindel, E., & Feldman, V. (1987). The impact of deaf children on their families. In E. Mindel & M. Vernon (Eds.), *They grow in silence: Understanding deaf children and adults* (pp. 1–29). Boston, MA: Little, Brown.

Mohay, H. (1983). The effects of cued speech on the language development of three deaf children. *Sign Language Studies, 38,* 25–47.

Moog, J., & Geers, A. (1985). EPIC: A program to accelerate academic progress in profoundly hearing-impaired children. *Volta Review, 87,* 259–277.

Moores, D. (1972). Neo-oralism and education of the deaf in the Soviet Union. *Exceptional Children, 38,* 377–384.

Moores, D. (1982). The language of hearing-impaired mentally retarded children. In. D. Tweedie & E. Shroyer (Eds.), *The multihandicapped hearing-impaired: Identification and instruction* (pp. 201–210). Washington, DC: Gallaudet University Press.

Moores, D. (1985a). Educational programs and services for hearing-impaired children: Issues and options. In F. Powell, T. Finitzo-Hieber, S. Friel-Patti, & D. Henderson (Eds.), *Education of the hearing-impaired child* (pp. 5–20). San Diego, CA: College-Hill.

Moores, D. (1985b). Early intervention programs for hearing-impaired children: A longitudinal assessment. In K. Nelson (Ed.), *Children's language: Volume V* (pp. 159–195). Hillsdale, NJ: Erlbaum.

Moores, D. (1987). *Educating the deaf: Psychology, principles, and practices* (3rd ed.). Boston, MA: Houghton Mifflin.

Moores, D., & Kluwin, T. (1986). Issues in school placement. In A. Schildroth & M. Karchmer (Eds.), *Deaf children in America* (pp. 105–123). San Diego, CA: College-Hill.

Moores, D., Kluwin, T., & Mertens, D. (1985). *High school programs for the deaf in metropolitan areas* (Research Monograph No. 3). Washington, DC: Gallaudet University Press.

Moores, D., Weiss, K., & Goodwin, M. (1978). Early intervention programs for hearing-impaired children. *American Annals of the Deaf, 123,* 925–936.

Morgan, A. (1987). Causes and treatment of hearing loss in children. In F. Martin (Ed.), Hearing disorders in children: Pediatric audiology (pp. 5–48). Austin, TX: Pro-Ed.

Morkovin, B. (1960). Experiment in teaching deaf preschool children in the Soviet Union. *Volta Review, 62,* 260–268.

Mosenthal, P. (1983). On defining writing and classroom writing competence. In P. Mosenthal, L. Tamor, & S. Walmsley (Eds.), *Research on writing: Principles and methods* (pp. 26–71). White Plains, NY: Longman.

Mosenthal, P., Tamor, L., & Walmsley, S. (Eds.). (1983). *Research on writing: Principles and methods.* White Plains, NY: Longman.

Mulholland, A. (Ed.). (1981). *Oral education today and tomorrow*. Washington, DC: Alexander Graham Bell Association for the Deaf.

Muma, J. (1986). *Language acquisition: A functionalistic perspective*. Austin, TX: Pro-Ed.

Murphy-Berman, V., Witters, L., & Harding, R. (1985). Hearing-impaired students' performance on the Piagetian liquid horizontality test. In D. Martin (Ed.), *Cognition, education, and deafness: Directions for research and instruction* (pp. 47–49). Washington, DC: Gallaudet University Press.

Myklebust, H. (1964). *The psychology of deafness* (2nd ed.). New York: Grune & Stratton.

Myklebust, H., & Brutton, M. (1953). A study of the visual perception of deaf children. *Acta Oto-Laryngologica*, Supplementum *105*, 1–126.

Naglieri, J. (1987). *Evidence for the planning, attention, simultaneous and successive cognitive processing theory*. Paper presented at the Annual Convention of the American Psychological Association, New York.

Naglieri, J., & Das, J. (in press). Planning-Arousal-Simultaneous-Successive (PASS): A model for assessment. *Journal of School Psychology*.

Naiman, D. (1979). Educating severely handicapped deaf children. *American Annals of the Deaf, 124*, 381–396.

Naiman, D. (1982). Educational programming for hearing-impaired mentally retarded adolescents. In D. Tweedie & E. Shroyer (Eds.), *The multihandicapped hearing-impaired: Identification and instruction* (pp. 148–161). Washington, DC: Gallaudet University Press.

Naremore, R. (Ed.). (1984). *Language science*. San Diego, CA: College-Hill.

Neville, H., & Bellugi, U. (1978). Patterns of cerebral specialization in congenitally deaf adults: A preliminary report. In P. Siple (Ed.), *Understanding language through sign language research* (pp. 239–260). New York: Academic Press.

Newport, E., & Meier, R. (1986). The acquisition of American Sign Language. In D. Slobin (Ed.), *The cross-linguistic study of language acquisition* (pp. 881–938). Hillsdale, NJ: Erlbaum.

Nicholls, G., & Ling, D. (1982). Cued speech and the reception of spoken language. *Journal of Speech and Hearing Research, 25*, 262–269.

Nickerson, R. (1975). Characteristics of the speech of deaf persons. *Volta Review, 77*, 342–362.

Niemoeller, A. (1978). Hearing aids. In H. Davis & S. R. Silverman, *Hearing and deafness* (4th ed.) (pp. 293–337). New York: Holt, Rinehart and Winston.

Nix, G. (1976). *Mainstream education for hearing-impaired children and youth*. New York: Grune & Stratton.

Northcott, W. (1973). *The hearing-impaired child in a regular classroom: Preschool, elementary, and secondary years*. Washington, DC: Alexander Graham Bell Association for the Deaf.

Northcott, W. (Ed.). (1984). *Introduction to oral interpreting: Principles and practices*. Baltimore, MD: University Park Press.

Novelli-Olmstead, T., & Ling, D. (1984). Speech production and speech discrimination by hearing-impaired children. *Volta Review, 86*, 72–80.

Nystrand, M., & Knapp, J. (1987). *Review of selected national tests of writing and reading*. University of Wisconsin, National Center on Effective Secondary Schools, School of Education, Madison. [Unpublished manuscript].

Obler, L., Zatorre, R., Galloway, L., & Vaid, J. (1982). Cerebral lateralization in bilinguals: Methodological issues. *Brain and Language, 15*, 40–54.

O'Brien, D. (1987). Reflection-impulsivity in total communication and oral deaf and hearing children: A developmental study. *American Annals of the Deaf, 132*, 213–217.

O'Connor, L. (1979). *Short-term memory and coding strategies in the deaf*. Unpublished doctoral dissertation, University of Northern Colorado.

Ogden, P. (1979). *Experiences and attitudes of oral deaf adults regarding oralism.* Unpublished doctoral dissertation, University of Illinois, Urbana-Champaign.

O'Neill, J., & Oyer, H. (1981). *Visual communication for the hard of hearing: History, research, methods* (2nd ed.). Englewood Cliffs, NJ: Prentice-Hall.

O'Neill, M. (1973). *The receptive language competence of deaf children in the use of the base structure rules of transformational generative grammar.* Unpublished doctoral dissertation, University of Pittsburg, Pennsylvania.

Orlansky, M., & Bonvillian, J. (1984). The role of iconicity in early sign language acquisition. *Journal of Speech and Hearing Disorders, 49,* 287–292.

Orlansky, M., & Bonvillian, J. (1985). Sign language acquisition: Language development in children of deaf parents and implications for other populations. *Merrill-Palmer Quarterly, 31,* 127–143.

Ottem, E. (1980). An analysis of cognitive studies with deaf subjects. *American Annals of the Deaf, 125,* 564–575.

Ouellette, S. (1985). *National project on higher education for deaf students.* Paper presented at a meeting of the Association on Handicapped Student Service Programs in Post-Secondary Education, Atlanta, Georgia.

Padden, C. (1980). The Deaf community and the culture of Deaf people. In C. Baker & R. Battison (Eds.), *Sign Language and the Deaf community: Essays in honor of William C. Stokoe* (pp. 89–103). Silver Spring, MD: National Association of the Deaf.

Padden, C., & Le Master, B. (1985). An alphabet on hand: The acquisition of fingerspelling in deaf children. *Sign Language Studies, 47,* 161–172.

Pascoe, D. (1986). *Hearing aids.* Austin, TX: Pro-Ed.

Paul, J., & Epanchin, B. (Eds.). (1982). *Emotional disturbance in children.* Columbus, OH: Merrill.

Paul, P. (1984). *The comprehension of multimeaning words from selected frequency levels by deaf and hearing subjects.* Unpublished doctoral dissertation, University of Illinois, Urbana-Champaign.

Paul, P. (1985). Reading and other language-variant populations. In C. King & S. Quigley, *Reading and deafness* (pp. 251–289). San Diego, CA: College-Hill.

Paul, P. (1987). Perspective on using American Sign Language to teach English as a second language. *Teaching English to Deaf and Second-Language Students (TEDSL), 5*(3), 10–16.

Paul, P. (1988a). The effects of viewing angle and visibility on speechreading comprehension ability. *Hearsay: The Journal of the Ohio Speech and Hearing Association,* Fall, 100–103.

Paul, P. (1988b). American Sign Language and English: A bilingual minority-language immersion program. *The Convention of American Instructors of the Deaf (CAID) News 'N' Notes, 1*(4), 3–5.

Paul, P. (in press). Depth of vocabulary knowledge and reading comprehension: Implications for hearing-impaired and learning-disabled students. *Academic Therapy.*

Paul, P., & Gramly, C. (1986). *Is reading in L1 really necessary for reading in L2, especially when L1 has no written form? A perspective on ASL and English.* Based on a paper presented at the Delaware Symposium on Language Studies VIII, University of Delaware, Department of Linguistics, Newark, Delaware, October, 1986. (ERIC Document Reproduction Service No. 285 320).

Paul, P., & O'Rourke, J. (1988). Multimeaning words and reading comprehension: Implications for special education students. *Remedial and Special Education (RASE), 9*(3), 42–52.

Paul, P., & Quigley, S. (1987a). Some effects of early hearing impairment on English language development. In F. Martin (Ed.), *Hearing disorders in children: Pediatric audiology* (49–80). Austin, TX: Pro-Ed.

Paul, P., & Quigley, S. (1987b). Using American Sign Language to teach English. In P. McAnally, S. Rose, & S. Quigley, *Language learning practices with deaf children* (pp. 139–166). San Diego, CA: Little, Brown.

Payne, J.-A., & Quigley, S. (1987). *Hearing-impaired children's comprehension of verb-particle combinations. Volta Review, 89,* 133–143.

Pearson, P. D. (1984). *Reading comprehension instruction: Six necessary changes.* (Reading Educ. Rep. No. 54). Champaign, IL: University of Illinois, Center for the Study of Reading.

Pearson, P. D. (1985). *The comprehension revolution: A twenty-four-year history of process and practice related to reading comprehension.* (Reading Educ. Rep. No. 57). Champaign, IL: University of Illinois, Center for the Study of Reading.

Pearson, P. D., Barr, R., Kamil, M., & Mosenthal, P. (1984). *Handbook of reading research.* White Plains, NY: Longman.

Pearson, P. D., & Valencia, S. (1986). *Assessment, accountability, and professional prerogative.* Paper presented at the 1986 National Reading Conference in Austin, Texas, December.

Pendergrass, R., & Hodges, M. (1976). Deaf students in group problem-solving situations: A study of the interactive process. *American Annals of the Deaf, 121,* 327–330.

Perigoe, C., & Ling, D. (1986). Generalization of speech skills in hearing-impaired children. *Volta Review, 88,* 351–366.

Perry, A., & Silverman, S. R. (1978). Speechreading. In H. Davis & S. R. Silverman, *Hearing and deafness* (4th ed.) (pp. 375–387). New York: Holt, Rinehart and Winston.

Pettito, L. (1986). *Language vs gesture: Why sign languages are NOT acquired earlier than spoken languages.* Paper presented at the 1986 Conference of Theoretical Issues in Sign Language Research, Rochester, New York.

Pflaster, G. (1980). A factor analysis of variables related to academic performance of hearing-impaired children in regular classes. *Volta Review, 82,* 71–84.

Phillips, W. (1963). *Influence of preschool training on language arts, arithmetic concepts, and socialization of young deaf children.* Unpublished doctoral dissertation, Columbia University, New York.

Piaget, J. (1952). *The origins of intelligence in children.* New York: Norton.

Piaget, J. (1955). *The language and thought of the child.* New York: Meridian Books.

Piaget, J., & Inhelder, B. (1969). *The psychology of the child.* New York: Basic Books.

Pintner, R. (1918). The measurement of language ability and language progress of deaf children. *Volta Review, 20,* 755–764.

Pintner, R. (1927). The survey of schools for the deaf—V. *American Annals of the Deaf, 72,* 377–414.

Pintner, R., Eisenson, J., & Stanton, M. (1941). *The psychology of the physically handicapped.* New York: Crofts.

Pintner, R., & Lev, J. (1939). The intelligence of the hard-of-hearing school child. *Journal of Genetic Psychology, 55,* 31–48.

Pintner, R., & Paterson, D. (1916). A measurement of the language ability of deaf children. *Psychological Review, 23,* 413–436.

Pintner, R., & Paterson, D. (1917). The ability of deaf and hearing children to follow printed directions. *American Annals of the Deaf, 62,* 448–472.

Pintner, R., & Reamer, J. (1920). A mental and educational survey of schools for the deaf. *American Annals of the Deaf, 65,* 451–472.

Poizner, H., Battison, R., & Lane, H. (1979). Cerebral asymmetry for American Sign Language: The effects of moving stimuli. *Brain and Language, 7,* 351–362.

Poizner, H., & Lane, H. (1979). Cerebral asymmetry in the perception of American Sign Language. *Brain and Language, 7,* 210–226.

Pollack, D. (Ed.). (1980). *Amplification for the hearing-impaired* (2nd ed.). New York: Grune & Stratton.

Pollack, D. (1984). An acoupedic program. In D. Ling (Ed.), *Early intervention for hearing-impaired children: Oral options* (pp. 181–253). San Diego, CA: College-Hill.

Pollack, D. (1985). *Educational audiology for the limited-hearing infant and preschooler* (2nd ed.). Springfield, IL: Thomas.

Poplin, D. (1972). *Communities: A survey of theories and methods of research.* New York: Macmillan.

Powers, A., Elliott, R., & Funderburg, R. (1987). Learning disabled hearing-impaired students: Are they being identified? *Volta Review, 89,* 99–105.

Powers, A., & Wilgus, S. (1983). Linguistic complexity in the written language of deaf children. *Volta Review, 85,* 201–210.

Premack, D. (1970). A functional analysis of language. *Journal of Experimental Analysis of Behavior, 14,* 107–125.

Premack, D. (1971). Language in chimpanzees? *Science, 172,* 808–822.

Pressnell, L. (1973). Hearing-impaired children's comprehension and production of syntax in oral language. *Journal of Speech and Hearing Research, 16,* 12–21.

Provence, A. (1974). Early intervention: Experiences in a services-centered research program. In D. Bergman (Ed.), *The infant at risk* (pp. 25–39). New York: Intercontinental Medical Books.

Public Law 94–142. (1975). *Public Law 94–142: The education of all handicapped children act of 1975.* November, 1975.

Pugh, C. (1946). Summaries from appraisal of the silent reading abilities of acoustically handicapped children. *American Annals of the Deaf, 91,* 331–349.

Quarrington, B., & Solomon, B. (1975). A current study of the social maturity of deaf students. *Canadian Journal of Behavioral Science, 7,* 70–77.

Quay, H., & Werry, J. (Eds.). (1979). *Psychopathological disorders of childhood* (2nd ed.). New York: Wiley.

Quigley, S. (1969). *The influence of fingerspelling on the development of language, communication, and educational achievement in deaf children.* Urbana, IL: University of Illinois, Institute for Research on Exceptional Children.

Quigley, S., & Frisina, R. (1961). *Institutionalization and psychoeducational development of deaf children* (CEC Research Monograph). Washington, DC: Council on Exceptional Children.

Quigley, S., Jenne, W., & Phillips, S. (1969). *Deaf students in colleges and universities.* Washington, DC: Alexander Graham Bell Association for the Deaf.

Quigley, S., & King, C. (1981–1984). *Reading milestones.* Beaverton, OR: Dormac.

Quigley, S., & King, C. (1982). The language development of deaf children and youth. In S. Rosenberg (Ed.), *Handbook of applied psycholinguistics: Major thrusts of research and theory* (pp. 429–475). Hillsdale, NJ: Erlbaum.

Quigley, S., & Kretschmer, R. E. (1982). *The education of deaf children: Issues, theory, and practice.* Austin, TX: Pro-Ed.

Quigley, S., & Paul, P. (1984a). *Language and deafness.* San Diego, CA: College-Hill.

Quigley, S., & Paul, P. (1984b). ASL and ESL? *Topics in Early Childhood Special Education, 3*(4), 17–26.

Quigley, S., & Paul, P. (1986). A perspective on academic achievement. In D. Luterman (Ed.), *Deafness in perspective* (pp. 55–86). San Diego, CA: College-Hill.

Quigley, S., & Paul, P. (1987). Deafness and language development. In S. Rosenberg (Ed.), *Advances in applied psycholinguistics,* Volume 1: *Disorders of first language development* (pp. 180–219). Cambridge: Cambridge University Press.

Quigley, S., & Paul, P. (1989). English language development. In M. Wang, M. Reynolds, & H. Walberg (Eds.), *The handbook of special education: Research and practice* (Vol. 3) (pp. 3–21). Oxford, England: Pergamon.

Quigley, S., Paul, P., McAnally, P., Rose, S., & Payne, J.-A. (in press). *Reading bridge.* San Diego, CA: Dormac.

Quigley, S., & Power, D. (Eds.). (1979). *TSA syntax program.* Beaverton, OR: Dormac.

Quigley, S., Steinkamp, M., Power, D., & Jones, B. (1978). *Test of syntactic abilities.* San Diego, CA: Dormac.

Quigley, S., & Thomure, R. (1968). *Some effects of hearing impairment upon school performance.* Urbana, IL: University of Illinois, Institute for Research on Exceptional Children.

Quigley, S., Wilbur, R., Power, D., Montanelli, D., & Steinkamp, M. (1976). *Syntactic structures in the language of deaf children* (Final Report). Urbana, IL: University of Illinois, Institute for Child Behavior and Development. (ERIC Document Reproduction Service No. ED 119 447)

Raffin, M. (1976). *The acquisition of inflectional morphemes by deaf children using Seeing Essential English.* Unpublished doctoral dissertation, University of Iowa, Iowa City.

Raffin, M., Davis, J., & Gilman, L. (1978). Comprehension of inflectional morphemes by deaf children exposed to a visual English sign system. *Journal of Speech and Hearing Research, 21,* 387–400.

Raimes, A. (1983). *Techniques in teaching writing.* New York: Oxford University Press.

Ratner, V. (1985). Spatial-relationship deficits in deaf children: The effect on communication and classroom performance. *American Annals of the Deaf, 130,* 250–254.

Rawlings, B., & Gentile, A. (1970). *Additional handicapping conditions, age at onset of hearing loss, and other characteristics of hearing-impaired students—United States: 1968–1969.* (Series D, No. 3). Washington, DC: Gallaudet University, Center for Assessment and Demographic Studies.

Rawlings, B., & King, S. (1986). Postsecondary educational opportunities for deaf students. In A. Schildroth & M. Karchmer (Eds.), *Deaf children in America* (pp. 231–257). San Diego, CA: College-Hill.

Reagan, T. (1985). The deaf as a linguistic minority: Educational considerations. *Harvard Educational Review, 55,* 265–277.

Redden, M. (1979). Summary report for a project titled *A design for utilizing successful disabled scientists as role models.* Washington, DC: American Association for the Advancement of Science.

Reich, C., Hambleton, D., & Houldin, B. (1977). The integration of hearing-impaired children in regular classrooms. *American Annals of the Deaf, 122,* 534–543.

Reich, P., & Bick, M. (1977). How visible is visible English? *Sign Language Studies, 14,* 59–72.

Reynolds, C. (1985). *The effects of instruction in cognitive revision strategies on the writing skills of secondary learning disabled students.* Unpublished doctoral dissertation, Ohio State University, Columbus.

Reynolds, H. (1986). Performance of deaf college students on a criterion-referenced, modified cloze test of reading comprehension. *American Annals of the Deaf, 131,* 361–364.

Reynolds, M., & Birch, J. (1977). *Teaching exceptional children in all America's schools: A first course for teachers and principals.* Reston, VA: Council for Exceptional Children.

Ries, P. (1973). Associations between achievement test performance and selected characteristics of hearing-impaired students in special education programs. In *Further studies in achievement testing, hearing-impaired students, United States, Spring, 1971* (pp. 3–22). (Series D, No. 13). Washington, DC: Gallaudet University, Center for Assessment and Demographic Studies.

Ries, P. (1986). Characteristics of hearing impaired youth in the general population and of students in special education programs for the hearing-impaired. In A. Schildroth & M. Karchmer (Eds.), *Deaf children in America* (pp. 1–31). San Diego, CA: College-Hill.

Rittenhouse, R. (1977). *Horizontal decalage: The development of conservation in deaf students and the effect of the task instructions on their performance.* Unpublished doctoral dissertation, University of Illinois, Urbana-Champaign.

Rittenhouse, R., Morreau, K., & Iran-Nejad, A. (1981). Metaphor and conservation in deaf and hard-of-hearing children. *American Annals of the Deaf, 126,* 450–453.

Robbins, N. (1983). The effects of signed text on the reading comprehension of hearing-impaired children. *American Annals of the Deaf, 128,* 40–44.

Robinson, H., & Robinson, N. (1965). *The mentally retarded child: A psychological approach.* New York: McGraw-Hill.

Rodda, M., & Grove, C. (1987). *Language, cognition, and deafness.* Hillsdale, NJ: Erlbaum.

Roeser, R. (1986). *Diagnostic audiology.* Austin, TX: Pro-Ed.

Roeser, R., & Yellin, W. (1987). Pure-tone tests with preschool children. In F. Martin (Ed.), *Hearing disorders in children: Pediatric audiology* (pp. 217–264). Austin, TX: Pro-Ed.

Rosenstein, J. (1961). Perception, cognition, and language in deaf children. *Exceptional children, 27,* 276–284.

Ross, M. (1977). Binaural versus monaural hearing aids. In F. Bess (Ed.), *Childhood deafness: Causation, assessment, and management* (pp. 235–249). New York: Grune & Stratton.

Ross, M. (1986a). *Aural habilitation.* Austin, TX: Pro-Ed.

Ross, M. (1986b). A perspective on amplification: Then and now. In D. Luterman (Ed.), *Deafness in perspective* (pp. 35–53). San Diego, CA: College-Hill.

Ross, M., Brackett, D., & Maxon, A. (1982). *Hard of hearing children in regular schools.* Englewood Cliffs, NJ: Prentice-Hall.

Ross, M., & Calvert, D. (1984). Semantics of deafness revisited: Total communication and the use and misuse of residual hearing. *Audiology, 9,* 127–143.

Ross, M., & Lerman, J. (1970). A picture identification test for hearing-impaired children. *Journal of Speech and Hearing Research, 13,* 44–53.

Ross, M., & Tomassetti, C. (1980). Hearing aid selection for preverbal hearing-impaired children. In D. Pollack (Ed.), *Amplification for the hearing-impaired* (2nd ed.) (pp. 213–254). New York: Grune & Stratton.

Rubin, A., & Hansen, J. (1986). Reading and writing: How are the first two *R's* related? In J. Orasanu (Ed.), *Reading comprehension: From research to practice* (pp. 163–170). Hillsdale, NJ: Erlbaum.

Rubin, R., & Balow, B. (1978). Prevalence of teacher identified behavior problems: A longitudinal study. *Exceptional children, 45,* 102–111.

Rumelhart, D. (1977). Toward an interactive model of reading. In S. Dornic (Ed.), *Attention and performance VI* (pp. 573–603). New York: Academic Press.

Sabatino, D. (1982). Preparing individual educational programs (IEPs). In D. Sabatino & L. Mann, *A handbook of diagnostic and prescriptive teaching* (pp. 19–70). Rockville, MD: Aspen.

Sabatino, D., & Mann, L. (1982). *A handbook of diagnostic and prescriptive teaching.* Rockville, MD: Aspen.

Sachs, J. (1967). Recognition memory for syntactic and semantic aspects of connected discourse. *Perception and Psychophysics, 2,* 437–442.

Salvia, J., & Ysseldyke, J. (1985). *Assessment in special and remedial education* (3rd ed.). Boston, MA: Houghton Mifflin.

Sanders, D. (1982). *Aural rehabilitation: A management model* (2nd ed.). Englewood Cliffs, NJ: Prentice-Hall.

Sapir, E. (1921). *Language.* New York: Harcourt, Brace, & World.

Sarachan-Deily, A. (1982). Hearing-impaired and hearing readers' sentence processing errors. *Volta Review, 84,* 81–95.

Sarachan-Deily, A. (1985). Written narratives of deaf and hearing students: Story recall and inference. *Journal of Speech and Hearing Research, 28,* 151–159.

Saur, R., & Stinson, M. (1986). Characteristics of successful mainstreamed hearing-impaired students: A review of selected research. *Journal of Rehabilitation of the Deaf, 20,* 15–21.

Schein, J. (1975). Deaf students with other disabilities. *American Annals of the Deaf, 120,* 92–99.

Schein, J. (1978). The deaf community. In H. Davis & S. R. Silverman, *Hearing and deafness* (pp. 511–524). New York: Holt, Rinehart and Winston.

Schein, J., & Delk, M. (1974). *The deaf population of the United States.* Silver Spring, MD: National Association of the Deaf.

Schiefelbusch, R. (Ed.). (1980). *Nonspeech language and communication: Analysis and intervention.* Baltimore, MD: University Park Press.

Schildroth, A. (1986). Residential schools for deaf students: A decade in review. In A. Schildroth & M. Karchmer (Eds.), *Deaf children in America* (pp. 83–104). San Diego, CA: College-Hill.

Schildroth, A., & Karchmer, M. (Eds.). (1986). *Deaf children in America.* San Diego, CA: College-Hill.

Schlesinger, H., & Meadow, K. (1972). *Sound and sign: Childhood deafness and mental health.* Berkeley, CA: University of California Press.

Schlesinger, H., & Meadow, K. (Eds.). (1976). *Studies of family interaction, language acquisition, and deafness* (Final Report). San Francisco, CA: University of California, Office of Maternal and Child Health, Bureau of Community Health Services.

Schlesinger, I. (1977). The role of cognitive development and linguistic input in language acquisition. *Journal of Child Language, 4,* 153–169.

Schloss, P., Smith, M., Goldsmith, L., & Selinger, J. (1984). Identifying current and relevant curricular sequences for multiply involved hearing-impaired learners. *American Annals of the Deaf, 129,* 370–374.

Schmitt, P. (1966). Language instruction for the deaf. *Volta Review, 68,* 85–105.

Schneiderman, C. (1984). *Basic anatomy and physiology in speech and hearing.* San Diego, CA: College-Hill.

Scott, K. (1978). Learning theory, intelligence, and mental development. *American Journal of Mental Deficiency, 82,* 325–336.

Scouten, E. (1967). The Rochester method: An oral multisensory approach for instructing prelingual deaf children. *American Annals of the Deaf, 112,* 50–55.

Scouten, E. (1984). *Turning points in the education of deaf people.* Danville, IL: Interstate Printers & Publishers.

Searls, E., & Klesius, K. (1984). 99 multiple meaning words for primary students and ways to teach them. *Reading Psychology: An International Quarterly, 5,* 55–63.

Shaver, K., Boughman, J., & Nance, W. (1985). Congenital rubella syndrome and diabetes: A review of epidemiologic, genetic, and immunologic factors. *American Annals of the Deaf, 130,* 526–532.

Shaver, K., & Vernon, M. (1978). Genetics and hearing loss: An overview for professions. *Rehabilitation Literature, 4*(2), 6–10.

Shelton, R., & Wood, C. (1978). Speech mechanisms and production. In P. Skinner and R. Shelton, *Speech, language, and hearing: Normal processes and disorders* (pp. 54–77). Reading, MA: Addison-Wesley.

Shepard, N., Davis, J., Gorga, M., & Stelmachowicz, P. (1981). Characteristics of hearing-impaired children in the public schools: Part I—Demographic data. *Journal of Speech and Hearing Disorders, 46,* 123–129.

Shroyer, E. (1982). A model of behavior management with multihandicapped hearing-impaired children. In D. Tweedie & E. Shroyer (Eds.), *The multihandicapped hearing-impaired: Identification and instruction* (pp. 53–60). Washington, DC: Gallaudet University Press.

Sigel, I., & Brinker, R. (1985). A synthesis from beyond the field of deafness. In D. Martin (Ed.), *Cognition, education, and deafness: Directions for research and instruction* (pp. 209–221). Washington, DC: Gallaudet University Press.

Silverman, S. R., Lane, H., & Calvert, D. (1978). Early and elementary education. In H. Davis & S. R. Silverman, *Hearing and deafness* (4th ed.) (pp. 433–482). New York: Holt, Rinehart and Winston.

Simmons, A. (1962). A comparison of the type-token ratio of spoken and written language of deaf and hearing children. *Volta Review, 64,* 417–421.

Singer, H., & Ruddell, R. (Eds.). (1985). *Theoretical models and processes of reading* (3rd ed.). Newark, DE: International Reading Association.

Skinner, B. F. (1953). *Science and human behavior.* New York: Free Press.

Slobin, D. (1979). *Psycholinguistics* (2nd ed.). Glenview, IL: Scott, Foresman.

Smith, C. (1975). Residual hearing and speech production in deaf children. *Journal of Speech and Hearing Research, 18,* 795–811.

Smith, D. (1981). *Teaching the learning disabled.* Englewood Cliffs, NJ: Prentice-Hall.

Smith, F. (1981). *Understanding reading* (2nd ed.). New York: Holt, Rinehart and Winston.

Snell, M. (Ed.). (1978). *Systematic instruction of the moderately and severely handicapped.* Columbus, OH: Merrill.

Snyder, L. (1984). Cognition and language development. In R. Naremore (Ed.), *Language science* (pp. 107–145). San Diego, CA: College-Hill.

Sternberg, R. (1984). Toward a triarchic theory of human intelligence. *Behavioral and Brain Sciences, 7,* 269–287.

Sternberg, R. (1986). *Intelligence applied.* New York: The Psychological Corporation.

Stewart, D. (1985). Language dominance in deaf students. *Sign Language Studies, 49,* 375–385.

Stewart, L. (1971). Problems of severely handicapped deaf: Implications for educational programs. *American Annals of the Deaf, 116,* 362–368.

Stewart, L. (1982). Developing the curriculum for severely disturbed hearing-impaired students. In D. Tweedie & E. Shroyer (Eds.), *The multihandicapped hearing impaired: Identification and instruction* (pp. 124–134). Washington, DC: Gallaudet University Press.

Stinson, M. (1974). Maternal reinforcement and help and the achievement motive in hearing and hearing-impaired children. *Developmental Psychology, 10,* 348–353.

Stinson, M. (1978). Effects of deafness on maternal expectations about child development. *Journal of Special Education, 12,* 75–81.

Stokoe, W. (1960). *Sign language structure: An outline of the visual communication systems of the American deaf. Studies in Linguistics Occasional Papers No. 8.* Washington, DC: Gallaudet University Press.

Stokoe, W. (Ed.). (1980). *Sign and culture: A reader for students of American Sign Language.* Silver Spring, MD: Linstok Press.

Stokoe, W., Casterline, D., & Croneberg, C. (1976). *A dictionary of American Sign Language on linguistic principles.* (rev. ed.). Silver Spring, MD: Linstok Press.

Stokoe, W., & Volterra, V. (Eds.). (1985). *SLR'83: Sign language research.* Silver Spring, MD: Linstok Press.

Streng, A. (1972). *Syntax, speech and hearing: Applied linguistics for teachers of children with language and hearing disabilities.* New York: Grune & Stratton.

Strong, M., & Charlson, E. (1987). Simultaneous communication: Are teachers attempting an impossible task? *American Annals of the Deaf, 132,* 376–382.

Strong, M., & Rudser, S. (1985). An assessment instrument for sign language interpreters. *Sign Language Studies, 49,* 343–362.

Stuckless, E. R., & Birch, J. (1966). The influence of early manual communication on the linguistic development of deaf children. *American Annals of the Deaf, 111,* 452–460; 499–504.

Stuckless, E. R., & Marks, C. (1966). *Assessment of the written language of deaf students.* Pittsburgh, PA: University of Pittsburgh, School of Education.

Stuckless, E. R., & Pollard, G. (1977). Processing of fingerspelling and print by deaf students. *American Annals of the Deaf, 122,* 475–479.

Sullivan, P., Scanlan, J., & La Barre, A. (1986). *Characteristics and therapeutic issues with abused deaf adolescents.* Presentation at the Second National Conference on Habilitation and Rehabilitation of Deaf Adolescents, Afton, OK.

Sullivan, P., Vernon, M., & Scanlan, J. (1987). Sexual abuse of deaf youth. *American Annals of the Deaf, 132,* 256–262.

Supalla, S., (1986). *Manually coded English: The modality question in signed language development.* Unpublished master's thesis, University of Illinois, Urbana-Champaign.

Suppes, P. Fletcher, J., & Zanotti, M. (1976). Models of individual trajectories in computer-assisted instruction for deaf students. *Journal of Educational Psychology, 68,* 119–127.

Taylor, I. (1980). The prevention of sensori-neural deafness. *Journal of Laryngology and Otology, 94,* 1327–1343.

Taylor, L. (1969). *A language analysis of the writing of deaf children.* Unpublished doctoral dissertation, Florida State University, Tallahassee.

Taylor, N. (1983). *Family literacy: Young children learning to read and write.* Exeter, NH: Heinemann.

Technical Assistance Paper. (1986). State of Florida Department of Education, Bureau of Education for Exceptional Students, Division of Public Schools, Tallahassee.

Terzian, A., & Saari, M. (1982). *Employment and related life experiences of deaf persons in New Jersey.* New Brunswick, NJ: Rutgers State University.

Thompson, G., & Weber, B. (1974). Responses of infants and young children to behavior observation audiometry (BOA). *Journal of Speech and Hearing Disorders, 39,* 140–147.

Thyan, P. (1979). Basic needs: Literacy, education and communicative relationships. *Journal of Rehabilitation of the Deaf, 12,* 64–68.

Tierney, R., & Leys, M. (1984). *What is the value of connecting reading and writing?* (Reading Education Report No. 55). Champaign: University of Illinois, Center for the Study of Reading.

Tierney, R., & Pearson, P. D. (1983). Toward a composing model of reading. *Language Arts, 60,* 568–580.

Travers, R. (1978). *An introduction to educational research* (4th ed.). New York: Macmillan.

Trybus, R. (1978). What the *Stanford achievement test* has to say about the reading abilities of deaf children. In H. Reynolds & C. Williams (Eds.), *Proceedings of the Gallaudet conference on reading in relation to deafness* (pp. 213–221). Washington, DC: Gallaudet University Press.

Trybus, R., & Karchmer, M. (1977). School achievement scores of hearing impaired children: National data on achievement status and growth patterns. *American Annals of the Deaf, 122,* 62–69.

Tweedie, D., & Shroyer, E. (Eds.). (1982). *The multihandicapped hearing impaired: Identification and instruction.* Washington, DC: Gallaudet University Press.

Upshall, C. (1929). *Day schools vs. institutions for the deaf.* New York: Teachers College, Columbia University.

U. S. Department of Education. (1983). *U. S. Department of Education/Office of Special Education Data Analysis System* (DANS), June 29, 1983 (TIA33B05).

Valencia, S., & Pearson, P. D. (1987). Reading assessment: Time for a change. *Reading Teacher, 40,* 726–732.

Vandell, D., Anderson, L., Ehrhardt, G., & Wilson, K. (1982). Integrating hearing and deaf preschoolers: An attempt to enhance hearing children's interactions with deaf peers. *Child Development, 53,* 1354–1363.

Vanderheiden, G., & Grilley, K. (1976). *Nonverbal communication techniques and aids for the severely physically handicapped.* Baltimore, MD: University Park Press.

van Uden, A. (1977). *A world of language for deaf children.* Part 1. *Basic principles: A maternal reflective method* (2nd ed.). Lisse, Nertherlands: Swets & Zeitlinger B. V.

Vernon, M. (1968). Fifty years of research on the intelligence of the deaf and hard of hearing: A survey of the literature and discussion of implications. *Journal of Rehabilitation of the Deaf, 1,* 4–7.

Vernon, M. (1969a). Sociological and psychological factors associated with hearing loss. *Journal of Speech and Hearing Research, 12,* 541–563.

Vernon, M. (1969b). *Multiply handicapped deaf children: Medical, educational, and psychological considerations.* CEC Research Monograph. Washington, DC: Council for Exceptional Children.

Vernon, M. (1982). Multihandicapped deaf children: Types and causes. In D. Tweedie & E. Shroyer (Eds.), *The multihandicapped hearing-impaired: Identification and instruction* (pp. 11–28). Washington, DC: Gallaudet University Press.

Vernon, M. (1987a). The primary causes of deafness. In E. Mindel & M. Vernon (Eds.), *They grow in silence: Understanding deaf children and adults* (2nd ed.) (pp. 31–38). Boston, MA: Little, Brown.

Vernon, M. (1987b). Outcomes: Deaf people and work. In E. Mindel & M. Vernon (Eds.), *They grow in silence: Understanding deaf children and adults* (2nd ed.), (pp. 187–195). Boston, MA: Little, Brown.

Vernon, M., & Hyatt, C. (1981). How rehabilitation can better serve deaf clients: The problem and some solutions. *Journal of Rehabilitation, 47,* 60–62, 79.

Vernon, M., & Koh, S. (1970). Early manual communication and deaf children's achievement. *American Annals of the Deaf, 115,* 527–536.

Vockell, E., Hirshoren, A., & Vockell, K. (1972). A critique of Auxter's "Learning disabilities among deaf populations." *Exceptional Children, 38,* 647–650.

Volta Review. (1985). Learning to write and writing to learn. *Volta Review, 87*(5), September. R. R. Kretschmer (Ed.). [Special Issue].

Volta Review. (1988). New reflections on speechreading. *Volta Review, 90*(5), September. C. De Filippo & D. Sims.

Wampler, D. (1972). *Linguistics of Visual English.* Santa Rosa, CA: Author. [Booklets].

Washburn, A. (1983). Seeing Essential English: The development and use of a sign system over two decades. *Teaching English to Deaf and Second-Language Students, 2*(1), 26–30.

Washington State School for the Deaf. (1972). *An introduction to manual English.* Vancouver, WA: Author.

Watson, B., Goldgar, D., Kroese, J., & Lotz, W. (1986). Nonverbal intelligence and academic achievement in the hearing-impaired. *Volta Review, 88,* 151–158.

Watson, J. (1913). Psychology as the behaviorists view it. *Psychology Review, 20,* 158–177.

Watts, W. (1979). Deaf children and some emotional aspects of learning. *Volta Review, 81,* 491–500.

Wechsler, D. (1974). *Wechsler intelligence scale for children–revised.* San Antonio, TX: Psychological Corporation.

Wedell-Monnig, J., & Lumley, J. (1980). Child deafness and mother-child interactions. *Child Development, 51,* 766–774.

Weir, R. (1963). Impact of the multiple handicapped deaf on special education. *Volta Review, 65,* 287–289, 325.

Welsh, W., Walter, G., & Riley, D. (1988). Earnings of hearing-impaired college alumni as reported by the internal revenue service. *Volta Review, 90,* 69–76.

Whitt, J., Paul, P., & Reynolds, C. (1988). Motivate reluctant learning-disabled writers. *Teaching Exceptional Children, 20*(3), 36–39.

Whorf, B. (1956). *Language, thought, and reality.* Cambridge, MA: Massachusetts Institute of Technology.

Wilbur, R. (1977). An explanation of deaf children's difficulty with certain syntactic structures in English. *Volta Review, 79,* 85–92.

Wilbur, R. (1987). *American Sign Language: Linguistic and applied dimensions* (2nd ed.). Boston, MA: Little, Brown.

Wilbur, R., & Goodhart, W. (1985). Comprehension of indefinite pronouns and quantifiers by hearing-impaired children. *Applied Psycholinguistics, 6,* 417–434.

Wilbur, R., Goodhart, W., & Fuller, D. (1989). Comprehension of English modals by hearing-impaired students. *Volta Review, 91,* 5–18.

Wilcox, J., & Tobin, H. (1974). Linguistic performance of hard-of-hearing and normal hearing children. *Journal of Speech and Hearing Research, 17,* 286–293.

Williams, A. (1982). The relationship between two visual communication systems: Reading and lipreading. *Journal of Speech and Hearing Research, 25,* 500–503.

Willingham, W., Ragosta, M., Bennett, R., Braun, H., Rock, D., & Powers, D. (1988). *Testing handicapped people.* Boston, MA: Allyn & Bacon.

Wilson, K. (1979). *Inference and language processing in hearing and deaf children.* Unpublished doctoral dissertation, Boston University, Massachusetts.

Wilson, W., & Thompson, G. (1984). Behavioral audiometry. In J. Jerger (Ed.), *Pediatric audiology* (pp. 1–44). San Diego, CA: College-Hill.

Witters-Churchill, L., Kelly, R., & Witters, L. (1983). Hearing-impaired students' perception of liquid horizontality: An examination of effects of gender, development, and training. *Volta Review, 85,* 211–225.

Wolfensberger, W. (1972). *Normalization: The principle of normalization in human services.* Toronto, CA: National Institute on Mental Retardation.

Wolff, A., & Harkins, J. (1986). Multihandicapped students. In A. Schildroth & M. Karchmer (Eds.), *Deaf children in America* (pp. 55–81). San Diego, CA: College-Hill.

Wolk, S. (1985). A macroanalysis of the research on deafness and cognition. In D. Martin (Ed.), *Cognition, education, and deafness: Directions for research and instruction* (pp. 202–208). Washington, DC: Gallaudet University Press.

Wolk, S., Karchmer, M., & Schildroth, A. (1982). *Patterns of academic and nonacademic integration among hearing-impaired students in special education* (Series R, No. 9). Washington, DC: Gallaudet University, Center for Assessment and Demographic Studies.

Wolk, S., & Schildroth, A. (1984). Consistency of an associational strategy used on reading comprehension tests by hearing–impaired students. *Journal of Research in Reading, 7,* 135–142.

Wolk, S., & Schildroth, A. (1986). Deaf children and speech intelligibility: A national study. In A. Schildroth & M. Karchmer (Eds.), *Deaf children in America* (pp. 139–159). San Diego, CA: College-Hill.

Wong, B. (1979a). The role of theory in learning disabilities research: Part I. An analysis of problems. *Journal of Learning Disabilities, 12,* 585–595.

Wong, B. (1979b). The role of theory in learning disabilities research: Part II. A selective review of current theories of learning and reading disabilities. *Journal of Learning Disabilities, 12,* 649–658.

Wood, F., & Lakin, K. (Eds.). (1982). *Disturbing, disorders, or disturbed?* Reston, VA: Council for Exceptional Children.

Woodward, J. (1986). *ASL is what it is not: Classroom use of ASL by teachers.* Paper presented at the American Sign Language Research and Learning Conference, Newark, California, April.

Woodward, J., Allen, T., & Schildroth, A. (1985). Teachers and deaf students: An ethnography of classroom communication. In S. DeLancey & R. Tomling (Eds.), *Proceedings of the First Annual Meeting of the Pacific Linguistics Conference* (pp. 479–493). Eugene, OR: University of Oregon.

Wrightstone, J., Aronow, M., & Moskowitz, S. (1963). Developing reading test norms for deaf children. *American Annals of the Deaf, 108,* 311–316.

Wulfsberg, R., & Petersen, R. (1979). *The impact of Section 504 of the Rehabilitation Act of 1973 on American colleges and universities.* Washington, DC: National Center for Education Statistics.

Yokoyama, O. (1986). *Discourse and word order.* Philadelphia: Benjamins.

Yoshinaga-Itano, C., & Synder, L. (1985). Form and meaning in the written language of hearing-impaired children. *Volta Review, 87,* 75–90.

Yussen, S., & Santrock, J. (1978). *Child development.* Dubuque, IA: Brown.

Zawolkow, E., & DeFiore, S. (1986). Educational interpreting for elementary- and secondary-level hearing-impaired students. *American Annals of the Deaf, 131,* 26–28.

Zemlin, W. (1968). *Speech and hearing science: Anatomy and physiology.* Englewood Cliffs, NJ: Prentice-Hall.

Index